Simplified Approach to
Operating Systems

VIVEK BHAMBRI
MCA, M. Phil
Assistant Professor
HOD, Department of Computer Sciences
Desh Bhagat Institute of Management and Computer Sciences, Mandi Gobindgarh

GAGAN MARKEN
MCA, M.Phil., M.Tech, MCSE
Assistant Professor
Department of Computer Sciences
Desh Bhagat Institute of Management and Computer Sciences, Mandi Gobindgarh

KHANNA BOOK PUBLISHING CO. (P) LTD.

::: *Publisher of Engineering and Computer Books* :::

Head Office : 4C/4344, Ansari Road, Darya Ganj, New Delhi-110002
Phone : 011-23244447/48 Fax : 011-23244447
Regd. Office : 1694-95, Nai Sarak, Delhi-110006
Phone : 011-23283211 Fax : 011-23256658
E-Mail : contact@khannabooks.com
Website : www.khannabooks.com, www.khannapublishers.com

Operating Systems

Vivek Bhambri

Copyright © Khanna Book Publishing Co. (P) Ltd.

This book is sold subject to the condition that it shall not, by way of trade or otherwise, be lent, resold, hired out, or otherwise circulated without the publisher's prior consent in any form of binding or cover other than that in which it is published and without a similar condition including this condition being imposed on the subsequent purchaser and without limiting the rights under copyright reserved above, no part of this publication may be reproduced, stored in or introduced into retrieval system, or transmitted any form or by any means (electronic, mechanical, photocopying, recording or otherwise), without the prior written permission of both the copyright owner and the above mentioned publisher of this book.

ISBN: 978-93-82609-15-5

First Edition: 2013

Published by:

Khanna Book Publishing Co. (P) Ltd.

4C/4344, Ansari Road, Darya Ganj, New Delhi-110 002

Phone: 011-23244448   Telefax: 011-23244447

E-mail: contact@khannabooks.com

Website: **www.khannabooks.com**

Regd. Off: 1694-95, 1st Floor, Nai Sarak, Delhi-110006 (India)

Phone: 011-23283211   Telefax: 011-23256658

Typesetted by:

M2W Media, Delhi

Printed in India by:

S.P.S. Printers & Binders, Delhi

PREFACE

Operating System is an essential component of a computer system. It lies at the heart of the Computer Science. It is the basis of what we perform, execute and achieve by using this machine, known as Computers. It is the force which drives the whole show forward. So the study of the design and architecture of operating systems is very important for the students undergoing studies on (in) Computer Science and Engineering.

The purpose of this book is to organize the known techniques and tools of designing and analyzing the operating systems in the simplest way possible and apart from that the aim is to enable the readers to think out of the box ideas to invent the better tools for the future systems. This book will work as a basic text book for the students at Under Graduation and Post Graduation Levels. The book explains the basic concepts, algorithms, techniques and design issues of the operating systems in general, i.e not related to any one particular operating system. The case studies on the most common operating systems, DOS, Windows, Unix and Linux have been provided so that the readers can co-relate the basic concepts with a particular system, they are using or wish to use. Multiple Choice Questions given at the end of the book provide a quick review of the whole text.

The book covers the complete syllabus of MCA, BCA, B.Tech and M.Sc(IT) Courses of Punjabi University, Punjab University, Punjab Technical University, Guru Nanak Dev University and Kurukshetra University.

Full care has been taken to explain the concepts in the best way possible, Suggestions for the further improvements are welcomed.

Wishing the readers a thoughtful learning experience.

All the best to student community for their future endeavors.

Mr. Vivek Bhambri

Mr. Gagan Marken

ACKNOWLEDGEMENT

A lot of people have helped us in this project and we relish the opportunity to thank them.

Our first gratitude is towards the Almighty for showering His blessings and making us capable of completing this project.

We are indebted to our parents, teachers and colleagues who guided and inspired us to do the work.

We express our heartfelt thanks to Dr. Shalini Gupta (Pro-VC, Desh Bhagat University) for her constant encouragement and cooperation in bringing out this book.

We express our deep gratitude to our family members for their constant support.

I, (Vivek Bhambri) thank my wife Nisha Bhambri, for her constant support and encouragement and for bearing a lot during my involvement in this project, further I thank Mr. Balram Krishan, Assistant Professor at Desh Bhagat Institute of Management and Computer Sciences, Mandi Gobindgarh, for his cooperation in this project.

I, (Gagan Marken) thank my brother Dr. Rohit Marken and all family members for their support.

The writing of a book of this nature would not have been possible without consulting the writings of many learned writers. We are thankful to all of them. We thank Mr. Mukul Seth, Managing Director, Khanna Book Publishing Co. for having confidence in us and our work.

We thank the whole team at Khanna Book Publishing Co. for converting our endeavors into reality.

Mr. Vivek Bhambri **Mr. Gagan Marken**

CONTENTS

Introduction to Operating Systems

Chapter 1

An operating system acts an intermediator between the user of the computer and the computer hardware. It provides an interface between the user and machine and provides an environment in which the user can run the programs efficiently. The primary objective of operating system is to make the computer system convenient to use and to utilize the hardware of the system in the most optimum way possible.

Like our body cannot work without the brain. The brain tells the other body parts how to work and how to interact with each other and the external environment surrounding us. It controls the various body parts and tries to manage them so that they can work efficiently. Without brain we will not be able to do anything. It can be termed as an interface between the human body and the external environment. Same is the case of an operating system. Operating System is like a brain for the computer system. It provides an interface between the computer hardware and the user. A computer system is comprised of various hardware components like memory, processor and various input and output devices. It is the job of an operating system that all these components should interact and coordinate with each other in order to achieve the common objectives and to make the system easy to use for the end user. The operating system performs the basic tasks such as receiving the input from the keyboard, processing the instructions and sending the output to the user. It is a layer which takes care of the technical aspect of the computer's operations. It shields the user from the machine level details and provides an abstract view to the user.

In a computer system, hardware is just a resource and it is the software which makes its workable. Hardware and software work hand in hand and one cannot work without the other. Operating system is the software that makes the hardware usable. Hardware provides "raw computing power." Operating system makes the computing power conveniently available to users, by making the optimum utilization of the hardware to achieve good performance. Operating systems can also be considered as a manager of the resources. An operating system determines which computer resources will be utilized for solving which problem and the order in which they will be used. Operating system may be considered as a software that controls the hardware.

Definition of Operating System: Operating system is a system software that provides an interface between user and machine and provides a platform for other programs to run. It is a set of integrated programs that controls the resources (the CPU, memory, I/O devices, etc.) of a computer system.

The operating system can be defined as an organized set of programs that controls and coordinates the use of the computer resources among the various users and tasks.

It acts as an interface between the user and the hardware. It schedules tasks, manages storage and handles communication with the external environment.

Primary objectives of an Operating System are:

1. To provide an interface between the user and machine.
2. To make the computer system convenient to use by providing a user friendly interface.
3. To hide the hardware level details from the user.
4. To manage the resources (i.e Allocation and Assignment) of computer resources efficiently.
5. To provide a platform to run application programs and utilities.
6. To monitor and keep track of the activities being run on the system.

As a foundation for all system softwares, an operating system performs various tasks like managing various programs running on the system, prioritizing them and handling the conflicting requests, controlling input and output devices, allocation and de-allocation of memory, managing the files and creating a user friendly environment for the end user. It forms a platform for other softwares, whether these are system softwares or application softwares.

In the nutshell, we can say that the operating system is the most important program that runs on your computer and without it your computer will not work. It provides a software platform on the top of which other application programs can run. The choice of operating system will determine that which particular applications the user can run on the system. The major key elements of an operating system are:

- A technical layer of software for driving the machine i.e the hardware of the system.
- A file system which provides a way of organizing files logically.
- A simple command interpreter which enables the users to run their own programs and to manipulate the files. Some operating system also provide text editors, compliers, debuggers and a variety of other tools.

The Operating System coordinates multiple applications and users (multiple processes) in a fair and efficient manner. The goal in OS development is to make the machine convenient to use (a software engineering problem) and efficient utilization of resources(a system and engineering problem). The memory area of the system is divided into system area and user area. Some operating system programs exist in the system area of memory permanently, while other programs are loaded in the transient area as and when required. The rest of the memory area is used by the user programs. The collection of operating system programs is also termed as the kernel. The objective of the operating system programs is to monitor and control the overall functioning of the computer system, so that these programs can be executed by the processor. So we can conclude that whether it is a system program or user program, both will be executed by the processor, so it needs to be switched from the system program to user program as and when required.

NEED OF AN OPERATING SYSTEM

Operating System is the first software we see when we turn on the computer and the last software we see when the computer is turned off. When the power is turned on to a computer, the first program that runs is usually a set of instructions kept in the Read Only Memory (ROM) that examines the system hardware to make sure everything is functioning as intended. The Power-On-Self-Test(POST) checks the CPU, memory and the other basic input and output systems for errors and stores the results in a special memory location. Once the POST has been successfully completed, the software loaded in ROM will begin to activate the computer's disk drives. When the computer activates the hard disk drive the bootstrap loader is the first piece of program that is activated. The bootstrap loader is a small program whose sole function is to load the operating system into the memory and allows it to begin its operations. The boot strap loader sets up the small drive programs that interface with and control and various hardware components of the system.

So operating system is an interface for a user to use the computer system. We cannot think of using a Computer without using an operating system. The operating system is supposed to ensure efficient use of computer system and to provide user convenience. However, these two requirements are conflicting with each other, providing fast execution of user's request could mean that other users of the system have not been entertained, it could also mean that resources have been allocated to a user even when the program is not using them, and at the same time other users or processes may be waiting for the resources, which will lead to under utilization of resources. So the operating system design has to trade off between user convenience and efficient utilization of resources. A combination of both objectives is the best strategy, which is known as effective utilization of the system. The operating system is needed as it performs the following jobs in order to provide the effective utilization of computer system:

Interface between User and Machine: The operating system provides an environment in which the user can work. For the execution of a program the user needs to interact with the internal hardware details, but the user having varying level of computer literacy are not competent enough to deal with the hardware directly. So some intermediator is required which can bridge this gap between the user and the machine and can provide an environment in which it will be easier for the user to interact with the machine. It hides the typical hardware level details from the user and provides an abstracted and easy to use view to the user.

A platform to run other programs: The user wishing to execute some job needs an interface and environment in which the user can execute its programs efficiently. To run a program, it is loaded into the RAM first and then CPU is assigned to it for the execution of the program. The program needs various resources from the system for its proper execution and if the environment is multiuser, then managing the resources is again a trival task. Apart from this, the program may need some other system applications and /or utilities for its execution. The complete environment for the program execution is created by the operating system, as it provides a platform to run the various user programs.

Resource Management: The program for its normal and successful execution needs some resources from the system. The most basic requirement is the need of processor, memory and input and output devices. These resources should be allocated to the program as and when required. Keeping track of which memory space has been allocated to which program and how to manage the free space, how to assign the processor to a particular job and if the environment is a multiuser environment, where a number of user share the resources, then this job becomes even more complex. So some manager is required which will manage these resources, i.e will allocate and de-allocate the resources as per the need of the user. This job of resource manager is performed by the operating system.

Need of abstraction: The abstraction is the feature that hides the lower level details and provides a set of higher level functions. The user being non-technical person does not know the internal hardware level details so operating system hides the internal details from the user and provides an environment in which the user can work and execute its jobs convenentially.

OPERATING SYSTEM COMPONENTS

The basic architecture of operating system can be visualized to be made up of number of layers. The operating system layer hides the internal details from the user and provides a convenient interface to run the other applications. To understand the architecture of an operating system, the computer can be divided into four major components:

1. **Computer Hardware:** The computer hardware is the actual computer system. It includes the major components like: Processor, Memory and Input and Output devices required to run the system. These are the basic computer resources for the system. It makes the basic internal layer of the architecture of an operating system. All of these components perform some particular job.

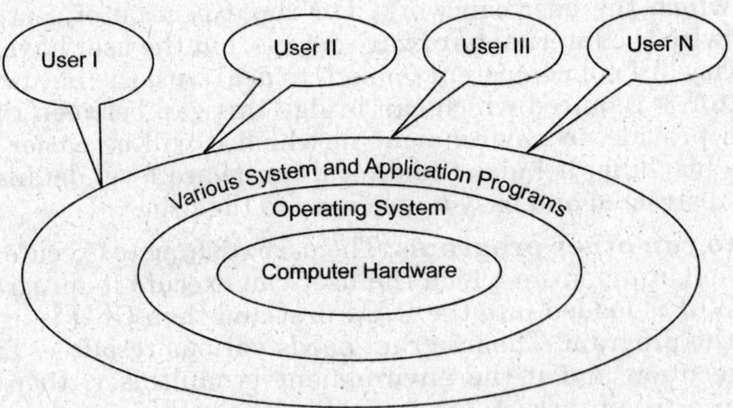

Figure 1.1: *Components of Operating System*

As the input devices receive the data and the instructions from the users, convert them into the form the computer can understand. The processor executes the instructions and the output devices finally show the results to the users. The memory unit performs the job of storing the data, where primary memory stores the data on the temporary basis and the secondary storage preserves the data on the permanent basis.

2. **Operating System:** It is the second layer of the architecture of operating system. It provides an interface between the internal computer hardware and various application and system programs being run by the user. It is the main component which controls and coordinates the use of various hardware components, application programs among the various users using the system. It provides an environment in which the other programs can work. The most common operating systems available in the market are: DOS, Windows, Unix and Linux. Operating System controls and coordinates the use of computer hardware, so that the various applications can be executed by the various users in a convenient way. And above all the operating system tries to make the efficient use of computer hardware. The ease of use and optimum resource utilization are the two major goals the operating system needs to achieve. If the environment is a single user environment, where a single user is using the system, in that case the focus is on ease of use and little attention is paid to resource utilization. In the contrary to this if the environment is a multiuser environment, where a number of users are using the same resources in shared mode, then the focus is on optimum utilization of the resources so that all the available resources viz. CPU time, memory and the other hardware and software resources can be used by all users in the best way possible, with none of them monopolizing any particular resource. Operating system works as an extended machine where it hides the internal hardware level details from the user and presents the users a virtual machine that is easier to use.

3. **System and Application Programs:** The user will be using the computer system for various applications to be carried out. The various application programs perform the specific tasks and help the user to get the desired results. The most common application programs being run on the system are Assembler, Complier, Word Processors, Spreadsheets, Accounting Packages, Web Browsers, Computer Games, Business Oriented Packages and any other application softwares for some specific function to be carried out by the user. The operating system provides a bridge between these applications and the computer hardware. Apart from these, there are some utilities which provide some add-on capabilities to the operating system. These utilities help the operating system in managing the system resources in a better and sophisticated way. These are installed as memory resident programs and assist in the various system management functions. The utilities are installed, configured and are periodically updated for a specific computer configuration. The various jobs performed by these utilities are: managing disk drives, disk optimization, antivirus protection and process execution related utilities.

4. **User:** The fourth component of the layered architecture of the operating system is the user. The various users who interact with the system are programmers, data base administrators, naïve users, online user and the end users. All these users have varying degree of computer literacy and depending upon their knowledge

they will need the interface. The operating system provides an interface so that all type of users can work and use the system in the best way possible.

OPERATING SYSTEM SERVICES

The operating system is designed to provide an interface between the user and the machine. As discussed earlier, the primary objective of an operating system is to provide an environment in which it will be convenient for the user to execute its jobs and the second major service is to manage the resources on behalf of the user. The services provided by the system can be broadly divided into two major areas: User Centric Considerations and System Centric Considerations. In the user centric considerations, user convenience and fast execution of user's requests is the important factor. It is important in the systems which involve user interaction while execution of the job and in the (case of) interactive and time bound jobs. On the other hand, in the system centric considerations, the efficient use of system and its resources is the major area of concern, it is important in non-interactive data processing jobs.

The major jobs done by an operating system may be enumerated as:

1. **To Provide an environment for Program Execution:** The user wishing to execute some job needs an interface and environment in which the user can execute its programs efficiently. This environment is provided by an operating system. The two major requirements for the program execution are processors and the memory. The allocation of the processor and mode of its allocation varies from system to system, as the processor may be dedicated to one program only or there may be multiple programs running on the machine, where scheduling of the processes and keeping a record of allocation of processors and release is to be kept. On the other side, program needs some memory space for its execution, how and from where the memory is to allocated and once the memory is not required, then how to manage the free memory space, so that it can be used by the other programs, is handled by the operating system. Apart from this, to run a program, it is loaded into the RAM first and then CPU is assigned to it for the execution of the program. So the management of processor and the memory is the major service provided by the operating system.
2. **To work as a Resource Allocator:** The computer has various resources like: Processor, Memory (Primary or Secondary) and various input and output devices. In a multiprogramming environment, where multiple jobs are running at a time the management of these resources to the various programs is a tedious job. Similarly, if the environment is multiuser, where multiple users are competing for the same set of resources, the task of resource allocation and de-allocation is even more tedious. This job of resource management is performed by operating system. Here the operating system works as a Resource Manager. Where it is the job of an operating system to allocate, de-allocate and keep a record of the resources (i.e which resource has been allocated to which process or the user) and to ensure that this job has been done to maximize the resource utilization and the user satisfaction. The major services provided by the operating system, as a resource manager are:

i. *Process Management:* In a multiprocessing environment, where more than one process is running on the system at the same time, managing these multiple processes is a very cumbersome job. As the various processes may be in the need of the processor, memory or the other resources at the same. Process management is a set of functions supporting the definition of inter-related process steps and management of their execution across a variety of hardware platforms. So operating system works as a process manager to manage these processes, so that processes can be managed properly and the conflicting requirements can be dealt properly. The operating system is responsible for the following activities in connection with process management:
   - Creation and Deletion of Processes.
   - Suspension and Resumption of Processes.
   - To devise mechanism for process scheduling i.e to decide when and for how long the CPU will be allocated to the program.
   - To devise mechanism for process synchronization
   - To devise mechanism for inter-process and intra-process communication.

ii. *Memory Management:* The user stores the programs and data in the memory. For this purpose both the primary and the secondary memory is used. Main memory has the programs and the data which can be used by the CPU for the execution directly. Whereas the secondary memory stores the data and programs on the permanent basis. Whenever a user wishes to execute a certain set of programs, then the required program is fetched from the secondary memory to the primary memory and hence the program is being executed by the CPU. It is the job of the memory management unit of the operating system to keep track of the available and occupied memory space. The major jobs of memory management unit are:
   - To check the memory requirement of a particular program.
   - To keep track of the free space available
   - To keep track of the memory utilization by various processes i.e to record that which memory unit is allocated to which program.
   - To decide which process should be loaded into memory when the memory space is free and to de-allocate the space when program does not need it any more.

iii. *Input-Output Management:* Each and every program needs some input and after processing of this input, the results obtained are produced as output to the user. It involves an interaction with various input and output devices. These I/O devices vary in their construction, operations and usage. To use these components the user must be able to have the required knowledge of hardware in general and all these devices in particular. The operating system helps the user in overcoming this major problem by providing an interface through which the user can use these devices easily. The operating system hides the internal hardware level details of these I/O devices from the user and hence makes the system easier to use.

iv. *Network Management:* When multiple computers are connected together in a network or in a distributed environment, the operating system works as a network resource manager, through which the multiple users in a network share the resources among themselves and coordinate with each other for the execution of the jobs. Even in a client server architecture the operating system plays a very important role.

3. **To help in File System Management:** The user while working on the system performs various types of functions on the file, where a file can be defined as a collection of related information. The various operations are creation of file, opening the file, storing the file, saving the file and deleting the file when its not required, moving the file from one place to other and many more. The operating system makes these jobs easier for the user by providing the facility of file management and manipulation. The file management module of an operating system takes care of file related activities as: accessing, naming, sharing and protection of files. The operating system is responsible for the following activities in connections with file management:
   - Creation and Deletion of Files.
   - Creation and deletion of directories.
   - To provide mechanism for manipulating files and directories.
   - To provide mechanism for mapping files onto secondary storage.
   - To provide mechanism for file backup on secondary storage.
   - To provide the support for file access.
4. **To facilitate Communication among Processes:** In a multiuser environment, the users need to communicate with each other to share data and other resources and even in multiprogramming environment where more than one programs is running on the system communicate with each other. This communication is handled by the operating system.
5. **Error detection and Protection:** While the system is executing its various jobs, it may be possible that some type of hardware or software error may occur. To avoid the hardware errors the operating system constantly monitors the performance of the system for detection of errors and then performs the remedial task to correct the errors. The major errors encountered are like bad sectors on hard disk, memory overflow and errors related to input and output devices. After identifying the errors the operating system performs appropriate actions so that the smooth execution of user's commands can be resumed. The module of error detection and correction is a critical part of the system which needs to be designed properly. The major jobs to be carried out by this module are:
   - Distinguish between authorized and unauthorized usage.
   - To provide a mechanism to impose controls when and wherever required.
   - To provide a mechanism to handle the unauthorized access.
6. **To keep an account of the System Resources:** In multiuser and / or multiprogramming environment, where programs from multiple users run at the same time, the resources of a system are used on shared basis by different programs and users. So keeping a record of system resources is of utmost importance. This job is done by the operating system. Such type of accounting will enhance the

system performance and fair allocation of the resources to various programs and/ or users.

7. **To create and maintain a Protection System:** Security in computer system deals with protecting the various resources and information of a computer system against destruction and unauthorized access. The protection is needed from external as well as internal sources. External security deals with protecting the system against external factors as fires, floods, earthquakes, leaking or stealing of the stored information. This can be achieved by adopting a proper back up procedure and applying security guards to protect the system. But, apart from that in a multiuser environment where the concurrent execution of various processes by various users is taking place at the same time, then these processes must not be allowed to interfere in one other's area. In order to achieve this objective, the operating system carries out the process of protection mechanism, through which the access of programs, processes or users is controlled. The operating system provides a system of protection by using the concept of user authentication (i.e if a user wish to access the computer, its authentication will be checked by the means of userid/password) and access control (where its ensured that all resources are not meant for all the users, so only those resources are allocated to the user which he is supposed to use) from the outside environment authenticating the user by means of passwords.

8. **To Work as a Command Interpreter:** As discussed earlier, user can not interact with the system hardware directly, it needs an interface through which the user requests can be fulfilled by the machine. This interface is the operating system, where it works as a command interpreter, where it receives the user's commands, interpret them and manage to get the command executed.

Table 1.1: Operating System Functions

Action	What the Operating System Does?
The User turn on the computer	Hardware Management
The User executes an application	Process Management
An Application reads data from a tape	Hardware Management (Device Management)
The Application waits for data	Process Management
The Process waits while other process runs	Process Management
The Process displays data on screen	Hardware Management
The User wishes to store data on the system	Hardware Management (Memory Management)
The User does not find the sufficient space for storing the data.	Hardware Management(Memory Management)
The Process writes data to tape	Hardware Management
The User quits and the process terminates	Process Management
The User turn off the computer	Hardware Management

ROLES PLAYED BY AN OPERATING SYSTEM

Keeping in view the various services provided by the operating system, the operating system is performing following roles:

1. **Operating System as a Parent:** Operating System, like a parent is always there whenever you need. As parents provide us the resources, support and stand by us in all the situations. In the Same way, operating system is providing all assistance for the successful execution of jobs, providing the required resources and support in all difficulties and problems encountered during the execution of the jobs.
2. **Operating System as a Magician:** A magician is person who performs various acts hiding the execution details from the user, and all that he performs looks like a black box to the user and by providing an illusion to the user the magician performs the jobs, same is the role of an operating system. Operating system provides each user with the illusion of a dedicated machine with an infinite memory and CPU time and in the presence of an operating system, the machine looks like a black box to the user, where he knows only what goes in and what goes out, remaining execution of the jobs and the management of resources is done by the operating system and all internal details are hidden from the user.
3. **Operating System as a Government:** The role of government in a country is to manage the resources for the benefit of the masses, to allocate the resources efficiently and fairly, to protect users from each other, and to provide safe and secure living. The operating system also performs the same job for the user. It allocates the system resources to various programs in such a way that all users and processes get the required share and all programs can run in parallel in coordination with each other, without interfering into each other's area so that various programs may run efficient in a safe and secure environment. Like a government operating system maintain law and order in the system.
4. **Operating system as a Teacher:** A teacher guides, inspires, makes complex tasks easier and stand by you through thick and thin. The operating system also performs the same job by guiding the user for the execution of the jobs and making the complex jobs easier for the user. Whether it is sharing of files, communicating with physically separated users or dealing with the hardware details of the machine, all these complex jobs are made simple with the help of an operating system.
5. **Operating system as a Call Center:** Operating system is like a call centre available around the clock, 365*24*7 and provides the same set of services everywhere. Moreover sometimes it provides the customized services as per the requirement of the user also.

SYSTEM CALLS

System calls provide the interface between a running program and the operating system. It can be defined as a request that a program makes to the operating system. Generally these system calls are made available as routines written in C and C++, although certain low level tasks (for example, the tasks which deals with the hardware details directly) may be written using assembly-language instructions. System calls occur in different ways depending upon the computer in use. In spite of identifying the desired system call, the exact type and amount of information required may vary according to the particular operating system and call used. System calls occur in different ways depending on the computer in use. First of all the desired system call is identified and the type and amount of information required vary from operating system to system and call to call. Like if we wish to get the input, we have to specify the file or the device to be used as the source and along with that address and the length of the memory buffer where the input is to be read is also to be specified. In the system call the device or the name of the file should be defined in the call. These all values are passed as the parameter to the system call. The system calls uses the special instruction called software interrupt instruction, which has the format: <SIinstruction> <interrupt code>

Where the interrupt code has standard meaning stored in the operating system. An interrupt occurs when a program executes this instruction and the interrupt code value is matched with the value saved already and the corresponding routine is executed. If system does not provide an operand in the interrupt instruction, then the program pushes a code available from the last instruction executed prior to the present instruction. The various methods to pass parameters are:

- **Pass Parameters in Registers:** The simplest method to pass the parameters is to pass them in registers.
- **Pass Parameters in a Block or Table:** In some cases, there may be more parameters than the registers available, then the parameters are stored in the table in the memory and the address of the table is passed as the parameter in the register.
- **Pass Parameters by Pushing them on the Stack:** The parameters may also be pushed on to the stack by the program, and can be popped off from the stack by the operating system. This method is very useful as here there is no limit on the number or the length of parameters being passed.
- **Types of System Calls:** The system calls can be divided into following categories:

  1. Process control
  2. File management or manipulation.
  3. Device management or manipulation.
  4. Information maintenance.
  5. Communications.

1. **Process Control:** The processes running in the system are under the direct control of the operating system and the operating system is responsible for controlling the execution of the processes, i.e when the process is running, and when the program ends normally or when the program is to be aborted (i.e forced to halt forcibly). This process control is being handled by the operating system by executing various system calls. In case the currently running program encounters an error trap then a dump of the memory is taken and then an error message is generated. The dump taken at this time is stored on the disk and then the debugger or the system program will be asked to check and rectify the error. Whether the process has been terminated normally or abnormally, the operating system must transfer the control to the command interpreter, so that it can read the next command. In a graphical user interface, an error message may pop up to alert the user and may ask and guide the user whereas in the batch processing system, the command interpreter terminates the entire job and then continues with the next job. The various actions in the category of process control are: end or abort a process, load and execute the process, creation and termination of the process, allocation and de-allocation of memory, wait for the resources etc.

2. **File Management:** As discussed earlier, the job of the operating system is to manage the file and directory structure. The files are created and are stored in the directories; files may be moved from one directory to the other. So, for the execution of these operations various system calls are issued. The system calls here require the name of the file, type of file, protection codes, accounting information and the some of the attributes which guide regarding the type of the operations to be performed. The most common system calls used for this purpose are get file attribute and set file attribute are required most of the times. Other system calls are the calls for moving or copying the file, read or write the file, repositioning the file.

3. **Device Management:** The operating system as we already know, works as a device manager. Where the device may be the various resources controlled by the operating system. These resources may be physical devices like processors, storage media or can be abstract or virtual devices like files. A process while execution may be in need of various resources like memory, disk drives and files etc. if the resources are available they can be granted and the control can be granted as per the need, otherwise the process will have to wait until the resources are not free for allocation. If multiple users are working at the same time, the request has to be made for the resource and after using the device it is to be released back, so that it can be allocated to other processes. So for all these functions the system calls are issued by the operating system, as and when required. The various system calls in this category are: request or release device, get and set device attributes, logically attach or detach the devices etc.

4. **Information Maintenance:** The processes running in a system or the processes of multiple number of users need to communicate with each other, so the system

calls exists for this purpose of transferring the information between the user programs and the operating system. Apart from this there are system calls to return the general information about the system, users and the processes running on the system. This information include, current system time and date, number of current users, the version of the operating system, CPU usage, amount of free and/or occupied memory space available. The various system calls in this category are: get or set time or date, get process, file or device attributes, set process, file or device attributes.

5. **Communication:** There are two models for inter-process communication:

   (a) *Message Passing Model:* In this model, the communicating process exchange information with each other. It is referred to as inter-process communication. Before the communication starts, the sender, receiver and the communication media to be used must be clear. The communication can be between two processes on the same system or the processes on the different computers. In the later case, the communication link has to be established through a communication network. The different systems in a network are identified by generating system calls to track the IP address, host id and the various processes are identified by process id and process name. The system calls get hosted and get processed are used for these operations. All these unique id's are translated into an identifier by which the operating system tracks a particular system in the network and then the particular process is tracked. The recipient process has to give its permission for the communication to take place with an accept connection call. If the recipient is available then the connection is established otherwise, wait for connection system call is issued. The sender (also known as the client) and the receiver (also known as the server) exchange messages by the system calls read message and write message, after the communication is over the connection is terminated by issuing a close connection system call.

   (b) *Shared Memory Model:* In this case, the processes use shared memory and the system calls are generated to create the memory regions for a user and/or process and then the system calls are used to allocate and de-allocate the memory regions. The processes and the users sharing a particular memory region should not be allowed to access each other's area. But if this model is to be used, then this restriction needs to be eliminated. The processes may share information by reading or writing data in the shared areas, it is worth mentioning here that the form of the data and locations to be shared is determined by the processes under question and not by the operating system. The map memory system call is used to get the access of memory regions owned by the other processes.

In either of these models, the various system calls used are: create, delete communication connection, send or receive messages, transfer status information, attach or detach remote devices. The operating systems use either of these methods and even both the methods are used by some operating systems. Message passing is useful when amount of data is to be exchanged is quite less. This method is easy to implement when inter-process communications needs to be established. On the other hand, shared memory model allows maximum speed and ease of communication. The system calls discussed can be broadly divided into following categories:

Various Classes of System Calls	Example
Resource	Check Availability of Resources Allocate and Deallocate the System Resources
Program	Execute/Terminate the program
File	Open/Close a file, Read/Write data in the file.
Information	Get any information pertaining to processes, users, resources etc.
Communication	Send/receive messages Setup the connection Terminate Connection.

Types of Operating Systems

Chapter 2

HISTORY AND EVOLUTION OF OPERATING SYSTEM

A computer needs an operating system to manage its hardware resources and to provide an interface to the user for making the system convenient to use. The earliest computer did not have any operating systems. The vendors were providing quite expensive tools for streamlining the various system activities.

The birth and evolution of operating systems have historically been closely tied to the architecture of the computers on which they run, with the growth of computer architecture through various successive generations led to the growth of operating systems.

The first true digital computer was designed by the English mathematician Charles Babbage (1792–1871). Although Babbage spent most of his life and fortune trying to build his "analytical engine," the analytical engine did not have an operating system. As an interesting historical aside, Babbage realized that he would need software for his analytical engine, so he hired a young woman named Ada Lovelace, as the world's first programmer. The programming language Ada® is named after her.

Through 1960's several concepts were developed which led to the growth of operating systems. The IBM 360 produced a family of mainframe computers that served consumers with differing capacity and prices, the 360 was designed to handle both scientific (i.e., numerical) and commercial computing. A single operating system was planned for these computers rather than developing separate programs for every individual model. The 360 was the first major computer line to use (small-scale) Integrated Circuits (ICs), thus providing a major price/performance advantage over the second-generation machines, which were built up from individual transistors. It was an immediate success, and the idea of a family of compatible computers was soon adopted by all the other major manufacturers. The greatest strength of the "one family" idea was simultaneously its greatest weakness. The intention was that all softwares, including the operating system, OS/360 had to work on all models. It had to run on small systems, which often just replaced 1401s for copying cards to tape, and on very large systems, which often replaced 7094s for doing weather forecasting and other heavy computing. It had to be good on systems with few peripherals and on systems with many peripherals. It had to work in commercial environments and in scientific environments. Above all, it had to be efficient for all of these different uses. There was no way that IBM (or anybody else) could write a piece of software to meet all those conflicting requirements. The result was an enormous and extraordinarily complex operating system. It consisted of millions of lines of assembly language written by thousands of programmers, and contained thousands upon thousands of bugs, which necessitated a continuous stream of new releases in an attempt to correct them. Each new release fixed some bugs and introduced new ones, so the number of bugs probably remained constant in time.

Despite its enormous size and problems, OS/360 and the similar third-generation operating systems produced by other computer manufacturers actually satisfied most of their customers reasonably well. They also popularized several key techniques absent in second-generation operating systems. Probably the most important of these was Multiprogramming.

Another major feature present in third-generation operating systems was the ability to read jobs from cards onto the disk as soon as they were brought to the computer room. Then, whenever a running job finished, the operating system could load a new job from the disk into the now-empty partition and run it. This technique is called Spooling (from Simultaneous Peripheral Operation On Line) and was also used for output.

Although third-generation operating systems were well suited for big scientific calculations and massive commercial data processing runs, they were still basically batch systems. Many programmers opined for the first-generation days when they had the machine only for a few hours, so they could debug their programs quickly. With third-generation systems, the time between submitting a job and getting back the output was often several hours, so a single misplaced comma could cause a compilation to fail, and the programmer to waste half a day.

This desire for quick response time paved the way for Time Sharing, a variant of multiprogramming, in which each user has an online terminal. In a timesharing system, if 20 users are logged in and 17 of them are thinking or talking, the CPU can be allocated in turn to the three jobs that want service. Since people debugging programs usually issue short commands (e.g., compile a five-page procedure) rather than long ones (e.g., sort a million-record file), the computer can provide fast, interactive service to a number of users and perhaps also work on big batch jobs in the background when the CPU is otherwise idle.

MULTICS was a mixed success. It was designed to support hundreds of users on a machine only slightly more powerful than an Intel 386-based PC, although it had much more I/O capacity.

One of the computer scientists at Bell Labs who had worked on the MULTICS project, Ken Thompson, subsequently found a small PDP-7 minicomputer that no one was using and set out to write a stripped-down, one-user version of MULTICS. This work later developed into the UNIX® operating system, which became popular in the academic world, with government agencies, and with many companies.

The desire for a free production (as opposed to educational) version of MINIX led a Finnish student, Linus Torvalds, to write Linux. This system was developed on MINIX and originally supported various MINIX features (e.g., the MINIX file system). It has since been extended in many ways but still retains a large amount of underlying structure common to MINIX, and to UNIX (upon which the former was based).

With the development of LSI (Large Scale Integration) circuits, chips containing thousands of transistors on a square centimeter of silicon, the age of the personal computer dawned. In terms of architecture, personal computers (initially called microcomputers) were not all that different from minicomputers of the PDP-11 class, but in terms of price they certainly were different. Where the minicomputer made it possible for a department in a company or university to have its own computer, the microprocessor chip made it possible for a single individual to have his or her own personal computer.

In 1974, when Intel came out with the 8080, the first general-purpose 8-bit CPU, it wanted an operating system for the 8080, in part to be able to test it. Intel asked one of its consultants, Gary Kildall, to write one. Kildall and a friend first built a controller for the newly-released Shugart Associates 8-inch floppy disk and hooked the floppy disk up to the 8080, thus producing the first microcomputer with a disk. Kildall then wrote a disk-based operating system called CP/M (Control Program for Microcomputers) for it. Since Intel did not think that disk-based microcomputers had much of a future, when Kildall asked for the rights to CP/M, Intel granted his request. Kildall then formed a company, Digital Research, to further develop and sell CP/M.

In 1977, Digital Research rewrote CP/M to make it suitable for running on the many microcomputers using the 8080, When IBM came back, Gates realized that a local computer manufacturer, Seattle Computer Products, had a suitable operating system, DOS(Disk Operating System). He approached them and asked to buy it (allegedly for $50,000), which they readily accepted. Gates then offered IBM a DOS/BASIC package, which IBM accepted. IBM wanted certain modifications, so Gates hired the person who wrote DOS, Tim Paterson, as an employee of Gates' fledgling company, Microsoft, to make them. The revised system was renamed MS-DOS (Microsoft Disk Operating System) and quickly came to dominate the IBM PC market.

By the time the IBM PC/AT came out in 1983 with the Intel 80286 CPU, MS-DOS was firmly entrenched and CP/M was on its last legs. MS-DOS was later widely used on the 80386 and 80486. Although the initial version of MS-DOS was fairly primitive, subsequent versions included more advanced features, including many taken from UNIX. CP/M, MS-DOS, and other operating systems for early microcomputers were all based on users typing in commands from the keyboard. That eventually changed due to research done by Doug Engelbart at Stanford Research Institute in the 1960s. Engelbart invented the GUI (Graphical User Interface), pronounced "gooey," complete with windows, icons, menus, and mouse. These ideas were adopted by researchers at Xerox PARC and incorporated into machines they built.

When Microsoft decided to build a successor to MS-DOS, it was strongly influenced by the success of the Macintosh. It produced a GUI-based system called Windows, which originally ran on top of MS-DOS (i.e., it was more like a shell than a true operating system). For about 10 years, from 1985 to 1995, Windows was just a graphical environment on top of MS-DOS. However, starting in 1995 a freestanding version of Windows, Windows 95, was released that incorporated many operating system features into it, using the underlying MS-DOS system only for booting and running old MS-DOS programs. In 1998, a slightly modified version of this system, called Windows 98 was released. Nevertheless, both Windows 95 and Windows 98 still contain a large amount of 16-bit Intel assembly language.

Another Microsoft operating system is Windows NT (NT stands for New Technology), which is compatible with Windows 95 at a certain level, but a complete rewrite from scratch internally. It is a full 32-bit system. The lead designer for Windows NT was David Cutler. Version 5 of Windows NT was renamed Windows 2000 in early 1999. It was intended to be the successor to both Windows 98 and Windows NT 4.0. So Microsoft came out with yet another version of Windows 98 called Windows Me (Millennium edition).

The other major contender in the personal computer world is UNIX (and its various derivatives). UNIX is strongest on workstations and other high-end computers, such as network servers. It is especially popular on machines powered by high-performance RISC chips. On Pentium-based computers, Linux is becoming a popular alternative to Windows for students and increasingly many corporate users. An interesting development that began taking place during the mid-1980s is the growth of networks of personal computers running network operating systems and distributed operating systems. In a network operating system, the users are aware of the existence of multiple computers and can log in to remote machines and copy files from one machine to another. Each machine runs its own local operating system and has its own local user (or users). Network operating systems are not fundamentally different from single-processor operating systems. They obviously need a network interface controller and some low-level software to drive it, as well as programs to achieve remote login and remote file access, but these additions do not change the essential structure of the operating system.

A distributed operating system, in contrast, is one that appears to its users as a traditional uniprocessor system, even though it is actually composed of multiple processors. The users should not be aware of where their programs are being run or where their files are located; that should all be handled automatically and efficiently by the operating system.

The Table 2.1 given below show the historical development of operating systems, and their features in various time slots:

Table 2.1

Type of Operating System	Period Beginning In	Major Concern	Goal	Mode of Execution
Batch Processing Systems	1960	CPU Idle time	Necessity and efficient use of computer system	One job is executed at a time, programs in a job are executed sequentially.

Multiprogramming Systems	1970	Resource Utilization	Necessity	The system interleaves execution of several programs in order to improve resource utilization and system performance.
Time Sharing Systems	1970	Response Time	Better Service through quick response time	The system interleaves the execution of processes to provide good response time to all processes.
Real Time Systems	1980	Meeting the Time Constraints	Better Service for time critical applications.	The system interleaves the execution of processes to provide good response time to all processes with sever time constraints.
Distributed Systems	1990	Sharing of Resources	Resource Sharing	Allows access to remote resources using networking. Execution of processes on different computers to achieve sharing and efficient use of resources.

In the era when the multiprogramming and batch processing systems came into existence, the major concern was the efficient use of a computer system. In batch processing system, the goal was CPU efficiency and the emphasis was on reducing the idle time of CPU, in multiprogramming systems the goal was extended to include other resources like memory and input/output devices apart from CPU, so the balanced utilization of system as a whole was the major concern. In the era of time sharing and real time systems the focus shifted from efficient use of system to the enhanced productivity and convenience to the user. Time sharing systems emphasized on providing better service to the user by reducing the response time for the requests of the user and real time systems focused on completing the jobs in fixed time constraints. With the passage of time, the need is felt to share the resources available at different sites having different set of resources, then the distributed systems came in to existence, where a user having lesser number of unsophisticated resources may work on the resources available at the other sites

POPULAR OPERATING SYSTEMS

1. **MS-DOS:** It is Microsoft Disk Operating System. It is used for IBM and IBM Compatible personal computers. It was launched by Microsoft and IBM in collaboration in year 1981. It was very popular in 1980's but its popularity started reducing by the beginning of 1990's. the various features of MS-DOS are:

   (a) It is a single user operating system.

(b) It is an operating system with Command User Interface (CUI).

(The detailed study of MS-DOS is available in the Case Studies Section given at the end of the book)

2. **Microsoft Windows:** It was invented by Microsoft. The basic idea behind its invention was to overcome the problems of MS-DOS. The first successful version of MS-Windows was Window 3.0 and was launched in the year 1990. The subsequent version of Windows Operating system are Windows 95, Windows 98, Windows 2000, Windows Me(Millenium Edition),Windows XP. It is one of the most successful operating system till date. The Main features of Windows Operating System are:

   (a) It is an operating system with graphical user interface(GUI), being GUI it is easy to learn and understand.

   (b) It is a complete operating system, which ensures that all programs are standardized and are easy to work on.

   (c) It is a single user, multitasking operating system, i.e a user may run more than one program at the same time

Windows NT: It is a multiuser, time sharing operating system designed by Microsoft. It is a powerful operating system, which can be used for powerful workstations, networks and data base servers. The main features of Windows NT operating system are:

(a) Its interface is GUI.

(b) It supports multiprogramming and multiprocessing.

(c) It supports networking and communication features. Any system using NT Operating System can work as network client or server.

(d) It enforces and ensures security mechanism.

(e) It is enriched with various types of software development and system administration tools.

(The detailed study of Windows Operating System is available in the Case Studies Section given at the end of the book)

3. **Unix:** It was developed in 1970's by Ken Thompson and Dennis Ritchie at Bell Laboratories. It was the first operating system written in high level language and the language used was C. Prior to the invention of Unix, the operating systems were written in assembly level language, due to which operating systems were machine dependent(i.e they could be used only on the systems for which they have been developed). The various features of Unix Operating System are:

   (a) Its interface is CUI i.e Command User Interface.

   (b) It is a multiuser operating system.

   (c) It is portable.

(d) It can be used on any type of system, starting from notebook computers to super computers.

(The detailed study of Unix Operating System is available in the Case Studies Section given at the end of the book)

4. **Linux:** It was developed by Linus Torvalds. He was a student at University of Helsinki,Finland. Earlier he wrote the first version of an Unix like Kernel and posted its code on the Internet and asked the programmers across the globe to improve and enhance it and hence the Linux Operating System came into existence. Torvalds holds the copyright but permits the free distribution of the source code. When someone submits a change, he and his team review it and depending upon the usability it is either added to the source code or it is rejected.

(The detailed study of Linux Operating System is available in the Case Studies Section given at the end of the book)

PERFORMANCE MEASUREMENT OF AN OPERATING SYSTEM

The operating system as discussed earlier also is responsible for providing a convenient environment in which user can execute the various programs. The ultimate aim is to make the efficient use of the computer system and to provide a user friendly environment. It is also important to measure these factors in quantitative terms so that various design principles can be compared, and the operating system best as per the user's requirements can be chosen and implemented. The various factors like user friendly interface, for the performance measurement of the operating system are non-quantifiable and hence can not be counted as such. As the attributes of user friendliness and convenience are relative terms and varies from user to user and environment to environment. The various attributes for performance measurement may be enumerated as:

- **Efficiency:** It deals with utilization of CPU time and disk space.
- **System Performance:** It is related to the throughput of the system i.e amount of work done per unit of time. The through put of a system is the number of jobs, programs, processes completed by it per unit of time.
- **User Service:** The next important criteria for the performance is how the system is providing the service to the user, the ultimate aim of the user is that his job must be executed at a fast rate, so two measures used in this context are:

  (a) *Turn around Time:* it is time slice between the submission of the job for processing and the time its results become available to the user.

  (b) *Response Time:* it is considered in interactive environments, it deals with the time between submission of sub requests by a user and the time at which the process response back to it.

SIMPLE BATCH PROCESSING SYSTEMS

The batch processing system was introduced to overcome the problems of early systems. Prior to batch processing systems, the early systems were in use. In these systems the manual loading mechanism was used in which jobs were manually loaded one after another in a computer by the computer operator. In these systems, the programs were written from the beginning to run on a specific computer. If the same program was to be used on a different machine, it was required to be rewritten from the beginning. Job to job transition was not automatic. In these systems, computer idle time was more, as computer remained idle while the operator loaded and unloaded jobs and prepared the system for the new job. The traditional batch processing system has been shown in the Figure 2.1(a) given below. The problem of more set up time present in traditional file processing system was reduced by processing the jobs in batches, which is known as batch processing mechanism. Batch of jobs was submitted together to the computer and job-to-job transition was done automatically by the operating system. The jobs in a batch are independent of each other and the jobs of different users may be present in a single batch. The responsibility of the programmer was to prepare a program, data and the corresponding control information and to submit it to the computer operator. The computer operator was used to submit this program in the form of punch cards to the computer and will provide the results. The role of operating system was to transfer control automatically from one job to another. To increase the efficiency of the system, instead of giving a single program to the computer for processing, a batch of these programmed cards can be given to the computer for processing. In a batch processing operating system interaction between the user and processor is limited or there is no interaction at all during the execution of work. Data and programs that need to be processed are bundled and collected as a 'batch' and executed together later on. Automatic job transition of jobs was handled by the 'Batch Monitor' which is also known as the kernel. The jobs were stored on the disk to create the pool of jobs for its execution as a batch. First the pooled jobs are read and executed by the batch monitor and then the jobs are grouped together by grouping the identical jobs in one batch. Then the batched jobs can be executed automatically one after another saving the time. By grouping the similar jobs in one batch, the set-up time for the execution of the jobs will be reduced, for example, if all the jobs which require C Complier have been batched together, then the C Complier is to be loaded once only for processing these jobs. This automatic transition from one job to another was made possible with the help of control statements written in job control language. When the operator gives a command to initiate the processing of the batch, the batch monitor starts the execution of first job of the batch, and after the execution of first job, it switches to the next job and this job to job transition is done automatically without the intervention of the user, and at the end of when all the jobs of one batch have been executed then the system switches to the next batch and at this time when the system switches from one batch to another, the user intervention is required. The working of batch processing system is shown in the Figure 2.1(b) given below.

Batch processing operating systems are ideal in situations where:

- There is large amount of data to be processed.

- The programs with similar data needs are to be processed.
- The jobs with similar type of processing are involved.

Like in Payroll Processing, Stock Control and Billing System.

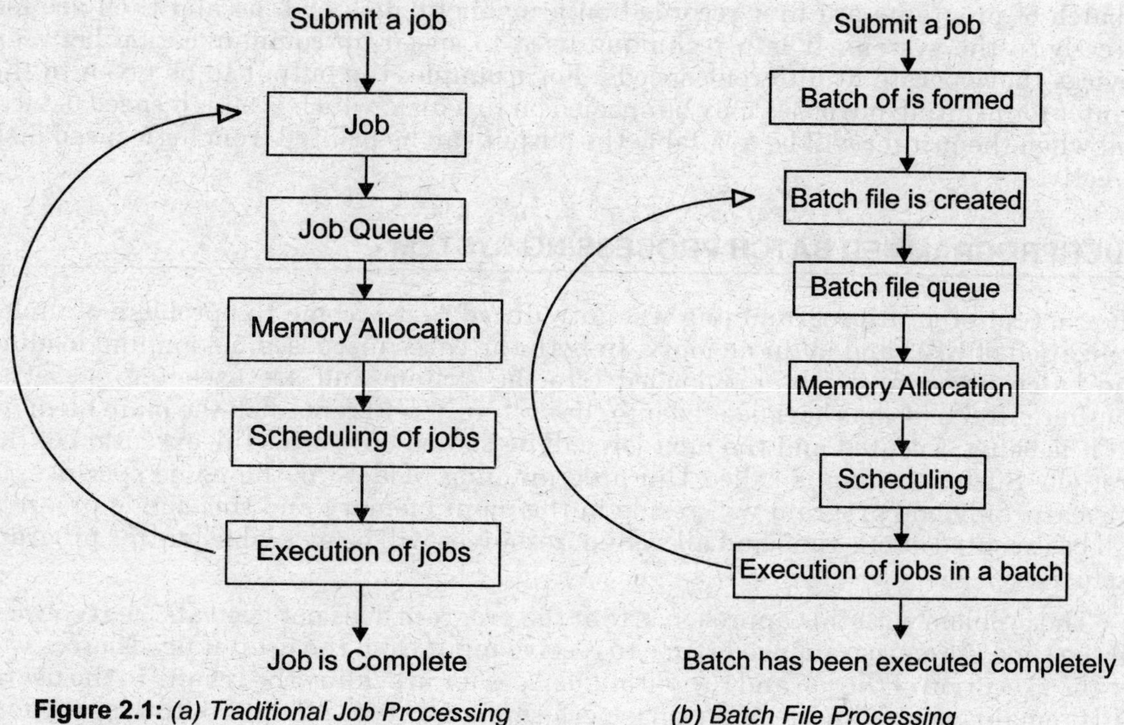

Figure 2.1: *(a) Traditional Job Processing* *(b) Batch File Processing*

Advantages

1. Batch processing systems help in reducing the idle time of system as job to job transition is automatic.
2. Batch processing system help in reducing the set up time, as jobs have been batched together.
3. Batch processing is useful for the jobs which require less or no user interaction.
4. Batch processing system provides improved system utilization due to reduced turn around time.
5. The workload of operator has been reduced and is shifted to the system.

Disadvantages

1. No interaction with user is possible, while the program is executed.
2. It requires mounting of tapes or cards, which is wastage of time.
3. CPU idle time will increase, when the transition from one job to another is taking place.

To overcome the limitation of job transition from one job to another and to reduce the idle time of CPU, the concept of automatic job transition and Spooling was developed. CPU used to be idle most of the times because input-output devices are slower as compared to the CPU. To overcome this mismatch of speed the concept of Spooling (Simultaneous Peripheral Operation On-line) was introduced, in which a batch of programs are first recorded on a magnetic disk or tape and then are fed directly to the system. It is a technique used to speed up communication between devices that operate at different speeds. For example, the output to be given to the printer for printing purposes may be spooled on to a disk, which is a high speed device, and when the printer will be available the output can be printed from high speed disk directly.

MULTIPROGRAMMED BATCH PROCESSING SYSTEM

The concept of multiprogramming was introduced to overcome the problem of under utilization of CPU and main memory. In both the cases discussed, i.e manual loading and batch processing, jobs are loaded into the system and are executed one after another. After a job has been loaded into the system, it will remain in the main memory till it is being executed and the next job will be loaded only after the execution of the first job. Such a system is called Uni-programming Model. As the name specifies, in this case, only one program will reside in the main memory and this single program will be executed at one time and all system resources will be available for this program exclusively.

The problem with this approach is that the program does not need all the resources all the time. As a program needs time to receive input from the user, it needs processor for the execution of the job and the output devices for providing the results to the users. CPU remains idle when the program is performing any type of input/output operation. So the program does not need the CPU all the time, but in uni-programmming system, CPU is dedicated to one program only, leading to the wastage of precious CPU time. So some mechanism is required to solve the problem of under utilization of CPU. Depending upon the CPU utilization, the jobs can be divided into two categories:

- **CPU Bound Jobs:** These types of jobs use CPU most of the time, and amount of input output operations is quiet less. In these types of jobs, the CPU utilization is very high. Programs which perform scientific/mathematical calculations fall in this category. Like processing of telephone bill of a user, needs just a command to send input, but rest of the job is to process the data depending upon usage and package opted, falls in the category of CPU bound jobs.
- **Input-Output Bound Jobs:** These types of jobs use Input-Output devices most of the time and the amount of processing required is low. In these types of jobs, CPU utilization is quiet less. Programs that are used for commercial applications fall in this category.

As discussed earlier, the CPU is not optimally utilized in the case of uni-programming systems; this problem is further enhanced if the jobs are input-output bound. To overcome this problem, the concept of multiprogramming was introduced.

Multiprogramming means interleaved execution of multiple jobs by the same computer.

In case of multiprogramming, two or more user programs can reside in the main memory at the same time and are being executed one after another. When one program is waiting for the input and output transfer, the other program can utilize the CPU, by doing so the CPU will be occupied in executing one job or the other and hence CPU will have some program to execute all the time and hence it will not be idle and overall CPU utilization will increase many fold.

Most of the times, the multiprogramming is visualized as the CPU is executing multiple jobs at the same time. But this notion is entirely wrong. Multiprogramming does not mean the execution of instructions from several programs at the same time, but it means that multiple programs reside in the main memory, and a part of one program is executed and then a part of another and so on. Remember, CPU can execute one instruction at a time, so out of many programs residing in the memory, only of them can use the CPU at a time. Execution of multiple programs at the same time is not possible at all.

Example of Multiprogramming Environment: The example given below in Figure 2.2 demonstrate a typical multiprogramming environment, where four jobs A, B, C and D are residing in the memory along with the operating system. Here job A is utilizing the CPU as it is being executed right now, job B is performing input/output operation(either it is receiving data through input device or is providing output through output device) and job C and D are waiting for CPU to become free. So these programs can be categorized into following three categories:

i. *Running:* The programs which are using the CPU, In this example program A is in the running state.

ii. *Blocked:* The programs which are performing any type of input/output operations are said to be in blocked state, in this example program B is in blocked state.

iii. *Ready:* The programs waiting for the CPU are said to be in ready state, in this example, Programs C and D are in Ready state.

As soon as job A leaves the control of CPU, CPU is given to program C or D (depending on the scheduling criteria followed) and if job B completes the operation related to input or output, its state changes to ready. So following this order the CPU will never be free and hence the idle time of CPU will reduce.

Main Memory

Pre-Requisites for Efficient Multiprogramming: In order to perform multiprogramming in an efficient manner, the following points should be kept in mind:

1. The size of main memory should be sufficient enough to accommodate a large number of jobs.

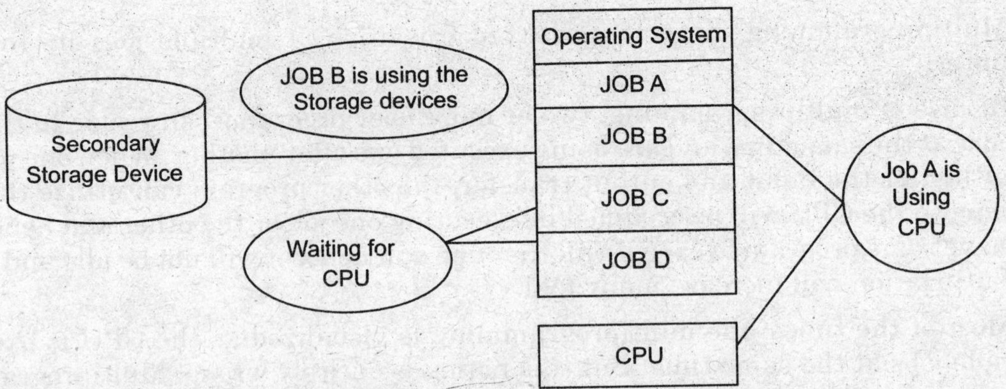

Figure 2.2: *Operations of a Multiprogramming System*

2. The different jobs available in the main memory should not be allowed to interfere with each other, so proper memory protection mechanism is to be implemented. It will prevent one job to go beyond its allocated area.
3. In multiprogramming system, when a job while executing needs input from user, CPU is taken from this job and after getting the required input it resumes the job from the point where the processing was stopped, so it requires preserving the job's status information when CPU is taken away from it and restoring this information back before CPU is given back to it again. It is made possible by maintaining Process Control Block (PSB) for each loaded process.
4. For effective execution of the concept of multiprogramming, a proper job mix of Input/output and CPU bound jobs should be maintained. It will facilitate the best utilization of CPU time.
5. When there are multiple jobs waiting for their turn to get the CPU (as in the example above jobs C and D are waiting for the CPU), then operating system must decide that CPU is to be given to which of these ready jobs. For handling this, proper scheduling algorithm should be used by CPU scheduler.
6. In many cases more than one job arrives at the same time, or there may be jobs which need to be executed at the priority basis, then program priority is assigned so that the jobs with high priority will be executed before the jobs with low priority.
7. Along with the implementation of priority scheduling, there comes the need of enforcing the preemption policy, where preemption is the forced de-allocation of the CPU from a program i.e the CPU is taken away from a low priority program when a high priority job arrives.

The major functions of multiprogramming system can be enumerated as Scheduling the jobs, memory and I/O management, where it deals with allocation and deallocation of memory and I/O devices as per the requirement and third important issue is resource sharing with proper protection mechanism, where one program is not allowed to interfere with the other programs. The Figure 2.3 shows the state transition diagram for a multiprogramming environment.

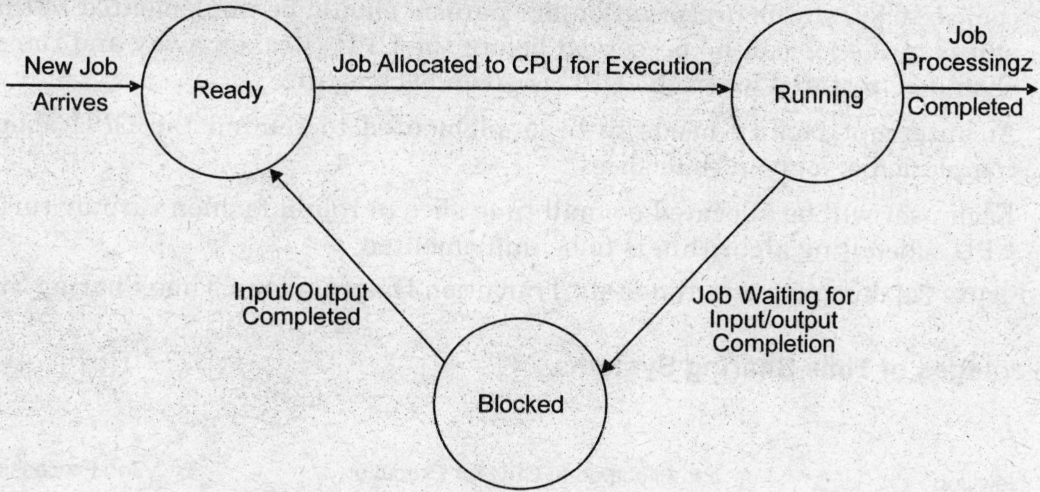

Figure 2.3: *State Transition Diagram for Multiprogramming Environment*

TIME SHARING SYSTEM

Time Sharing systems are the systems in which number of users interact with the system and use system resources at the same time and all the users feel that he/she is using the system exclusively. The user thinks that he is the sole user of the system. This mechanism uses multiprogramming with a special scheduling algorithm. The multiprogramming feature allows a number of programs to reside in the memory and scheduling algorithm allocate a short CPU time to various user process one by one. Each process will get a small amount of CPU time for the execution of the job and this small time duration is termed as time slot or time slice or time quantum. The CPU will be taken away from the process when the allocated time slice expires. On the other hand the process can also leave the CPU when the duration of the job is less than the time allocated or the job needs to perform some input/output operation. The time slice is of the order of milliseconds or microseconds. For successful operation of time sharing systems, the following points should be kept in to consideration:

1. Multiple users should be allowed to use the system at the same time in an interactive mode.
2. The system should have large memory space available so that the programs of a number of users can be stored in the system.
3. As the time sharing systems will be using multiprogramming feature, so proper memory protection mechanism should be implemented so that one job should not interfere with the other job.

4. In time sharing system, the CPU will be taken away from the process when the allotted time slice expires and is given back when the next turn of the process comes, so job status preservation mechanism should be implemented so that the status of the job can be preserved before the CPU is taken away and the status should be restored when the CPU is given back again.
5. An interrupt facility needs to be implemented to remind the CPU about the completion of a given time slice.
6. Each user will be allocated a small time slice in round fashion turn by turn, so a CPU scheduling algorithm is to be implemented.

Figure 2.4 demonstrates the State Transition Diagram for a Time Sharing System.

Advantages of Time Sharing Systems

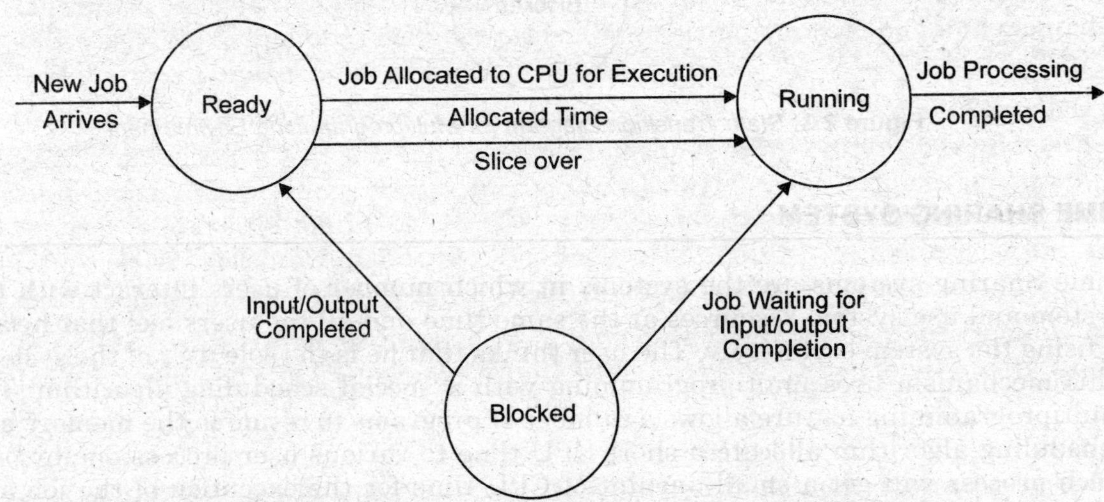

Figure 2.4: *State Transition Diagram for Time Sharing Systems*

1. The time sharing systems help in reducing the idle time of CPU, as it is a fact that the user is not using the CPU all the time, user will be receiving the input and/or delivering the output in between the processing. During the time I/O operation is being performed, the CPU remains idle. But using time sharing system, this time can be allocated to other process and hence it will ensure the better utilization of CPU time.
2. In time sharing system, all the programs will be put into execution very soon and all the programs will be under active state, so the response time will improve drastically.
3. A number of distant users may be sharing the same set of resources, which is a benefit to the small users, who will be able to access a large number of sophisticated resources.

Example of Time Sharing System

Lets us consider a scenario where three processes P1, P2 and P3 are running at the same time, and the time duration of these processes is 5, 4 and 2 milliseconds respectively.

Case I: If the processes are executed one after another then first of all P1 will be executed and it will take 5 ms and then P2 will run and will end its execution at the end of 9 ms and then P3 will finally complete its execution at the end of 11 ms. And the waiting time of P1 = 0 and P2 = 5 ms and for P3 = 9 ms.

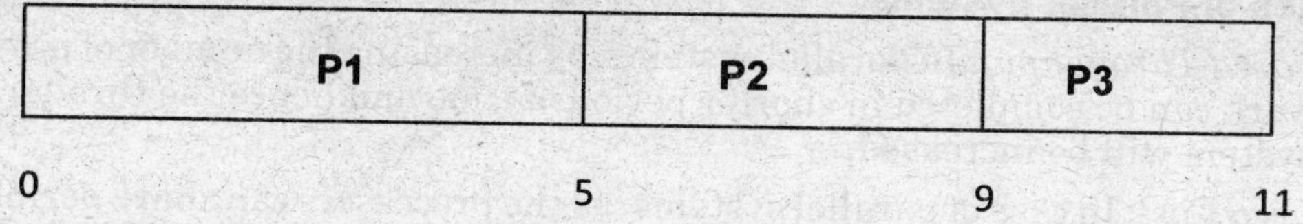

Case II: If the processes are executed using time sharing mode with a time slice of 1 ms, then P1 will be executed for 1 ms and then P2 will get the CPU for 1 ms and then P3 will be executed for 1 ms and after that P1 will get the CPU again. The execution of these processes has been shown below as:

P1	P2	P3	P1	P2	P3	P1	P2	P1	P2	P1	
0	1	2	3	4	5	6	7	8	9	10	11

So waiting time of P1 is again 0 and for P2 it is 1 ms and for P3 it is 2 ms. And moreover the P2 will be completed at the end of 10 ms and P3 will be completed at the end of 6 ms. It is clearly evident from the example that by using time sharing systems the waiting time and the job completion time (also known as the turn around time) of processes P2 and P3 will reduce and moreover the CPU utilization will improve to a greater extent.

PARALLEL SYSTEMS

These systems are referred to as the systems in which a number of processors work in parallel. These are also called multiprocessor systems; such systems have more than one processor working in a close connection with each other, sharing common computer bus, the clock and may be memory and peripheral devices. These systems are used to interface multiple networked computers to complete task in parallel. A parallel operating system works by dividing sets of calculations into smaller parts and distributing them between the machines on a network. The basic architecture of these systems allows coordinating distributed loads between multiple computers in a network. These systems use software to manage all the different resources of the computer like memory, cache, processing power to run in parallel. A given task is distributed between the machines on a network and the routing software share its memory by assigning the same address space to all the networked computers or distribute its memory by assigning a different address space to each system. To facilitate communication between the processor cores and memory arrays, routing software has to either share its memory by assigning the same address space to all of the networked computers, or distribute its memory by assigning a different address space to each processing core. Sharing memory allows the operating system to run very quickly, but it is usually not as powerful. When using distributed shared memory, processors have access to both their own local memory and the memory of other processors; this distribution may slow the operating system, but it is often more flexible and efficient.

Advantages of Parallel Systems

i. *Increased Throughput:* In parallel systems, by increasing the number of processors the work can be completed in shorter period of time and hence the through put of the system will be increased.

ii. *Reduced Cost:* In case of parallel systems, as the processors can share peripherals, cabinets and power supplies, the cost of multiprocessor system will be quiet less as compared to multiple single systems. If several programs are to operate on the same set of data, it is economical to store data on one disk and to have all the processors share them, rather than to have many computers with local disks and many copies of data.

iii. *Reliability:* As the functions can be distributed properly among several processors, then the failure of one processor will not halt the system because other processors will take over the work of the failed system. In this case the overall performance of the system will be slowed down to some extent.

The multiple processor parallel systems can be divided into two categories:

- **Symmetric:** In such systems, each processor runs an identical copy of the operating system and these copies communicate with each other as and when required. The major benefit of this system is that many processors can run at the same time, without causing any deterioration in the performance. Windows NT, Unix and Solaris operating systems follow this mechanism.
- **Asymmetric:** In such systems, each processor is assigned a specific task, a master processor controls the system and other processors abide by the instructions of the master processors. The normal master-slave model is used in this case, the master processor schedules and allocates the work to the slave processors. Sun Operating System Version 4 follow this mechanism.

DISTRIBUTED SYSTEMS

In these systems, the computation has been distributed among multiple systems (processors). It is a loosely coupled collection of autonomous computers connected by a network using system software to produce a single integrated computing environment. In these systems, the software and data may be distributed around the system, programs and files are stored on different storage devices, which are located at different geographical locations, accessible to each other. It is defined as a system consisting of two or more nodes where each node is a computer system with its own memory, processor, some networking hardware and the ability to perform some control functions of an operating system. These systems make the best use of multiple resources and presence of a network to provide the benefits of resource sharing among computers, reliability of operations, speed up of execution of applications and better and fast communication between the users and processes. The processors do not share memory or a clock; these processors have their own local memory. The processors communicate with each other through various communication lines and by using the appropriate communication protocol. The processors in these systems may vary in size and function. These may include small microprocessors, workstations, minicomputers and large general purpose computer systems. However the chances of failure of system and its subsequent effects needs that these systems should be designed with special design techniques in mind.

The following are the key features of a distributed system:

- They are loosely coupled and the remote access is many times slower than local access.
- The nodes in a distributed environment are autonomous.
- Network connections are maintained using system software and the remote access requires explicit message passing between nodes i.e messages are passed from CPU to CPU.
- These systems use protocols for reliability, flow control, failure detection, etc., implemented in software.

Advantages of Distributed Systems

i. *Sharing:* In the distributed systems, a number of sites are connected to each other, then they will be able to share the resources with each other. It provides the facility of sharing data at the remote sites, processing information in a distributed database, using remote specialized hardware etc.

ii. *Reliability:* In distributed system environment, if one site stops working, then the remaining sites will keep on carrying the jobs. These systems offer enhanced availability of resources through redundancy of resources and communication paths. Hence there will be no threat of failure and ultimately the overall reliability of the system will increase.

iii. *Increase in Computation Speed:* In distributed environment, a single job can be divided in to number of parts and then can be distributed among the various sites and these sites will be executing their own part at the same time, it will increase the computation speed of the processes and hence the throughput will increase and turn around time (time between submission of the job and getting its final results) will decrease. So a number of jobs can be executed in a stipulated time.

iv. *Better Communication among Systems:* In many cases, the programs need to exchange data with one another. Distributed systems facilitate the sharing and communication of data among the various sites.

v. *Incremental Growth:* In distributed environment it is easy to add the new nodes at a cheaper rate as compared to set up the central systems.

Main techniques used in Distributed Operating Systems:

- **Distributed Control:** as the name specifies the control functions of a distributed system are performed by several computers instead of being performed by a single computer, it ensures that if any one node fails in the distributed environment, it does not affect operations of the entire system.
- **Transparency:** it is applicable to both the resources and services, where a user should be able to access them without having to know which node in the distributed system has initiated it. i.e the location of the nodes is hidden for all the processes.
- **Remote Procedure Calls:** These calls are used by an application to execute a procedure in another computer over the distributed system.

Disadvantages of Distributed Systems

Apart from the various benefits of distributed systems, these systems also suffer from some limitations also, which have been enumerated as:

1. The communication in a distributed environment is dependent on the availability and reliability of the underlying network.
2. The performance of the network is also a major issue to be taken into consideration.
3. The data transfer rate from one node to another may cause delay in communication.
4. The communication between two nodes is dependent on the total network bandwidth available for the communication.
5. As data and its processing are distributed over a complete network then there are higher security risks as the intruders have large number of access points for tempering with the data.

Differences between Distributed and Parallel Operating Systems

Distributed Operating systems are also referred to as Loosely Coupled systems whereas parallel processing systems are referred to as tightly coupled systems, where a loosely coupled system is one in which the processors do not share memory and each processor has its own local memory whereas in a tightly coupled system there is a single system wide primary memory shared by all the processors.

The processors of distributed operating systems can be placed far away from each other to cover a wider geographic area which is not the case with parallel processing systems.

The number of processors that can be usefully deployed is very small in a parallel processing operating system whereas for a distributed operating system a large number of processors can be used to increase the efficiency and productivity of the system.

REAL TIME SYSTEMS

Real time systems are the systems which has well-defined, fixed time constraints. In these systems, the processing needs to be done within the fixed defined time frame, otherwise the system will fail. These systems are also known as real time processing systems. These systems impose rigid time requirements on the operation of the processor or flow of data and hence can be used as a control device in a dedicated application. A real time application is a program that responds to activities in an external system within a maximum time determined by the external system. A real time system is said to be functioning accurately only if it can provide the accurate results within fixed time constraints, where as in time sharing systems, the systems should respond quickly but fixed rigid time constraints are not there and even in batch processing systems, there is no constraint on time at all.

Systems that control scientific experiments, industrial control systems, control of nuclear power plants, oil refining, chemical processing and traffic control systems, air, reservation of tickets etc and medical imaging systems fall in the category of real time systems. The main features of real time systems can be enumerated as:

1. These systems allow the creation of multiple processes within an application.
2. These systems allow the priorities to be assigned to the processes.
3. In these systems the user can define interrupt and interrupt processing tasks.
4. These systems use priority based scheduling algorithms.
5. These systems use deadline oriented scheduling algorithms.
6. These systems provide facility to implement the fault tolerance mechanisms.

Real Time systems can be classified into two categories

(a) *Hard Real Time Systems:* These systems adhere to strict time constraints and ensure that critical tasks will complete in time. These systems are dedicated to processing real time applications and meet the response requirements of the application under all conditions.

(b) *Soft Real Time Systems:* In these systems, a critical real-time task is tried to be completed with the best effort possible, but does not guarantee that the task will be completed in all circumstances. It means that the time constraints may or may not be met.

PERSONAL COMPUTER SYSTEMS

These are the systems which are used by a single user only. These systems came into existence due to the increasing need and dependency of users on the computers for the day to day operations and decreasing cost of the hardware. Due to the reduced cost the computers have become affordable for one and all. These personal computers came into existence in 1970s and less expensive and smaller as compared to the mainframe computers. Earlier these systems were neither multiuser nor multitasking, but later on the required features have been included in these systems. The major goal of these systems is to maximize user convenience and lesser emphasis has been given to CPU and /or peripheral utilization. With the advancement in the technology, these systems now a days provide almost all major services required. These systems have adopted all the latest technologies developed and used by the large operating systems.

Features of Personal Computer Systems are

1. These are single user systems.
2. Resource Utilization is not the major concern.
3. The main emphasis is on the better facilities to the users, like better user interface and better services.
4. These systems may not be having all facilities which are present on other mainframe systems (Due to advancement in the technology and reduction in the hardware cost, the PC systems have been upgraded to support all latest features).

NETWORK OPERATING SYSTEMS

An operating system that provides the connectivity among a number of autonomous computers is called a network operating system. A network operating system is a software application that provides a platform for both the functionality of an individual computer and for multiple computers within an interconnected network. It controls other software and computer hardware to run applications, share resources, protects data and establishes communication. These systems support the use of network of machines and provide an environment where users are aware of using a set of computers, which facilitates the use of remote resources located over the network. A network operating system provides printer sharing, common file system and database sharing, application sharing, and the ability to manage a network name directory, security, and other housekeeping aspects of a network. These operating systems include special functions for connecting computers and devices into a network. In these systems, the computers are connected by external interfaces that run under the control of software. Each computer in the network run an autonomous copy of operating system and communicate with each other to allow various types of facilities like sharing of data, files, peripherals, memory and hard disk and apart from that remote execution of programs. The main features of network operating systems are:

1. These systems provide features such as support for processors, protocols, automatic hardware detection and support for multiprocessing of applications.
2. These systems provide security features such as authentication, login restrictions and access control.

3. These systems provide name, directory services, file, print and web and back up services.
4. These systems support internetworking.

The most important services provided by a network operating system is the file service. It allows a user of a computer to access the files and other storage objects from any other remote computer connected to the network. The files stored in one or more computers are called the file servers and computers that access these files are called workstation. The two most common types of network operating systems are:

- **Peer To Peer:** This type of network operating systems allows users to share resources and files located on their computers and to access shared resources found on the other computers. In these systems, all computers are considered equal and have same set of privileges to use the resources available on the network. These systems are designed basically for small to medium local area networks.
- **Client/Server:** These network operating systems allow the network to centralize functions and applications in one or more dedicated file servers. The file server becomes the heart of the system also known as the server, it is responsible for providing access to resources and providing security. The workstations also known as the clients, on the other hand, have the access to resources available on the file servers. These network operating systems allow multiple users to share the resources at the same time irrespective of their physical location.

The most common example of such a system is a set of workstations connected together through a local area network, where every workstation has its own operating system, each user has its own workstation in exclusive use and cooperate with each other to allow a variety of facilities including sharing of files, hardware resources and execution of jobs. A user can connect to the servers or other workstations by authenticating them through login and passwords.

The common network operating systems are: Novell Netware, Windows NT/2000, Linux, Unix, Sun Solaris.

Chapter 3

Process Management

One of the primary job of an operating system is to execute the user programs and apart from that it needs to take care of various system tasks, which are required as a basis for the execution of user programs. Earlier the uni-programming model was followed where only one program was executed at a time. This single program used to have the full control of the system and had access to all the system resources. But now a days, multiple programs can be loaded into the system and can be executed at the same time, which requires the proper management of various programs. The user makes use of processes to achieve the execution of the programs either in sequential or concurrent manner. The programs in execution are termed as a process. The system has two types of processes running in the systems:

- Operating System Processes, which are responsible for the execution of the system code,
- User Processes, which are responsible for the execution of user processes.

The operating system is capable of executing both types of processes at the same time and the operating system manages the allocation and de-allocation of the resources for these processes, whenever it is required. By making the multiple processes run at the same time, the productivity of the user will increase because of reduced turnaround time and the idle time of CPU will decrease, which will result in enhancement of the overall productivity of the system and efficient utilization of the user time.

DEFINITION OF PROCESS

A process can be defined as a program in execution or a unit of work given for processing to the system, it actually performs the actions specified in the program. It can be visualized as an instance of application execution, where an application may be system application or may be a program written by the user. The user may run many different applications at the same time or even can run the various instances of same application at the same time, each running application is a process. The process will be alive only for the duration of execution of the application.

A program is a passive entity that does not perform any action by itself, it has to be executed to realize the actions specified in it. When a process is executed, the CPU executes the instructions in the program, when CPU wishes to switch from one process to another, the kernel saves the status information of the currently running process and loads the status of the process to be executed now and the old status is reloaded when the same process is scheduled again.

Components of a Process: A process is an active entity and the process definition comprises of following components:

1. **Process ID:** It is a unique name/id assigned to the program under execution.
2. **Code:** Is the code of the program itself.
3. **Data:** It corresponds to data and files used in execution of the program.
4. **Stack:** It is used to store the parameters and the return addresses of the functions called.
5. **Resources:** It enlists the set of resources allocated by the system for the execution the process.
6. **State Information:** It specifies the various CPU states, it contains information about the current instruction to be executed, the address of the next instruction to be executed and current status of CPU registers,

A process is more than a code of the program, which just contains the text section as stored on the disk and may be considered as a dead or passive entity, where as the process is considered as an active entity and consists of:

- **Text Section:** which contains the program code,
- **Program Counter:** which shows the execution of current activity.
- **Processor Register:** which show the temporary data.
- **Stack:** which hold the temporary data, return addresses and local variables.
- **Data Section:** which contains the global variables.

There may be many processes residing in the system, they need the processor when they have been scheduled for the execution. And apart from the processor, the process may need the other resources like memory, input and output devices or may be the data. The operating system must store all this information about the processes. To manage this, the system maintains the Process Control Block and the Process environment for each process.

The process environment comprises of resource information, file pointers, code, data and stack, address space of a process and all other information required for accessing and controlling the resources allocated to the process. The contents of process environment change during execution of the process. The operating system creates a process environment by allocating memory to the process, loading the process code in the allocated memory and setting up its data space. The various components of program environment are listed in the Table 3.1 given below, and the contents of the process environment change during execution of a process due to actions like file open and close and run time creation and destruction of data by the process.

Table 3.1 Components of Program Environment

Component	Description
Code and Data	It contains the code of the program, including its functions and procedures and its data, including the stack.
Memory Allocation Information	Information concerning memory areas allocated to the process, it is used to implement memory accesses made by the process.
Status of file processing activities	Pointers to the files opened by the process.
Process Interaction Information	It stores the information required to manage the interactions between the processes like interprocess messages, signal handlers, ids of parent and child processes.
Resource Information	Information concerning resources allocated to a process.

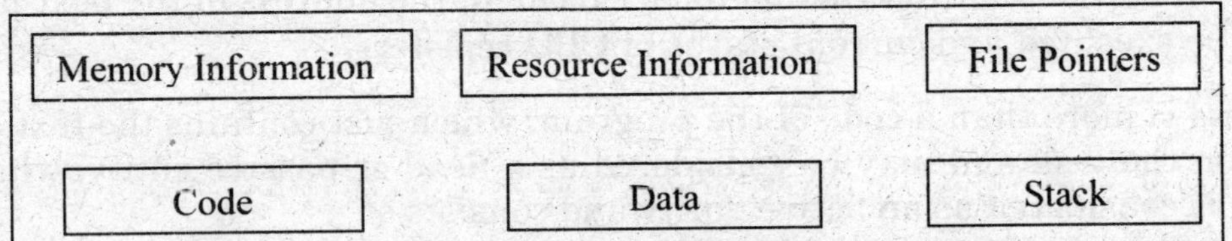

Figure 3.1: *Process Environment*

Two or more processes may be associated with a same program, but they are considered as the two separate entities. Lets us consider the case, if a user has invoked several copies of the same program then each one of these will be considered as a separate process. They will have same text section, but their data section will be different. A process is an executing program, including the current values of the program counter, registers, and variables. The subtle difference between a process and a program is that the program is a group of instructions whereas the process is an activity. The program and process may have following types of relationships:

One-to-One: A one-to-one relationship exists when a single execution of a sequential program is in process. During the execution the control flows between the main program and set of functions according to the logic given in the program. If several executions of this program are in progress at the same time, then relationship will be many-to-one.

Many-to-Many: At many instances, specially designed programs i.e the programs containing concurrent programming feature, informs the operating systems about the parts of the program which are to executed concurrently. The system considers each of these executions as a process. So the relationship between the processes and the program is many-to-one. Such a program is termed as a concurrent program and the processes that co-exist at the same time are called concurrent processes. These processes can interact with each other during execution.

Creation of Child Processes: When the operating system initiates the execution of a program by creating a process corresponding to it, it is known as the main process and this main process may create other processes, which are termed as the child processes, moreover, this child process may create other processes, resulting in a hierarchical tree like structure, where the main process is at the root of the tree. For example: the user is running a program to extract data from the database using some techniques of data mining, then the process will have three steps: first to extract the data from the data base, copying the data from the specified location and then to write the data. The execution of the data_miner program will create three processes namely data_extract, data_copy and data-write as shown in the Figure 3.2.

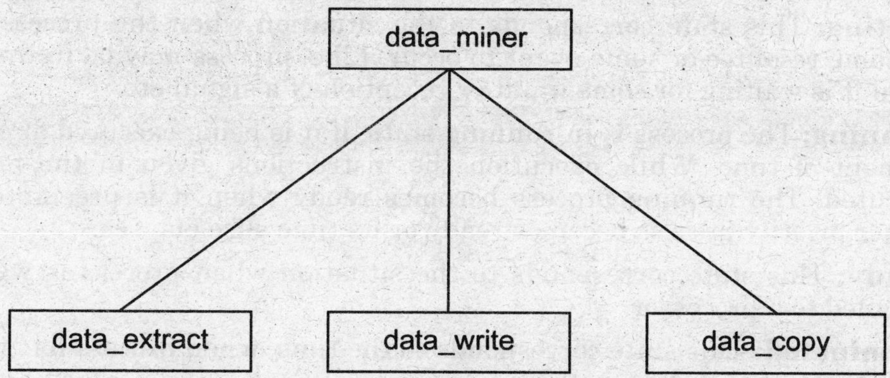

Figure 3.2: *Parent Child Relation between Processes*

Benefits of Child Processes: The creation of child processes by the program under consideration is:

(a) As the child processes are created by the parent process, it facilitates the concept of multi-tasking, which enables the interleaved execution of various processes at the same time. As a result of which the computation speed will increase resulting in faster execution of user programs and more user requests can be entertained at the same time.

(b) Critical Jobs can be performed on the priority basis, as the child processes created by the main parent process can be assigned higher priority as compared to the parent and other child processes and hence can be executed at the earliest. This facilitates the execution of time critical jobs at the priority basis.

(c) When some un-trusted program is to be executed under some abnormal conditions, then such processes can be executed as child processes, because if some error occurs during the execution the operating system will abort the execution of child process or the child process itself, without affecting the other processes in the tree.

PROCESS STATES

The process while in execution will pass through various states during its complete life time. The state is defined according to the current activity performed by a particular process at a particular moment of time. Depending on the criteria of the present activity status, the process can be in any of the following states:

- **New:** This state corresponds to the time when the process is created but it has not been admitted to the pool of executable processes by the operating system. Normally the new process has not been loaded into the main memory although its process control block has been created.
- **Waiting:** This state corresponds to the situation when the process is waiting for some resource or some event to occur. Like, process may be in waiting state, when it is waiting for some input or reception of a signal etc.
- **Running:** The process is in running state, if it is being executed at a particular moment of time. While execution the instructions given in the program are executed. The running process becomes ready when it is preempted either a higher priority process becomes ready or its time slice elapses.
- **Ready:** This state corresponds to the situation when process is waiting to be assigned to a processor.
- **Terminated:** This state corresponds to the time, when process has finished the execution.

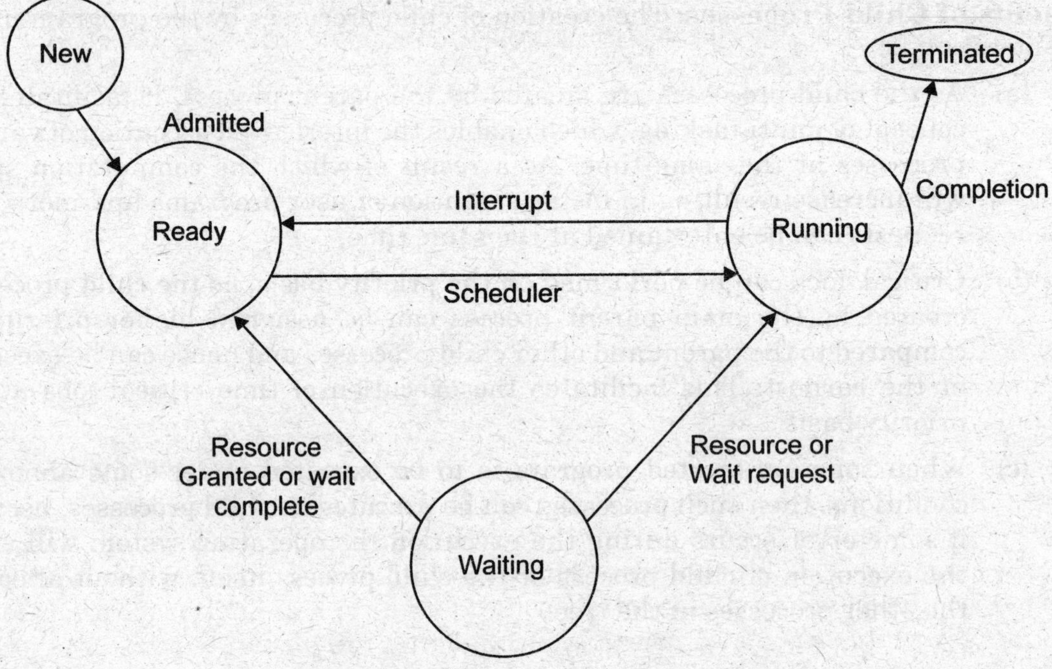

Figure 3.3: *State Transition Diagram for a Process*

It is worth mentioning here, that only one process may be in running state on any processor at any particular moment of time, although many processes may be in ready or waiting states. The Figure 3.3 given below show the different states of a process during its complete life time. A new process is put in ready state after all resources required by it have been allocated, it may enter the running, waiting and ready states a number of times and in the end it reaches the terminated state.

Table 3.2 shows the reasons behind the transition of a process from one state to another.

Table 3.2 Reason behind State Transitions

State Transition	Reason
Ready -> running	The process goes in execution state, process starts or resumes execution of its instructions.
waiting -> ready	The process was in waiting state, as it was waiting for some I/O event to occur, when such an event occurs, the process changes its state from waiting to ready.
Running -> ready	The running process is preempted and processor is taken from the running process, as processor decides to execute some other process. The reason behind this transition are: • A high priority process arrives • A high priority process already in the system, becomes ready. • The time slice of the running process has elapsed.
Running -> waiting	The running process may be in need of some I/O or may require the occurence of some event for its normal execution, so the running process goes into waiting state, until the resource request or the event required has not occurred. The reasons for a process to go into waiting state are: • Process requires an I/O operation. • Process requires some resource. • Process wish to wait for a particular interval of time. • Process waits till some action by other process occurs.
Running -> terminated	The process is terminated, when its execution is complete. The reasons for process termination are: • The process being executed completes it task assigned and goes into termination state, it may also happen when the process thinks that it will not be able to complete its execution (may be due to insufficient resources/incorrect data or inability to access data required) and issues a 'terminate me' system call. These both cases are of self termination by a process. • Process may be terminated by its parent process, it happens when the parent process realizes that the execution of the child process is not required.

	• The process if exceeds the limit of resource utilization may be terminated by the operating system. • During the process execution if some abnormal condition occurs (like overflow, data access violation, security breach, execution of invalid instruction), then the process is terminated. • The process during execution is indulged in a deadlock and the system is not able to recover from the deadlock, so the only choice to recover from the deadlock is the process termination.

PROCESS CONTROL BLOCK

The various parameters which come in to action, as the process is invoked are depicted in process control block, also called as task control block. This block show complete information about the present status of a particular process. It is a kernel data structure that contains information regarding the resources being allocated to a process. The basic information is pertaining to following three fundamental functions:

(a) **Scheduling:** this is related to selecting a process to be executed next depending upon the scheduling policy implemented.

(b) **Dispatching:** it deals with creation of an environment for the execution of the process.

(c) **Context Save:** it is used to store the information when the CPU switches from one process to another. The process may release the CPU when its execution has been completed or may be preempted to make the processor available to the other high priority processes. It preserves the process states so that the process can be executed from the point it has been suspended when it resumes the execution again.

The various pieces of information contained in the process control block are explained in table 3.3:

Table 3.3: Contents of Process Control Block

S.No	Information	Purpose
1.	Process ID	It specifies the id of the process, which has been assigned to it as soon as it has been invoked. If a process creates some other child process then the ids of both the parent and the child processes are also preserved.
2.	Process Priority	It specifies the priority number of the process, as various processes are assigned the priority. It is a numeric value that is assigned at the time of process creation. This value may change during the execution of the process

3.	Process State	It shows the current state of the process at a particular moment of time, the process may be in any of the five states: new, ready, running, waiting or terminated.
4.	Program counter	It shows the address of next instruction to be executed for the current process.
5.	PSW [Program Status Word]	It is a collection of control registers in the system, the common fields of a program status word are: interrupt mask, memory protection information, program counter etc. the PSW in the PCB is a snapshot of PSW when the CPU was last released by the process. When the process is loaded back its PSW is loaded along with it.
6.	CPU Registers	A process may use various registers during its execution, the number, type and size may vary from one system to another (as it depends on the architecture of the system). But the common registers, whose contents are stored in the program counter are: Accumulators, index registers, stack pointers and general purpose registers. The data of these registers must be preserved when we move from one process to another.
7.	CPU Scheduling Information	The CPU will use various methods to manage the various processes running in the system, it needs to schedule them, as to decide which process will be executed when, this information will be stored here, which includes the process priority, access to scheduling queues.
8.	Accounting Information	This includes the record of various systems used, when they are used and for how much duration and in what amount. It includes CPU time, Account Numbers, Process ID, Time Limits, Duration for which the I/O devices are used etc.
9.	I/O Status Information	It shows the list of I/O devices allocated to a particular process.
10.	Memory Allocation Information	It shows the allocation details of a particular memory unit to the current process, how much memory of which type has been allocated to a particular process for how much duration. Values of the base and limit registers, page and segment table is mentioned.
11.	ID of the Parent Process	If the process is created by some other process, then id of the parent process is mentioned so that the output of the process can be returned back to the parent process.
12.	Event Occurrence Information	The process may be in waiting state, when it is waiting for the occurrence of some event. This field stores the information regarding the event for which it was waiting. When the required event occurs the process state is changed from waiting to the ready state.

As soon as a particular program is invoked for the execution, its process control block is invoked for that program. For the different programs, different PCB's will be there. And when the system is executing various programs at the same time, as discussed earlier also that CPU can run only one program at a time, so CPU switches from one process to another almost instantaneously and at that time the PSB of the previous process is stored and the PCB of the new process is invoked. This process is termed as context switching. The context switching may be defined as the process of saving an executing thread or process and transferring the control to another thread or process. In context switching following tasks are done:

Saving the state i.e the PCB of the old process i.e the currently running program, this process is termed as context save. The context save performs the house keeping function when a process releases CPU or is preempted by some other process. It involves the saving of the information regarding the process control block and the process environment.

Loading the state i.e the PCB of the new program. Whenever this switching takes place, the current state of the first process is stored in the PCB of that process, so that whenever the system returns back to the first process after the execution of the second process, the previous states of first process can be reused.

During the time the context switching is taking place, the system is doing nothing, so sometimes it is also considered as an overhead. The concept of context switching can be visualized better with the help of the following diagram and the corresponding example. The time required for context switch is dependent on the hardware support and varies from machine to machine, depending upon the memory speed, number of registers available and existence of special instructions etc.

Example: Let the CPU is executing a process P1 at a particular moment of time, and the various parameters regarding this process has been initialized and stored in its PCB named as PCB1. While its execution is in progress, another process P2 comes in the system for the execution and then the operating system will send the interrupt signal to process P1, so that the execution of P1 can be stopped momentarily and the process P2 can be executed. When P2 will be invoked for execution its PCB named as PCB2 will be initialized. But before invoking P2 into action and its corresponding PCB i.e PCB2, the operating system will save the current status of PCB1 so that after the execution of P2, the execution of P1 can be restarted from the point where it had been suspended. The complete process of context switching has been shown in the Figure 3.4 given below.

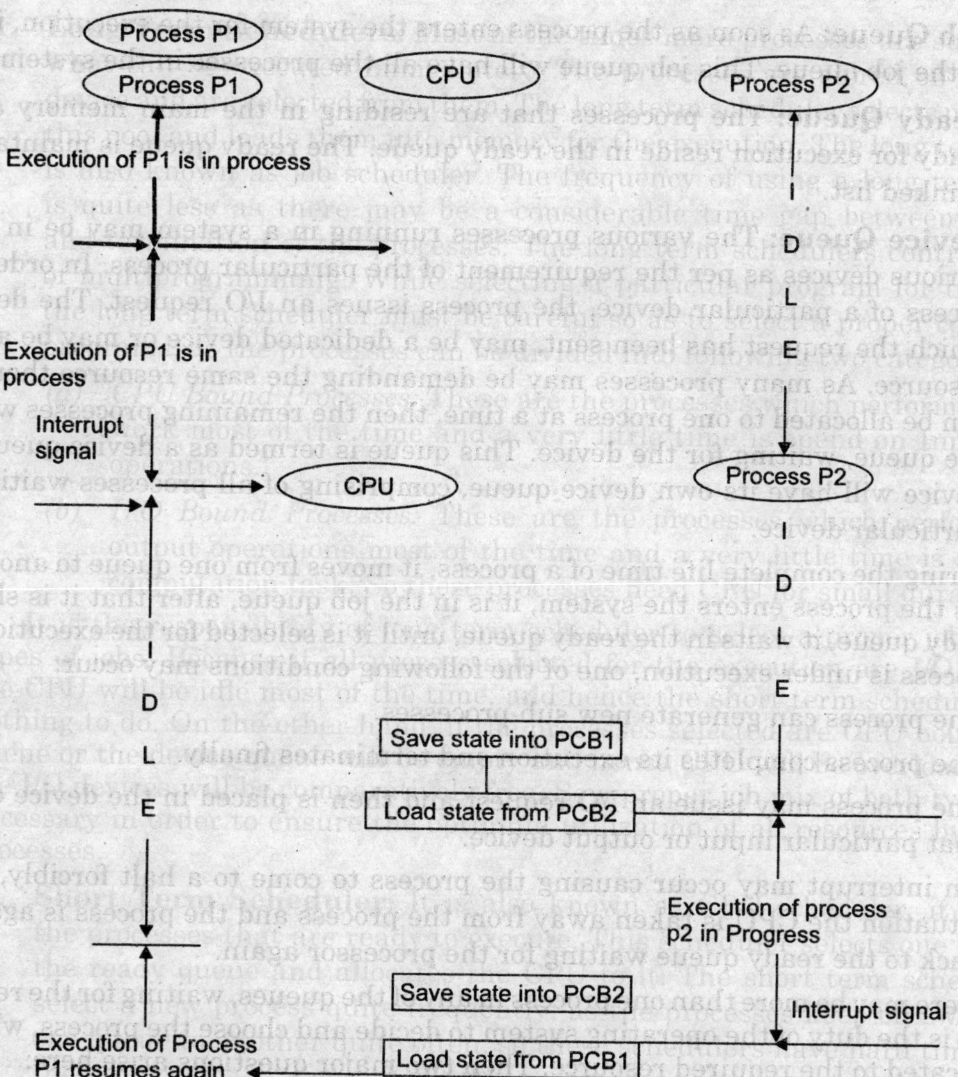

Figure 3.4: *Context switching from one Process to Another*

PROCESS SCHEDULING

The operating systems now a days, support the features of multiprogramming and also work on time sharing basis also. This is helpful to maximize the CPU utilization and overall performance of the system. In the uni-programming model, as only one program will be running at a time, so there will be no need for scheduling. As more than one program is running in the system at the same time, the need is to schedule the various processes, so that various processes can share the resources in a graceful manner, without leading to any type of conflict or deadlock. During the execution of the program, it passes through various queues, as mentioned below:

1. **Job Queue:** As soon as the process enters the system for the execution, it is put in the job queue. This job queue will have all the processes in the system.
2. **Ready Queue:** The processes that are residing in the main memory and are ready for execution reside in the ready queue. The ready queue is maintained as a linked list.
3. **Device Queue:** The various processes running in a system may be in need of various devices as per the requirement of the particular process. In order to get access of a particular device, the process issues an I/O request. The device for which the request has been sent, may be a dedicated device or may be a shared resource. As many processes may be demanding the same resource then device can be allocated to one process at a time, then the remaining processes will be in the queue, waiting for the device. This queue is termed as a device queue. Each device will have its own device queue, comprising of all processes waiting for a particular device.

During the complete life time of a process, it moves from one queue to another. As soon as the process enters the system, it is in the job queue, after that it is shifted to the ready queue, it waits in the ready queue, until it is selected for the execution. Once the process is under execution, one of the following conditions may occur:

1. The process can generate new sub-processes.
2. The process completes its execution and terminates finally.
3. The process may issue an I/O request and then is placed in the device queue of that particular input or output device.
4. An interrupt may occur causing the process to come to a halt forcibly, in such situation the CPU is taken away from the process and the process is again send back to the ready queue waiting for the processor again.

There may be more than one process in any of the queues, waiting for the resources, then it is the duty of the operating system to decide and choose the process, which will be allocated to the required resource. Then two major questions arise here:

1. How to choose a process from the various processes in the queue?
2. Who will choose the process?

The first question is related to the procedure or criteria for the selection of a particular process, out of the various processes waiting in the queue and second one is related to that who will do it.

Both of these jobs are taken care of by the operating system and Schedulers do this job with the help of various scheduling algorithms.

Schedulers: The scheduler is a program which schedules the execution of the process. These can be divided into two categories:

1. Long Term Schedulers.
2. Short Term Schedulers.

1. **Long Term Schedulers:** Most of the times more processes are submitted than what can be executed immediately. The processes are stored on mass storage device and are selected from them. The long term scheduler selects processes from this pool and loads them into memory for the execution. The long term scheduler is also known as job scheduler. The frequency of using a long term scheduler is quite less as there may be a considerable time gap between the creation and termination of the processes. The long term schedulers control the degree of multiprogramming. While selecting a particular program for the execution, the long term scheduler must be careful so as to select a proper combination of programs, as the processes can be divided into following two categories:
   (a) *CPU Bound Processes:* These are the processes which perform computation work most of the time and a very little time is spend on Input or output operations.
   (b) *I/O Bound Processes:* These are the processes which perform input or output operations most of the time and a very little time is spend on the computation task. So these processes need CPU for small durations only.

It is the responsibility of long term scheduler to select a proper job mix of both types of jobs. Because if all process selected for the execution are I/O bound, then the CPU will be idle most of the time, and hence the short term scheduler will have nothing to do. On the other hand, if the processes selected are CPU bound, then I/O queue or the device queue will be empty and hence CPU will be overloaded, whereas the I/O devices will be comparatively free. So a proper job mix of both types of jobs is necessary in order to ensure the optimum utilization of all resources by the various processes.

2. **Short Term Scheduler:** It is also known as CPU scheduler, it selects from the processes that are ready to execute. This scheduler selects one process from the ready queue and allocates the CPU to it. The short term schedulers must select a new process quite frequently; as the processes keep on switching from one queue to another quite often, so these schedulers have hard time managing these processes at a very fast rate.

Difference between Long Term and Short Term Schedulers

Long Term Schedulers (Job Schedulers)	**Short Term Schedulers (CPU Schedulers)**
These select the processes from the secondary storage device and loads them into the memory for the execution.	These select one process out of the various processes that are ready to execute and allocates the CPU to one of them.
The process scheduled by long term scheduler executes for long duration of time.	The process scheduled by short term scheduler executes for small duration of time.

Long term scheduler executes less frequently, as job once scheduled will execute for long duration.	Short term scheduler executes more frequently, as jobs need to be scheduled at small intervals of time.
These schedulers may be slow as compared to short term schedulers.	These schedulers must be fast as compared to the long term schedulers.

VARIOUS OPERATIONS ON PROCESSES

Process management is one of the primary jobs of the operating systems. In the environment where multiple programs run on the system at the same time, the management of these processes becomes even more important. There must be some provision of process creation and deletion and moreover this should be done automatically, as far as possible. The operating system should perform this job for the user, in order to create a user friendly and convenient environment and to ensure the efficient utilization of system resources. The various operations possible on the processes are:

Process Creation: As discussed earlier, there will be a large number of user programs stored in the system and they are executed as and when required, when the program is executed, it becomes a process. So a process is created as soon as the program comes in to execution. The system call create_process, is used to create a new process and assigns to it a priority and assigns a unique identifier known as process_ id and this id is returned to the caller. While a process is under execution it will create many new processes and the newly created processes may create several more new processes in turn. The process creating a new process is called the parent process and the newly created process is termed as the child process, and this child process in turn will create many new other child processes and this complete structure can be visualized as a tree. Whenever a process is created, it receives various physical and logical resources, data as the input and this data input can be passed to the child process by the parent process. The parent and child processes may share all resources or they may share subset of parent's resources and they may not share any of the resources at all. Restricting a child process to a subset of the parents resources prevents any process from overloading the system by creating too many child processes. Whenever a process creates a new child process, then it may be possible that the parent continues to execute concurrently with its child processes or the parent waits until some or all of its child processes have been terminated.

Process Termination: Upon completion of the task assigned to a process, it terminates and the operating system deletes this process by running the system call-exit. During this process all the resources allocated to the process for its execution (like memory, files and I/O devices or buffers) are returned back to the operating system. If a child process is terminated, then it will return data i.e output to its parent process. Upon deletion of a parent process, all of its child processes are also terminated, such a mechanism is called cascading termination. But if a child process is terminated, then deletion of parent does not happen along with. The users are not allowed to delete the processes of the other users. Only the parent process can cause the termination of its child processes. The parent can terminate the child process if the task assigned to the child process has been completed or is not required any more or the child exceeds the resources allocated to it. The termination of the process may be normal or forced. In case of normal termination, the process terminates by using an exit system call. The process terminates gracefully by completing and executing its last statement and all the resources allocated to it are freed. On the other hand, if the termination of the process is a forced one, then the process is terminated by its parent process forcibly by executing an abort System call.

Status Checking: The user may need to check the status of the process at any stage during its execution, it can be checked by the system call check_status, and will return the user the value depicting the present status of the process i.e whether it is alive or terminated.

INTER-PROCESS COMMUNICATION

It is the technique to allow the processes to communicate with each other and to synchronize their actions. It allows the cooperating processes to share and transfer data from one process to another. Interprocess communication is useful in distributed environment where communicating processes may reside on different computers connected with a network. For example, a Web browser retrieving data from a distant server. The interaction between processes will facilitate the sharing of data among processes and hence will speed up the execution of the processes. The various types of process interactions possible are:

- **Sharing of data:** The various processes running may need to share data among themselves and can work on same piece of information. The problem with this sharing is that if number of processes update the same data item at the same time, it will lead to data inconsistency and may create havoc among processes. So before going for the data sharing, the processes must design some mechanism dealing with when and how the data should be shared, so that it can be handled safely.
- **Message Passing:** The processes may interact with each other by sending and receiving messages and valuable information can be exchanged through this mode. The sender will put the information to be transferred in the message and the receiver will receive the same and will act as per his requirement (the receiving process may store, delete or act on the message). The sender and receiver must agree upon the issue that when and how the messages are to be passed.
- **Synchronization:** The processes deliberating for the common cause must coordinate their activities and must perform the jobs in the desired fashion only. The coordination among the processes lead to efficient utilization of resources and faster execution of user's requests.
- **Special Signals:** The processes communicating with each other may need to convey some short message for the smooth execution of the processes. So the signals are used for this purpose, which convey an exceptional situation so that the desired action can be taken. It is being handled with the help of interrupt

signals and the receiver handles it with signal handler. When the signal is sent to a process, the operating system interrupts the execution of the currently running process and the handles the signal handler.

There are two fundamentally different approaches in IPC:

Approach I: Processes are residing on the same computer: in this approach the processes communicating with each other are residing on the same computer. The communication is made possible through the operating system kernel. In this case the processes can share memory either in the user space or in the system space.

Approach II: Processes are residing on different computers: In this approach the processive communicating are residing on different computers separated geographically and the communication in this case will be made possible with the help of communication medium.

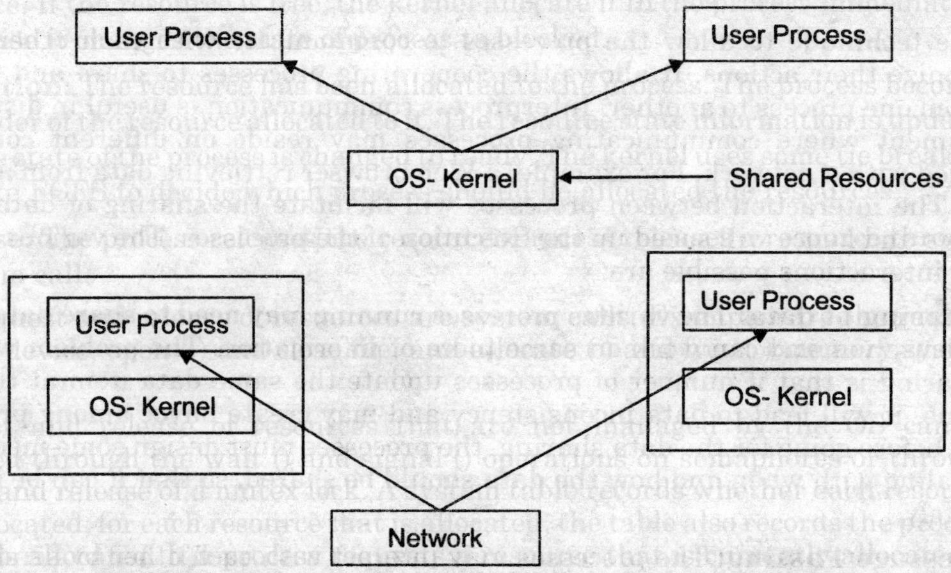

Figure 3.5: *Different Approaches in Inter-Process Communication*

The approach I and II have been shown in the Figure 3.5

One method for the processes to communicate with each other is that these processes share a common buffer pool and the other method for communication between the processes is through Interprocess communication which can be implemented by message scheme communication.

Message Passing: This facility provided by the operating system allows the processes to communicate with each other without the need of sharing of memory space. Two basic operations which can be implemented by any inter process communication system are: send ( ) used to send a message and receive ( ) used to receive a message.

Message-based inter-process communication can be

- **Unidirectional:** In this scheme messages can be passed in one direction at a time, here, one process is the sender and the other is the receiver.
- **Bidirectional:** In this scheme messages can be passed in any direction and each process can act as either a sender or as a receiver.

Messages can be blocking or nonblocking

- **Blocking:** In this system the receiver sends an acknowledgement to the sender to notify that the message has been received.
- **Non-blocking:** In this system, enables the sender to continue with other processing

Message Size: Messages sent by a process can be of fixed size or variable size.

- **Fixed Size Messages:** In this scheme, the sender can send messages of a fixed size only. The implementation of this scheme will be easy, but the restriction makes the programming task difficult.
- **Variable Size Messages:** In this scheme, the sender can send messages of any size. The implementation of this scheme will be difficult, but the programming task becomes easier.
- **Communication Links:** In order to make the inter process communication between the processes possible, there must exist a communication link between them.

Apart from the physical implementation of the links, another important issue is to study how the links are established logically. Where the operating system has to decide how the links will be implemented, can a link be attached with more than one process or not, what will be the capacity of a link, can the link accommodate the fixed sized or variable sized messages.

Types of Message Communication: The processes wishing to communicate with each other, must have some mechanism for the communication. Various types of communication schemes possible are:

1. **Direct Communication:** The process which wishes to communicate with other process must name the receiver i.e the name of the sender and the receiver must be clearly mentioned. For this communication the following two system calls are used:
   - Send (B, Message) , which is run to send a message to the process B.
   - Receive (A, Message), which is run to receive a message from the process A.

If a process A sends a message to process B by executing the above mentioned system calls then the operating system copies the messages into buffer and waits till the process B executes the receive ( ) system call. When B executes a receive call, the operating system delivers the message to B, then process B interepts and receives and executes the message sent by A. if more than one message has been sent to B, then the operating system delivers them in first come first served order. The communication link established in the case of direct communication will have following properties:

- The processes must know the identity of each other and the link must be established automatically between each pair of processes.
- The link must be associated with exactly two processes.
- There must be exactly one link between each pair of processes.
- The link established may be unidirectional or bi-directional.

Implementation Issues

Issue I: Naming of Sender and Receiver Processes: In order to make the communication between two processes possible, they must know each other. For this purpose the sender and receiver processes must be named or must be provided some id so that they can be recognized during the communication. If the processes are concurrent processes within a program, then it will be easy for them to know each other. But if the processes belong to different programs, they will not be able to recognize each other, so here, the operating system must provide the facility by which processes can find the name of any other process. It is mandatory for the sender to know the receiver, but the converse is not true i.e it is not necessary that the receiver must know the sender, as in many cases the receiver is required to execute the command given by the sender, as happens if the receiver is a server who is liable only to execute the command send by the sender, then he may not know the identity of the sender. Based on this criteria, the addressing schemes can be divided into following categories:

(a) *Symmetric Addressing Scheme:* In this addressing scheme, both the sender and receiver processes must name each other. The message format in this case will be of following format:

- send (senderid, message)
- receive (receiverid, message)
- *senderid and the receiverid are the ids of these processes assigned by the operating system.*

(b) *Asymmetric Addressing Scheme:* In this addressing scheme, only the sender names the receiver but the receiver need not to know the sender. The message format in this case will be of following format:

- send (senderid, message)
- receiver (message)

Issue II: Message Delivery Protocol: Protocol is a set of rules and conventions followed by the process undergoing communication. The protocols determine the message data formats and action of processes while sending and receiving messages. A message delivery protocol has the following elements:

(a) Conventions concerning data formats

(b) Rules regarding the actions to be performed by the sender and receiver.

When the communication between the sender and the receiver is taking place, then what actions are performed till a message is delivered. The following two scenarios may happen:

- A sender process is blocked till the message is delivered to the receiver. For this purpose a blocking protocol is used. The sender process ensures that message sent by it has been delivered, before it continues its execution and on the other hand the operating system, ensure that the message remains in the user area until it is delivered.
- In the second option, the sender continues its execution after performing a send operation irrespective of whether the message has been delivered or not for this purpose a non-blocking protocol is used. In this case the sender is free to continue its execution immediately after sending the message. But the major limitation of this method is that sender has no means of knowing that whether its message has been delivered to receiver or not, or when it has been delivered or when it is safe to reuse the memory area containing the message. To overcome this problem, the operating system does not hold undelivered messages in sender's memory area, but allocates a buffer in the system area and copies the message to that buffer area.
- Rules for Handling Exception Conditions: It is responsibility of the protocol being used to ensure that the message send should reach its destination safe and secure, and if due to any of the reasons some fault occurs, then the system itself should handle this exceptional condition by its own. In a single machine environment, messages are implemented in the shared memory and if failure occurs, the entire system will fail, but in a distributed environment, the chances of communication errors will be very large and if such a situation occurs, then the failure of one site does not effect the entire network. In both of these situations, the system should handle these exceptional conditions. The various exceptional conditions that may occur are:
  - The receiver process does not exist.
  - Either the sender or the receiver has terminated before the message is processed.
  - The message has been lost somewhere in the communication network due to hardware failure or due to some fault in the communication line.
  - The operating system has not accepted a send call because it has run out of buffer memory.

Whenever any of the above mentioned exceptional condition occurs, then the operating system must be able to detect it and hence should perform some remedial action in order to ensure smooth communication between the processes. The operating system may perform any of the following actions:

- The process executing a send or receive call which has lead to some exception may be aborted.
- If exception has occurred due to non-availability of buffer space, then process may be blocked till some buffer space becomes available.

2. **Indirect Communication:** the indirect communication is made feasible through the mailboxes also named as ports. The messages are sent and received with the help of mailboxes. The mailbox can be visualized abstractly as an object which works as a repository for inter-process communication, in a mail box, message can be stored by the sender and subsequently can be removed from the mailbox by the receiving process. The mailbox has following features:
   - A mailbox has unique id.
   - The processes communicate with each other through mailbox only. Sender sends the message to mailbox and then it is received from the mailbox by the receiver.
   - The process willing to send the message must know the id of mailbox to which the message is to be sent.
   - Each mailbox has an owner process who created that particular mailbox and only the owner process can receive the messages from its mailbox.
   - The processes communicate with each other with the help of a number of different mailboxes.
   - For the communication to be made possible between the processes, they must have a shared mailbox and they must know each other's identity.
   - The link between the mailboxes may be unidirectional or bidirectional.

Creation of Mailbox: The operating system may provide a set of prefixed mailboxes names or may allow the user processes to name the mailboxes. Let a process A1 wishes to create a mailbox and the process A2 will use it to send the message to A1. The process A1 will give a unique name to its mailbox and A2 will use this name instead of the process id in its send command.

- **The command used by A1:** create mailbox (india) – the process has created a mailbox and has named it as india.
- **The command used by A2:** send (india, <text>) – the process is sending a message and will be stored in the mailbox india, which was created by the process A1.

The mailbox can be created by the operating system or by a particular process. If the mailbox is owned by a process, then it can be attached to or can be defined as a part of the process and then there will be processes who can only receive messages from this mailbox and there will be processes which can only send messages to the mailbox. As soon as the owner process terminates, the mailbox created by it is also destroyed. On the other hand, if the mailbox is owned by the operating system, then it has no individual existence of its own. It exists as an independent entity and is not attached to any particular process, the operating system facilitates the processes to create a new mailbox, send and receive messages through mailbox and ultimately destroy the mailbox when it is not required. The process who creates the mailbox is the owner of that mailbox and only that process is authorized to receive messages through this mailbox. The process can pass the receive right to other processes also and in that case there will be multiple processes who can receive the messages through the same mailbox.

Communication through Mailbox

For sending and receiving the messages: the system calls used in this indirect communication are:

- send (A, message) – to send a message to mailbox A.
- receive (A, message) – to receive a message from mailbox A.

The biggest advantage of using this technique is that the senders need not to know the name of the receiver and a single process may have multiple mailboxes, which will allow to differentiate between different kind of messages.

BASIC CONCEPTS OF THREADS

A thread is known as a Lightweight Process (LWP). It is a basic unit of CPU utilization and consists of:

- A program counter.
- A register set and
- A stack space.

It shares its code section, data section and operating system resources with other threads. It is the smallest scheduling unit of concurrency to run on a processor. The thread is similar to a sequential program; it has a beginning, a sequence and an end. The thread has no individual existence it can run within a program only. It has its own stack and CPU state. A single program will have multiple threads running at the same time and performing different tasks. A thread runs within the context of a program and uses all the resources allocated to that program. A thread executes with in a program and has its own stack space and the program counter. Threads simplify the programming as in a reservation system, there may be a thread dedicated for seat allocation, separate thread for checking the availability of a seat, and separate thread for adding new records. All these threads can be programmed independently. Threads may be managed by the operating system or by a user application. Examples: Win32 threads, C-threads, Pthreads . Figure 3.6 show that there is some information common to all processes and some information that is used and maintained by each thread individually.

Need of threads: When the system implements the concept of concurrency, it implements the concept of switching, where one program switches from one state to other to and fro. It incurs a huge cost. The process switching overhead has two components: execution related overheads and Resource related overhead. The overhead incurred due to switching of processes from one state to another and due to state preservation of the processes in PCB are termed as execution related overheads. The process is allocated some resources and the resources may be de-allocated as and when required, so this whole house keeping regarding the resources also adds to process switching overhead. When an event occurs, switching from the execution of the running process Pi to the execution of the process Pj occurs. If both P1 and P2 belong to same application, they share the code, data and resources, but they differ in the values contained in the CPU registers and stacks. Most of the flow of information while saving, loading and reloading the information is redundant; to avoid this redundancy the concept of threads is used. An application may create many threads to obtain concurrency and to simplify its functioning. They are used to perform concurrent servicing requests received by a server. The threads provide a low cost method for implementing the concurrency. It reduces the switching overhead by eliminating the resource related overhead in some situations.

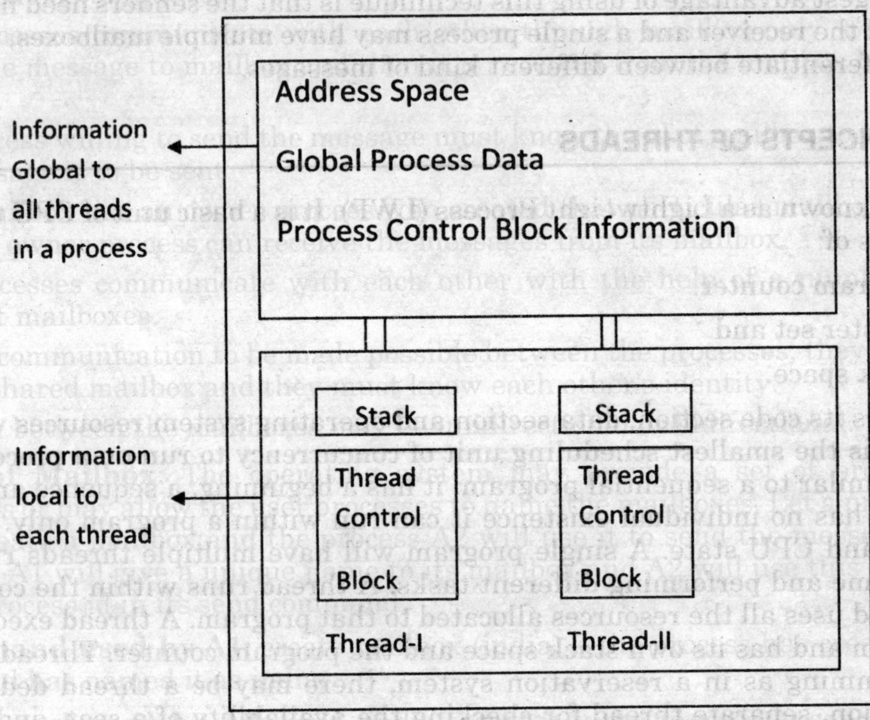

Figure 3.6: *Heavy Weight Process*

Threads operate in the same way as a process and have the states like a process, ready, blocked, running or terminated. When a thread is created, it is put in the ready state as its parent process is already running, it enters the running state when it is scheduled to run, it does not go into waiting state as it does not request for any resource, it may go into waiting state due to process synchronization. The threads of a same process share code, data and resources with one another.

- Like processes, threads also share the processor time.
- Like a process, only one thread will be active at a time.
- Like a process can create the child processes, the thread can also create the child threads.
- If one thread is in the blocked state then other threads can work.

The diagram given below in Figure 3.7 (a) show relationship between threads and processes. The process P1 has four threads shown by curved lines. The operating system kernel allocates a stack and thread control block to each thread. The threads execute within the environment of P1. So the operating system saves the CPU state and stack pointer while switching from one thread to another. The threads divide process states into two categories, resource state and execution state, where resource state is maintained by the process and the execution state is taken care of by the thread.

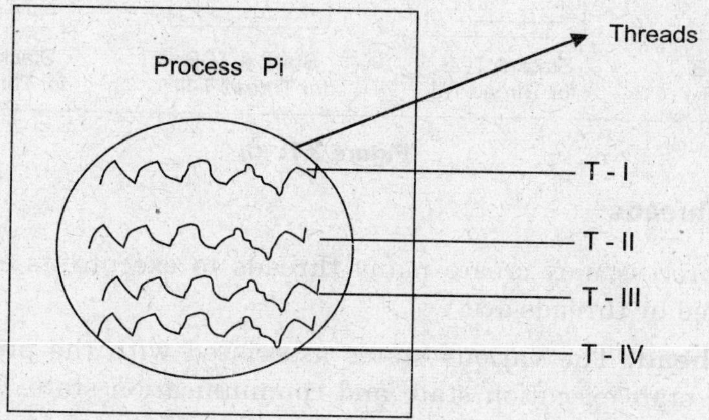

Figure 3.7: *(a) Threads in a Process.*

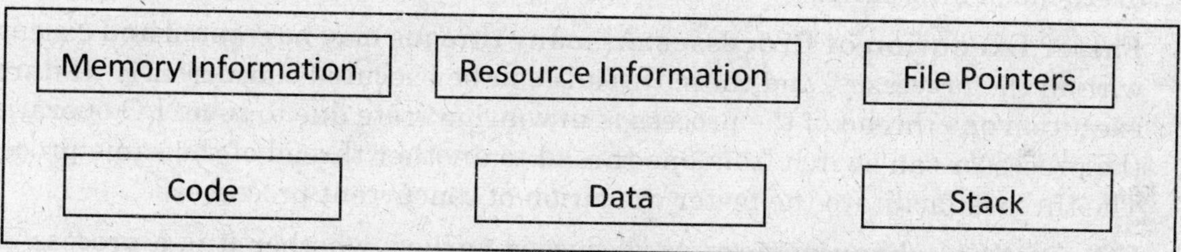

Figure 3.7: *(b) Environment of Process Pi*

Figure 3.7 (b) and (c) show the environment of Process Pi and the Process Control Block of Process Pi and 3.7 (d) shows the stack and task control block for various threads.

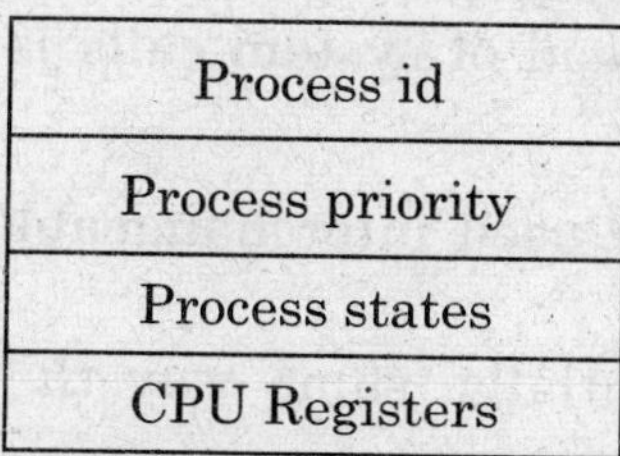

Figure 3.7: *(c) Process Control Block of process Pi*

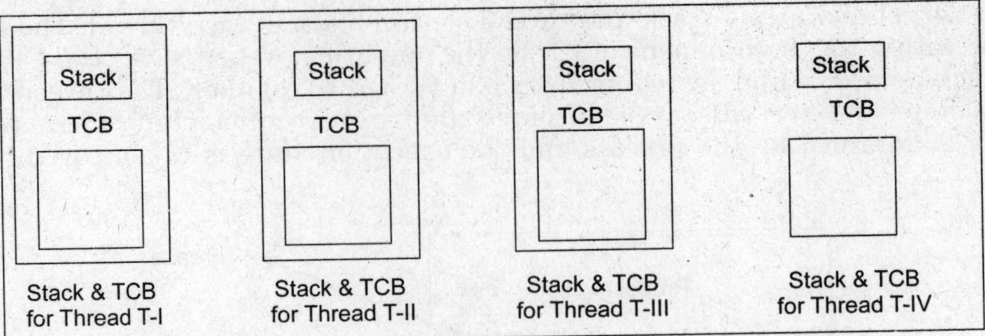

Figure 3.7: *(d)*

Advantages of Threads

An application process may create many threads to execute its code. The various advantages offered by threads are:

1. **Low Overhead:** The various states associated with the process/thread may be resource state/execution state and communication state. The resource and communication states are not a part of the thread states, so switching between execution states is done for the threads of the same process, which leads to low overhead of switching.
2. **Faster Execution of Processes:** As many threads may be created and executed with in the processes, and these threads can be executed concurrently. If during execution one thread of the process is in waiting state due to some I/O operation, the processor can switch from one thread to another thread of the same process. The threads facilitate the faster execution of concurrent processes.
3. **Efficient Synchronization:** As discussed earlier, whether it is a process or a thread, both have to communicate and synchronize with one another to make the interprocess/inter thread communication effective and efficient. When the processes do this job, the kernel is involved as the system calls are issued to and from the kernel. But if this process is to be carried out for the threads, they communicate and synchronize through shared memory so system calls are not required, hence the overhead of system calls is reduced which leads to faster execution of processes.

The processes and threads are used interchangeably also, as these have following similiartities:

- The processes run sequentially, same way the threads within a process run sequentially.
- Like processes, threads also share CPU.
- The threads have same states as of processes i.e new, ready, running, waiting, and terminated.

- As processes create their sub-processes called the children, the threads can do the same job.
- If one process is in blocked state, another process can run. In the same way if one thread is in blocked state, another thread can run.

DIFFERENCE BETWEEN PROCESSES AND THREADS

Process	Threads
The processes are independent of each other, processes will have their own stack space and address space	Threads are not independent of each other, all threads of a task share the same address space.
The processes implement the concept of protection, as the processes cannot read/write into the space of the other process, so the processes provide a secure way of communication	There is no concept of protection in the threads, as threads share the same address space, so one thread can read/write into the space of the other thread. So the threads do not provide a secure way of communication.
The processes may be created and owned by a multiple users and these processes may or may not be cooperating with each other.	The threads will be created and owned by a particular process, which created it and all threads of a program are under the control of that process.
The process needs to be protected from the other processes.	The threads of a program are created to assist each other, so they do not require mutual protection.
The process creation and its termination is time consuming.	The creation of a thread in the existing process and its termination (when it is not required) is less time consuming.
The switching time i.e the time to switch from one process to another is large.	The switching time i.e the time to switch from one thread to another is quite less as compared to the time required for processes.
Process require large number of system resources.	Threads require lesser number of resources.

CPU Scheduling

Chapter 4

BASIC CONCEPTS OF SCHEDULING

In uni-programming environment, where only a single program is run by the processor at a time, all the resources required for the execution of the process are allocated to the process. The problem with this approach is that the program does not need all the resources all the time. As a program needs time to receive input from the user, it needs processor for the execution of the job and the output devices for providing the results to the users. CPU remains idle when the program is performing any type of input/output operation. So the program does not need the CPU all the time, but in uni-programming system, CPU is dedicated to one program only, leading to the wastage of precious CPU time. To overcome the problem of under utilization of CPU, the concept of multiprogramming operating systems is used which allow more than one process to be loaded into the executable memory at a time and the processes share the CPU time. Multiprogramming means interleaved execution of multiple jobs by the same computer. In case of multiprogramming, two or more user programs can reside in the main memory at the same time and are being executed one after another. When one program is waiting for the input and output transfer, the other program can utilize the CPU, by doing so the CPU will be occupied in executing one job or the other and hence CPU will have some program to execute all the time and hence it will not be idle and overall CPU utilization will increase many fold. Even the operating system itself needs multiprogramming to execute its own processes.

In order to make the concept of multiprogramming feasible, the processor is to be allocated to the multiple processes according to some schedule, so that all processes get the fair amount of the CPU time. So the CPU is allocated to various processes turn by turn when processor is allocated to one process the other processes have to wait. But the successful execution of this concept, the various jobs and the allocation of processor to these jobs needs to be scheduled. So the allocation of CPU to various processes is termed as CPU scheduling.

The CPU scheduling is possible due to the fact that process execution consists of cycle of CPU execution and I/O wait. These two phases appear alternatively. The process execution begins with CPU burst followed by I/O burst and this process continues till the process is executed completely. However the duration of CPU and I/O burst vary from process to process. It is the job of scheduler to schedule the execution of various processes.

A process, which is a program in execution, can be in any of the following states during its execution:

- **New:** This state corresponds to the time when the process is created but it has not been admitted to the pool of executable processes by the operating system. Normally the new process has not been loaded into the main memory although its process control block has been created.
- **Waiting:** This state corresponds to the situation when the process is waiting for some resource or some event to occur. Like, process may be in waiting state, when it is waiting for some input or reception of a signal etc.
- **Running:** The process is in running state, if it is being executed at a particular moment of time. While execution the instructions given in the program are executed. The running process becomes ready when it is preempted either a higher priority process becomes ready or its time slice elapses.
- **Ready:** This state corresponds to the situation when process is waiting to be assigned to a processor.
- **Terminated:** This state corresponds to the time, when process has finished the execution.

It is worth mentioning here, that only one process may be in running state on any processor at any particular moment of time, although many processes may be in ready or waiting states. The Figure 4.1 given below show the different states of a process during its complete life time. A new process is put in ready state after all resources required by it have been allocated, it may enter the running, waiting and ready states a number of times and in the end it reaches the terminated state.

CPU scheduling has the basic goals to manage the resources of system. Resources range from CPU time to disk space to channel I/O time.

During the execution of the program, it passes through various queues, as mentioned below:

- **Job Queue:** As soon as the process enters the system for the execution, it is put in the job queue. This job queue will have all the processes in the system.
- **Ready Queue:** The processes that are residing in the main memory and are ready for execution reside in the ready queue. The ready queue is maintained as a linked list.
- **Device Queue:** The various processes running in a system may be in need of various devices as per the requirement of the particular process.

In order to get access of a particular device, the process issues an I/O request. The device for which the request has been sent, may be a dedicated device or may be a shared resource. As many processes may be demanding the same resource then device can be allocated to one process at a time, then the remaining processes will be in the queue, waiting for the device. This queue is termed as a device queue. Each device will have its own device queue, comprising of all processes waiting for a particular device.

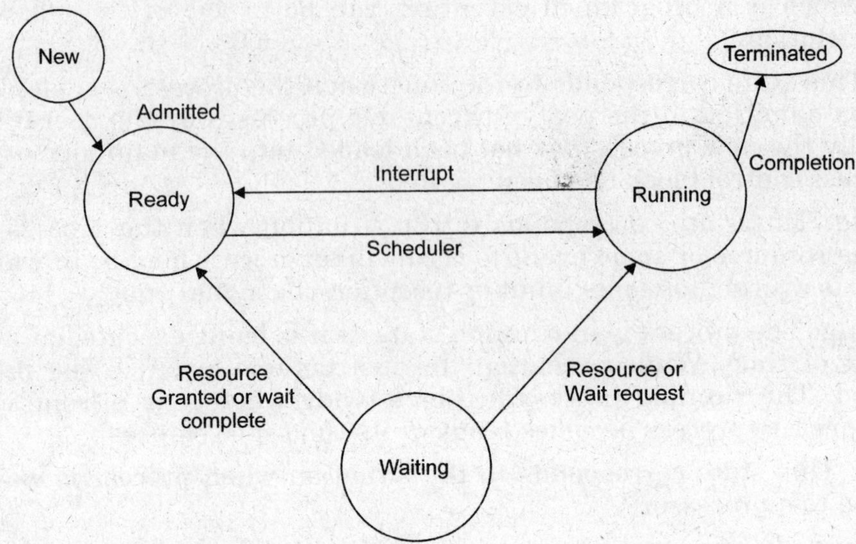

Figure 4.1: *State Transition Diagram for a Process*

During the complete life time of a process, it moves from one queue to another. As soon as the process enters the system, it is in the job queue, after that it is shifted to the ready queue, it waits in the ready queue, until it is selected for the execution. Once the process is under execution, one of the following conditions may occur:

1. The process can generate new sub-processes.
2. The process completes it execution and terminates finally.
3. The process may issue an I/O request and then is placed in the device queue of that particular input or output device.
4. An interrupt may occur causing the process to come to a halt forcibly, in such situation the CPU is taken away from the process and the process is again send back to the ready queue waiting for the processor again.

There may be more than one process in any of the queues, waiting for the resources, then it is the duty of the operating system to decide and choose the process, which will be allocated the required resource. Then two major questions arise here:

1. How to choose a process from the various processes in the queue?
2. Who will choose the process?

The first question is related to the procedure or criteria for the selection of a particular process, out of the various processes waiting in the queue and second one is related to that who will do it?

Both of these jobs are taken care of by the operating system and Schedulers do this job with the help of various scheduling algorithms. It is assumed here that there is a pool of runnable processes competing for the processor and the job of scheduler is to distribute the scarce time period of the processor to different processes fairly, so that the overall performance of the system can be optimized. The scheduling policy used in an operating system influences user service, efficient use of resources and system performance. These algorithms use the techniques of preemption, reordering the request and variation of time slice to achieve the desired goals.

The concept of schedulers and their various types have already been explained in the Chapter 3. The present chapter concentrates on various scheduling algorithms.

The Figure 4.2 given below shows the basic concept of scheduling. All requests waiting to be serviced are kept in a list of pending requests. All newly arrived processes are kept in this list. To execute a process, the scheduler selects one of the processes from these processes (depending on the scheduling algorithm used). The selected request is handed over to the processor for the execution. The job will free the CPU when either it has completed its execution or it has been preempted by the scheduler. If it has completed the execution then the results are shown to the user and if it has been preempted it is put back in the list of pending requests. The major events of scheduling are arrival, scheduling, preemption and completion.

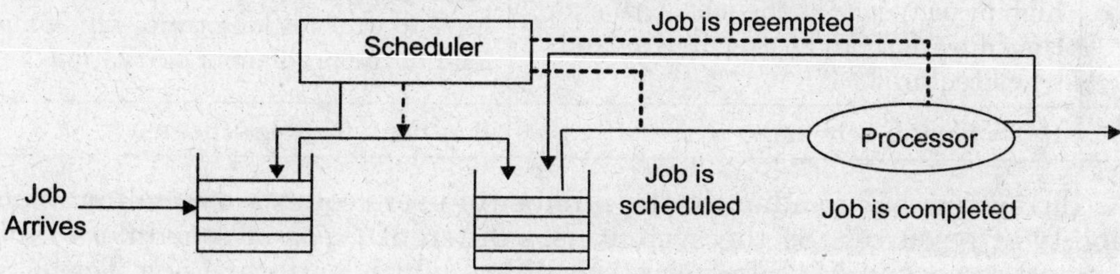

Figure 4.2: *Concept of Scheduling*

Types of Scheduling

1. **Non-Preemptive Scheduling:** In this type of scheduling, the CPU is allocated to a process, the process keeps the processor until it releases the CPU either by terminating or by switching to the waiting state. It is not removed from the processor until it has completed its service time. The context_switch () is called only when the process terminates or blocks. This scheduling method is used by the Microsoft Windows Environment. This method does not require any special hardware like timer, which is required in preemptive scheduling.

2. **Preemptive Scheduling:** In this case the CPU can be taken away forcibly from the process to which it has been allocated and can be allocated to some other process. This is handled by sending an interrupt signal to the running process. This preemption incurs a cost. The preemptive algorithms are driven by the notion of prioritized computation. The process with the highest priority should always be the one currently using the processor. If a process is currently using the processor and a new process with a higher priority enters, the ready list, the process on the processor should be removed and returned to the ready list until it is once again the highest-priority process in the system.

Difference between Preemptive and Non-Preemptive Scheduling:

S.No	Preemptive Scheduling	Non-Preemptive Scheduling
1.	In preemptive Scheduling the CPU can be taken away from a process after being allocated to it. The processor is taken away when either a high priority process has arrived or the time allocated to this process has elapsed.	In Non-Preemptive Scheduling, once the CPU has been allocated to a process, the processor can not be taken away from that process.
2.	This type of scheduling involves the overhead of context switch, i.e the processor is moved from one process to another. It incurs a cost.	It is less costly as compared to Preemptive Scheduling.
3.	It is efficient in the context that the high priority jobs or the jobs with short time duration can be executed as and when required.	Short jobs or high priority jobs may have to wait for long time, which may lead to the problem of starvation.
4.	It is a flexible scheme.	It is not a flexible scheme.

As the system has to adapt to the number of user requests depending upon the availability of resources. So the system uses different types of schedulers i.e Long Term, Short term and Medium term scheduler, which perform Long Term, Short Term and Medium Term Scheduling respectively.

Long-Term Scheduling

The long-term scheduler decides which jobs or processes are to be admitted to the ready queue (in the Main Memory); that is, when an attempt is made to execute a program, its execution is decided by the long-term scheduler. Long term scheduler will decide about how low and high degree of processes runs simultaneously and how CPU handles these processes. It decides when to admit an arrived process for scheduling based on its nature, whether it is CPU bound or I/O bound and availability of resources. In modern operating systems, real time processes get enough CPU time and priority to finish their tasks. The long term queue exists in the Hard Disk or the "Virtual Memory". In batch multiprogramming, the decision may be based on the different requirements of the competing jobs and the resources currently available. Interactive multiprogramming often does not have this level of scheduling at all; it is up to the user to decide which job steps to run (is to be executed next). Long-term scheduling is also important in large-scale systems computer clusters, supercomputers and render farms.

Medium-term Scheduling

The medium-term scheduler is mainly used to remove running process from main memory and place that process into queue and vice versa. This process is called as swapping out. Decision to remove the process from main memory depends on various factors like if process is idle for some time, process is taking too much memory as compared to what has been allocated to it, creating large number of page faults or process has low priority as compared with the new process. In this process, process can be placed back in main memory from ready queue when memory is free and resources are available.

Short-term scheduling

Short-term scheduling, decides how to share the system resources among all the processes that are to be executed currently. It decides which process is executed (allocated a CPU) next following a clock interrupt, an I/O interrupt, an operating system call or another form of signal. Short term scheduler makes decision frequently. When a process arrives from long term scheduler or medium term scheduler, it arrives in the preview of short term scheduler. This scheduler can be preemptive and can forcibly remove the process from ready queue. Often the short term scheduler executes at least once every 10 millisecond. If it takes 1 millisecond to decide to execute a process for 10 millisecond, the 1/ (10 + 1) = 9% of the CPU is being wasted simply for scheduling the work. Therefore, it must be very fast.

SCHEDULING CRITERIA

There exists a number of scheduling algorithms, which may be suitable for one environment or the other. There are various criterias which can be used to compare the efficiency of various scheduling algorithms. The major criterias that can be used are:

1. **Processor Utilization:** The user wish to keep the processor as busy as possible, that is, we want to reduce the idle time of the CPU. The processor utilization may vary from 0 to 100 percent. It can be calculated as:

   Processor busy time / (Processor busy time + Processor Idle Time))

2. **Throughput Time:** It is the measure of work done in a unit time interval. One measure of work is the number of processes that are completed per unit of time, and it is known as the throughput. For long processes, this rate may be one process per hour; for short transactions, it may be 10 processes per second. For efficient systems, A high through put is desirable. The through put depends on the job mix i.e the number of CPU bound and I/O bound processes. If all the processes are CPU bound, through put will be less as compared to I/O bound processes, as these processes require CPU for small durations only, so more processes can be completed in a given time. The throughput can be increased by having the jobs with a proper job mix.

3. **Turnaround Time:** It is the total time taken for the execution of a process. It is the sum of time spent waiting in the ready queue, executing and the time spent for I/O. It can be calculated as:

Turn Around Time = Time of Completion of the process – Time of Submission of the Process.

It should be minimum as far as possible.

4. **Waiting Time:** It is the time spent by the process waiting in the ready queue. It should be minimum as far as possible.

5. **Response Time:** It is the amount of time it takes to start responding to a request. This criterion is important for interactive systems. In an interactive system, turnaround time may not be the best criterion. Often, a process can produce some output fairly early and can continue computing new results while previous results are being given as the output to the user. Thus, the response time measures the time from the submission of a request until the first response is produced. It can be calculated as:

   Time when the first response is received – Time of submission of the request.

The objective is to maximize the CPU utilization and through put and to minimize the turnaround time, waiting time and response time.

A typical scheduler is designed to select one or more primary performance criteria and rank them in order of importance. One problem in selecting a set of performance criteria is that they often conflict with each other. For example, increased processor utilization is usually achieved by increasing the number of active processes, but then response time decreases. A scheduling algorithm that maximizes throughput may not necessarily minimize turnaround time. In most cases, we optimize the average measure. However, under some circumstances, it is desirable to optimize the minimum or maximum values rather than the average. For example, to guarantee that all users get good service, we may want to minimize the maximum response time. If for some reasons, system has to degrade under load, this should be done gracefully.

SCHEDULING ALGORITHMS

CPU Scheduling deals with the problem of deciding which process from the ready queue is to be allocated the CPU. There are various types of scheduling algorithms. In multiprogrammed batch systems the primary concern is the efficiency. Since no user is waiting at a terminal, preemption is not crucial and if it is used, each process is given a long time period before being preempted. For interactive systems, preemption is crucial for fairness and rapid response time to short requests. Preemption is typically not important in real time systems, since all the processes are cooperating and are programmed to do their task in a prescribed time frame.

First-Come, First Served Scheduling: It is a non preemptive scheduling policy. Where the processes are executed on the first come first served basis. The process that requests the CPU first is allocated the CPU first. The implementation is handled by FIFO queue. When a process enters the ready queue, its process control block is linked onto the tail of the queue, when the processor is free, the processor is allocated to the process which is the first member in the queue.

Consider the following set of processes that arrive at time 0, with the length of CPU burst time given in seconds.

Process	Burst Time
P1	16
P2	4
P3	3
P4	2

These processes are executed on first come first served basis and the execution is shown in the following Gantt Chatt:

P1	P2	P3	P4
0	16	20	23 25

The turn around time for these processes will be:

Process	Turn around Time
P1	16
P2	20
P3	23
P4	25
Average Turn Around Time	(16 + 20 + 23 + 25) = 84/4 = 21

The waiting time for the various processes will be:

Process	Waiting Time
P1	0
P2	16
P3	20
P4	23
Average Waiting Time	(0 + 16 + 20 + 23) / 4 = 59/4 = 14.75

If the processes arrive in the order: P2, P4, P3 and P1, then the corresponding Gantt Chart will be:

P2	P4	P3	P1
0	4	6	9 … 25

The turn around time for these processes will be:

Process	Turn around Time
P1	25
P2	04
P3	09
P4	06
Average Turn Around Time	(25 + 04 + 09 + 06) = 44/4 = 11

The waiting time for the various processes will be:

Process	Waiting Time
P1	9
P2	0
P3	6
P4	4
Average Waiting Time	(9 + 0 + 6 + 4) / 4 = 19/4 = 4.75

Advantages: It is easy to understand and implement. It is suitable for batch processing systems.

Limitations

- Waiting time can be large if short requests arrive after the long ones.
- It is not appropriate for time sharing systems, which require that the CPU should be allocated for an equal amount of time interval.
- To get the best output out of this algorithm, the jobs should be of proper job mix.

Shortest Job First Scheduling

In shortest job first scheduling algorithm, when the CPU is available, it is assigned to the process that has the smallest next CPU burst. If two processes have the same length then FCFS will break the tie. The scheduling is done on the basis of shortest next CPU burst, as the scheduling is done on the basis of next CPU burst of a process, rather than its total length. Sort jobs by execution time needed and run the shortest first. This is a Non-preemptive algorithm (if processes arrive at the same time). In this method, the processor is assigned to the process with the smallest next processor burst time. Therefore, we need to know the length of its next processor burst time for each process.

Consider the following set of processes

Consider the following set of processes that arrive at time 0, with the length of CPU burst time given in seconds.

Process	Burst Time
P1	16
P2	4
P3	3
P4	2

These processes are executed on first come first served basis and the execution is shown in the following Gantt Chatt:

P2	P4	P3	P1

0 4 6 9 25

The turnaround time for these processes will be:

Process	Turn around Time
P1	25
P2	09
P3	05
P4	02
Average Turn Around Time	(25 + 09 + 05 + 02) = 41/4 = 10.25

The waiting time for the various processes will be:

Process	Waiting Time
P1	09
P2	05
P3	02
P4	00
Average Waiting Time	(09 + 05 + 02 + 00) / 4 = 16/4 = 4

The shortest job first algorithm may be preemptive also. The choice arises when a new process arrives at the ready queue while a previous process is still executing. The new process may have a shorter next CPU burst than what is left of currently executing process. A preemptive shortest job first algorithm will preempt the currently executing process, whereas a non-preemptive algorithm will allow the currently running process to finish its CPU burst. Preemptive scheduling is also known as shortest remaining time first scheduling. Permit a process that enters the ready list to preempt the running process if the time for the new process (or for its next burst) is less than the remaining time for the running process (or for its current burst).

Consider the following set of processes:

Process	Arrival Time	Burst Time
P1	0	16
P2	1	4
P3	2	5
P4	3	6

The process P1 arrived at 0, as it is the only process in the queue, so the processor will be allocated to it. At time 1, the process P2 arrives and it has the burst time of 4 seconds and the remaining time of P1 is 15, as the remaining time of P1 is more than P2, so process P1 is preempted and P2 is scheduled for execution. At time 2, the P3 arrives and has the burst time of 5 seconds, as the burst time of P3 is more than P2, so it not preempted and P2 continues with the processing. At time 3, P4 arrives, as it has burst time of 6 seconds which is more than the processes P2, P1 and P3, so P2 is not preempted.

The execution of processes is shown in the following Gantt Chatt:

P1	P2	P3	P4	P1

0 1 5 10 16 31

The turnaround time for these processes will be:

Process	Turn around Time (Time of Completion of Job – Time of Submission of Job)
P1	31 – 0 = 31
P2	5 – 1 = 04
P3	10 – 2 = 08
P4	16 – 3 = 13
Average Turn Around Time	(31 + 04 + 08 + 13)/4 = 56/4 = 14

The waiting time for the various processes will be:

Process	Waiting Time
P1	16 – 1 =15
P2	1 – 1 = 0

P3	5 – 2 = 3
P4	10 – 3 = 7
Average Waiting Time	(15 + 0 + 3 + 7)/4 = 25/4 = 6.25

Advantages: It is the optimal algorithm and gives minimum average waiting time.

Disadvantages: It may be difficult to know the burst time of the process in the beginning.

Priority Scheduling

In priority scheduling a priority is associated with each process and the processor is allocated to the process with the highest priority. The processes with equal priority are handled on first come first served order.

The priority is signified as some integer value, where 0 may be considered as high priority or may be considered as low priority.

Consider the following processes:

Process	Priority	Burst Time
P1	4	16
P2	1	4
P3	2	5
P4	3	6

The execution of processes is shown in the following Gantt Chatt:

P2	P3	P4	P1

0 4 9 15 31

The turnaround time for these processes will be:

Process	Turn around Time
P1	31
P2	04
P3	09
P4	15
Average Turn Around Time	(31 + 04 + 09 + 15) = 59/4 = 14.75

The waiting time for the various processes will be:

Process	Waiting Time
P1	15
P2	0
P3	4
P4	9
Average Waiting Time	(15 + 0 + 4 + 9)/4 = 25/4 = 6.25

Priorities can be defined in any of following ways:

1. **Internally,** defined priorities use some quantitative measure to calculate the priority of a process. Like the memory requirements, burst time, the number of open files and the ratio of average I/O burst to average CPU burst can be used to compute the priority of the process. We can visualize the shortest job first algorithm as a priority algorithm where,

   $$\text{Priority} = \frac{1}{\text{Next CPU Burst}}$$

   The larger the CPU burst, the lower is the priority.

2. **Externally,** the priorities are defined on the basis of some external factors, like importance of the process, or some other economic or political factors related to the execution of the process. Like the process created by the Head of the Institution can be given high priority over the processes created by the staff members or the students.

Priority scheduling can be preemptive or non-preemptive. Whenever a process comes in the ready queue, its priority is compared with the priority of already running process, if preemptive scheduling algorithm is followed then upon arrival of a high priority process, the low priority process will be preempted and the processor will be allocated to the newly arrived process. But in case of non-preemptive algorithm the newly arrived high priority process will be put in the ready queue.

The biggest problem with the priority scheduling algorithm is of starvation. It can leave a low priority process to be waiting for the processor indefinitely. In a heavily loaded system, it may be possible that high priority processes keep on arriving and the low priority jobs are not given any chance for execution, so they keep on waiting for the processor for an infinite time. To overcome this problem, the concept of aging is used, in which the priority of the process waiting since long is increased by some constant value, so that low priority jobs can be converted into high priority jobs and hence can be executed.

Round Robin Scheduling

This scheduling algorithm was designed particularly for the time sharing systems (discussed in Chapter 2). In time sharing systems, the processes are allocated the processor on time sharing basis and a fixed time slot known as time slice or time quantum is allocated to each process. After the completion of the time slice, the processor is allocated to some other process and this process continues till the process is executed completely. Time quantum is usually a small duration of time of the order of 10 to 100 millseconds. The processor executes the ready queue in a circular fashion. It can be visualized as the preemptive version of FCFS.

Consider the processes given below, let the time slice is of 4 millseconds.

Process	Burst Time
P1	16
P2	4
P3	5
P4	6

The execution of processes is shown in the following Gantt Chatt:

P1	P2	P3	P4	P1	P3	P4	P1

0 4 8 12 16 20 21 23 31

In round robin scheduling the processes will be considered in as in a circular queue and will be executed in the order P1, P2, P3, P4, P1, P2, P3, P4...........

First of all P1 will be executed for 4 seconds and then it is the turn of P2 it needs CPU for 4 seconds only, then it comes the turn of P3, it needs CPU for 5 seconds, but as the time slice is of 4 seconds then it will be allocated the CPU for 4 seconds and the remaining execution of P3 has been delayed and the process is put in the queue again. Then same this happens with P4. Here one circle of the queue is over and the remaining burst time of processes for the second round is :

Process	Burst Time
P1	8
P2	0
P3	1
P4	2

In the second round the process P1 will be executed for 4 seconds, P2 does not need the CPU, P3 needs it for 1 second and P4 requires it for 2 seconds and in the third round, neither P2, P3 and nor P4 need the CPU, only P2 needs it and it will be allocated to it for 7 seconds (as per its requirement).

The turnaround time for these processes will be:

Process	Turn around Time
P1	31
P2	08
P3	21
P4	23
Average Turn Around Time	(31 + 08 + 21 + 23)/4 = 20.75

The waiting time for the various processes will be:

Process	Waiting Time
P1	0 + (16 – 4) + (23 – 20) = 0 +12 + 3 = 15
P2	4
P3	8 + (20 – 12) = 8 + 8 = 16
P4	12 + (21 – 16) = 12 + 5 = 17
Average Waiting Time	(15 + 4 + 16 + 17)/4 = 13

The performance of this algorithm depends on the size of the time slice, if time slice is large, then this algorithm becomes same as the first come first served algorithm and the performance degrades. On the other hand if time slice is quite less, then the number of context switches will be more. So a balance between these two is to be maintained to ensure the best output.

Exercises on Scheduling Algorithms

Example 1: The following processes P1, P2 and P3 arrive for execution at the times indicated below. The burst time of each process is mentioned. Find average turnaround time for the various processes are Find the turn around and waiting time for processes if they follow:

(a) FCFS

(b) SJF

Process	Arrival Time	Burst Time
P1	0.0	8
P2	0.4	4
P3	1.0	1

(a) *FCFS*

P1	P2	P3

0 8 12 13

The turn around time for these processes will be:

Process	Turn around Time
P1	08 – 0 = 8
P2	12 – 0.4 = 11.6
P3	13.0 – 1.0 = 12

The waiting time for the various processes will be:

Process	Waiting Time
P1	0
P2	8 – 0.4 = 7.6
P3	12 – 1 = 11
Average Waiting Time	(0 + 7.6 + 11) / 3 = 18.6/3 = 6.2

Case II: *Shortest Job First Scheduling Algorithm:*

P1	P3	P2	P1

0 0. 1.0 2 5.4 13

The turn around time for these processes will be:

Process	Turn around Time
P1	13 – 0 =13.
P2	5.4 – 0.4 = 5
P3	2 – 1 = 1
Average Turn Around Time	(13 + 5 + 1)/3 = 19/3 = 6.33

The waiting time for the various processes will be:

Process	Waiting Time
P1	5.4 – 0.4 = 5
P2	2 – 1 = 1
P3	0
Average Waiting Time	(5 + 1 + 0) / 3 = 6/3 = 2

Example 2: Five jobs arrive at a computer center at almost the same time. There estimated running time has been mentioned below along with their externally defined priorities, where higher the value means higher the priority. For each of the following scheduling algorithm determine the process turnaround and waiting time for each process, while ignoring the process switching overhead.

(a) FCFS (where the order of arrival of jobs is 10, 6, 2, 4, 8)

(b) Shortest Job First.

(c) Priority Scheduling.

(d) Round Robin Scheduling.

Process	Priority	Burst Time
A	3	10
B	5	6
C	2	2
D	1	4
E	4	8

For round robin scheduling assume that the system is Multiprogrammed with time sharing and each job gets its fair share of the CPU time.

Solution: The time slice as fair share = (10 + 6 + 2 + 4 + 8)/5 = 30/5 = 6.

(a) FCFS: If the jobs are executed according to FCFS, the corresponding Gantt Chart is:

A	B	C	D	E
0	10	16	18	22 – 30

The turn around time for these processes will be:

Process	Turn around Time
A	10
B	16
C	18
D	22
E	30
Average Turn Around Time	(10 + 16 + 18 + 22 + 30)/5 = 96/5 = 19.2

The waiting time for the various processes will be:

Process	Waiting Time
A	0
B	10
C	16
D	18
E	22
Average Waiting Time	(0 + 10 + 16 + 18 + 22) /5 = 66/5 = 13.2

(b) *SJF:* If the jobs are executed according to SJF Scheduling, the corresponding Gantt Chart is:

C	D	B	E	A

0 2 6 12 20 30

The turn around time for these processes will be:

Process	Turn around Time
A	30
B	12
C	02
D	06
E	20
Average Turn Around Time	(30 + 12 + 02 + 06 + 20)/5 = 70/5 = 14

The waiting time for the various processes will be:

Process	Waiting Time
A	20
B	06
C	00
D	02
E	12
Average Waiting Time	(20 + 06 + 00 + 02 + 12) /5 = 40/5 = 08

(c) *Priority Scheduling:* If the jobs are executed according to Priority Scheduling Algorithm, the corresponding Gantt Chart is:

B	**E**	**A**	**C**	**D**

0 6 1 24 26 30

The turn around time for these processes will be:

Process	Turn around Time
A	24
B	06
C	26
D	30
E	14
Average Turn Around Time	(24 + 06 + 26 + 30 + 14)/5 = 100/5 = 20

The waiting time for the various processes will be:

Process	Waiting Time
A	14
B	00
C	24
D	26
E	06
Average Waiting Time	(14 + 00 + 24 + 26 + 06) /5 = 70/5 = 14

(d) *Round Robin Scheduling:* If the jobs are executed according to Round Robin Scheduling Algorithm while keeping priority in mind, the time slice will be as calculated as the fair share for each process, and it is 6 units of time and the corresponding Gantt Chart is:

B	E	A	C	D	E	A

0 6 1 18 20 24 26 30

The turn around time for these processes will be:

Process	Turn around Time
A	30
B	06
C	20
D	24
E	26
Average Turn Around Time	(30 + 06 + 20 + 24 + 26)/5 = 106/5 = 21.2

The waiting time for the various processes will be:

Process	Waiting Time
A	12 + (26 – 18) = 12 + 8 = 20
B	00
C	18
D	20
E	06 + (26 – 12) = 06 + 12 = 18
Average Waiting Time	(14 + 00 + 24 + 26 + 06) /5 = 70/5 = 14

Multilevel Queue Scheduling

This algorithm partitions the ready queue into several separate queues. For this purpose the processes are divided in the categories of foreground and background processes, these processes are permanently assigned to one queue depending on their particular characteristics like process priority, process type, memory requirement.

Each queue has its own scheduling algorithm. Like an interactive process at the foreground may use the round robin scheduling while the batch jobs at the background may use shortest job first scheduling.

In addition to it there will be some scheduling among the queues, which is commonly implemented as fixed priority scheduling. Like foreground queue may have absolute priority over background queue.

The Figure 4.3 given below show an example of multilevel queue scheduling with four queues, namely,

- System Processes.
- Interactive Processes.
- Batch System Processes.
- End-User Processes.

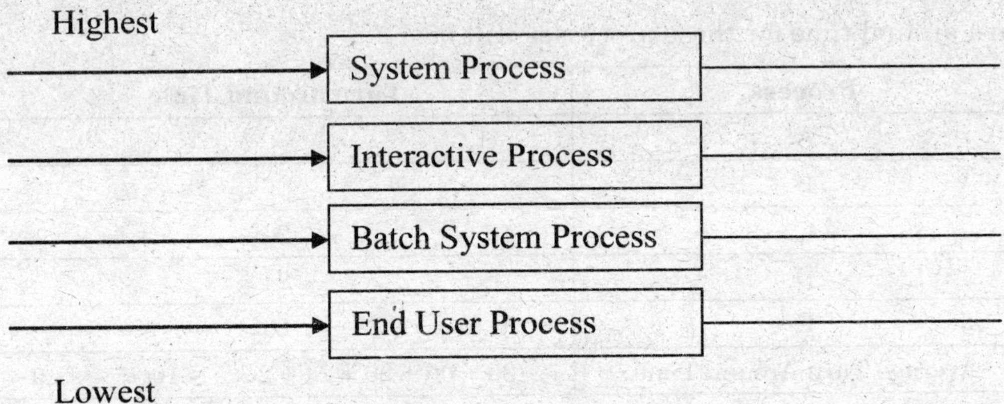

Figure 4.3: *Multi Level Queue*

The advantage of this algorithm is that the processes are permanently assigned to a queue at the entry to the system. As processes do not change their basic nature, this method leads to a low scheduling algorithm.

On the other hand, it is an inflexible approach as the processes can not change their queues, so may lead to starvation, if any of the high priority queues are not getting empty.

Multilevel Feedback Queue Scheduling

This scheduling method allows the processes to move between the queues. The ready queue is divided into multiple queues of different priorities. The idea is to separate the processes with different CPU burst. If a process uses too much of CPU time, it will be moved to a low priority queue. The I/O bound and interactive processes will be in the higher priority queues and CPU bound processes will be in low priority queues. After a suitable time interval, the processes are moved from low priority queue to high priority queue, by using the concept of aging.

The Figure 4.4 given below show the implementation of a multilevel feedback queue scheduling with three queues. The scheduler will execute the processes in the high priority queue, these processes will have smallest CPU time slice, after a process from the top queue has completed its assigned time slice, and then it is placed in next lower level queue. Similarly, the process which consumes the larger CPU time slice is moved to the higher queue. Here the scheduler will execute all processes in queue 0, after all the processes in this queue has been executed, the processes in queue 1 will be executed. A process that arrives for queue 1 will preempt a process in queue 2, and a process that arrives for queue 0 will preempt a process in queue 1. A process entering the ready queue is put in queue 0, a process in queue 0 is given a time slice of 4 seconds, if it does not completes its job in this time, it is moved to the end of queue 1. If queue 0 is empty, the process at the head of queue 1 is given a time slice of 8 seconds. If it does not complete its task in the given time period, then it is preempted to the queue 2 where the processes are executed on first come first served basis.

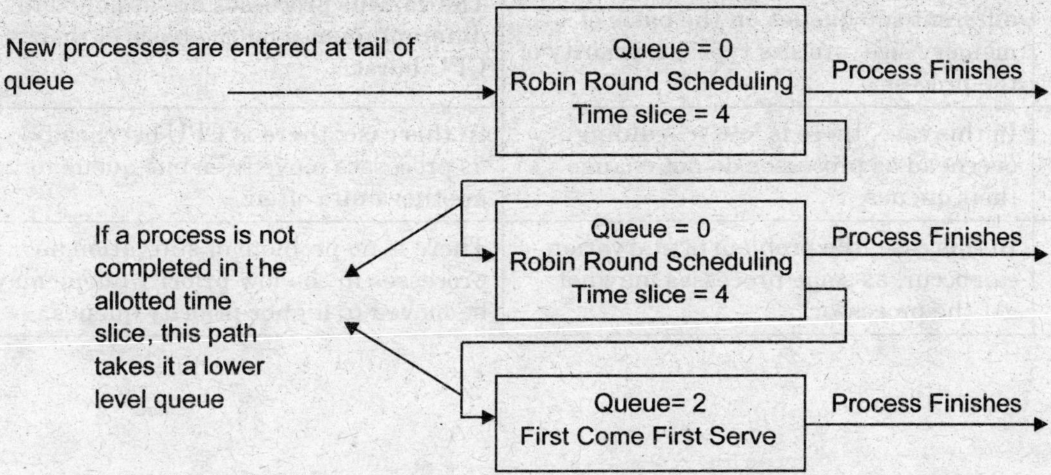

Figure 4.4: *Multilevel Feedback Queue*

The major parameters for these algorithms are:

- Number of queues to be fixed.
- The scheduling algorithm for each queue.
- How and when to upgrade the processes from low priority queue to high priority queue and vice versa.
- Method for assigning a process to a queue as it comes for some service.

Advantages

- It allows processes to move from one queue to the another. It is suitable for I/O bound processes, as they do not have to wait for long.
- It prevents starvation, as the low priority jobs can be moved to high priority queues.
- It is flexible.

Limitations

- How to define the best scheduler i.e to determine the parameters depending on which it will be defined.
- As the processes are moved from one queue to another, it is an overhead.
- It is the most complex scheduling algorithm.

Difference between Multilevel Queues and Multilevel Feedback Queues

S.No	Multilevel Queues	Multilevel Feedback Queues
1.	In multilevel queues the various processes can not move between different queues.	In multilevel feedback queues the processes in different sub queues can move between different queues.
2.	The various processes are assigned to different sub queues on the basis of memory size, process types or priority of the process.	The various processes are assigned to different queues on the basis of their CPU burst.
3.	In this case, there is low scheduling overhead as processes do not change their queues.	In this case, there is CPU overhead as processes move from one queue to another quite often.
4.	In this case, the problem of starvation can occur, as some processes may not get the processor.	There is no problem of starvation as processes in the low priority queue may be moved to higher priority queues.

Deadlocks

INTRODUCTION TO DEADLOCKS

A deadlock is situation where two or more processes are competing for the same resource. A deadlock situation occurs only in sharable resources. If any resource is exclusively meant for a particular action, then there are no chances of any kind of deadlock. When a process demands resource for its execution and the resource is held by some other process, then the demanding process goes into waiting state. If the waiting goes for infinite time, it is termed as a deadlock. Deadlock is a common situation in multiprogramming, parallel computing and distributed computing. In real life scenario, two persons are dialing each other's phone number at the same time and are getting a busy tone every time is a simple example of deadlock. The occurrence of deadlocks affects the performance of operating system.

This scenario in software systems process management is referred to as Deadlock and in its simplest form it will occur if process 1 is allocated resource A and later on it requires resource B and process 2 is allocated resource B and later on it requires resource A, such a situation is termed as a deadlock.

Example

- Process-1 requests the printer, gets it.
- Process-2 requests the CD ROM, gets it.
- Process-1 requests the CD ROM, waits.
- Process-2 requests the printer, waits.
- Process-1 and Process-2 are deadlocked.

Assumptions for Deadlocks

1. A process must request a resource before using it. It must release the resource after using it. The process follows the steps: request-->use-->release.
2. A process cannot request a number more than the total number of resources available in the system. For example; if the system has only four tape drives, a process cannot request five tape drives.

For the resources of the system, a resource table shall be kept, which shows whether each resource is free or if it is allocated, to which process it is allocated. For every resource, queues shall be kept, indicating the names of processes waiting for that resource.

A system has a number of resources which are to be distributed among a number of competing processes. These resources are the commodities necessary to get work done. The resources of similar types are grouped together, which consist of number of instances of a particular type. If the system has two printers then resource type printer will have two instances. If a request for a particular resource type has been made, then the request can be satisfied by any instance of that resource. Under the normal mode of operation, a process may utilize a resource in only the following sequence:

1. **Request:** It is the first step in which the request for a resource is made by a process. It may or may not be entertained. If the request cannot be granted immediately, then the requesting process must wait until it can acquire the resource. If the resource is free, the kernel allocate it to the process immediately, otherwise it changes the state of process to blocked.
2. **Allocation:** The resource has been allocated to the process. The process becomes the holder of the resource allocated to it. The resource state information is updated and the state of the process is changed to ready. The kernel uses some tie breaking rule like FCFS to decide which process should be allocated the resources.
3. **Release:** The process releases the resource. Process releases a resource through a system call.

The request and release of resources are system calls. Examples are the request and release device, open ( ) and close file, and allocate ( ) and free ( ) memory system calls.

Request and release of resources that are not managed by the OS can be accomplished through the wait () and signal () operations on semaphores or through acquisition and release of a mutex lock. A system table records whether each resource is free or allocated; for each resource that is allocated, the table also records the process to which it is allocated. If a process requests a resource that is currently allocated to another process, it can be added to a queue of processes waiting for this resource. A process whose resource request has just been denied will normally sit in a tight loop requesting the resource, then sleeping, then trying again.

The notion of a process is central to operating systems, but is notoriously hard to define. To a first approximation, a process is the execution of a program. It is a fundamental entity that requires resources in order to accomplish its task, which is required to run the program to completion. If the request for a resource cannot be satisfied at the moment, then it can be added to the queue of processes waiting for the resource. The set of processes will be in deadlock state when every process in the set is waiting for an event currently held by the other processes.

One can picture processes as actors simultaneously performing one-act plays in a theater; stage props are their resources. As actors need props, they request them from the property manager (the operating system resource allocator). The manager's job is to satisfy two conflicting goals on behalf of the actors. The processes can be categorized into following sets:

1. **Reusable:** These are the resources which can be safely used by one process at a time and is not consumed by that use. Processes obtain these resources, use them and after they have released the resource, it can be allocated to the other processes. The resources like processors, memory, files, devices, databases, and semaphores falls in the category of reusable resources.
2. **Consumable:** These are the resources which once allocated to a process will be consumed by that process. When a resource is acquired by a process, the resource ceases to exist afterwards. The resources like interrupts, signals, messages, and information in I/O buffers fall in this category.
3. **Preemptable:** The resources which can be taken from a process and can be allocated to some other process. It can be performed without any ill effects. It normally happens when a high priority job arrives, then the resource is taken from the low priority process and can be allocated to high priority process. Memory, CPU, I/O devices fall in the category of preemptable resource.
4. **Nonpreemptable:** The resources which cannot be taken away from its current owner without causing the computation to fail. Like printer, CD-R (W)floppy disk are the nonpreemptable resources.

In general, deadlocks occur while sharing reusable and nonpreemptable resources. Potential deadlocks that involve preemptable resources can usually be resolved by reallocating resources from one process to another.

Deadlocks can occur on hardware resources or on software resources. Unlike other problems in multiprogramming systems, there is no efficient solution to the deadlock problem in the general case. A programmer who is developing multithreaded applications must pay particular attention to this problem. Multithreaded programs are good candidates for deadlock because multiple threads can compete for shared resources.

Definition and Characteristics of Deadlock

Definition: A set of processes are in a deadlock state if every process in the set is waiting for an event that can only be caused by some other process in the same set. Thus, each process is waiting for an event that cannot occur. This situation arises if the following conditions are satisfied:

A deadlock involving a set of processes S is a situation in which each process Pi in S satisfies the following two conditions:

- Process Pi is blocked on some event Ej.
- Event Ej can be caused only by actions of other processes in S.

Each process capable of causing event Ej for which process Pi waits itself belongs to S. this property makes it impossible for the event Ej to occur, making process Pi wait indefinitely. Every other process in S also waits indefinitely.

Necessary Conditions for Occurrence of Deadlocks.

A deadlock occurs if and only if the following four conditions hold in a system simultaneously.

1. **Mutual Exclusion:** At least one of the resource must be held in a non-sharable (that is, only a limited number of processes can use it at a time and if it is requested by a process while it is being used by another one, the requesting process has to wait until the resource is released.
2. **Hold and Wait:** There must be at least one process that is holding at least one resource and waiting for other resources that are currently being hold by other processes.
3. **No Preemption:** No resource can be preempted before the holding process completes its task with that resource. The resource can be released only voluntarily.
4. **Circular Wait:** There exists a set of processes: {P1, P2, ...,Pn} such that:

   P1 is waiting for a resource held by P2

   P2 is waiting for a resource held by P3

   Pn – 1 is waiting for a resource held by Pn

   Pn is waiting for a resource held by P1

   These four conditions must hold for a deadlock to occur.

Representation of Deadlock Using Resource Allocation Graph

The deadlocks can be described with the help of a directed graph, also known as the resource allocation graph, Resource allocation graph consists of a set of vertices V and set of edges E. The set of vertices V can be partitioned into two different types of nodes: P the set of active processes and R is the set of all resource types.

There are two types of edges used in resource allocation graph:

1. **Request Edge:** This edge indicates the request of a process for acquisition of a particular resource. It will be a directed edge from the process Pi to the resource type Rj and is denoted by Pi -> Rj, it shows that the process Pi is requesting for the resource type Rj and is currently waiting for that resource.
2. **Assignment Edge:** This edge indicates the allocation of resource to a particular process. It will be a directed edge from the resource type Rj to the process Pi and is denoted by Rj -> Pi, it shows that the resource Rj is allocated to the process Pi.

Pictorial Representation of a Resource Allocation Graph uses following symbols:

1. The process is represented by a circle.
2. The resource type is represented by a square, as the resource type may have more than one instance, each instance may be represented by a dot within the square.

P1 holds one copies of resource R1 and P2 holds one copy of resource R2 and request one copy of R1.

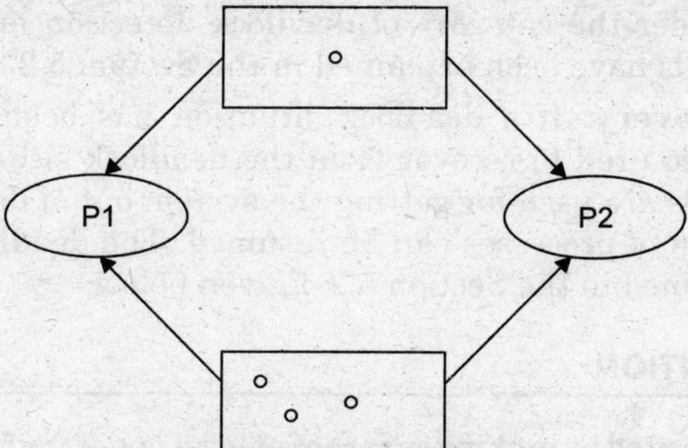

Figure 5.1: *Resource Allocation Graph*

The figure given below show a resource allocation graph with set P, R and E

Where P is the set of processes {P1, P2, P3}

R is the set of resources {R1, R2}, where the resource R1 has one instance, R2 has three instances.

E is the set of edges {P1 -> R2, R2 -> P2, R2->P3, P2 ->R1, R1 -> P1}

This resource allocation graph consists of a loop but does not have a cycle.

METHODS FOR HANDLING DEADLOCKS

The solutions to the deadlock problem fall into following categories:

1. **Deadlock Prevention:** The user ensures that the system does not enter into the deadlock, for this purpose either the deadlock prevention or a deadlock avoidance scheme can be used. Deadlock prevention is a set of methods to ensure that at least one of the conditions necessary for the occurrence of deadlock does not hold. These methods specify the way in which the requests can be made so that deadlock does not occur. It may lead to less efficient resource utilization in order to guarantee no deadlocks. The deadlock prevention mechanisms have been explained in the Section 5.2.1 given below.
2. **Deadlock Avoidance:** This method requires that the operating system may be given some information in advance about the resources required by the process during its total life time. Each request made by a process requires that the system consider the resources currently available, the resources allocated to each process and the future requests of the various processes, to decide whether the current request can be entertained or not. The deadlock avoidance methods have been explained in the Section 5.2.2 given below.

3. **Deadlock Detection:** If the system has failed to implement the deadlock prevention or deadlock avoidance algorithm, then deadlock may occur. Then, the user or system need to detect that deadlock has occurred. The methods used for this falls under the category of deadlock detection methods. The deadlock detection methods have been explained in the Section 5.2.3 given below.
4. **Deadlock Recovery:** If a deadlock situation has been detected, then some mechanism is required to recover from the deadlock situation, so the deadlock recovery methods are used for getting the system out of deadlock and hence the normal execution of processes can be resumed. The deadlock recovery methods have been explained in the Section 5.2.4 given below.

DEADLOCK PREVENTION

Deadlocks can be prevented by making sure that at least one of the four required conditions for the occurrence of deadlock should not occur. It can be achieved as follows:

1. **Mutual Exclusion:** It holds for non-sharable resources. Like a printer can be shared by a number of processes. As the shared resources are not involved in the mutually exclusive access, so these are not involved in the deadlock. The shared resources such as read-only files do not lead to deadlocks, as these can be accessed by a number of users or processes at the same time. It is not possible to prevent the deadlock by denying the mutual exclusion condition, as some of the resources are non-sharable.
2. **Hold and Wait:** To ensure that hold and wait condition does not occur, it must be ensured that a process requests a resource it must not be holding any other resource. It can be achieved by any of the following methods:
   (a) The first method require that the processes request all resources at one time, i.e the process should request all the resources required for the successful execution of the process in the beginning and these must be allocated to that process in the beginning itself. This can be wasteful of system resources if a process needs one resource early in its execution and doesn't need some other resource until much later. It leads to poor resource utilization, as some of the resources allocated to a process have not been used for a long time.
   (b) The second method require that processes holding resources must release them before requesting new resources, and then re-acquire the released resources along with the new ones in a single new request i.e, the process should request the resources when it has no resources allocated to it. This can be a problem if a process has partially completed an operation using a resource and then fails to get it re-allocated after releasing it.
3. **No Preemption:** This condition says that there will be no preemption of resources that have already been allocated. It can be handled as:
   (a) The first approach is that if a process is forced to wait when requesting a new resource, then all other resources previously held by this process are

implicitly released, (preempted), forcing this process to re-acquire the old resources along with the new resources in a single request.

(b) Another approach is that when a resource is requested, the user checks whether it is available, if these are available they are allocated. If they are not available, it is checked whether they have been allocated to some other process that is waiting for the additional resources. If it is so, we preempt the desired resources from the waiting process and allocate them to the requesting process. If the resources are not either available or held by a waiting process, the requesting process must wait. While it is waiting, some of its resources may be preempted, but only if another process requests them.

Either of these approaches may be applicable for resources whose states are easily saved and restored, such as registers and memory, but are generally not applicable to other devices such as printers and tape drives.

4. **Circular Wait:** One way to avoid circular wait is to number all resources, and to require that processes request resources only in strictly increasing (or decreasing) order. Let there is set R of various resources as {R1, R2 .... Rn}, each resource is assigned a unique integer number. In order to request resource Rj, a process must first release all Ri such that i >= j. One big challenge in this scheme is to determine the relative ordering of the different resources.

DEADLOCK AVOIDANCE

The deadlock prevention method tries to prevent the deadlock by ensuring that one of the necessary conditions for the occurrence of deadlock does not hold and it achieves it by deciding the way in which requests should be made. But this method of deadlock prevention may lead to poor resource utilization and low throughput.

An alternative method that can be used is the method of deadlock avoidance, which considers the additional information about how the resources should be requested. With the knowledge about the request and release of resources by various processes, the user can decide whether the process should wait or not. In this method, to avoid the deadlock, the system considers:

- The resources currently available.
- The resources currently allocated to each process.
- The resource requests for the future and the order in which these will be freed.

A deadlock avoidance algorithm examines the resource allocation state to ensure that there can never be a circular wait condition. The resource allocation state is defined by the number of available and allocated resources, the maximum demands of the processes.

The deadlock avoidance algorithms calculate safe paths for completion of all processes. Before a resource is allocated to a given process, the operating system first checks whether at least one path is available after allocation is made. If no path is available then the requesting process must wait until the resource can be safely allocated to the process. To avoid deadlocks in multiprogramming system, it is necessary to have some advance information of the resource usage of task. Due to unpredictability of a process in a transaction oriented system, it is not possible to have advance information of all the resources that may be required by process.

Given some additional information on how each process will request resources, it is possible to construct an algorithm that will avoid deadlock states. The algorithm will dynamically examine the resource allocation operations to ensure that there won't be a circular wait on resources. When a process requests a resource that is already available, the system must decide whether that resource can immediately be allocated or not. The resource is immediately allocated only if it leaves the system in a safe state. A state is safe if the system can allocate resources to each process in some order avoiding a deadlock. A deadlock state is an unsafe state.

Safe State: An allocation state is safe if there is an ordering of processes, a safe sequence, is a sequence in which each process gets the resources up to its maximum in some order and still avoid a deadlock. The system will be in safe state if there exists a safe sequence. A sequence of processes is a safe sequence for the current allocation state if for each process Pi, the resources that Pi can still request can be satisfied by currently available resources and the resources held by all Pj with j< i. if the processes required by Pi are not available then Pi can wait until all Pj have finished. When they have finished Pi can get all of its needed resources, complete its processing , return its allocated resources and finally terminate. When Pi terminates, Pi+1 can get the needed resources and can terminate finally. If no such sequence exists, then system state is said to be unsafe. A safe state is not a deadlock state, and a deadlock state is an unsafe state. Not all unsafe states are deadlocks , however an unsafe state may lead to deadlock. If the state is safe, the operating system can avoid deadlock states. In an unsafe state, the operating system cannot prevent processes from requesting resources such that a deadlock occurs.

Example: Consider a system with 12 tape drives. Assume there are three processes : p1, p2, p3. Assume we know the maximum no. of tape drives each process may request:

p1 : 10, p2 : 4, p3 : 9

Suppose at time t0, 9 tape drives have been allocated as follows:

p1 : 5, p2 : 2, p3 : 2

So, we have three more tape drives which are free.

This system is in a safe state because it we sequence processes as: <p2, p1, p3>, then p2 can get two more tape drives and it finishes its job, and returns four tape drives to the system. Then the system will have 5 free tape drives. Allocate all of them to p1, it gets 10 tape drives and finishes its job. p1 then returns all 10 drives to the system. Then p3 can get 7 more tape drives and it does its job.

Example: It is possible to go from a safe state to an unsafe state: consider the above example.

At time t1, p3 requests one more tape drive and gets it. Now, the system is in an unsafe state.

There are two free tape drives, so only p2 can be allocated all its tape drives. When it finishes and returns all 4 tape drives, the system will have four free tape drives.

p1 is allocated 5, may request 5 more --> has to wait

p3 is allocated 3, may request 6 more --> has to wait

so a situation of deadlock occurs. Here we allocated p3 one more tape drive and this caused a deadlock.

Method I for Deadlock Avoidance

In order to ensure that the system does not fall into a deadlock, the deadlock avoidance method is used. In this method a resource allocation graph is maintained where each resource is having only one instance, this graph is same as discussed earlier. But in addition to request and assignment edges a new edge called as claim edge is used, it an edge from the process to the resource Pi -> Rj, shows that the process Pi may request resource Rj some time in future. The edge resembles a request edge in direction but is shown by a dashed line. When the process Pi requests the resource Rj, it is converted into a request edge. Same way when a resource Rj is released by Pi, the assignment edge Rj ->Pi is converted to a claim edge Pi -> Rj. If the graph has no cycles, then the system will be in a safe state. If cycle exists, then the allocation will lead the system into an unsafe state.

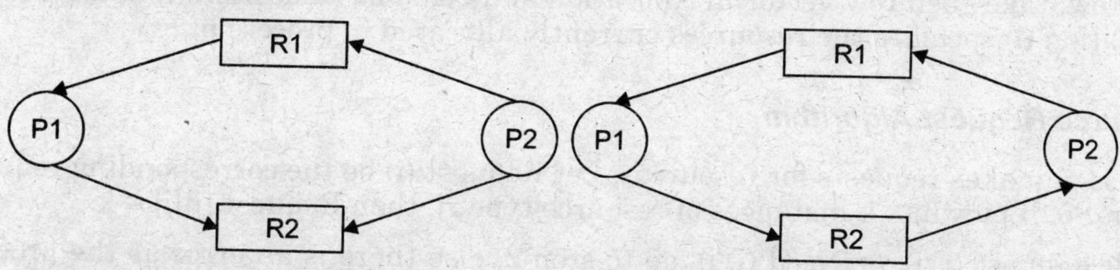

Figure 5.2: *Resource Allocation Graph for Deadlock Avoidance.*

Figure 5.3: *An Unsafe State in a Resource Allocation Graph.*

The resource allocation graph shown in Figure 5.2 show that P2 requests R2. Although R2 is currently free, we cannot allocate it to P2, as this action will create a cycle in the graph. A cycle shows that the system is in unsafe state. If P1 requests R2 and P2 requests R1, then deadlock will occur. As shown in the Figure 5.3.

Method II for Deadlock Avoidance

The method I of resource allocation graph is applicable only if there is one instance of a resource type, but normally there exist multiple instances of the resources. This algorithm considers each request and examines whether it leads to a safe state or not. The algorithm is divided into two parts: Safety Algorithm and Resource Request Algorithm. The safety algorithm provides a sequence in which if processes are processed will lead the system into a safe state. While the resource request algorithm ensures whether a process requesting the resource should be granted the resource right now or the process have to wait for the resource. The resource will be granted only if the allocation of the resource corresponding to this request will lead to a safe state or to an unsafe state. If upon granting the request the system goes into an unsafe state, then the request should not be granted and the process should wait.

The various data structures used in the algorithm are: (m : number of resource types, n : number of processes).

1. **Available [m]:** One dimensional array of size m. It indicates the number of available resources of each type. For example, if Available [i] is k, there are k instances of resource ri are available.
2. **Max [n, m]:** Two dimensional array of size n*m. It defines the maximum demand of each process from each resource type. For example, if Max [i, j] is k, that means process pi may request at most k instances of resource type rj.
3. **Allocation [n, m]:** Two dimensional array of size n*m. It defines the number of resources of each type currently allocated to each process.
4. **Need [n, m]:** Two dimensional array of size n*m. It indicates the remaining need of each process, of each resource type. If Need [i, j] is k, process pi may need k more instances of resource type rj.

   Note that Need [i, j] = Max [i, j] – Allocation [i, j].

   Now, take each row vector in Allocation and Need as Allocation (i) and Need (i).

(Allocation (i) specifies the resources currently allocated to process pi.)

Resource Request Algorithm

Process pi makes requests for resources. Let Request (i) be the corresponding request vector. So, if pi wants k instances of resource type rj, then Request [i][j] = k.

1. If Request (i, j) <= Need (i, j), go to step 2, else there is an error as the process is requesting for the amount greater than its need and maximum claim made earlier.
2. If Request (i, j) <= Available [j], go to step 3, else pi must wait as the resources are not available.
3. If the requested resources have been allocated to the process Pi, the following updations are performed:

   Available [j] = Available [j] – Request (i, j), for all j.

   Allocation (i, j) = Allocation (i, j) + Request (i, j), for all j.

   Need (i, j) = Need (i, j) – Request (i, j), for all j.
4. If the resulting resource allocation state is safe. The transaction is completed and process Pi is allocated the resources and if the new state is unsafe, then Pi must wait for Request [i, j] and all old resource allocation state is restored.

Safety Algorithm

This algorithm is used to find out that whether the system is in safe state or not.

The algorithm follows as

Let Work and finish be vectors of length m and n respectively, Initialize Work = Available and finish [i] = false, for all i.

1. Find an i such that both,
   Finish [i] = false,
   Need [i, j] <= Work.
   If no such i exists, go to step 4.
2. Work = Work + Allocation,
   Finish [i] = True, and then go to step 1.
3. If Finish [i] = true for all i, then system is in safe state.

Banker's algorithm based on the following assumptions

1. System has a limited number of resources.
2. Each process must use the resource for a limited period of time.
3. Each process must declare the maximum number of instances of each resource type that it may need, when it comes to execution.

Example 1: Let a system has 5 processes and 4 resources, the allocation and the maximum requirement of the various resources has been mentioned as below:

Process/ Resources	Allocation Matrix				Maximum Number of Resources Required			
	A	B	C	D	A	B	C	D
P1	3	0	1	1	4	1	1	1
P2	0	1	0	0	0	2	1	2
P3	1	1	1	0	4	2	1	0
P4	1	1	0	1	1	1	0	1
P5	0	0	0	0	2	1	1	0

Available Resources

Resources	A	B	C	D
	1	0	2	0

Find

(a) The contents of Need Matrix.

(b) The safe sequence for the above mentioned processes.

Solution:

The Contents of Need Matrix can be calculated as:

(a) Need = Maximum Number of Resources Required – Resources allocated

Process/Resources	A	B	C	D
P1	1	1	0	0
P2	0	1	1	2
P3	3	1	0	0
P4	0	0	0	0
P5	2	1	1	0

(b) How to obtain the Safe Sequence?

Step 1: Check and find the process which satisfy the following condition, i.e

Need < = Work (Available)

Here these values are: Available is (1, 0, 2, 0)

Starting from the first process, P4 satisfies this equation as (0, 0, 0, 0) < = (1, 0, 2, 0)

So the solution set = {P4}

And Work = Work + Allocation

Work = (1, 0, 2, 0) + (1, 1, 0, 1) = (2, 1, 2, 1)

Step 2: Check and find the process which satisfy the following condition, i.e

Need < = Work (Available)

Here the updated value of Work is (2, 1, 2, 1)

The process P1 satisfies this condition as: Need of P1 (1, 1, 0, 0) <= (2, 1, 2, 1)

So the solution set becomes {P4, P1}

And Work is updated as Work = Work + Allocation

Work = (2, 1, 2, 1) + (3, 0, 1, 1) = (5, 1, 3, 2).

Step 3: Check and find the process which satisfy the following condition, i.e

Need < = Work (Available)

Here the updated value of Work is (5, 1, 3, 2).

The process P2 satisfies this condition as: Need of P2 (0, 1, 1, 2) <= (5, 1, 3, 2)

So the solution set becomes {P4, P1, P2}

And Work is updated as Work = Work + Allocation

Work = (5, 1, 3, 2) + (0, 1, 0, 0) = (5, 2, 3, 2).

Step 4: Check and find the process which satisfy the following condition, i.e

Need < = Work (Available)

Here the updated value of Work is (5, 2, 3, 2).

The process P3 satisfies this condition as: Need of P3 (3, 1, 0, 0) <= (5, 2, 3, 2)

So the solution set becomes {P4, P1, P2, P3}

And Work is updated as Work = Work + Allocation

Work = (5, 2, 3, 2) + (1, 1, 1, 0) = (6, 3, 4, 2).

Step 5: Check and find the process which satisfy the following condition, i.e

Need < = Work (Available)

Here the updated value of Work is (6, 3, 4, 2).

The process P5 satisfies this condition as: Need of P5 (2, 1, 1, 0) <= (6, 3, 4, 2)

So the solution set becomes {P4, P1, P2, P3, P5}

And Work is updated as Work = Work + Allocation

Work = (6, 3, 4, 2) + (0, 0, 0, 0) = (6, 3, 4, 2).

Which is equal to the total number of instances for A, B and C.

The safe sequence is <P4, P1, P2, P3, P5>

Example 2: Let a system has 5 processes and 3 resources, the allocation and the maximum requirement of the various resources has been mentioned as below:

Process/ Resources	Allocation Matrix			Maximum Number of Resources Required			Available Resources		
	A	B	C	A	B	C	A	B	C
P0	0	1	0	7	5	3	3	3	2
P1	2	0	0	3	2	2			
P2	3	0	2	9	0	2			
P3	2	1	1	2	2	2			
P4	0	0	2	4	3	3			

Find:

(a) The contents of Need Matrix.

(b) The safe sequence for the above mentioned processes.

(c) If a request for one additional instance of resource A and 2 more instances of resource B arrives from process P1, can it be granted or not?

Solution:

(a) The contents of Need Matrix can be calculated as:

Need = Maximum Number of Resources Required – Resources allocated

Process/Resources	A	B	C
P0	7	4	3
P1	1	2	2
P2	6	0	0
P3	0	1	1
P4	4	3	1

How to obtain the Safe Sequence?

Step 1: Check and find the process which satisfy the following condition, i.e

Need < = Work (Available)

Here these values are: Available is (3, 3, 2)

Starting from the first process, P0 does not satisfy this condition as (7, 4, 3) is not less than or equal to Available (3, 3, 2).

Process P1 satisfies this equation as (1, 2, 2) < = (3, 3, 2)

So the solution set = {P1}

And Work = Work + Allocation

Work = (3, 3, 2) + (2, 0, 0) = (5, 3, 2)

Step 2: Check and find the process which satisfy the following condition, i.e

Need < = Work (Available)

Here the updated value of Work is (5, 3, 2)

The process P3 satisfies this condition as: Need of P3 (0, 1, 1) <= (5,3,2)

So the solution set becomes {P1, P3}

And Work is updated as Work = Work + Allocation

Work = (5, 3, 2) + (2, 1, 1) = (7, 4, 3).

Step 3: Check and find the process which satisfy the following condition, i.e

Need < = Work (Available)

Here the updated value of Work is (7, 4, 3)

The process P4 satisfies this condition as: Need of P4 (4, 3, 1) <= (7, 4, 3)

So the solution set becomes {P1, P3, P4}

And Work is updated as Work = Work + Allocation

Work = (7, 4, 3) + (0, 0, 2) = (7, 4, 5).

Step 4: Check and find the process which satisfy the following condition, i.e

Need < = Work (Available)

Here the updated value of Work is (7, 4, 5)

The process P0 satisfies this condition as: Need of P0 (7, 4, 3) <= (7, 4, 5)

So the solution set becomes {P1, P3, P4, P0}

And Work is updated as Work = Work + Allocation

Work = (7, 4, 5) + (0, 1, 0) = (7, 5, 5).

Step 5: Check and find the process which satisfy the following condition, i.e

Need < = Work (Available)

Here the updated value of Work is (7, 5, 5)

The process P2 satisfies this condition as: Need of P2 (6, 0, 0) <= (7, 5, 5)

So the solution set becomes {P1, P3, P4, P0, P2}

And Work is updated as Work = Work + Allocation

Work = (7, 5, 5) + (3, 0, 2) = (10, 5, 7).

Which is equal to the total number of instances for A, B and C.

The safe sequence is <P1, P3, P4, P0, P2>

(b) Suppose that process P1 requests an additional instance of resource type A and two instances of resource type C so the request (1, 0, 2). To decide whether this request can be granted or not, we check that Request <= Available, i.e (1, 0, 2) <= (3, 3, 2), which is true and if the request has been fulfilled then the new states of the system becomes

Process/ Resources	**Allocation Matrix**			**Maximum Number of Resources Required**			**Available Resources**		
	A	B	C	A	B	C	A	B	C
P0	0	1	0	7	5	3	2	3	0
P1	3	0	2	3	2	2			
P2	3	0	2	9	0	2			
P3	2	1	1	2	2	2			
P4	0	0	2	4	3	3			

Although the request can be allocated, but have to make sure that whether the system will be in safe state or not. So we execute the safety algorithm to find the safe sequence as follows:

(a) Need Matrix of resources can be calculated as:

Need = Maximum Number of Resources Required – Resources allocated

Process\Resources	A	B	C
P0	7	4	3
P1	0	2	0
P2	6	0	0
P3	0	1	1
P4	4	3	1

(b) How to obtain the Safe Sequence?

Step 1: Check and find the process which satisfy the following condition, i.e

Need < = Work (Available)

Here these values are: Available is (2, 3, 0)

Starting from the first process, P0 does not satisfy this condition as (7, 4, 3) is not less than or equal to Available (3, 3, 2).

Process P1 satisfies this equation as (0, 2, 0) < = (2, 3, 0)

So the solution set = {P1}

And Work = Work + Allocation

Work = (2, 3, 0) + (3, 0, 2) = (5, 3, 2)

Step 2: Check and find the process which satisfy the following condition, i.e

Need < = Work (Available)

Here the updated value of Work is (5, 3, 2)

The process P3 satisfies this condition as: Need of P3 (0, 1, 1) <= (5, 3, 2)

So the solution set becomes {P1, P3}

And Work is updated as Work = Work + Allocation

Work = (5, 3, 2) + (2, 1, 1) = (7, 4, 3).

Step 3: Check and find the process which satisfy the following condition, i.e

Need < = Work (Available)

Here the updated value of Work is (7, 4, 3)

The process P4 satisfies this condition as: Need of P4 (4, 3, 1) <= (7, 4, 3)

So the solution set becomes {P1, P3, P4}

And Work is updated as Work = Work + Allocation

Work = (7, 4, 3) + (0, 0, 2) = (7, 4, 5).

Step 4: Check and find the process which satisfy the following condition, i.e

Need < = Work (Available)

Here the updated value of Work is (7, 4, 5)

The process P0 satisfies this condition as: Need of P0 (7, 4, 3) <= (7, 4, 5)

So the solution set becomes {P1, P3, P4, P0}

And Work is updated as Work = Work + Allocation

Work = (7, 4, 5) + (0, 1, 0) = (7, 5, 5).

Step 5: Check and find the process which satisfy the following condition, i.e

Need < = Work (Available)

Here the updated value of Work is (7, 5, 5)

The process P2 satisfies this condition as: Need of P2 (6, 0, 0) <= (7, 5, 5)

So the solution set becomes {P1, P3, P4, P0, P2}

And Work is updated as Work = Work + Allocation

Work = (7, 5, 5) + (3, 0, 2) = (10, 5, 7).

Which is equal to the total number of instances for A, B and C.

The safe sequence is <P1, P3, P4, P0, P2> and as the safe sequence is available the request for the additional resources can be granted.

Example 3: Let a system has 5 processes and 4 resources, the allocation and the maximum requirement of the various resources has been mentioned as below:

Process/ Resources	**Allocation Matrix**				**Maximum Number of Resources Required**			
	A	B	C	D	A	B	C	D
P0	0	0	1	2	0	0	1	2
P1	1	0	0	0	1	7	5	0
P2	1	3	5	4	2	3	5	6
P3	0	6	3	2	0	6	5	2
P4	0	0	1	4	0	6	5	6

Available Resources

Resources	A	B	C	D
	1	5	2	0

Find the contents of need matrix; Find the Safe sequence for the above mentioned processes.

Solution:

(a) Need of resources can be calculated as:

Need = Maximum Number of Resources Required – Resources allocated

Process/Resources	A	B	C	D
P0	0	0	0	0
P1	0	7	5	0
P2	1	0	0	2
P3	0	0	2	0
P4	0	6	4	2

(b) How to obtain the Safe Sequence?

Step 1: Check and find the process which satisfy the following condition, i.e

Need < = Work (Available)

Here these values are: Available is (1, 5, 2, 0)

Starting from the first process, P0 satisfies this equation as (0, 0, 0, 0) < = (1, 5, 2, 0)

So the solution set = {P0}

And Work = Work + Allocation

Work = (1, 5, 2, 0) + (0, 0, 1, 2) = (1, 5, 3, 2)

Step 2: Check and find the process which satisfy the following condition, i.e

Need < = Work (Available)

Here the updated value of Work is (1, 5, 3, 2)

The process P2 satisfies this condition as: Need of P2 (1, 0, 0, 2) <= (1, 5, 3, 2)

So the solution set becomes {P0, P2}

And Work is updated as Work = Work + Allocation

Work = (1, 5, 3, 2) + (1, 3, 5, 4) = (2, 8, 8, 6).

Step 3: Check and find the process which satisfy the following condition, i.e

Need < = Work (Available)

Here the updated value of Work is (2, 8, 8, 6)

The process P3 satisfies this condition as: Need of P3 (0, 0, 2, 0) <= (2, 8, 8, 6)

So the solution set becomes {P0, P2, P3}

And Work is updated as Work = Work + Allocation

Work = (2, 8, 8, 6) + (0, 6, 3, 2) = (2, 14, 11, 8)

Step 4: Check and find the process which satisfy the following condition, i.e

Need < = Work (Available)

Here the updated value of Work is (2, 14, 11, 8)

The process P4 satisfies this condition as: Need of P4 (0, 6, 4, 2) <= (2, 14, 11, 8)

So the solution set becomes {P0, P2, P3, P4}

And Work is updated as Work = Work + Allocation

Work = (2, 14, 11, 8) + (0, 0, 1, 4) = (2, 14, 12, 12)

Step 5: Check and find the process which satisfy the following condition, i.e

Need < = Work (Available)

Here the updated value of Work is (2, 14, 12, 12)

Start looking from the first process, the process P0 satisfies this condition as:

Need of P1 (0, 7, 5, 0) <= (2, 14, 12, 12)

So the solution set becomes {P0, P2, P3, P4, P0}

And Work is updated as Work = Work + Allocation

Work = (2, 14, 12, 12) + (1, 0, 0, 0) = (3, 14, 12, 12).

Which is equal to the total number of instances for A, B and C.

The safe sequence is <P0, P2, P3, P4, P0>

DEADLOCK DETECTION

If the system does not employ either a deadlock prevention or deadlock avoidance algorithm, then a deadlock situation may occur. In order to recover from deadlock state, the user should be able to detect the deadlock. There should be mechanisms to detect whether a deadlock exists in the system and if yes, methods to recover the system from such a state should be known.

There are two algorithms for deadlock detection, the first one considers that there is only one instance of each resource type and the second one considers that there are multiple instances of each resource type.

Algorithm I: *Single Instance of each Resource Type:* If all resources have only a single instance, then we can define a deadlock detection algorithm that uses a wait for graph. An edge Pi to Pj in a wait for graph implies that process Pi is waiting for process Pj to release a resource that Pi needs. An edge Pi -> Pj exists in a wait for graph if and only if the corresponding resource allocation graph contains two edges Pi -> Rq and Rq -> Pj for some resource Rq. Deadlock exists in the system iff a cycle appears in a wait for graph.

Figure 5.4(a) the resource allocation graph and the fig. 5.4 (b) show the wait-for-graph for the resource allocation graph in Figure (a). in order to detect deadlock, the system maintains the wait for graph and periodically invoke an algorithm that searches for a cycle in the graph.

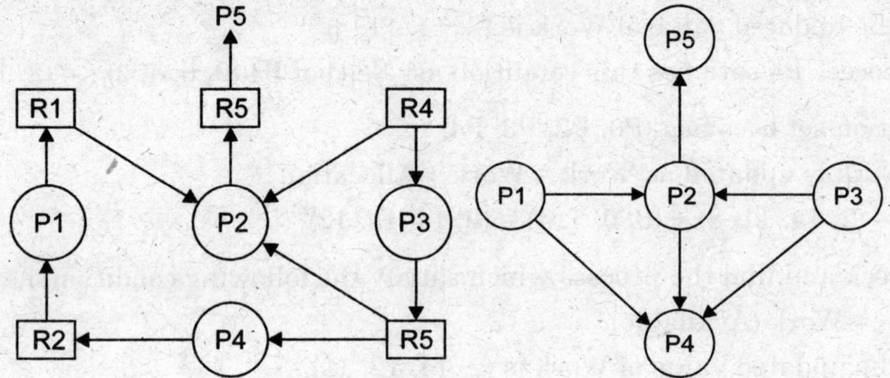

Figure 5.4: *(a) Resource Allocation Graph (b) Corresponding Wait for Graph*

Algorithm II: *Multiple Instances of a Resource Type:* If the resources have multiple instances then the following algorithm is used to detect the deadlock. This algorithm is quite similar to the banker's algorithm described for deadlock avoidance. This algorithm requires to maintain the following data structures: (m: number of resource types, n : number of processes).

1. **Available [m]:** One dimensional array of size m. It indicates the number of available resources of each type. For example, if Available [i] is k, there are k instances of resource ri.
2. **Max [n, m]:** Two dimensional array of size n*m. It defines the maximum demand of each process from each resource type. For example, if Max [i, j] is k, that means process pi may request at most k instances of resource type rj.
3. **Allocation [n, m]:** Two dimensional array of size n*m. It defines the number of resources of each type currently allocated to each process.
4. **Need [n, m]:** Two dimensional array of size n*m. It indicates the remaining need of each process, of each resource type. If Need [i, j] is k, process pi may need k more instances of resource type rj.

Algorithm for Deadlock Detection

Let Work and finish be vectors of length m and n respectively, Initialize Work = Available. If allocation is not equal to Zero then Finish[i] = false, else finish[i] = true, for all i.

1. Find an i such that both,

   Finish[i] = false,

   Request [i ,j] <= Work.

   If no such i exists, go to step 3.

2. Work = Work + Allocation,
   Finish[i] = True, and then go to step 1.
3. If Finish[i] = false for all i, then system is in a deadlock state.

Example: Let us consider the system with 5 processes and 3 resources. Resource type A has 7 instances, B has 2 instances and C has 6 instances. At time t0 the resource allocation state is given below:

Process/Resources	Allocation Matrix			Request for Resources		
	A	B	C	A	B	C
P0	0	1	0	0	0	0
P1	2	0	0	2	0	2
P2	3	0	3	0	0	0
P3	2	1	1	1	0	0
P4	0	0	2	0	0	2

Available Resources

Resources	A	B	C
	0	0	0

The system is not in a deadlock state, the safe sequence is <P0, P2, P3, P1, P4>

(a) How to obtain the Safe Sequence?

Step 1: Check and find the process which satisfy the following condition, i.e

Request < = Work (Available)

Here these values are: Available is (0, 0, 0)

P0 satisfies this equation as (0, 0, 0) < = (0, 0, 0)

So the solution set = {P 0}

And Work = Work + Allocation

Work = (0, 0, 0) + (0, 1, 0) = (0, 1, 0)

Step 2: Check and find the process which satisfy the following condition, i.e

Request < = Work (Available)

Here the updated value of Work is (0, 1, 0)

The process P2 satisfies this condition as: Request of P2 (0, 0, 0) <= (0, 1, 0)

So the solution set becomes {P0, P2}

And Work is updated as Work = Work + Allocation

Work = (0, 1, 0) + (3, 0, 3) = (3, 1, 3).

Step 3: Check and find the process which satisfy the following condition, i.e

Request < = Work (Available)

Here the updated value of Work is (3, 1, 3)

The process P3 satisfies this condition as: Request of P3 (1, 0, 0) <= (3, 1, 3)

So the solution set becomes {P0, P2, P3}

And Work is updated as Work = Work + Allocation

Work = (3, 1, 3) + (2, 1, 1) = (5, 2, 4).

Step 4: Check and find the process which satisfy the following condition, i.e

Request < = Work (Available)

Here the updated value of Work is (5, 2, 4)

The process P1 satisfies this condition as: Request of P1 (2, 0, 2) <= (5, 2, 4)

So the solution set becomes {P0, P2, P3, P1}

And Work is updated as Work = Work + Allocation

Work = (5, 2, 4) + (2, 0, 0) = (7, 2, 4).

Step 5: Check and find the process which satisfy the following condition, i.e

Request < = Work (Available)

Here the updated value of Work is (7, 2, 4)

The process P2 satisfies this condition as: Request of P4 (0, 0, 2) <= (7, 2, 4)

So the solution set becomes {P0, P2, P3, P1, P4}

And Work is updated as Work = Work + Allocation

Work = (7, 2, 4) + (0, 0, 2) = (7, 2, 6).

Which is equal to the total number of instances for A, B and C.

If P2 makes an additional request for an instance of type C then the new Request Matrix becomes:

Process/Resources	Allocation Matrix			Request for Resources		
	A	B	C	A	B	C
P0	0	1	0	0	0	0
P1	2	0	0	2	0	2
P2	3	0	3	0	0	1
P3	2	1	1	1	0	0
P4	0	0	2	0	0	2

The request of process P0 is less than or equal to the available vector, can be allowed to finish. After P0 executes, Avail will be (0, 1, 0). Now neither P1 nor P2 can be allowed to finish, as its request is not less than or equal to available. Thus P1 and P2 are deadlocked, as their Finish is still false.

DEADLOCK RECOVERY

Once a deadlock has been detected, the system should be recovered from this state of deadlock. The recovery from the deadlock should be done on the priority basis, otherwise it will degrade the system performance and if no correction mechanism is applied there is a possibility that total system may fail. The recovery can be automatic or may be handled manually. To perform the recovery one or more processes may be aborted to break the circular wait, the other option is to preempt some resources from one or more of the deadlocked processes. The various recovery mechanisms that can be applied are:

1. **Recovery through Process Termination:** In this method either all or some of the processes involved in the deadlock are terminated. If all the processes are terminated, the deadlock cycle will be broken definitely. This method will incur a huge cost, as many of the processes may be near completion or the results of the partial computations may be discarded. Another method is to abort one process at a time, until the deadlock is eliminated. After the abortion of a process, a deadlock detection algorithm must be run to check whether any of the processes are still deadlocked or not.

This method is not that easy as the process may be in use, while it is terminated and may lead the system into an inconsistent state. The decision about the choice of the process to be aborted depends on the following factors:

(a) The priority of the process.

(b) The number and type of resources used by the process.

(c) How much percentage of the process has been completed?

(d) How many resources the process needs in order to complete?

(e) What is the nature of the process- that is whether it is a batch program or an interactive one.

2. **Recovery through Preemption:** In this method some of the resources are preempted from a process and are allocated to other processes till the deadlock is broken. The various issues to be taken into account in this method are:

3. **Selection of the process to be preempted:** The first issue is to decide which resources or the processes are to be preempted. The choice should incur the

minimum cost, i.e if a process has completed almost 90-95 % of its execution, should not be preempted.

4. **Rollback:** This issue deals with the problem that what should be done with the preempted processes, one option is to roll back this process to some earlier safe state and restart its execution from that point.

5. **Starvation:** There must be some method to ensure that starvation should not occur i.e a particular process should not be deprived of some of the resources, and the same process should not become the target for preemption. To make it possible, a counter can be used to count the number of times the resources have been taken away from a process.

Process Synchronization

Chapter 6

INTRODUCTION TO PROCESS SYNCHRONIZATION

To maximize the overall system performance more than one process need to interact with each other, where they share data or coordinate their activities with each other. But these processes must work in coordination with each other so that the common goal is achieved or we can say that there must be synchronization in their actions and the concept is termed as process synchronization. Process synchronization makes sure that processes perform their actions in a desired order. In this approach, processes cooperate with each other for completion of their tasks. A cooperating process is one that can affect or be affected by the other processes executing in the system. Cooperating processes may either share a logical address space (that is, both code and data), or be allowed to share data only through files. The former case is achieved through the use of lightweight processes or threads. A process is independent if it cannot affect or be affected by the other processes executing in the system. On the other hand, a process is cooperating if it can affect or be affected by the other processes executing in the system. The cooperation among the processes is achieved either by sharing or by communication. Like the transactions processed in a banking system are cooperating, as they share common database, update and read same data on shared basis. The basic properties of cooperating processes are:

1. They share or exchange a common object or message.
2. They are non-deterministic.
3. They are not reproducible.
4. Their execution may lead to race conditions.

Need of Process Cooperation: There are several reasons for providing an environment that allows process cooperation:

1. Information sharing
2. Computation speedup
3. Modularity
4. Convenience

Types of Synchronization

1. Data Access Synchronization
2. Control Synchronization.

1. **Data Access Synchronization** makes sure that shared data should not loose its identity while updation or retrieval of data by several processes. It is possible if the accesses to the shared data are performed in mutually exclusive manner. It avoids the occurrence of race conditions and safeguards the consistency of the shared data.
2. **Control Synchronization** ensures that the interacting processes perform their actions in a desired order, i.e if a process should perform some actions ti only after some processes have executed a set of actions {tj} or only when a set of conditions {ck} hold.

Computer systems provide atomic instructions for data access synchronization and control Synchronization.

To perform process synchronization, a control on processes should be there. When a process needs to synchronize its data, it has to wait for the completion/termination of other running processes or when other process holds its execution for some time.

Concurrent access to shared data may result in data inconsistency. If processes shared data in an unordered or uncoordinated manner, then race condition may arise. Where race condition is that when several processes access and manipulate the same data concurrently and the outcome of the execution depends on the particular order in which the access takes place. So to avoid the occurrence of race condition the processes should be executed in mutually exclusive manner. The basic technique to implement synchronization is to block a process until a suitable action is performed by other process or until a condition is satisfied. The data access synchronization is implemented by blocking a process until another process finishes accessing shared data and control synchronization is implemented by blocking a process until another process performs a specific action. If we are implementing the concept of process synchronization, then effective execution speed of a process cannot be estimated due to the factors like time slicing, process priorities and I/O activities in the processes.

THE CRITICAL SECTION PROBLEM

Consider a system with a number of sequential processes running asynchronously sharing some data. Instructions of co-operating processes can be interleaved arbitrarily.

Example:

Process P1:

P1 reads variable A (A = 40)

P1 writes A+10 into A (A = 50)

Process P2:

P2 updates variable A (A = 20)

P2 reads variable A (50 instead of 20)

The order of execution of these processes may vary from execution to execution, two such scenarios may be:

Case I	Case II
P1 reads variable A (A = 40) P1 writes A + 10 into A (A = 50) P2 updates variable A (A = 20) P2 reads variable A (Its value is 20)	P1 reads variable A (A = 40) P2 updates variable A (A = 20) P1 writes A+10 into A (A = 50) P2 reads variable A (50 instead of 20)

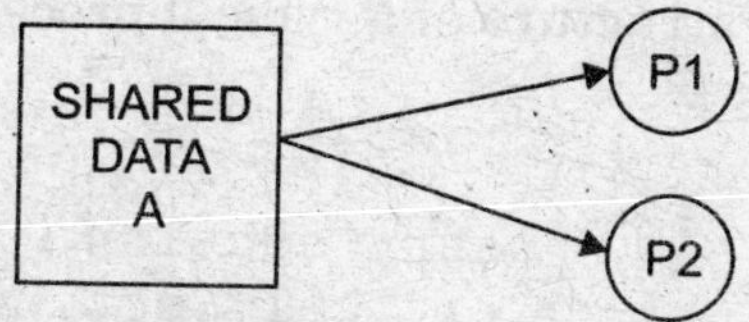

Figure 6.1: *Shared Variable Accessed by Processes P1 and P2*

Thus, the output of interleaved execution depends on the order in which the access takes place. So the shared variables should not be updated at the same time, but if the processes are executed concurrently, they will access and manipulate the data at the same time, it will be possible only through the mechanism of synchronization.

Solution: Allow only one process to execute in its critical section at a time. (Mutual Exclusion)

Critical Sections

The idea of critical section is introduced to avoid the occurrence of race condition.

Definition: A section of code or set of operations in which process may change the shared variables, update a common file or some data is known as the critical section of that process.

A critical section for a data item is the section of code that should not be executed concurrently either with itself or with the critical section for that data item.

The processes that execute concurrently, they must ensure that execution of the critical section should be made atomic, that means that either the operations in the critical section should happen completely or not at all, that means we can say that the processes should not be interrupted in between.

The synchronization mechanism ensures that the critical section of a process should not be executed concurrently with the critical section of the other processes. That means if one process is executing in its critical section, no other process is allowed to execute in its critical section. So the execution of critical sections by the processes is mutually exclusive in time. The critical section problem is to design a protocol that processes should use when they are cooperating. Each process must request if it wishes to enter into its critical section, this request is implemented in the entry section and following this is the exit section and the remainder section of code or set of operations of a process that does not belong to its critical section is termed as remainder section. The parts of a process may be divided into following Sections:

1. **Entry Section:** The code requesting entry into the critical section.
2. **Critical Section:** The code in which only one process can execute at any one time.
3. **Exit Section:** The end of the critical section, releasing or allowing others to execute.
4. **Remainder Section:** Rest of the code after the critical section.

Figure 6.2 Show the general structure of a typical process.

```
do
{
Entry section
Critical Section
Exit Section
Remainder Section
} while;
```

(a): Structure of a Process.

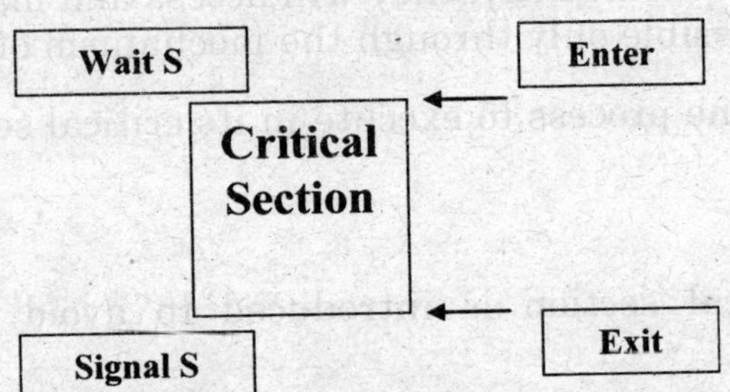

Figure 6.2: *(b): Representation of Critical Section*

Characteristic Properties of the code that form a Critical Section are:

1. Codes that reference one or more variables in a "read-update-write" fashion while any of those variables is possibly being altered by another thread.
2. Codes that alter one or more variables that are possibly being referenced in "read-update-write" fashion by another thread.
3. Codes use a data structure while any part of it is possibly being altered by another thread.
4. Codes alter any part of a data structure while it is possibly in use by another thread.

SOLUTION FOR CRITICAL SECTIONS PROBLEM

Criteria for a Solution of the Critical Section Problem

The solution to the critical section problem must satisfy the following criteria:

1. Only one process at a time can enter the critical section.
2. A process that halts in non-critical section cannot prevent other processes from entering the critical section.
3. A process requesting to enter a critical section should not be delayed indefinitely.
4. When no process is in a critical section, any process that requests to enter the critical section should be permitted to enter without delay.
5. Make no assumptions about the relative speed of processors (or their number).
6. A process remains within a critical section for a finite time only.

A solution to the critical section problem must satisfy the following three conditions:

Mutual Exclusion: Only one process at a time can be executing in their critical section i.e If process P_i is executing in its critical section, then no other processes can be executing in their critical sections. Along with this the implementation should ensure that any process wishing to enter a critical section will not be delayed indefinitely i.e starvation will not occur. It will ensure that critical sections should be focused and short and if a process somehow halts/waits in its critical section, it must not interfere with other processes.

Progress: If no process is currently executing in their critical section, and one or more processes want to execute their critical section, then only the processes not in their remainder sections can participate in the decision, and the decision cannot be postponed indefinitely, i.e. processes cannot be blocked forever waiting to get into their critical sections. It ensures that the wish of a process to enter into its critical section will be entertained fairly and the opportunity will be provided in a finite time.

Bounded Waiting: A bound must exist on the number of times that other processes are allowed to enter their critical sections after a process has made a request to enter its critical section and before that request is granted. This property limits the number of times other processes can be favored over a given process Pi.

Types of Solutions to Critical Section Problem

- **Software Solutions:** These solutions consider the usage of algorithms to provide a solution to the problems of critical section.
- **Hardware Solutions:** These solutions rely on some special hardware machine instructions.
- **Operating System Solutions:** These solutions provide some functions and data structures to the programmer through system/library calls.

Software Solutions for Critical Section's Problem

Dijkstra's Algorithms

No assumptions may be made concerning the hardware instructions or the number of processors the hardware supports. However, it is assumed that the primitive machine language instructions (load, store, compare, etc.) are executed atomically. If two primitive machine language instructions are executed simultaneously, then the result is equivalent to their sequential execution in an unknown order.

1. No assumptions may be made on the relative speeds of the n processes executing in the system.
2. When a process is in its non-critical section (non-CS) of code, it may not prevent other processes from entering their own critical sections (CS).
3. When a decision must be made to admit one of a number of candidate processes to its CS, the decision cannot be postponed indefinitely.
4. So, we shall try to develop protocols to solve the CS problem and our solutions will not violate Dijkstra's constraints.

In the following discussions, a number of algorithms have been proposed as a solution to the CS problem. For simplicity, only two processes, p0 and p1 shall be considered to be existing in the system, unless it is stated otherwise.

Algorithm - 1

Let the processes share a common integer variable turn, which is 0 or 1. If turn = 1, p1 is allowed to execute in its CS. Otherwise, p0 is allowed to execute in its CS.

```
{ for p1 }
repeat
while turn <> 1
do;
CS
turn : = 0;
non-CS
until false;
```

This algorithm ensures that only one process at a time is in its Critical Section (mutual exclusion). However, it violates Dijkstra's constraint-3, because it requires strict alternation of processes in the execution of the CS.

Example:

turn = 0 and p1 wants to execute its CS.

It can't do so, even though p0 may not want to execute in its CS at that time.

Algorithm - 2

Algorithm-1 failed to remember the state of each process. It could only remember which process is allowed to enter its CS next. Now, replace turn with the following shared variable:

```
type flagarray: array [0..1] of boolean;
var flag: flagarray;
Initially set all elements of flag to
false.
If flag [i]=true, then process pi is
executing its CS.
{ for p1 }
repeat
while flag [0] do ;
flag [1]:= true ;
CS
flag [1]:= false ;
non-CS
until false;
```

This algorithm does not ensure that only one process at a time will be executing is CS.

Example:

p0 executes while, finds that flag[1] = false

p1 executes while, finds that flag[0] = false

p0 sets flag[0] = true, and enters its CS

p1 sets flag[1] = true, and enters its CS.

Now, p0 and p1 are both in their Critical Sections.

Algorithm - 3

```
{ for p1 }
repeat
flag [1]:= true ;
while flag [0] do ;
CS
flag [1]:= false ;
non-CS
until false;
```

This algorithm ensures mutual exclusion, but violates constraint - 4.

For example,

p0 sets flag[0] to true,

p1 sets flag[1] to true. => Deadlock will occur.

Dekker's Algorithm: This algorithm uses two shared variables. Dekker's algorithm is the first known correct solution to the mutual exclusion problem in concurrent programming. The solution is attributed to Dutch mathematician Th. J. Dekker by Edsger W. Dijkstra in his manuscript on cooperating sequential processes. It allows two threads to share a single-use resource without conflict, using only shared memory for communication.

```
var turn: integer; (is either 0 or 1)
flag: array [0..1] of boolean;
initialize flag [0] = flag [1] = false,
turn is either initialized to 0 or 1.
{ for p1 }
repeat
flag [1]:= true
while flag [0] do
if turn = 0 then
begin
flag [1]:= false
while turn = 0 do ;
flag [1]:= true
end
CS
turn:=0
flag [1]:= false
non-CS
until false
```

It avoids the strict alternation of a naïve turn-taking algorithm, and was one of the first mutual exclusion algorithms to be invented.

Dekker's algorithm satisfies the mutual exclusion condition and it also guarantees that mutual blocking cannot occur. (Dijkstra's constraints 3 and 4 are valid).

Eisenberg and Mc Guire's algorithm

This is a correct solution for the n-process case, developed by Eisenberg and McGuire. Earlier solutions had been proposed by Dijkstra, Knuth, and DeBruijn. This solution improves on the previous ones by reducing the bound on how many turns a process may have to wait to the minimum possible, n-1. The basic concept used is that the turn variable and status flags are used as in Dekker's algorithm for the 2-process case. The flags now have three possible values: WAITING for a process in the entry protocol, waiting for the resource' ACTIVE for a process in the critical section, using the resource; and IDLE for other cases. Process priority is maintained in circular order beginning with the one holding the turn. Each process begins the entry protocol by scanning all processes from the one with the turn up to itself. These are the only processes that might have to go first if there is competition. If the scan finds all processes idle, the process advances tentatively to the ACTIVE state. We check one more time to be sure that there are no active processes.

Bakery Algorithm: (Lamport, 1974)

Each process receives a number depending on its creation time and a number before entering into its critical section. Upon a request, the process with the lowest number is served next i.e allowed to enter its critical section.

This algorithm is actually developed for a distributed environment. So, it does not guarantee that two processes do not receive the same number. In case of a tie, the process with the lowest name is served first. (As process names are unique). While exiting from its critical section, the process sets its number to zero.

Shared data structures

- *Choosing:* an array of Boolean values, initialized to false,
- *Number:* an array of integer values, initialized to zero.

This algorithm ensures mutual exclusion as if Pi is in its critical section, it implies that any other process Pj will have a number j != 0 and [j] will be greater than [i] and thus at this time only Pi can execute its critical section. If Pj tries to enter its critical section, it will be looping in second as its number is greater than the number Pi.

```
var choosing: array [0..n-1] of boolean;
number : array [0..n-1] of integer;
initially: all entries of choosing are false
number = 0
notation : (i) (a,b) < (c,d) if a < c,
or if a = c and b < d
 (ii) max (a0, a1, a2, ... , an-1) is k such that
k >= ai ; for i=0,1,...,n-1
{ for pi of n processes }
Algorithm:
repeat
choosing[i]:=true;
number[i]:=max (number[0],number [1],...number[n-1])+1;
choosing[i]:=false;
for j=0 to n-1 do
begin
while choosing[j] do ;
while number[j] <> 0 and
```

```
 (number[j],j) < (number[i],i) do ;
end;
CS
number[i] := 0 ;
non-CS
until false;
```

It ensures the progress property, as whenever a process exits from its critical section, it makes its number zero and it takes a new number to contest with the other processes trying to enter their critical section. So all processes will get an equal chance to enter its critical section after a finite time. Advantage of this algorithm is that no assumption has been made regarding the relative speed of the processes and the processes are served on first come first served basis and equal opportunity is given to all processes for execution.

Limitations of Software Solutions for Critical Section Problem

1. All these solutions are complicated to program.
2. The processes that are requesting to enter in their critical section are busy waiting, so they consume the processor's time needlessly.
3. If the currently running critical section is long, then it is desirable to block processes that are waiting to enter into their critical section.

Hardware Solution (Synchronization Hardware): Apart from the software support to handle critical section problem, the hardware features can also be exploited to make the programming task easier and can improve the efficiency of the system. The following are some hardware instructions that can be used effectively in solving the critical section problem:

Disable Interrupts: The first solution is that each thread disable all interrupts just before entering its critical section and re-enable them when leaving. The interrupts are disabled while a process is modifying a shared variable. It ensures that no other process will make unexpected modifications to the shared variables. This ensures that the operating system will not get a timer interrupt and have its scheduler preempt the thread while it is in the critical section. Figure 6.3 given below show the structure of this solution.

```
repeat
Disable Interrupts
Critical Section
Enable Interrupts
Remainder Section
forever
```

Figure 6.3: *Hardware Solution through Interrupts*

Advantages

1. This is a simple to implement.
2. It is best suited for a uni processor system.

In short, this is clearly not a good idea for the general welfare of the operating environment. However, because of its extreme simplicity, this was a common approach to mutual exclusion in operating system kernels, at least before multiprocessors spoiled the fun.

Disadvantages

As the multiprogramming is not utilized during the execution of critical section, the performance of the system is degraded.

This solution is not acceptable for a multiprocessor machine, as in order to disable interrupts, all processors are required to communicate with each other, which will be a time consuming process and will hamper the efficiency of the system.

This method gives the thread too much control over the system. Moreover, it is something that can only be done if the thread is executing in kernel mode; user processes are disallowed from disabling interrupts. Consider what happens if the logic in the critical section is incorrect and interrupts are never enabled? The operating system will not get its timer interrupt and will not be able to preempt the thread and let any other process run. The system will have to be rebooted. Even if the thread does re-enable interrupts after the critical section, what happens if the critical section itself has a dependency on some other interrupt, thread, or system call? For example, the logic in the critical section may need to read data from a file on a disk but the operating system will not get the disk interrupt that tells it that data is ready. Finally, if you're on a multiprocessor system, disabling interrupts will only disable them on one processor, so the technique does even work on these systems.

Hardware Instructions

Many processors provide hardware instructions to read, modify and store a word atomically. Most of the processors have specific instructions that aid in programming critical sections. The key to these instructions is that the operations that they perform are atomic, meaning that they are indivisible. A system interrupt cannot come in and preempt the instruction after the first part of its operation is finished, Different processors offer different instructions that help with critical sections. We will look at three variations of these atomic instructions:

1. Test-and-set
2. Compare-and-Swap
3. Fetch-and-Increment

1. **Test and set:** A test-and-set instruction reads the contents of a memory word into a register, writes a value of 1 into that location, and returns the previous contents of the memory. The crucial item here is that this operation is guaranteed

to be atomic: indivisible and non-interruptible. The code given below show a way to define test-and-set instruction. The major benefit of this instruction is that it can be executed atomically, so two Test-and-set instructions can be executed at the same time, each on a different processor.

```
int test_and_set (int *x)
{
  last_value = *x;
  *x = 1;
 return last_value;
}
```

Test-and-set always sets a lock but it lets the user know if it was already set at the time the user executed the instruction. If the lock was already set when the user ran test-and-set then somebody simply got the lock before it he did; you don't have it. If the lock was not set when the user ran the instruction (i.e., the instruction returned a zero), then it is now set and have the lock. The following code show the implementation of mutual exclusion with time-and-set.

```
while (test_and_set (&lock)) ; /* wait for the lock */
/* do critical section */
lock = 0; /* release the lock */
```

2. **Compare and Swap:** The compare-and-swap instruction compares the value of a memory location with an "old" value that is given to it. If the two values match then the "new" value is written into that memory location. The Figure 6.4 given below shows the definition of compare and swaps instruction.

```
int compare_and_swap (int *x, int old, int new)
{
 int save = *x; /* current contents of the
memory */
 if (save == old)
 *x = new;
 return save; /* tell the caller what was read
*/
}
```

Figure 6.4: *Definition of Compare and Swap Instruction*

With compare-and-swap, we're telling it the value we last read from that memory location and what we'd like to set it to provided that somebody did not change the contents since we last read it. If they did, our new value will not be set since our idea of the old value was not correct. The return value tells us what the contents of the memory location were when the compare-and-swap instruction was executed. An example of how we control entry to and exit from a critical section using compare-and-swap is:

```
    while (compare_and_swap (&locked, 0, 1) != 0) ; /* spin until
locked == 0 */
    /* if we got here, locked got set to 1 and we have it */
    /* do critical section */
    locked = 0; /* release the lock */
```

In order to provide the fulfillment of the requirement of mutual exclusion, Pi can enter its critical section only if either waiting[i] == false or key == false. The Figure 6.5 given below show the implementation of mutual exclusion with the swap instruction.

```
do
{
key = true;
While ( key == true)
Swap (lock,key);
Critical Section;
Lock = false;
Remainder section;
}, while;
```

Figure 6.5: *Implementation of Mutual Exclusion with swap Instruction.*

3. **Fetch and increment:** The final atomic instruction is fetch-and-increment. This instruction simply increments a memory location but returns the previous value of that memory location.

```
int fetch_and_increment (int *x)
{
   last_value = *x;
   *x = *x + 1;
   return last_value;
}
```

The return value, last_value corresponds to the number on your ticket while the machine is now ready to generate the next higher number. To implement a critical section, we grab a ticket (myturn) and wait our turn. Our turn arrives when the turn-o-matic machine shows our number and the deli clerk calls it (turn == myturn):

4. **Lockstep Synchronization:** We can keep a shared lock variable and set it to 1 if a process is in a critical section and 0 otherwise. When a process wants to enter its critical section, it first reads the lock. If the lock variable is 0, the process sets the lock to 1 and executes its critical section. If the lock is 1, the process waits until it becomes 0. The following code implements it:

```
while (locked) ; /* loop, waiting for locked == 0 */
locked = 1; /* set the lock */
/* do critical section */
locked = 0; /* release the lock */
```

Advantages

- This solution is extremely simple to understand, implement, and trace.

Disadvantages

- The really big problem with this approach is that a race condition exists for reading and setting the lock. After the while loop sees that locked is zero, the thread could be preempted. Another thread that is waiting for the critical section will also see that locked is zero and will also exit its while loop and enter the critical section. When the first thread is given a chance to continue running, it is already out of the while loop and simply sets locked = 1, unaware that somebody else already entered the critical section and set locked to 1. This attempt at a solution involves keeping a shared variable (turn) that tells which thread will be executed next. Each thread that may want to access the critical section is given a unique number and the turn variable cycles through these numbers. In the simple case of only two threads, we can use the numbers 0 and 1. For instance, thread 0 gets to run its critical section when turn is 0 and thread 1 gets to run its critical section when turn is 1.

SEMAPHORES

Semaphores are synchronization tools introduced by Dijkstra (1965). A semaphore is an integer variable with two associated operations: down (also known as p or wait) and up (known as v or signal). It is a special kind of synchronization data that can be used only through specific synchronization primitives. It ensures lack of race conditions.

Definition: A semaphore is a shared integer variable with non-negative values that can be subjected only to following operations:

- Initialization which is specified as a part of its declaration.
- The indivisible operations wait and signal, these can be defined as:

Sempaphore -> P (), an atomic operation that waits for semaphore to become positive, then decrements it by 1, it is also known as wait operation.

Semaphore -> V (), an atomic operation that increments semaphore by 1, it is termed as signal operation.

The definition of wait is:

```
operation wait (s)
begin
if (s > 0)
then s = s-1;
else block the process on s;
}
```

When a process performs a wait operation on a semaphore, the operation checks whether the value of semaphore is greater than zero. It it so, it decrements the value of semaphore and lets the process continue its execution, else it blocks the process on semaphore.

The definition of signal is:

```
operation signal (s)
{
begin
if some processes are blocked on s
then activate one blocked process;
else S++;
}
```

A signal operation on a semaphore activates a process blocked on the semaphore. The programming language or operating system ensures the indivisibility of the wait and signal operations. It ensures that race conditions cannot arise over a semaphore. Processes use wait and signal operations to synchronize their execution w.r.t to one another. The initial value of a semaphore determines how many processes can get past the wait operation. A process that does not get past a wait operation is blocked on the semaphore.

Characteristics of Semaphores:

1. These have integer values, except they have no negative values.
2. The operations possible are wait and signal.
3. These cannot read or write a value except to set it in beginning.
4. The operations wait and signal are atomic, that means the operations in these instructions can be executed in a single execution cycle.

Uses of Semaphores

The following are the uses of semaphores in the concurrent systems:

1. **Mutual Exclusion:** Mutual exclusion can be implemented using a semaphore that is initialized to 1. A process performs a wait operation on the semaphore before entering the critical section and a signal operation on exiting from it. The Figure 6.6 given below show the implementation of a critical section in processes Pi and Pj, using a semaphore named sema. It is initialized to 1. Each process performs a wait operation on it before entering the critical section and a signal operation after exiting from its critical section. The first process going to perform wait (sema), finds that the value of sema is greater than zero, so it decrements sema by 1 and goes onto enter its critical section. When the second process performs wait (sema), the value of sema is zero, and hence the process is blocked

on sema. It is activated when the first process executes signal (sema) and enters its critical section. If no process is blocked on sema when a signal (sema) operation is performed, the value sema becomes 1. It permits a process that performs a wait in future to enter its critical section directly. The special type of semaphores used to implement the mutual exclusion are binary semaphores. It is often called as mutex. A binary semaphore is initialized to 1 and takes only the values 0 and 1 during execution of the program.

Process Pi	Process Pj

begin
repeat
wait (sema)
{ critical section}
signal (sema)
{remainder section}
forever;
end.
	repeat
	wait (sema)
	{critical section}
	signal (sema)
	{remainder section}
	forever;

Figure 6.6: *Working of Processes Pi and Pj.*

2. **Bounded Concurrency:** It implies that a function may be executed concurrently by n processes, where n lies between 1 and c (a constant), as 1<=n <=c. A semaphore initialized to c can be used to implement bounded concurrency. Every process willing to perform an operation performs a wait (sema) before performing the operation and a signal (sema) after performing it. Upto c processes can concurrently perform an operation. Semaphores used to perform bounded concurrency are called counting semaphores. Figure 6.7 given below show how a set of concurrent processes share three printers.

Process P0	Process Pj

begin
repeat
wait (printers)
{ use a printer}
signal (printers)
{remainder section}
forever;
end.
	repeat
	wait (printers)
	{use a printer}
	signal (printers)
	{remainder section}
	forever;

Figure 6.7: *Working of Concurrent Processes Pi and Pj.*

3. **Signaling:** It is used when a process Pi wishes to perform an action ai only after process Pi has performed an action aj. It is implemented using a semaphore initialized to 0. Pi performs a wait on the semaphore before performing action ai. Pj performs a signal on the semaphore after it performs action aj. This mechanism

ensures that Pi executes ai only after Pj executes aj. The Figure 6.8 given below show that process Pi performs a wait (syn) before executing an action ai and Pj performs a signal (syn) after executing action aj. Semaphore syn is initialized to zero and hence Pi will get blocked on wait (syn) if Pj has not already performed a signal (syn). It would proceed to perform action ai only after process Pj performs a signal. In the code given below var syn:semaphore = 0,

Process Pi	Process Pj

begin
repeat
wait (syn)
{perform action ai}
end.
	....
	{perform action aj}
	signal (syn)
	{remainder section}
	forever;

Figure 6.8: *Working of Concurrent Processes Pi and Pj.*

This is a protected integer variable that can facilitate and restrict access to shared resources in a multi-processing environment.

Types of Semaphores

The two most common kinds of semaphores are:

1. Binary semaphores.
1. Counting Semaphores and

1. **Binary Semaphores:** Binary Semaphores, as the name implies, represents two possible states (generally 0 or 1; locked or unlocked). These are a special form of semaphore used for implementing mutual exclusion. They can be used to solve the critical section problem as described above, and are sometimes known as mutexes, because they provide mutual exclusion. For Example: To control access to a shared device between tasks. A printer is a good example. The user does not want two tasks sending to the printer at once, so a binary semaphore is created to control access to the printers. When a device wishes to print, it attempts to "take" the semaphore. If the semaphore is available, the task gets to print. If the semaphore is not available, the task will have to wait for the printer.

```
do {
waiting (mutex):
//critical section
signal (mutex):
//remainder section
}
while (TRUE):
```

2. **Counting Semaphores:** These semaphores can take on any integer value, and are usually used to count the number remaining of some limited resource. The counter is initialized to the total number of such resources available in the system, and whenever the counting semaphore is greater than zero, then a process can enter a critical section and use one of the resources. When the counter gets to zero (or negative in some implementations), then the process blocks until another process frees up a resource and increments the counting semaphore with a signal call. The binary semaphore can be seen as just a special case where the number of resources initially available is just one. Counting Semaphores are used when you might have multiple devices (like 3 printers or multiple memory buffers).

Problems with Semaphores: *The semaphores suffer from the following problems:*

1. **Deadlocks:** One important problem that can arise while using semaphores to block processes waiting for a limited resource is the problem of deadlocks, which occur when multiple processes are blocked, each waiting for a resource that can only be freed by one of the other (blocked) processes, as illustrated in the following example.

P0	P1
Wait (S);	Wait (Q);
Wait (Q);	Wait (S);
....	....
....	....
....	....
Signal (S);	Signal (Q);
Signal (Q);	Signal (S);

2. **Starvation:** Another problem to consider is that of starvation, in which one or more processes gets blocked forever, and never get a chance to take their turn in the critical section. For example, in the semaphores above, we did not specify the algorithms for adding processes to the waiting queue in the semaphore in the wait ( ) call, or selecting one to be removed from the queue in the signal ( ) call. If the method chosen is a FIFO queue, then every process will eventually get their turn, but if a LIFO queue is implemented instead, then the first process to start waiting could starve.

Memory Management

Chapter 7

MEANING OF MEMORY MANAGEMENT

Memory management is the act of managing computer memory. As the processor can be shared by a number of processes and the concept of CPU scheduling help to improve the CPU utilization and the response time for the user's jobs. Same way a number of programs of a number of users are stored in the memory, i.e they share a common memory space. Due to which the obvious requirement of memory management comes into existence. The von Neumann principle for the design and operation of computers requires that a program has to be primary memory resident to execute. Also, a user requires to revisit his programs often during its evolution. However, due to the fact that primary memory is volatile, relatively expensive, but a user needs to store his program in some non-volatile storage space like secondary memory, which is cheap and is of large capacity. All computers provide a non-volatile secondary memory available as an online storage. The programs which the user wants to execute must be present in the main memory. But as the main memory is too small to accommodate all data and programs permanently, the computer system must provide secondary storage as a back up to the main memory. Programs and files may be disk resident and downloaded whenever their execution is required. Therefore, some form of memory management is needed at both primary and secondary memory levels.

The essential requirement of memory management is to provide ways to dynamically allocate portions of memory to programs at their request, and freeing it for reuse when no longer needed. The main jobs covered under the memory management module are:

1. To check the memory requirement of a particular program.
2. To keep track of the free space available.
3. To keep track of the memory utilization by various processes i.e to record that which memory unit is allocated to which program.
4. To decide which process should be loaded into memory when the memory space is free and to de-allocate the space when program does not need it any more.
5. To protect the processes from each other so that they should not interfere with each other's operations.

Main memory requires careful management. Several methods have been devised that increase the effectiveness of memory management. Virtual memory systems separate the memory addresses used by a process from actual physical addresses, allowing separation of processes and increasing the effectively available amount of RAM using paging or swapping to secondary storage. The quality of the virtual memory manager can have an extensive effect on overall system performance. Following is the detail of requirement of memory for different operating systems.

Operating system	Minimum memory requirment	Recommeded memory
Windows 1	256 KB	-
Windows 2.03	320 KB	-
Windows 3.0	896 KB	1
Windows 3.1	2.6 MB	4
Windows 95	8 MB	16
Windows NT 4.0	32 MB	96
Windows 98	24 MB	64
Windows ME	32 MB	128
Windows 2000 Prof.	64 MB	128
Windows XP HOME	64 MB	128
Windows XP Prof.	128 MB	256

Figure 7.1: *Details of requirement of different operating systems*

Secondary memory may store program scripts, executable process images and data files. It may store applications, as well as, system programs. In fact, a good part of all OS, the system programs which provide services (the utilities for instance) are stored in the secondary memory. These are requisitioned as needed. Primary memory is a precious resource that frequently cannot contain all active processes in the system The memory management system decides which processes should reside (at least partially) in main memory. It monitors the amount of available primary memory and may periodically write processes to a secondary device called the swap device to provide more space in primary memory. At a later time, the kernel reads the data from swap device back to main memory. For swapping the data and return back process's data, kernel maintains kernel process table and kernel region table. File description table synchronize with kernel process table and kernel region table as shows in figure 7.2

The main motivation for management of main memory comes from the support for multiprogramming. Several executables processes reside in main memory at any given time. In other words, there are several programs using the main memory as their address space. Also, programs move into, and out of, the main memory as they terminate, or get suspended for some IO, or new executables are required to be loaded in main memory. So, the OS has to have some strategy for main memory management.

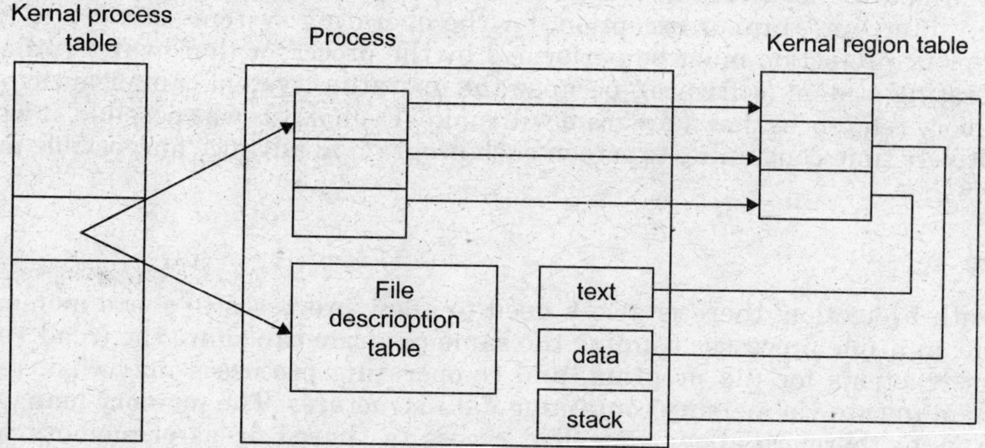

Figure 7.2: *Working of Kernel with Process.*

MEMORY MANAGEMENT POLICIES

The memory management is intended to satisfy the following five requirements:

- Relocation
- Protection
- Sharing
- Logical Organization
- Physical Organization
- Relocation

In a multi-programming system, the execution of a single process is often unrelated to others. When a process is first created, it is difficult (if not impossible) to know where its image will be Placed when initially loaded into memory. Similarly, when a process is swapped-out (Suspended), it is unlikely that the process will be swapped-in back to exactly the same memory location. Memory management determines where both instructions and data are located, i.e. how a process's memory references (requests) translate into actual physical memory addresses.

Protection

Each process must be protected from either accidental or deliberate interference from other processes. Thus, program in processes should not be able to reference memory locations in a process, for reading or writing purposes, without permission. Although compilers for high-level programming languages offer some support (e.g. constrained control, static array bound references), but most of the data references are dynamic. Memory references made by a process must be checked at run-time to ensure that they lie within the bounds of memory allocated by the operating system. Checks are performed by hardware at run-time, and invalid references generate an access violation interrupt, trap, or exception, for the operating system software to handle. The memory protection must be performed by the processor (hardware) rather than the operating system (software), because the operating system cannot anticipate all the memory references that a program will make. Even if this was possible, it would be prohibitively time-consuming to screen each program in advance for possible memory violations.

Sharing

Even with protection, there is also a need to allow processes to share memory. For example, multiple processes running the same program can share the (read +execute only) instructions for the program, and co-operating processes may wish to share and communicate via memory containing data structures. The memory management system must therefore allow controlled access to shared areas of memory without compromising essential protection.

Logical Organization

Although processes in memory often occupy linear sequences of addresses, programs are organized into modules, some of which are unmodifiable and some of which contain data that may be modified. If the operating system and computer hardware can effectively deal with user program and data in the form of modules, a number of advantages can be realized.

- Modules can be written and compiled independently with all references from one module to another resolved by the system at run time (termed late binding).
- Different degrees of protection can be given to different modules.
- It is possible to introduce mechanisms by which modules can be shared among processes.

Physical Organization of Memory

Computer memory is divided into at least 2 parts: Main memory and Secondary memory. Main memory provides fast access at relatively high cost and it is volatile. Secondary memory is slcwer and cheaper than main memory and is non- volatile. Thus secondary memory of large capacity can be provided to allow for long term storage of programs and data while a smaller memory holds program and data currently in use. The relationship between primary memory (RAM) and secondary memory (disk) is straightforward, Old techniques termed overlays permitted reuse of a process's memory, but they were unnecessarily complex. Moreover, in a multi-programmed system, the programmer cannot predict the size or location of a process's memory. The task of moving information between main and secondary memory is clearly the responsibility of the operating system.

Memory is made up of a large array of words each with its own address. The processor fetches the instructions from memory according to the value of program counter. Each instruction is then saved in the RAM when it is executed, so each instruction has its location/address in the memory. Each instruction is executed by following step by step procedure, known as the instruction cycle. It has following steps:

- To fetch the instruction from memory.
- To decode the instruction.
- To get operands from the memory
- To execute the instruction.

After the execution of the instruction, the output is stored in the memory.As discussed earlier, the programs are moved from the secondary storage to the primary storage for the execution. This movement is handled by the memory management scheme used. The collection of processes waiting in the secondary memory for the execution form an input queue. A process from the queue is selected and it goes through the instruction cycle mentioned above and when the process terminates, the memory space allocated to it is declared available. The another major issue is to assign the addresses for the various programs and their results. The addresses used by the user are termed as symbolic addresses or logical addresses. Address binding is done to map these logical addresses into actual physical addresses in memory. The binding of instructions and data to memory addresses can be done at the various stages of program execution differently as follows:

Compile Time: binding at compile time will generate absolute addresses. It requires that it must be known that where the process will reside in memory. That is if it is known that the user program will reside at location M, then the generated complier code will be start at M and will extend up from there. The problem with this scheme is that if the starting location of the process in the memory changes, then the entire process must be recompiled to generate the absolute address again.

Load Time: If it is not known at compile time that where the process will be stored in the memory, then the compiler will generate a relocatable code, which will be converted into absolute addresses at the load time. If there is a change in the starting address the user need to reload the user code to the new address, this method of putting the code to the new location is termed as relocation.

Execution Time: If the processes can be moved during its execution from one memory segment to another, then the binding can be delayed until the execution time. For making this method possible good hardware support is required. This method can increase the total run time of a process due to the movement of process during execution time. The concept of dynamic relocation is used to make it possible.

The linker binds a program to a memory location starting on the load origin of the program, so the program can be executed correctly only if it occupies a memory area whose starting address is equal to its load address. But to make it execute correctly from some other memory location it needs to be relocated by changing all memory addresses used in it. For this purpose, a special register known as relocation register is used, where every address used in the program is relocated as follows:

Effective Address = Address used by the program + Contents of Relocation Register

The memory management unit is responsible for mapping the logical addresses to the physical addresses. This concept is known as relocation.

Dynamic Loading: It is a technique used to make efficient utilization of memory space, in which a routine is not loaded until it is called. As the entire program and data of a process can not reside in the physical memory, due to its limited size, the concept of dynamic loading is used, in which all routines are kept on disk in relocatable format. The main program is loaded into memory and is executed. When a routine needs some another routine, it checks if the required routine has already been loaded or not, if it has not been loaded yet, then relocatable linking loader is called to load the desired routine and the corresponding data structures are updated accordingly. The biggest advantage of this scheme is that a routine is loaded only if it is required.

OVERLAYS

If a process is restricted to a partition that is too small, the overlay software technique can help it, although the operating system would not provide much assistance. The idea of overlays is to keep in memory only those instructions and data that are needed at given time. When other instructions are needed, they are loaded into space occupied previously by instructions that are not required any more. Figure 7.3 shows process A trying to cram into a small partition that starts at 20K and runs for 8K. The first 8K of A are placed at locations 20K to 28K; the last 5K are placed at 23K to 28K, overlapping some of the first part. This cramming is a private affair of process A, which has created a new level of address translation by using the same region of virtual store for different purposes at different times." A's virtual store has length of only 8K, but its pseudo-store has length 13K. The process divides its pseudo-store into regions called overlays. Each overlay can fit into virtual space by itself. In fact, several overlays may be able to fit at the same time into virtual space. The process assigns each overlay a fixed place in virtual store. This region may overlap with the region given to some other overlay. At any given time during execution, some overlays are present and others are in backing store. The ones that are present do not overlap.

Whenever an access is made to an area in pseudo-store, either the overlay it needs is currently in virtual store, in which case the access is performed easily, or it is not. In the latter case, the process undertakes the necessary steps to remove the overlays that occupy the place where the desired one needs to reside and then to bring the required overlay into that position. The hardware does not support overlays. Checking every reference would be unacceptably slow in software. Therefore, only procedure calls are allowed to require new overlays. Procedure invocation and return are therefore more expensive than they would be otherwise, because not only the status of the destination overlay be examined, but it may also have to be brought into virtual store. One could place every procedure in its own overlay. Instead, the programmer might specify the overlay structure in order to keep the number of cross-overlay calls to a minimum and to make sure that overlays that do call each other can be placed simultaneously in virtual store. Compilers can be of great assistance, too.

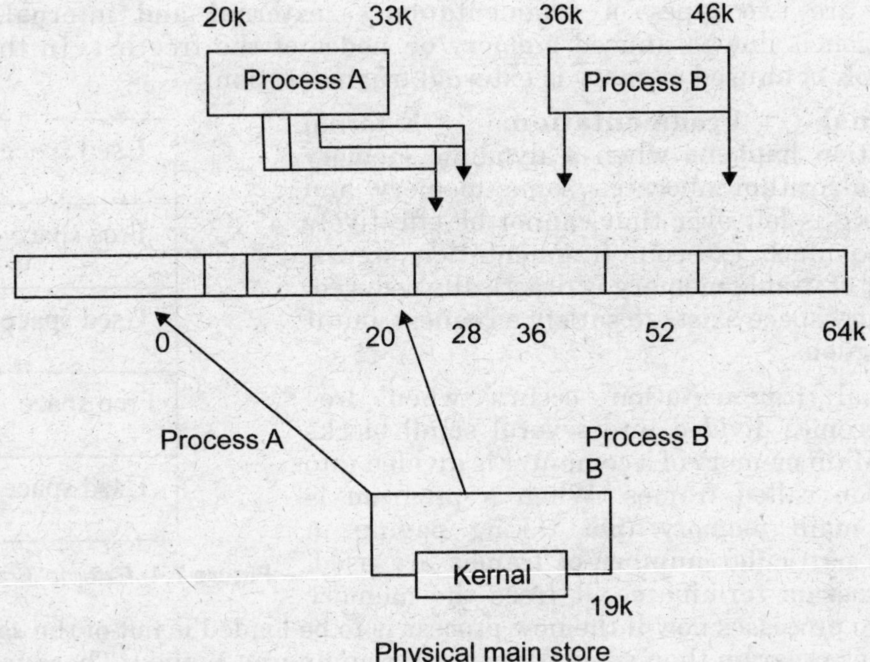

Figure 7.3: *Overlays*

Algol like languages are especially suited to overlays because the hierarchical nature of name scopes means that during execution of any one procedure, only variables local to that procedure or to enclosing procedures can be accessed. Therefore, each procedure can be given an overlay that starts in virtual store right after all the overlays for its enclosing procedures. They will all be in store at the same time, but other procedures at the same level will be absent. Unfortunately, overlays will often be swapped out when room is still available in virtual store, because some other overlay that must reside at the same location has been accessed. Overlays work well only in applications where the execution of the program goes through well defined phases, each of which requires different program units. Thrashing can result from the inappropriate use of overlays.

FRAGMENTATION AND ITS TYPES

Fragmentation is a concept that pops up in a lot of places in systems programming. Fragmentation occurs when a user program has allocated memory, but doesn't use it. Fragmentation is often reported in terms of the percentage of allocated memory that is wasted. For example, suppose a program has a code segment of 4K, a global segment of 1K, a heap of 8K and a stack of 1K. Moreover, suppose that malloc () has 6K on its free list. Then the fragmentation of the program is 6/ (4 + 1 + 8 + 1) = 43%. This isn't too bad since the total memory usage of the program is 14K. Were that 14M, or were there 1000 such programs running on the machine at the same time, the fragmentation would be very wasteful.

There are two types of fragmentation -- external and internal. External fragmentation is due to unused memory on nodes of the free list. In the example above, the 6K of unused memory is external fragmentation.

External Fragmentation: External Fragmentation happens when a dynamic memory allocation algorithm allocates some memory and a small piece is left over that cannot be effectively used. If too much external fragmentation occurs, the amount of usable memory is drastically reduced. Total memory space exists to satisfy a request, but it is not contiguous.

Used space
Free space
Used space
Free space
Used space

Figure 7.4: *External Fragmentation*

External fragmentation occurs when free memory becomes divided into several small blocks over time. Main memory of a computer is divided into small section called frames. When a program is loaded in main memory (not taking paging in account), a particular number of frames are used. When a program terminates, it frees the memory between two processes now if the new process is to be loaded is not of the same length as the earlier program then some frames will remain unassigned. These frames keep on increasing when more no of processes enter or exit from the main memory.

Internal Fragmentation: Internal fragmentation is the space wasted inside of allocated memory blocks because of restriction on the allowed sizes of allocated blocks. Allocated memory may be slightly larger than requested memory; this size difference is memory internal to a partition, but not being used.

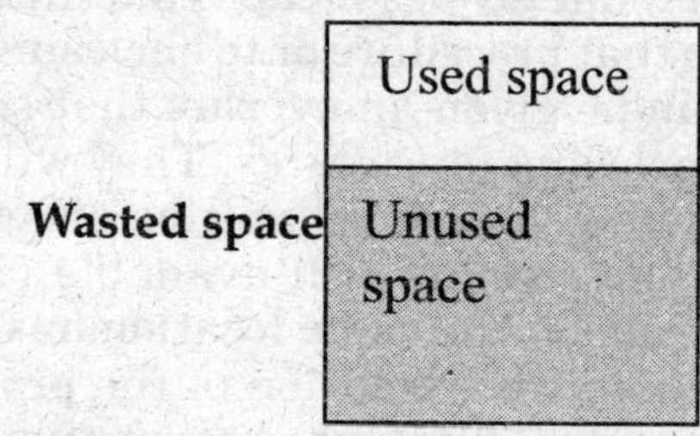

Figure 7.5: *Internal Fragmentation*

Internal fragmentation occurs when more storage is allocated than is actually requested. This left over space, known as slack space, causes a degradation of system performance. For example, space can be left over between the last byte of the file and the first byte of the next sector. This slack space can add up and eventually cause system performance to degrade.

PARTITIONED MEMORY MANAGEMENT SCHEME

The core task of memory management is to bring programs into main memory for execution by the processor. In all multiprogramming systems, this task involves a scheme called Virtual Memory. Virtual memory is based on the use of one or both of the techniques: Segmentation and Paging. Virtual memory decisions based on fixed partitioning and unequal size partitioning. In figure 7.4, example of partitioning of memory as fixed size and not fixed size is shown.

Fixed Partitioning

In modern operating systems offering memory management, the operating system itself occupies a fixed portion of main memory, and the remainder is available for multiple user/application processes. The simplest technique is to consider main memory being in fixed-sized partitions, with two clear choices: equal sized partitions, or unequal sized partitions.

Operating system	Operating system with 512k
512k	128k
512k	256k
512k	320k
512k	512k
512k	576k
512k	768k
512k	1M
512k	
(a) Equal-size partitions	(b) Un Equal-size partitions

Figure 7.6: *Shows equal size and unequal size partitions*

Any new process whose size is less than or equal to a partition's size may be loaded into that partition. Equal sized partitions introduce two problems:

1. A process's requirements may exceed the partition size, and
2. A small process still occupies a full partition. Such wastage of memory is termed as internal memory fragmentation. The initial choice of partition, the placement algorithm, is of course trivial with Equal-sized partitions.

Unequal sized partitions

With unequal – size partitions, there are two possible ways to assign processes to partitions. The simplest way is to assign each process to the smallest partition within which it will fit. In this case a scheduling queue is needed for each partition, to hold swapped – out processes destined for that partition. The advantage of this approach is that processes are always assigned in such a way as to minimize wasted memory within a partition. This technique seems optimum for individual and not whole. When it is time consuming to load a process into main memory, the smallest available partition that will hold the process is selected. If all partitions are occupied, than a swapping decision must be made. Preference may be given to the swapping out of the smallest partition that will hold the incoming process. The use of Unequal – size partitions provides a degree of flexibility to fixed partitioning. But it also has certain disadvantages:

1. The number of partitions specified at the time of system generation limits the number of active processes in the system.
2. Because partition sizes are present at the time of system generation, small jobs do not use partition space efficiently.

Dynamic Partitioning

Dynamic partitioning overcomes some shortcomings of fixed partitioning: partitions are of variable length and number. When a process commences, it occupies a partition of exactly the required size, and no more.

Initially, main memory is empty except for the operating system. (Figure 7.7,a). The first three processes are loaded in, starting where the operating system ends, and occupy just enough space for each process (Figure 7.7, b, c, and d)). This leaves a "hole" at the end of a memory that is too small for a fourth process. At some point, none of the processes in memory is ready. The operating system therefore swaps out process 2 (Figure 7.7, e), which leaves sufficient room to load a new process, process4 (Figure 7.7, f). Because process4 is smaller than process2, another small hole is created. Because there is insufficient room in memory for process2, the operating system swaps process1 out (Figure 7.7,g) and swaps process2 back in (Figure 7.7, h). This method starts out well, but eventually it leads to a situation in which there are a lot of small holes in memory.

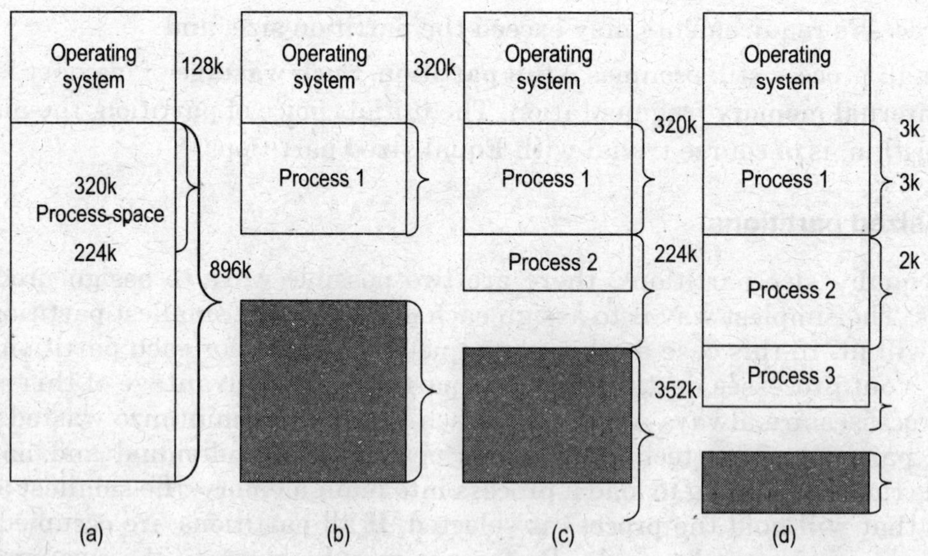

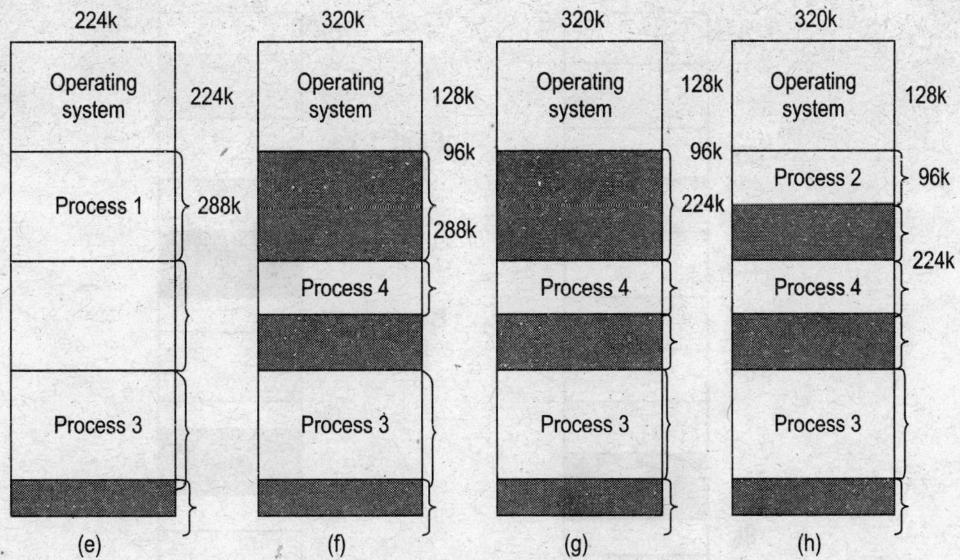

Figure 7.7: *Shows dynamic programming*

As time goes on, memory becomes more and more fragmented, and memory use declines. External Fragmentation- referring to the fact that the memory that is external to all partitions becomes increasingly fragmented. Technique used to overcome external fragmentation is Compaction. The operating system shifts the processes so that they are contiguous and so that all the free memory is together in one block. Difficultly with this technique is that it is a time consuming procedure, and leads to the wastage of processor time. wasteful of processor time.

Placement Algorithm

One obvious question suggested by dynamic partitioning is —Where do we place a new process? Three simple algorithms exist:

- Best fit
- First fit
- Next fit

(a) *First-fit:* find the first unused block of memory that can contain the process, searching from Address 0.

(b) *Best-fit:* chooses the block that is closest in size to the request.

(c) *First-fit:* find the first unused block of memory that can contain the process, searching from Address 0.

(d) *Best-fit:* chooses the block that is closest in size to the request.

(e) *Next-fit:* Begins to scan memory from the location of the last placement and chooses the next available block that is large enough.

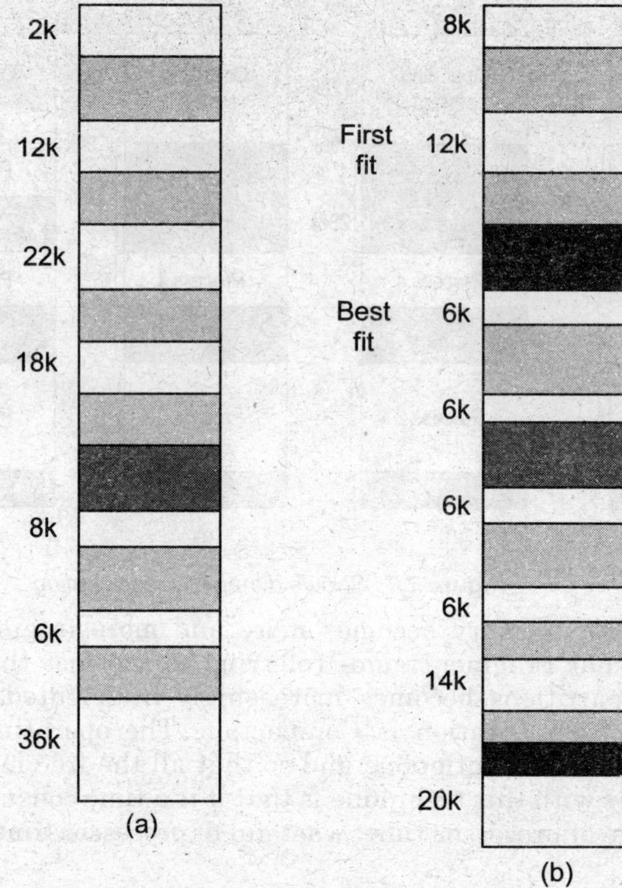

Figure 7.8: *Example memory Configuration before and after Allocation of 16 KB Block*

Figure 7.8 (a) shows the example of placement and swapping-out operations. The last block that was used was a 22KB block from which a 14KB partition was created. Figure 7.8 (b) shows the difference between the best, first, and next-fit placement algorithms in satisfying a 16KB allocation request. Best – fit will search the entire list of available blocks and make use of the 18KB block, leaving a 2KB fragment. First –fit results in a 6KB fragment, and next – fit results in a 20KB fragment.

VIRTUAL STORAGE SPACE AND MAIN MEMORY PARTITIONS

Programming models assume the presence of main memory only. Therefore, ideally we would like to have an unlimited (infinite) main memory available. In fact, an unlimited main memory shall give us a Turing machine capability. However, in practice it is infeasible. So the next best thing is attempted. CPU designers support and generate a very large logical addressable space to support programming concerns. However, the directly addressable main memory is limited and is quite small in comparison to the logical addressable space. The actual size of main memory is referred as the physical memory.

The logical addressable space is referred to as virtual memory. The notion of virtual memory is a bit of an illusion. The OS supports and makes this illusion possible. It does so by copying chunks of disk memory into the main memory as shown in Figure 7.9. In other words, the processor is fooled into believing that it is accessing a large addressable space. Hence, the name virtual storage space is used. The disk area may map to the virtual space requirements and even beyond. Besides the obvious benefit that virtual memory offers a very large address space, there is one other major benefit derived from the use of virtual storage. We now can have many more main memory resident active processes. During much of the lifetime of its execution, a process operates on a small set of instructions within a certain neighborhood. The same applies for the data as well. In other words a process makes use of a very small memory area for doing most of the instructions and making references to the data. So, technically, at any time we need a very small part of a process to really be memory resident. For a moment, let us suppose that this small part is only 1/10th of the process's overall requirements. Note in that case, for the same size of physical main memory, we can service 10 times as many memory resident programs.

The next question then is how do we organize and allocate these small chunks of often required areas to be in memory. In fact, this is where paging and segmentation become important.

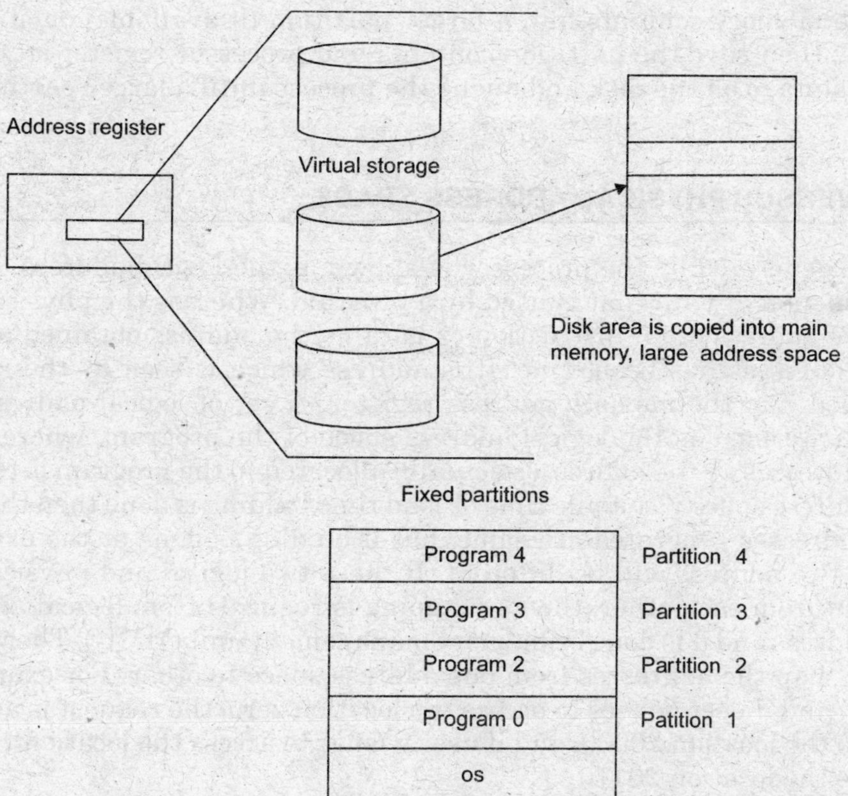

Figure 7.9: *Shows transfer of physical memory as virtual memory*

Getting back to the issue of loading multiple processes into memory at the same time, we can divide memory into multiple fixed partitions (segments). The partitions could be of varying sizes and they would be defined by the system administrator when the system starts up. This was the approach used in IBM System/360's OS/MFT. A new program gets placed on a queue for the smallest partition that can hold it. Any unused space within a partition remains unused. This is internal fragmentation.

In figure 7.7, If any partitions have no programs to run then the memory in that partition is always wasted. This is called external fragmentation. External fragmentation refers to areas of storage that are not allocated and are therefore unused. A modification of the multiple queue approach is to use a single queue. All incoming jobs go on this queue. When a partition is free, the memory manager searches the entire queue for the biggest job for that available partition. This gives small jobs poor service, a problem that can be partially remedied by defining more small partitions when the partitions are configured. Overall, a system using multiple fixed partitions is simple to implement but does not make good use of memory. It also messes up the scheduler's decision of what processes should run since partitions dictate which processes could be loaded into the system in the first place. Finally, this method of allocation requires knowing just how big the process will get. If there isn't enough room in the partition, then the operating system will have to move the memory contents into a larger partition (if available) or, if no partition is available, then save the partition contents and processor register state onto some temporary storage on the disk and queue the process until a larger partition becomes available.

LOGICAL VERSUS PHYSICAL ADDRESS SPACE:

An address generated by the processor is known as the logical address, it is address of the instruction or data that is used by a program. Whereas the physical address is the effective address of an instruction or data i.e the address obtained after binding of logical addresses has been done. It is address which is seen by the memory unit and is loaded into the memory address register. A set of logical addresses used by a program is termed as the logical address space of the program, whereas the set of physical addresses i.e the addresses actually allocated to the program is termed as the physical address space.if compile time or load time binding is done then the logical and physical addresses generated are same, but if binding is done at the execution time then these two address will be different. If these two logical and physical addresses are different from each other, then a mapping is required from logical address to the physical address and it is done by memory management unit (MMU). There are various methods to map the addresses from one address space to other. For example, if base is at 20000, and if user wishes to access the location zero, the request is automatically relocated to the location 20000, and if user wishes to access the location 110, it will be relocated to the location 20110.

SWAPPING

Multiprogrammed CPUs timeshare between processes, allowing each to run for a set period of time before being descheduled. What if there is not enough memory to hold all the processes that want to run? The first solution that comes to mind is to move processes that have been blocked or descheduled to disk to make room for other ones that want to run. When it is their turn to run again, they can be brought back into memory. The method of dynamically moving processes between memory and disk is called swapping.

Partitions in swapping do not have to be fixed, as was the case with the previous method. One problem that arises as a result of swapping with variable-sized partitions is the creation of holes in memory. Holes are areas of unused memory between partitions. They are usually too small to hold a process and too scattered out to be of any use whatsoever.

The solution is to combine all the holes together, allowing a process to move into that space on the next cycle. This technique is called memory compaction. Since memory compaction has a large overhead (takes a considerable amount of time to complete), various other algorithms are used by the memory manager to allocate processes to holes.

These are described below:

- **First fit:** Looks for the first hole that is big enough for the process and uses it. It breaks it into two depending on the process's size.
- **Next fit:** Same as first fit, except that the next time a process wants to find a hole, it starts from right after the last hole that was filled as opposed to the beginning.
- **Best fit:** Looks for the hole that has the closest size to that of the process, instead of breaking up a big hole that may be used by a big process at a later stage.
- **Worst fit:** Looks for the largest available hole to break up for a process. This algorithm reasons that a larger hole that is broken up will have part of it left behind to be useful to another process as opposed to best fit, which looks for a hole that is just the right size for a process, but will leave behind a very small and possibly unusable hole.
- **Quick fit:** A separate list is maintained of different sized holes. When a process requests access to memory, the list is searched and the process is assigned to one that is closest to its size.

All of the above algorithms suffer from large overheads. Implementing them is expensive (in terms of CPU time). Merging segments (recall, a segment is a block of addresses containing a process) in memory has to be done every time a process exits, otherwise memory becomes fragmented into lots of holes.

KINDS OF MEMORY ALLOCATION

Contiguous Allocation

A file contains a file header, which associates the file with its disk sectors. Also, a file system needs a disk allocation bitmap to represent free space on disk, one bit per block. Blocks are numbered in cylinder-major order, so that adjacent numbered blocks can be accessed without seeks or rotational delay.

Block number (s)	Sector number (s)	Track number (s)	Cylinder number (s)
0	0-7	0	0
1	8-15	0	0
..			
31	247-255	0	0
32	0-7	1	0
..			
511	247-255	15	0
512	0-7	0	1

Figure 7.10: *Contiguous Allocation*

For contiguous allocation, file blocks are stored contiguously on disk. A user specifies the file size in advance, and the file system will search the disk allocation bitmap according to various allocation policies (e.g., first-fit and best-fit policies) to locate the space for the file as described in figure 7.10. The file header contains the first block of the file on disk, and the number of blocks in the file. Contiguous allocation provides fast sequential access. A random disk location in a file can be trivially computed by adding an offset to the first disk block location of the file. The disadvantages are external fragmentation and difficulties to grow files.

Linked Allocation

For linked-list allocation, each file block on disk is associated with a pointer to the next block. Perhaps, the most popular example is the MS-DOS file system, which uses the file attribute table (FAT) to implement linked-list files. A file header points to the table entry of the first file block, and the content of the file block contains the table entry number of the next block as shown in figure 7.11. A special marker is used to indicate the end of the file.

One advantage of the linked-list approach is that files can grow dynamically with incremental allocation of blocks. However, sequential accesses may suffer since blocks may not be contiguous. Random accesses are horrible and involve multiple sequential searches. Finally, linked-list allocation is unreliable, since a missing pointer can lead to loss of the remaining file.

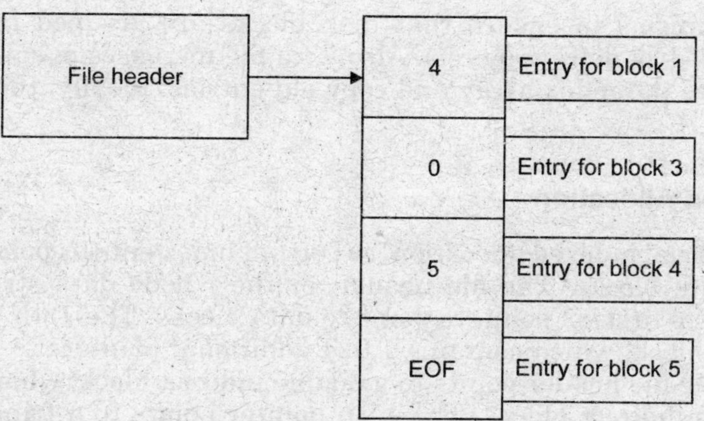

Figure 7.11: *Shows linked list allocation*

Segment-Based Allocation

Segment-based allocation uses a segment table to allocate multiple regions of contiguous blocks. The file header points to a table of begin-block and end-block pairs.

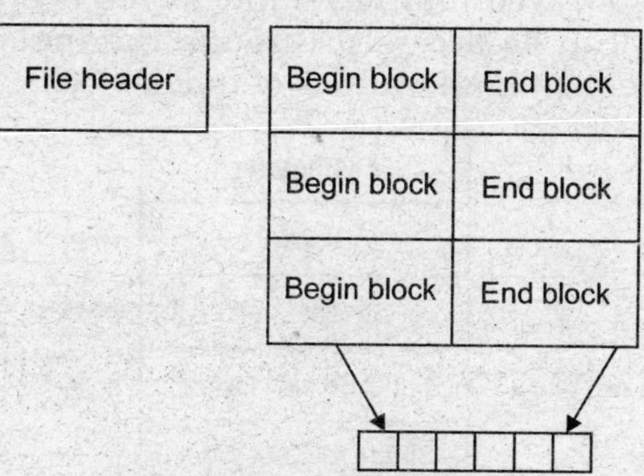

Figure 7.12: *Segment Allocation*

As shown in figure 7.12, Segment-based allocation provides the flexibility to break the allocation into a number of contiguous disk regions, while it still permits contiguous allocation to reduce disk seek time. However, as the disk becomes increasingly fragmented, in the extreme case, segment-based allocation needs a bigger and bigger table to locate piece-wise contiguous blocks. As an extreme case, segment-based allocation can potentially need one table entry per disk block. In addition, under this scheme, random accesses are not as fast as the contiguous allocation, since the file system needs to locate the pair of begin block and end block that contains the target byte before making the disk accesses.

Indexed Allocation

Indexed allocation uses an index to directly track the file block locations as shown in figure 7.13. A user declares the maximum file size, and the file system allocates a file header with an array of pointers big enough to point to all file blocks.

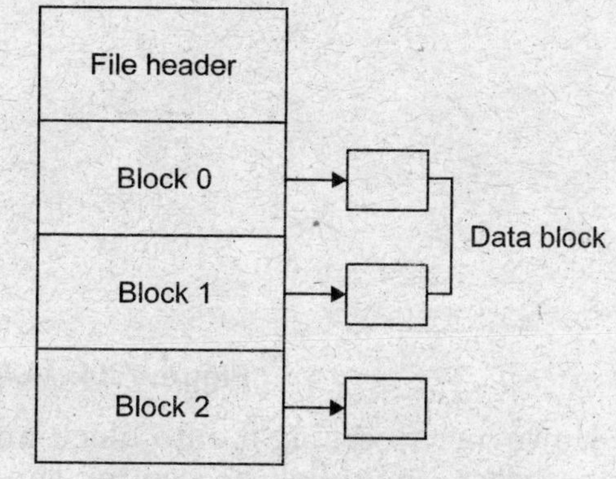

Figure 7.13: *Indexed Allocation*

Although indexed allocation provides fast disk location lookups for random accesses,file blocks may be scattered all over the disk. A file system needs to provide additional mechanisms to ensure that disk blocks are grouped together for good performance (e.g., disk defragmenter). Also, as a file increases in size, the file system needs to reallocate the index array and copy old entries. Ideally, the index can grow incrementally.

Multilevel Indexed Allocation

Linux uses multilevel indexed allocation, so certain index entries point to index blocks as opposed to data blocks. The file header, or the i_node data structure, holds 15 index pointers. The first 12 pointers point to data blocks. The 13th pointer points to a single indirect block, which contains 1,024 additional pointers to data blocks. The 14th pointer in the file header points to a double indirect block, which contains 1,024 pointers to single indirect blocks. The 15th pointer points to a triple indirect block, which contains 1,024 pointers to double indirect blocks as described in figure 7.14. This skewed multilevel index tree is optimized for both small and large files. Small files can be accessed through the first 12 pointers, while large files can grow with incremental allocations of index blocks.

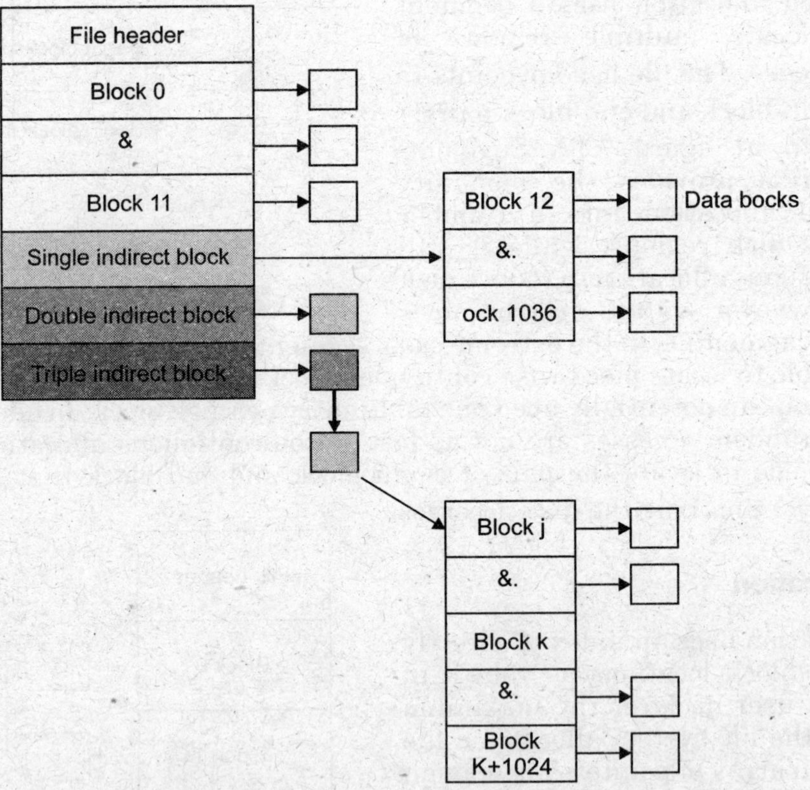

Figure 7.14: *Multilevel Indexed Allocation*

However, accessing a data block under the triple indirect block involves multiple disk accesses—one disk access for the triple indirect block, another for the double indirect block, and yet another for the single indirect block before accessing the actual data block. Also, the number of pointers provided by this data structure cap the largest file size. Finally, the boundaries between the last four pointers are somewhat arbitrary. With a given block number, it is not immediately obvious as to of which of the 15 pointers to follow.

Inverted Allocation

If we use a disk as a device for backups (e.g., tape), the storage capacity may be the primary concern, and the speed of disk may not matter (as long as it is faster than tape). Since backup storage keeps track of all modifications, a small modification to a large file results in storing the entire modified file,. Inverted allocation allocates a disk block by hashing the file block content to a disk block location as shown in figure 7.15. By doing so, different file blocks of the same content (e.g., empty blocks) can share the same disk block for storage. For example, if one block is modified in a N-block file, the storage requirement for both files is N + 1 blocks.

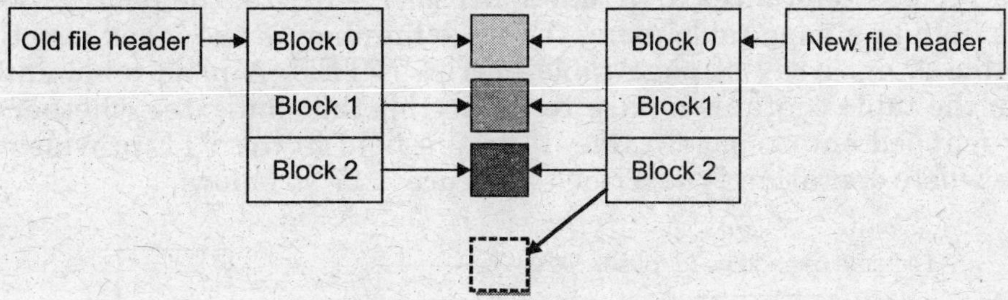

Figure 7.15: *Inverted Allocation*

PAGING

Paging is a memory management technique that does not let the amount of physical memory limit the size of our process. The process feels like it owns the entire address space of the processor. It allows memory allocation to be non-contiguous and has no external fragmentation problems, simplifying memory management and obviating any need for compaction. Help to keep more processes in memory than the sum of their memory needs so that we can keep the CPU utilization as high as possible. Help to keep just the parts of a process that we are using in memory and the rest on the disk.

If the blocks that we divide memory into pages of equal size, then we have a paging system. If the blocks are of different sizes, then we have a segmentation system. In this section, we will examine how paging works. Implementing this requires a more sophisticated memory management unit architecture in the processor. With paging, we divide physical memory into equal-sized blocks. These are called page frames. A logical address space is also divided into blocks of the same size, called pages as shown in figure 7.16. Every memory access is translated from a page to a page frame by the memory management unit. A page may be placed in any available page frame. The memory management unit maps a page to the page frame in which that page resides.

The size of each page is constant and is a power of two. Therefore, a fixed number of high bits in the memory reference (virtual address) identifies the page number and a fixed number of lower bits in the address identifies the displacement, or offset.

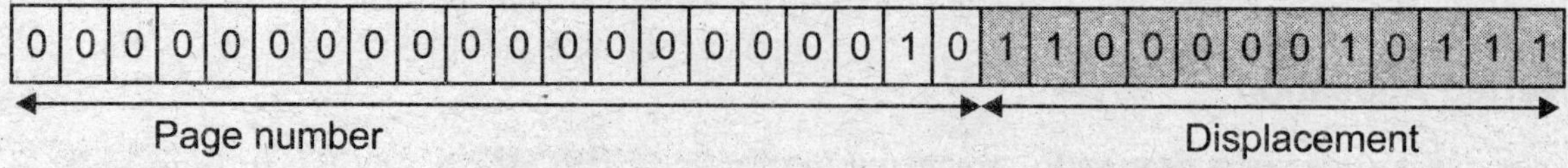

Figure 7.16: *Virtual address decomposition*

For instance, if the page size is 4K bytes, the offset in the page will be 12 bits (log24096 = 12). This means that if we have a 32-bit virtual address, the page field will be 20 bits (32-12), corresponding to 1M pages. An address of 0x00002c37 will correspond to page 2, offset 0xc37. If this isn't obvious, convert the address to binary. Grab the top 20 bits as the page number and the bottom 10 as the offset.

When a process references a virtual address (v = (p, d)), the paging system (the MMU) looks up p in a page table using the page number as the index into this table. The page table is an array of page table entries (PTEs). A page table entry (PTE) for page p in the table contains a page residence bit that indicates whether the page is currently mapped onto a page frame. If it is, a field in the PTE provides the page frame f. The whole operation is described in figure 7.17 as below:

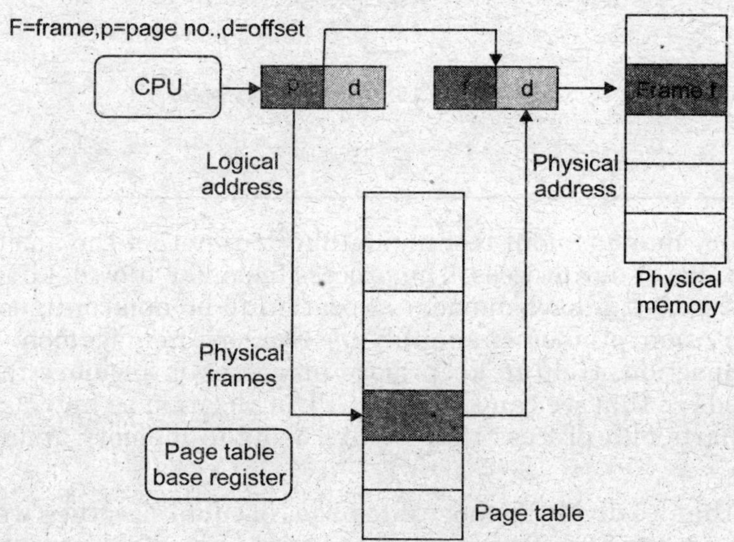

Figure 7.17: *Page Setup Table*

Direct Mapping

The page-table based system just described is a direct mapped paging system as shown in figure 7.18. With a paging system that uses direct mapping, the page table contains an entry for every page (page table entry, or PTE) in the process' virtual address space. The most significant bits of the virtual address are used as an index into the page table. Before starting a process, the operating system loads the starting address for the page table for that process into a page table base register. Ideally, the page table should be in high speed memory so that the page translation can be done within an instruction cycle. Unfortunately, the page table can be somewhat large (e.g., a 4 GB address space and 4 KB pages yields a page table of 1M entries) — and you need a page table per process. Hence, it is not feasible to use memory that's on the MMU (integrated into the CPU chip). If we use main memory, however, we end up spending an extra memory access cycle accessing the page table. The effective speed of every machine instruction that makes a single memory reference is now twice as slow!. An instruction that makes two memory references now has to make four. We need something better.

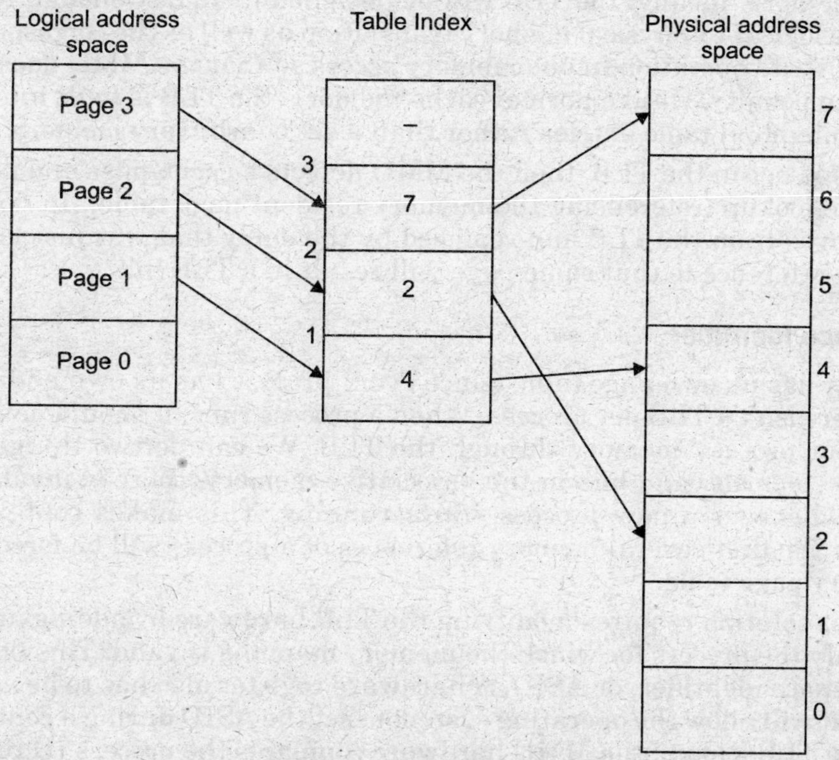

Figure 7.18: *Page mapping*

Associative Mapping

Associative memory, also known as content addressable memory, is very high speed, expensive memory that, unlike regular memory, is queried by the contents of a key field versus an address-based lookup.

Within the memory management hardware, associative memory is used to construct the translation look aside buffer, or TLB (Translation look aside buffer). Each entry in the TLB contains the information that would be found in a page table as well as the page number (which is used as the query key). Every entry in the TLB is compared with the key (the page number that were looking up) simultaneously. This approach is known as associative mapping. Associative memory is fast but also expensive (more transistors and more chip real estate). For it to work well, it has to be co-located in the processor's memory management unit. Given how big page tables can get and that we need a page table per process, the TLB will not be used to store entire page tables but rather act as a cache for frequently-accessed page table entries instead. This is a combined associative and direct mapped approach to page translation and is used by practically every processor being made today. The hope with the TLB is that a large percentage of the pages we seek will be found in the TLB. The percent of references that can be satisfied with a TLB lookup is called the hit ratio. A hit ratio close to 100% means that almost every memory reference is translated by associative memory. Ideally, the TLB will be designed to be fast enough to allow the CPU to do the logical-to-physical memory translation as well as the corresponding real memory read/write operation in one memory access so that the MMU does not create a performance penalty. Unlike normal cache memory, the TLB is built into the MMU and caches individual table entries rather than a set of arbitrary memory locations.

If a page is not in the TLB, then the MMU detects a cache miss and performs an ordinary page lookup (referencing the memory-resident page table). In doing so, one entry is removed from the TLB and replaced by the entry that was just looked up so that the next reference to that same page will result in a TLB hit.

Address Space Identifier

Every process has its own page table (since every process has its own address space). However, there isn't a TLB per process. When a process runs, it should not be allowed to access other process' memory through the TLB. We can do two things. The easy solution is to clear all valid bits in the associative memory, thereby invalidating the entire TLB whenever a new process starts running. This makes context switches costly since a the first several memory references of a process will be forced to access the in-memory page table.

A cleaner solution requires modifying the TLB hardware by adding another field in it to identify the process for which the memory mapping is valid. This field is called the address space identifier, or ASID. A hardware register also has to be added to the processor that will allow the operating system to set the ASID during a context switch. When doing a TLB lookup, the MMU hardware compares the process ID register with the TLB field to only accept matches from the proper process. This solution allows us to save time on context switches since there's a chance that the TLB already contains mappings of frequently used pages for the switched-in process.

Memory Protection and Statistics

In addition to managing logical-to-physical memory page translations, each page table entry can contain fields for additional information, allowing the management unit to enforce memory access permissions and track memory access. Some common elements in a page table include:

- **valid/invalid:** (residence bit) is there a page frame mapped to this region of memory?

- **read-only:** is the process allowed to write to this page?
- **execute:** is the process allowed to execute code from this page?
- **dirty:** has the page been modified since the bit was cleared?
- accessed: has the page been accessed since the bit was cleared? This can help us decide if a page is still being actively referenced.

Memory sharing

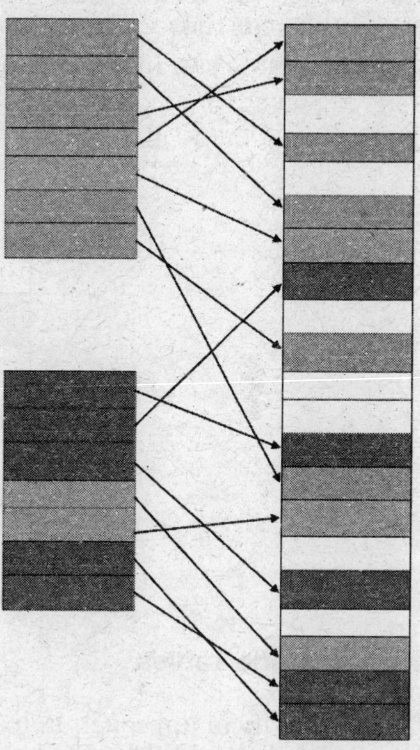

While a virtual memory system allows each process to have its own private address space and ensures that a process cannot stray into any regions that have not been explicitly mapped in the page table, it also makes it easy to share regions of memory as shown in figure. By simply having page table entries for different processes point to the page frame, the operating system can create regions of memory that are shared by two or more processes. The only caveat is that the shared regions have to be multiples of a page; fractional pages cannot be shared. In doing this, the operating system is responsible for keeping track that certain page frames belong to multiple processes. Shared page frames should only be considered unused when the last process that has them mapped exits.

Multilevel Page Tables

Virtual memory allows each process to have its own private address space. The page table for the process maps memory references from this virtual private address space onto page frames in real memory. Because a process can conceivably access any memory location in its address space, the page table has to be big enough to cover every page within that space, whether that page is actually mapped to real memory or not. A 32-but system with 4 KB pages means that we have 20-bit pages and, therefore, a 20-bit index into the page table. This means that the page table needs to have 1,048,576 (220) entries. Even if we skimp on extra flags and assume that each entry is only 24 bits, the page table now consumes 3 MB per process (with a 64-bit address space, each page table will consume approximately 28,672 TB!).

The vast bulk of processes use only a very small part of their address space, although the regions that are used may be scattered. For example, the stack may be at a different end of memory than the text and heap.It's a waste to maintain an entire page table since large regions of it will be unused and empty.

To optimize memory use for a sparse page table, we can arrange the page table in a hierarchy (figure 7.19). The virtual address is divided into three parts. The high-order bits index into a top-level page table (index table). This table contains the base address of a partial page table: the pages that contain those high-order bits. The middle-bits are an offset into this partial page table. This partial page table contains page table entries. If a large-enough region of memory is not used, then the partial page tables for those regions don't need to be created and the corresponding entries in the index table can indicate that there is no valid mapping.

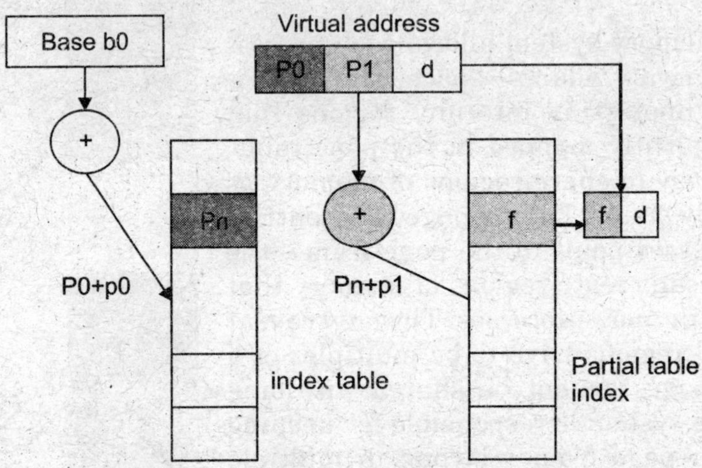

Figure 7.19: *Multilevel page table*

Inverted Page Tables

The hierarchical approach helps to deal with large address spaces. The hierarchy can be extended to additional layers (e.g., a three-level or even a four-level page table) at the cost of an extra memory read per table lookup. A four-level page table will require four memory reads just to find the page translation and then one more memory access for the actual read/write operation. This effectively makes memory access five times slower whenever there's a cache miss.

With a large address space, the potential number of pages is huge with a larger address space (e.g., 64 bit). The number of page frames, however, is more manageable since it is limited by the physical memory on a system. We can design a paging system that is indexed by page frames such that the ith entry into an inverted page table contains information on the contents of page frame i. The number of entries in such a table will always be equal to the number of page frames on the system and will be independent of the virtual address space or the number of processes. The problem is that it isexpensive to search through such a table since there is no direct index onto the desired entry; we only know the page number but the table is indexed by page frames. By using a hash table, we can achieve an access time that is much better than linear search through the table. Moreover, we can couple this inverted page table with a TLB as we did with with page tables to gain the benefits of cached entries for frequently accessed pages. Inverted page tables are not used on today's x86-64,

Intel 32-bit, or ARM architectures but have been used on systems such as the IBM System/38, PowerPC,Intel Itanium, and UltraSPARC.

System Memory Map

In today's operating system, the view of memory is split into two logical regions: kernel memory and process memory. Kernel memory is the memory that is reserved for the operating system kernel's code, data, and stack. Its location in the virtual address space remains constant, typically in the top part of the address space. On 32-bit Linux systems, kernel memory is configurable (PAGE_OFFSET) and is generally set to the top 1 GB of the address space. On Microsoft Windows 7 systems, the top 2 GB of the address space is dedicated to kernel memory on 32-bit systems (8 TB on 64-bit systems).

Process memory represents the remainder of the address space and is available to user processes. In physical memory, page frames will be allocated to various processes. In virtual memory, however, we are looking at memory from the viewpoint of the context of the process. The view of memory is defined by the page table for the process and contains mappings to the pages relevant to that specific process as well as mappings to the kernel.

When a mode switch occurs, either because of an interrupt or system call, the current page table does not change: we experience a mode switch and not a context switch. Execution is transferred to the kernel, which can, if it needs to, access memory in the context of the process that generated the mode switch. A page table will generally be set up to disallow user-mode execution access to regions of the address space that are mapped to kernel memory. Most memory management units allow one to set kernel-only access permissions to a page.

Page Allocator and Kernel Memory Management

With page-based virtual memory, processes can freely get available discontiguous pages as they need more and more memory. The page table for a process can provide the illusion of contiguity by making the virtual address space contiguous. There are special cases, however, where physically contiguous pages are needed. For example,devices that use DMA (direct memory access) interact with memory over the system b us and hence bypass the processor and its memory management unit. If devices on the system rely on DMA, it is crucial that all DMA operations take place either within a page or across contiguous pages. For this reason, it is useful for an operating system to be able to handle requests for contiguous pages for those special cases when such pages are needed. For the most part, these allocations are requested for kernel memory space.

To add to the complexity, some computer architectures (e.g., older Intel) allow peripherals to perform DMA only for addresses below 16 MB. Linux deals with different memory requests via a zone allocator, where a request for memory is accompanied by an prioritized list of acceptable "zones", or types, of memory. The three currently supported zones are:

- DMA: memory that is accessible for DMA.

- NORMAL: general purpose memory
- HIGHMEM: memory regions strictly for system use (e.g., file system buffers, user space, etc.)

For most of today's computer architectures, there is no distinction between the regions.To keep track of pages, the Linux operating system uses a technique called the Buddy System within each zone and maintains an array called free_area of lists of free pages.The first element of the array is a list of free single-page regions; the second element is a list of free two-page regions (free adjacent pages); the third element is a list of free four-page regions; etc., up through the tenth element, which contains a list of free regions of 512 contiguous pages.

SEGMENTATION

A variation on variable partition multiprogramming is to allocate each of the components of a process separately (e.g., code, data, heap, stack). This is known as segmentation. By taking this approach, we break up a process into smaller chunks and increase our chances of finding free memory. Certain regions, such as code and static data, will not grow in size and will never have to be reallocated. It's unlikely that the entire process will have to be moved to a larger whole but rather just the heap or stack segments. To get this to work, however, means that we cannot use a single base register to offset all memory operations. The offsets are different depending on which segment of the process is being addressed. The memory management unit that handles segmentation has to take this into account. Each process will have a number of segment registers associated with it, one for each region of the process (e.g., code, data, stack). The processor's hardware will need to be designed to select the appropriate register for each type of memory reference as in figure 7.20. An example of processors that support a segmentation model is the family of Intel processors starting from the 8086 and 8088 and continuing through today's 64-bit systems.

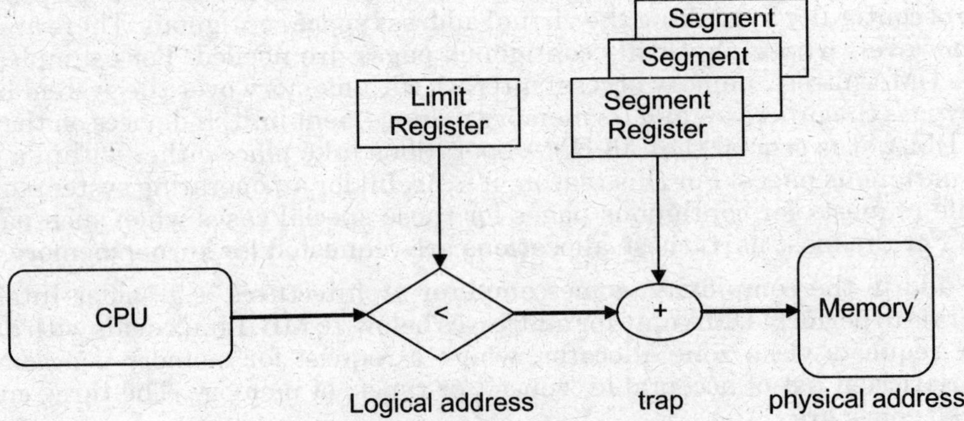

Figure 7.20: *Segmentation hardware*

Allocation Algorithms

If more than one region of memory is able to accommodate a segment (or process), the operating system needs to make a decision on how to pick the best segment. Several approaches are possible.

First fit

Scan segments of memory until you find a hole that fits. Break the hole into one segment for the process and another segment that will be a hole containing the leftover memory. This algorithm has the advantage of a small search.

Next fit

This algorithm is just like First Fit except that it searches from where it left off the previous time (and then wraps around). In practice it exhibits worse performance than First Fit.

Best fit

The Best Fit technique searches the list for the hole that best fits the process. It's slower than First Fit since the entire list must be searched. It also produces tiny holes that are often useless.

Worst fit

Since best fit doesn't perform well, you would think its inverse would. The Worst Fit algorithm searches for the largest hole on the assumption that the hole remaining after allocation will be big enough to be useful. It also doesn't yield good performance.

Quick fit

The Quick Fit algorithm maintains separate lists for common sizes (e.g. 4K holes, 12K holes, ...). It's fast but has the drawback that finding neighbors for merging is difficult.

Advantages of Segmentation

Simplifies handling of growing data structures: If the programmer does not know how large a particular data structure will be, it is necessary to guess unless dynamic segment sizes are allowed. With segmented virtual memory, the data structure can be assigned its own segment, and the operating system will expand or shrink the segment as needed. Allows programs to be altered and recompiled independently, without requiring the entire set of programs to be relinked and reloaded due to use of multiple segments.Lends itself to sharing data among processes – a programmer can place a utility program or a useful table of data in a segment that can be referenced by other process.

Lends itself to protection, because a segment can be protected to contain a well-defined set of procedures or data, the programmer or system administrator can assign access privileges in a convenient fashion.

Organization Of Segmentation

- Each process has its own segment table and when all its segments are loaded in main memory, the segment table for a process is created and loaded into main memory.
- Each entry contains the starting address of the corresponding segment and length of the segment.
- A bit is needed to determine if segment is already in main memory.
- Another bit is needed to determine if the segment has been modified since it was loaded in main memory.

Chapter 8

Virtual Memory

INTRODUCTION

The data and the instructions are read from the main memory and then after the execution of the instruction is over they are written back onto the memory. But what happens when the program in consideration is larger than the size of the available memory? Virtual Memory is a concept that addresses this issue by allowing a program than is even larger than the size of the available free memory to be loaded and executed and eliminate the chances of external fragmentation.

The data and instructions of any process (a program in execution) or thread of execution within a process must be available to the CPU by residing in physical memory at the time of execution. Virtual Memory refers to the concept in which a process of a larger size than available memory can be loaded and executed by loading the process in parts. It is an illusion that a computer system has more memory than it actually has. The Operating System maps the programmer's virtual addresses to real hardware storage addresses. Mapping implies the correspondence between the virtual addresses and the physical addresses using virtual translation mechanisms as decided by the Operating System. The program memory is divided into pages and the available physical memory into frames. The page size is always equal to the frame size. The page size is generally in a power of 2 to avoid the calculation involved to get the page number and the offset from the CPU generated address.

In the virtual memory systems, the addresses that the application programs deal with are known as virtual addresses. These virtual addresses used by the application program are mapped to physical addresses by translation of these virtual addresses. This is taken care of by the virtual memory system's address translation mechanism by mapping these virtual addresses to frame addresses using the Page Map Tables. This is what we call the physical address in the main memory that can be used to refer to the contents from the memory. The process address space implies the number of unique addresses needed to hold both the process and its data. The virtual address space refers to the memory space of the virtual addresses.

The virtual address contains a page number and an offset. This is mapped to the physical address by a technique of address resolution after searching the Page Map Table. In order to maintain the accounting information of which pages are loaded into which frames, the Operating System maintains a Page Map Table. This table contains the following:

- The Page Number
- The Offset
- The Frame Number
- The Reference Bit
- The Presence Bit
- The Dirty/Modified Bit

The Page Number refers to the number of the pages in the virtual addressing mechanism for the page. The offset indicates the relative address of a particular instruction in the page from the base of that page. The frame number indicates the number of the physical frame in the memory that is divided into equal sized frames. Note that the page size and the frame size are always equal so that a page can be easily mapped onto a frame in the main memory. The reference bit indicates whether the page is being referenced. The presence bit indicates whether the page is in memory. The modified bit is set if the page has been modified after being loaded in memory. The Page table is process specific and each process is allocated its own Page Table. There is another table called the Page Table Register that contains the references to the Page Tables in memory. Therefore, there is one Page Table Register for the entire system, but there can be multiple Page Map Tables, each belonging to a particular process.

Virtual Page Address Translation

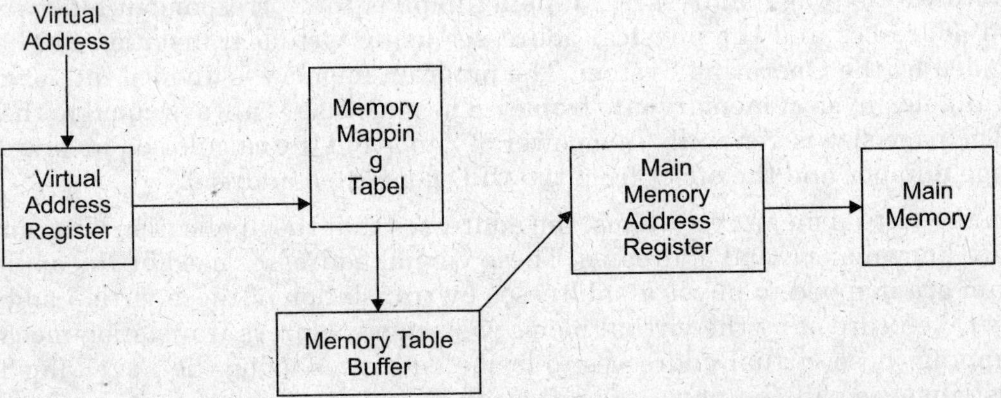

Figure 8.1: *Memory Table for Mapping a Virtual Address to Physical Address*

This mechanism translates a virtual Page Number to a Physical Frame No. This translation is taken care of by a specific hardware called the Memory Management Unit (MMU) that is contained in the CPU. The MMU is a hardware device responsible for handling memory access requests that come from the CPU. Note that the addressing model in this case is defined by the CPU. In order to facilitate faster page table lookups, the Operating System makes use of "Translation Look aside Buffers"

(TLB) and ensures that the Page Tables are updated with each Page Fault. A TLB is a buffer (or cache) in a CPU that contains parts of the page table of a particular process that translates the virtual address to a physical address. The Figure 8.1 given below show the mapping of a virtual address to the physical address. It is a dynamic operation which means that every address is translated immediately as a word is referenced by the processor

Advantages and Disadvantages of Virtual Memory Systems

The primary advantage or objective of Virtual Memory systems is the ability to load and execute a process that requires a larger amount of memory than what is available by loading the process in parts and then executing them. The disadvantage is that Virtual Memory systems tend to be slow and require additional support from the system's hardware for address translations. It can be said that the execution speed of a process in a Virtual Memory system can be equal, but never exceed, the execution speed of the same process with Virtual Memory turned off. Hence, we do not have an advantage with respect to the execution speed of the process. The advantage lies in the ability of the system to eliminate external fragmentation. The other disadvantage of Virtual Memory systems is the possibility of Thrashing due to excessive Paging and Page faults. It may be noted that Trash Point is a point after which the execution of a process comes to a halt; the system is busier paging i.e pages in and out of the memory than executing them.

DEMAND PAGING

In Virtual Memory Systems the pages are not loaded in the memory until they are "demanded" by a process; hence the name, Demand Paging. Demand paging allows the various parts of a process to be brought into physical memory as the process needs them to execute.

In virtual memory systems, demand paging is a type of swapping in which pages of data are not copied from disk to RAM until they are needed. In contrast, some virtual memory systems use anticipatory paging in which the operating system attempts to anticipate which data will be needed next and copies it to RAM before it is actually required. For a process to execute, all the structures for data, text, and so on have to be set up. Pages are not loaded in memory until they are "demanded" by a process. Thus we get the term "demand paging." Demand paging allows the various parts of a process to be brought into physical memory as the process needs them to execute. Rather than swapping the whole process into memory we use a lazy swapper. A lazy swapper never swaps a page into the memory unless it is required. When a process is to be swapped in, the pager guesses the pages required by the process, so instead of swapping in the whole process, the pager brings only those pages which are required into the memory. So the pages which are not required are not read and hence the amount of physical memory required will be reduced and there will be substantial reduction in the swap time. This system requires the special hardware that will find out that which pages are in memory and which is on the disk. To make it happen, valid-invalid bit scheme method can be used. Which says, when the bit is set to valid, so page is in the memory and if it is invalid, it shows that either it is not valid or it is valid but is currently on the disk. The Figure 8.2 given below show the concept of Page table, where the pages not in the memory have been marked as invalid?

Subscript	Logical Memory
0	A
1	B
2	C
3	D
4	E

Logical Memory

Subscript	Frame	Valid- Invalid Bit
0	4	v
1		i
2	1	v
3		i
4		i

Page Table

Subscript	Data
0	
1	C
2	
3	
4	A

Physical Memory

Figure 8.2: *Page Table When Some Pages are not in Memory*

If all the pages required are in the memory then the execution of the process proceeds normally. But the problem arises when we wish to access a page that is not brought into the memory. Access to such a page which has been marked as invalid will cause a page fault trap. The following is the procedure to handle the page fault:

1. The system checks whether the reference made is valid or invalid, it is done by checking the internal table stored along with the process control block.
2. If the reference is invalid, the process is terminated. If it is valid, but the required page has not been brought into the memory, so the process to bring the page in begins.
3. A free frame is brought and a disk read operation is done to read the desired page into the newly allocated frame.
4. When disk read is complete, both the internal table and the page tables are updated to indicate that the page is in the memory now.
5. The process can now access the page as it is now available in the memory.

When ever an interrupt occurs due to a page fault in a process, its state is saved and we can start the process from exactly the same place and state, from where it was interrupted. The page not available in the memory can be brought in by using the concept of demand paging. The process will keep on creating a page fault until all the pages required by it are not in the memory. But a page is not brought into the memory until it is required, it is known as the concept of pure demand paging.

PERFORMANCE OF DEMAND PAGING

When the CPU executes an instruction that is not available in the memory, a Page Fault occurs. This means a page is being referenced, but the same is not present in the memory. The Operating System is now responsible for bringing the appropriate page into memory from the disk. The total turnaround time of a process is divided into CPU time and IO time. Disk I/O takes a longer time than CPU and the process must wait until the page has been fetched from the disk. A module of the Operating System called the Page Fault Handler is given the control. It gets the Page Table address and the page number of the faulting page along with the information needed to bring the required page into the main memory from the backing store. The information also includes the disk address of the page in the backing store. A longer IO is detrimental to the performance of the system as a whole because the CPU would remain idle for a considerable amount of time which is not feasible for a good Operating System design. So, the CPU would schedule another process that could execute at the same point of time when the Disk IO is being performed so that the CPU idle time can be avoided.

The Operating System searches for the page in the File Map Table that contains the page number and the corresponding disk address of the page. After acquiring the disk address, the OS schedules a disk read operation to get the page from the disk/physical storage. The Memory Map Table is then searched to locate the first free frame for that page to be loaded. After getting the free frame number, the OS updates the Page Map Table with the frame number and the reference bit. Now the presence bit is set to indicate the presence of the page in memory. The CPU is now instructed to restart the execution. If the probability of the page fault is "p" and the memory access time is "ma," then the total time required is (1 – p) x ma + p x page fault time.

Besides Demand Paging, there is another concept related to paging operation in the name of Anticipatory Paging. This implies that the Operating System guesses the pages that can be referenced and fetches them from the backing store to put onto the main memory even before they need to be referenced. To compute the effective access time, the user must know that how much time is required to service a page fault.

PAGE REPLACEMENT ALGORITHMS

Once the main memory fills up, a page must be swapped out to make room for the new pages to be swapped in. This concept is known as page replacement. The problem is to decide which pages are to be swapped out to make a room for the new processes; it is decided by various algorithms known as page replacement algorithms.

In the page replacement scheme, if no frame is free, then we find out that is not used currently and free it. The frame can be freed by writing its content to the swap space and changing the entry in the page table and the related data structures to show that the page is not in the memory now. Then the freed frame can be allocated to the new page. The process can be enumerated as:

1. Find the location of the desired page on the disk.
2. Find a free frame, if it is available it is allocated to the process,

Else, use a page replacement algorithm to select a frame which is to be freed, this frame is known as a victim frame. Then the contents of this victim frame are written back on the disk. And the page table and frame table entries are updated accordingly.

3. Read the desired page into the newly free frame, and again the page table and frame table entries are updated accordingly.
4. The normal execution of the process can be restarted again.

If no frames are free, two page transfers are required. This situation will double the page fault service time and will increase the effective access time. This overhead can be reduced by the use of a modify (dirty) bit. Each page or frame may have a modify bit associated with it in the hardware. The modify bit for a page is set by the hardware whenever any word or byte in the page is written into, indicating that the page has been modified. When we select a page for replacement the modify bit is checked, if bit is set, it means that the page has been modified as it was read in from the disk. So we write that page to the disk. If the modify bit is not set, the page has not been modified as it was read into memory. Figure 8.3 shows the process of page replacement. The step by step procedure is:

1. The victim page will be swapped out from the main memory to make the room for the new page.
2. The entry of this swapped out page is updated in the page table, to show that it is no more in the main memory, for this purpose the valid-invalid bit is changed from valid to invalid.
3. The required page is swapped into the memory.
4. The entry of this swapped in page is updated in the page table, to show that it is now present in the main memory, for this purpose the valid-invalid bit is changed from invalid to valid.

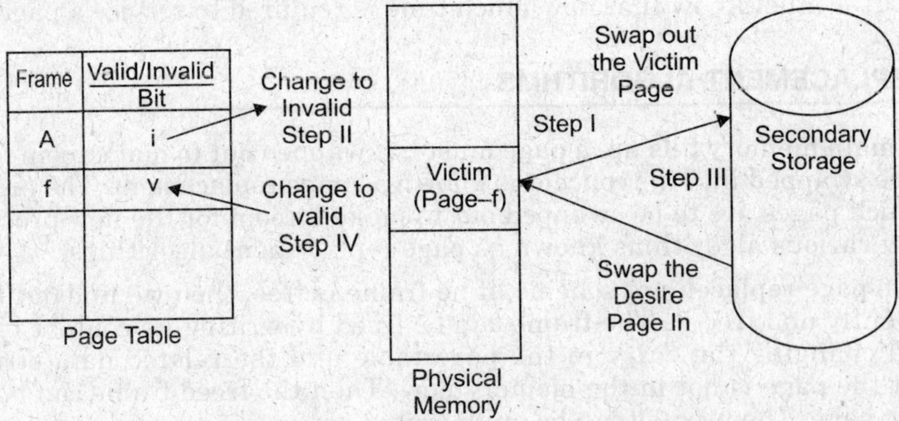

Figure 8.3: *The Concept of Page Replacement.*

The overall objective of page replacement policy is that the pages should be replaced in such a way that the page fault should be minimum as far as possible.

The various page replacement algorithm exists which vary in the number of page faults incurred by them. The evaluation of these algorithms has been done by running them for a particular string of memory references. For a given page size, to access a particular page the user must know the page number not the entire address. If a page p is in memory then immediately following references will not fault. The page faults can be calculated if the number of frames in a page increases. As the number of frames available increases, the number of page faults decreases.

First-In, First-Out (FIFO)

First-in, first-out is the easiest page replacement policy. Rather than choosing a victim page at random, the oldest page (or first-in) is the first to be removed. A FIFO queue is maintained to hold all pages in the memory. The new page brought in the memory will be inserted at the tail of the queue and the page for replacement will be chosen from the head of the queue. It is a general result that as the number of frames increases the page fault goes down.

Example 1: Consider the following reference string 4, 0, 1, 2, 0, 3, 0, 8, 2, 3, 0, 3, 2, 1, 2, 0, 4, 0, 1 and the page is having three frames then this reference string will be executed following FIFO policy as under:

If number of frames = 3,

Arrival of Requests	4	0	1	2	0	3	0	8	2	3	0	3	2	1	2	0	4	0	1
Data in the Frames	4	4	4	2		2	2	8	8	8	0			0	0		4	4	4
		0	0	0		3	3	3	2	2	2			1	1		1	0	0
			1	1		1	0	0	0	3	3			3	2		2	2	1
Page Fault	Y	Y	Y	Y	N	Y	Y	Y	Y	Y	Y	N	N	Y	Y	N	Y	Y	Y

Figure 8.4

Total Number of Page Faults = 15

As in Figure 8.4, The first three references will cause the page faults as all these frames are empty in the beginning. The next reference is for the page number 2, there is no space for the new page, so some page needs to be replaced, as the algorithm is following the first in first out policy, so the page entered first will be the one to be removed, so page number 4 will be removed. The next reference is for page number 0, it is already in the frame, so no operation (NOP) will be there. The next reference is for page number 3, as it not in the frames, it has to be brought in, so the page number 0 will be replaced.

If number of frames = 4, then the page faults for the above mentioned memory reference string can be calculated as given below in Figure 8.5.

Arrival of Requests	4	0	1	2	0	3	0	8	2	3	0	3	2	1	2	0	4	0	1
Data in the Frames	4	4	4	4		3		3			3			3	2		2		
		0	0	0		0		8			8			8	8		4		
			1	1		1		1			0			0	0		0		
				2		2		2			2			1	1		1		
Page Fault	Y	Y	Y	Y	N	Y	N	Y	N	N	Y	N	N	Y	Y	N	Y	N	N

Figure 8.5

Total Number of Page Faults = 10

If number of frames = 5, then the page faults for the above mentioned memory reference string can be calculated as in Figure 8.6;

Arrival of Requests	4	0	1	2	0	3	0	8	2	3	0	3	2	1	2	0	4	0	1
Data in the Frames	4	4	4	4		4		8									8	8	8
		0	0	0		0		0									4	4	4
			1	1		1		1									1	0	0
				2		2		2									2	2	1
						3		3									3	3	3
Page Fault	Y	Y	Y	Y	N	Y	N	Y	N	N	Y	N	N	N	N	N	Y	Y	Y

Figure 8.6

Total Number of Page Faults = 09

Example 2: Consider the following reference string 7, 8, 4, 9,7, 8, 3, 7, 8, 4, 9, 3 and the page is having three frames then this reference string will be executed following FIFO policy as under:

If number of frames = 3, the execution is shown in Figure 8.7 below,

Arrival of Requests	7	8	4	9	7	8	3	7	8	4	9	3
Data in the Frames	7	7	7	9	9	9	3			3	3	
		8	8	8	7	7	7			4	4	
			4	4	4	8	8			8	9	
Page Fault	Y	Y	Y	Y	Y	Y	Y	N	N	Y	Y	N

Figure 8.7

Total Number of Page Faults = 9

If number of frames = 4, the execution is shown in Figure 8.8

Arrival of Requests	7	8	4	9	7	8	3	7	8	4	9	3
Data in the Frames	7	7	7	7			3	3	3	3	9	9
		8	8	8			8	7	7	7	7	3
			4	4			4	4	8	8	8	8
				9			9	9	9	4	4	4
Page Fault	Y	Y	Y	Y	N	N	Y	Y	Y	Y	Y	Y

Figure 8.8

Total Number of Page Faults = 10.

This example shows an unexpected result, as the number of frames increased from 3 to 4, the page faults have also increased from 9 to 10. This is not a usual result. This anomoly is known as the Belady's Anomaly, which states that as the number of frames allocated increases the page fault also increase.

Optimal Algorithm

This algorithm was invented to overcome the limitations of FIFO algorithm. This algorithm states, replace the page that will not be used for the longest period of time. This algorithm claims to have lowest page fault and does not suffer from the belady's anomaly. This algorithm works on the policy of looking forward and works on the future demands for a particular page.

Example 1: Consider the following reference string 4, 0, 1, 2, 0, 3, 0, 8, 2, 3, 0, 3, 2, 1, 2, 0, 4, 0, 1 and the page is having three frames then this reference string will be executed following FIFO policy as under:

If number of frames = 3, the execution is shown in Figure 8.9

Arrival of Requests	4	0	1	2	0	3	0	8	2	3	0	3	2	1	2	0	4	0	1
Data in the Frames	4	4	4	2		2		2			2			2			4		
		0	0	0		0		8			0			0			0		
			1	1		3		3			3			1			1		
Page Fault	Y	Y	Y	Y	N	Y	N	Y	N	N	Y	N	N	Y	N	N	Y	N	N

Figure 8.9

Total Number of Page Faults = 9

The first three references will cause the page faults as all these frames are empty in the beginning. The next reference is for the page number 2, now which page is to be removed from the frame buffer to make a place for the page number 2, according to optimal policy, the user will select the page which will not be used for the longest duration of time in the future, out of the present pages in the frame {4, 0, 1}, the page number 4 will not be used in the near future, so it will be the victim to be replaced, as the page number 0 and 1 will be referenced in the near future recently. Moving in this way, the Figure 8.9 show the order of reference and the consecutive page faults and total number of page faults come out to be 9, which quite less as compared to one in FIFO policy (that was 15 in Figure 8.4)

This algorithm is difficult to implement as it require the knowledge about the future references.

If number of frames = 4, the execution is shown in Figure 8.9.

Arrival of Requests	4	0	1	2	0	3	0	8	2	3	0	3	2	1	2	0	4	0	1
Data in the Frames	4	4	4	4		3		3						1			1		
		0	0	0		0		0						0			0		
			1	1		1		8						8			4		
				2		2		2						2			2		
Page Fault	Y	Y	Y	Y	N	Y	N	Y	N	N	N	N	N	Y	N	N	Y	N	N

Total Number of Page Faults = 8.

Clearly, the page faults have reduced from 9 to 8, as the frame size increased from 3 to 4.

Example 2: Consider the following reference string 7, 8, 4, 9, 7, 8, 3, 7, 8, 4, 9, 3 and the page is having three frames then this reference string will be executed following FIFO policy as under:

If number of frames = 3, the execution is shown in Figure 8.10

Arrival of Requests	7	8	4	9	7	8	3	7	8	4	9	3
Data in the Frames	7	7	7	7			7			4	4	
		8	8	8			8			8	9	
			4	9			3			3	3	
Page Fault	Y	Y	Y	Y	N	N	Y	N	N	Y	Y	N

Figure 8.10

Total Number of Page Faults = 7

If number of frames = 4, the execution is shown in Figure 8.11

Arrival of Requests	7	8	4	9	7	8	3	7	8	4	9	3
Data in the Frames	7	7	7	7			7				9	
		8	8	8			8				8	
			4	4			4				4	
				9			3				3	
Page Fault	Y	Y	Y	Y	N	N	Y	N	N	N	Y	N

Figure 8.11

Total Number of Page Faults = 6.

This example shows a usual, as the number of frames increased from 3 to 4, the page faults have decreased from 7 to 6. So Belady's Anomaly is not present.

Least Recently Used (LRU)

This algorithm replaces a page which has not been used since long in the recent past, i.e it replaces the page which has not been used for the longest period of time. LRU assumes that a page recently referenced will most likely be referenced again soon. To measure the "time" elapsed since a page has been a part of the reference stream, a backward distance is stored. This distance must always be greater than zero, the point for the current position in the reference stream, and can be defined as infinite in the case of a page that has never been referenced. Thus, the victim page is defined as the one with the maximum backward distance; if two or more points meet this condition, a page is chosen arbitrarily. Actual implementation of the backward distance number can vary, and does play an important role in the speed and efficiency of this algorithm. This can be done by sorting page references in order of their age into a stack, allowing quick identification of victims. However the overhead associated with sorting does not generally justify the speed of identification, unless specific hardware exists to perform this operation. Many operating systems do not assume this hardware exists. and instead increment an age counter for every active page during the page stream progression.

Example 1: Consider the following reference string 4, 0, 1, 2, 0, 3, 0, 8, 2, 3, 0, 3, 2, 1, 2, 0, 4, 0, 1 and the page is having three frames then this reference string will be executed following LRU policy as under:

If number of frames = 3, the execution is shown in Figure 8.12

Arrival of Requests	4	0	1	2	0	3	0	8	2	3	0	3	2	1	2	0	4	0	1
Data in the Frames	4	4	4	2		2		8	8	8	0			1		1	4		4
		0	0	0		0		0	0	3	3			3		0	0		0
			1	1		3		3	2	2	2			2		2	2		1
Page Fault	Y	Y	Y	Y	N	Y	N	Y	Y	Y	Y	N	N	Y	N	Y	Y	N	Y

Figure 8.12

Total Number of Page Faults = 13

The first three references will cause the page faults as all these frames are empty in the beginning. The next reference is for the page number 2, now which page is to be removed from the frame buffer to make a place for the page number 2, according to least recently reduced, the user will select the page which have not be used for the longest duration of time in the recent past, out of the present pages in the frame {4, 0, 1}, the page number 4 has not been used recently, so it will the victim to be replaced, as the page number 0 and 1 has been referenced recently. Moving in this way, the Figure show the order of reference and the consecutive page faults and total number of page faults come out to be 13, which quite less as compared to one in FIFO policy (that was 15 in Figure 8.4).

If number of frames = 4, the execution is shown in Figure 8.13

Arrival of Requests	4	0	1	2	0	3	0	8	2	3	0	3	2	1	2	0	4	0	1
Data in the Frames	4	4	4	4		3		3						3			4		
		0	0	0		0		0						0			0		
			1	1		1		8						1			1		
				2		2		2						2			2		
Page Fault	Y	Y	Y	Y	N	Y	N	Y	N	N	N	N	N	Y	N	N	Y	N	N

Figure 8.13

Total Number of Page Faults = 8.

As the number of frames has been increased from 3 to 4, the page faults have been reduced from 13 to 8.

Example 2: Consider the following reference string 7, 8, 4, 9,7, 8, 3, 7, 8, 4, 9, 3 and the page is having three frames then this reference string will be executed following FIFO policy as under:

If number of frames = 3, the execution is shown in Figure 8.14

Arrival of Requests	7	8	4	9	7	8	3	7	8	4	9	3
Data in the Frames	7	7	7	9	9	9	3			4	4	4
		8	8	8	7	7	7			7	9	9
			4	4	4	8	8			8	8	3
Page Fault	Y	Y	Y	Y	N	N	Y	N	N	Y	Y	Y

Figure 8.14

Total Number of Page Faults = 8

If number of frames = 4, the execution is shown in Figure 8.15

Arrival of Requests	7	8	4	9	7	8	3	7	8	4	9	3
Data in the Frames	7	7	7	7			7			7	7	
		8	8	8			8			8	8	
			4	4			3			3	9	
				9			9			4	4	
Page Fault	Y	Y	Y	Y	N	N	Y	N	N	Y	Y	N

Figure 8.15

Total Number of Page Faults = 7.

This example shows a usual, as the number of frames increased from 3 to 4, the page faults have decreased from 8 to 7. So Belady's Anomaly is not present.

Stack Algorithms

One would naturally expect the behavior of static paging algorithms to be linear; after all, they are static in nature. Instinct tells us that by increasing the available physical memory for storing pages, and thus decreasing the needed number of page replacements, that the performance of the algorithm would increase. However, with most simple algorithms this is not necessarily the case. In fact, by increasing the available physical memory, some algorithms such as FIFO can decrease in page fault performance seemingly at random. This occurrence is referred to as Belady's Anomaly, and is a primary factor in considering the practicality of any static algorithm. The predictable change in performance with an increase in physical memory is obviously not something to be taken for granted. It can be proven, however, that if any algorithm with allocation of size m has pages that are guaranteed to be a subset of the allocation m + 1, it will not be subject to Belady's Anomaly; this is what is referred to as the inclusion property. Static algorithms that meet this requirement are called Stack Algorithms, named rightly so for the process of stacking subsets of pages as available allocations increase. Not only are Stack Algorithms more useful, since they are guaranteed not to degrade in performance as available resources increase, their page faulting behavior is also easy to predict.

Dynamic Page Replacement Algorithms

All of the static page replacement algorithms considered have one thing in common: they assumed that each program is allocated a fixed amount of memory when it begins execution, and does not request further memory during its lifetime. Although static algorithms will work in this scenario, they are hardly optimized to handle the common occurrence of adjusting to page allocation changes. This can lead to problems when a program rapidly switches between relatively large and relatively small page sets or localities.

Depending on the size of the memory requirements of a program, the number of page faults may increase or decrease rapidly; for Stack Algorithms, we know that as the memory size is decreased, the number of page faults will increase. Other static algorithms may become completely unpredictable. Generally speaking, any program can have its number of page faults statistically analyzed for a variety of memory allocations. At some point the rate of increase of the page faults (derivative of the curve) will peak; this point is sometimes referred to as the hysteresis point. If the memory allocated to the program is less than the hysteresis point, the program is likely to thrash its page replacement. Past the point, there is generally little noticeable change in the fault rate, making the hysteresis the target page allocation.

Since a full analysis is rarely available to a virtual memory controller, and that program behavior is quite dynamic, finding the optimal page allocation can be incredibly difficult. A variety of methods must be employed to develop replacement algorithms that work hand-in-hand with the locality changes present in complex programs. Dynamic paging algorithms accomplish this by attempting to predict program memory requirements, while adjusting available pages based on reoccurring trends. This policy of controlling available pages is also referred to as "prefetch" paging, and is contrary to the idea of demand paging. Although localities (within the scope of a set of operations) may change, it is likely that within the global locality (encompassing the smaller clusters), locality sets will be repeated

Evaluation of Algorithms

Methodology of Evaluation: It quickly becomes obvious when evaluating algorithms that a common benchmark is difficult to identify; although standards such as Belady's Optimal Algorithm or Perfect Prediction can be used as performance benchmarks across static and dynamic algorithms, they are certainly not the end-all of judgment. One of the largest concerns when comparing algorithms is not only their speed, but the relative cost in resources necessary to accomplish them. Depending on the implementation, many algorithms may not even be feasible due to hardware restrictions, or performance decreases due to limited hardware support. Other design considerations, such as the size of pages present on the system can also affect algorithm performance.

We can assume that a sufficient architecture for implementing virtual memory does exist, such as a virtual memory manager, and that a single page replacement generally takes some fixed average time. In reality, page reads from a secondary memory may vary widely due to the storage medium or system-wide demand for access to that device, by the relatively slow performance of secondary devices.

THRASHING

A process is thrashing if it is spending more time than executing. The high paging activity is called thrashing. If the process does not have the sufficient number of frames, it will quickly page fault. At this point, some of the pages are to be replaced. As all pages are in active use, it must replace a page that will be needed again very soon. So it will fault again and again. This process continues to fault, replacing pages for which it then faults brings back the pages again. Thrashing results in severe performance problems. The operating system is responsible for monitoring the CPU utilization. If CPU utilization is too low, we increase the degree of multiprogramming by adding the new process. There we can use a global page replacement algorithm which will replace pages with no regard to the process to which they belong. Now if the process needs more frames, it starts faulting and try to take frames from the other processes. These processes needed those pages so they also start faulting and taking frames from the other processes. These faulting processes must use the paging device to swap pages in and out. As they queue up for the paging device, the ready queue becomes vacant, so processes start waiting for the paging device, so the CPU utilization decreases. To overcome the problem of low CPU utilization the scheduler starts picking up the new processes, these new processes will try to acquire the new frames from the running processes which will result in more page faults and the queue for the paging device will increase. So CPU utilization decreases even more. So the system will try to increase the degree of multiprogramming even more. In such a situation, Thrashing has occurred and system performance drops down to a larger extent. In such a situation, the system is not doing work, because the processes are spending more time in performing the activity of paging in and paging out.

As the degree of multiprogramming increases, CPU utilization also increases, when it reaches the maximum limit and the degree of multiprogramming is increased after this point, the problem of thrashing appears and the CPU utilization drops sharply. In order to stop the thrashing the degree of multiprogramming must be reduced. The ill effects of thrashing can be reduced by using a local replacement algorithm, according to which if one process starts thrashing, it cannot steal the frames from the other processes and cannot cause the other processes to thrash also.

Chapter 9

File Management

File system is an integral part of any operating system. Files are used to store data and programs. The programs and data related to operating system and the users of the computer are stored in the files. The major component of file system is a collection of files, where each file stores the relevant data and the other one is the directory structure which organizes and provides information about the files in the system. The file management system allows the users to create files, assign them meaningful names, manipulate them and to specify that how these can be shared among the users. It visualizes a file as an entity that is owned by the user, can be shared by the authorized users and can be stored reliably permanently. The main characteristics of the file system are:

- The organized arrangement of files and the directories.
- Easy and fast access to the files.
- Reliable storage of the files and hence the data.
- The provision of sharing of files among users with the implementation of proper access privileges.

CONCEPT OF FILES

A file is a named collection of related information that is recorded on secondary storage device. It contains a sequence of bits, bytes, lines or records, the meaning of which is defined by the creator of the file. A file may be considered as the smallest allotment of the logical secondary storage, where data cannot be stored in the system memory, unless it has not been written into a file. The file creator stores the information in the file. Various types of information may be stored in a file; it may be source programs, object programs, executable programs, text or numeric data, graphic images, sound clips. The structure of the file is defined by its type. The information about the files is stored in a directory which is also stored in the secondary storage device. The directory entry stores the name of the file and its unique identifier, where the identifier will work as a pointer to the other attributes of the file. Files are mapped on the physical devices by the operating system. The storage devices used here are nonvolatile so that the data is the file can be retained even if the system reboots or any power failure occurs.

File Attributes

File attributes are the characteristics of a file that are important to its user and to the operating system itself. Each and every file created in the system is assigned a particular name, so that the user can easily track the file. The name of the file is usually a collection of characters, e.g a file created in MS-WORD can be named as computer.doc. The file created by the user may be stored on secondary storage device or may be stored on some removable storage media or may be transmitted over the network. The attributes of a file may vary from the operating system to operating system, but normally, the most common attributes are shown in the table 9.1 given below:

Table 9.1 Description of Various File Attributes

S.No	File Attribute	Description
1.	Name	To identify a particular file, it is named, it is given in human readable form and most of the time it is symbolic of the purpose or the data stored in the file.
2.	Identifier	The unique tag, normally a number that identifies a file in the file system, it is non-human readable form.
3.	Type	The type of the file depends on the data stored in it. It may be a text file, image file or system file.
4.	Location	It specifies the location of the file in the system
5.	Size	The current size of the file in terms of bytes in mentioned in this attribute
6.	Protection	To provide a controlled access, the access permission of various users is stored, i.e the information regarding who can read or write data from or into the file.
7.	Time and Date	Time and date of file creation, last modification, last usage will be stored for tracking in various aspects.
8.	User Identification	The information about the user who created, who used or who tried to use the file is stored so that protection and security of the files can be maintained.
9.	Creator	It shows the id of the user who created it.
10.	Owner	It shows the current owner of the file.
11.	Protection Information	It shows who can access the file and in what way.
12.	Access Flag	It shows the type of the access possible on the file, where the access may be sequential access or random access.
13.	Creation time	It shows the date and time when the file was created.

S.No	File Attribute	Description
14.	Time of last access	It shows the data and time when the file was accessed for the last time.
15.	Time of last change	It shows the date and time when the file was changed.
16.	Read only Flag	This shows that whether the file is read only or write operation can also be performed. • 0 for read/write • 1 for read only.
17.	System Flag.	This shows whether the file is a normal file or a system file. • 0 for normal file • 1 for system file.
18.	Archive Flag	This shows that whether the backup of the file has been taken or not. • 0 if file back up has been taken. • 1 if file back is still to be taken.
19.	Random access Flag	It shows that whether the file supports sequential access or direct access. • 0 for sequential access only. • 1 for random access.
20.	Maximum Size	It shows the maximum size to which the file may grow to.

File Operations

The operating system is responsible for creating and maintaining the files. Further it ensures that files can be accessed by the authorized users only and is responsible to delete the file when it is not required. The various operations possible on a file are:

Table 9.2 Description of Various File Attributes

S.No	Operation	Description
1.	Create	This operation is used to create a file. It is a two step process: Space for the file is to be searched Entry for the new file is made in the directory.
2.	Open	This operation is used to open a file. As before using a file either for reading or writing, it must be opened.
3.	Close	This operation is used to close the file when it is not required any more.
4.	Write	This operation is used to write data into a file. Given the name of the file in which data is to be written, the system searches for that file in the directory and the data is written to the location in the file where the write pointer is kept.

S.No	Operation	Description
5.	Read	This operation is used to read data from a file. Given the name of the file from which data is to be read, the system searches for that file in the directory and the data is read from the location in the file where the read pointer is kept to the location where next read is to take place. The same pointer may be used by the system for the read and write operations, which will save space and will reduce the system complexity.
6.	Seek	This operation is used to position the pointer to a particular location, directory is searched for the appropriate entry and current file position is set to the desired location. After the pointer has been positioned to the desired location, then any other required operation(read/write etc.) can be done.
7.	Delete	This operation deletes a particular file and the corresponding entry from the directory is erased and the space allocated to the file is freed.
8.	Truncate	This operation is used to erase the contents of the file but the existence of the file remains as such, that means file length is reduced to zero, but the other file attributes remain the same.
9.	Rename	This operation is used to rename the existing file
10.	Append	This operation is used to add new information to the end of the file. This is considered similar to write operation, but the difference is that by using a write call we can write data any where in file, but by using append, the data can be written only at the end of the file.
11.	Copy	This operation is used to copy the content of a file to another file. It is basically a composite operation in which following sub-operations will be performed: • Create the new file • Read data from the original file. • Write data into the new file.
12.	Getattributes	This operation is used to know the attributes of a file, like its owner, type, size and the other properties related to a file.
13.	Setattributes	This operation is used to set the attributes of a file, for example: the user may wish to set the file to read only, which means the file can only be read by the user and the data cannot be written into it.

File Types

The files can be of various types depending upon the type of data that can be stored in it. The operating system may or may not support a particular file type. The data stored in the files may be executable programs, object modules, text data, documents, spreadsheets, photo and video clips. Broadly, the files can be divided into two categories:

Structured files: These are the files consisting of records and fields, where a record is a meaningful collection of related fields and a field contains a single data item. Each record in a file has a key field, which is unique. If operating system recognizes and accept a particular file type, only then it will be able to perform various operations on the file. To recognize the type of a file easily, the type of the file is included in its name itself. In this case file name is divided as:

<file name> . <extension>

Where file name is the name of the file given by the user. And the extension gives an idea about the type of file and hence the type of the content stored in the file and in some cases the extension also gives an idea about the operation that can be performed on the file. For example, if a user is willing to open a file named as india.doc, then the operating system checks the extension of file and come to know what to do with the file, for opening this file the operating system will open this file in the word processor it has.

Same way if the user is willing to open the file 'photo.jpg', the extension show that it is an image file, then operating system will open this file in whatever the default image viewer has been installed on the system. Normally in MS-DOS, the name of the file can be of 8 characters and the extension may be of up to three characters. The Table 9.3 below shows the common file types, the three character long abbreviation for the extension and the function of that particular file type. In unix operating system a file may have two or more extensions like 'operating.doc.z' where z indicates that the file has been zipped.

Table 9.3: Various File Extensions

S.No	Extension	Function
1.	.exe, .com, .bin	Ready to run machine language program, executable file
2.	.obj,o	Complied machine language program, not linked yet., also called object file.
3.	.bak	Backup file
4.	.bat	Batch File, Commands batched for the command interpreter
5.	.doc	Documentation file (Microsoft Word Document)
6.	.lib	Library of files use d by the linker
7.	.ps, .gif	ASCII or binary file ready for printing or viewing
8.	.arc, .zip	Related files grouped into one file, sometimes compresses for archiving or storage.
9.	.bin	Executable binary program
10.	.c, .cpp, .java, .pas	Source Code in various languages like C, C++, Java and Pascal.

S.No	Extension	Function
11.	.dat	Data file
12.	.mpeg, .mov	Audio or Video Information.
13.	.hlp	Text for HELP command
14.	.txt	Plain text file.
15.	.rtf	Rich Text Format File
16.	.log	Log File
17.	.docx	Microsoft Word Open XML Document
18.	.pps, .ppt	PowerPoint Slide Show
19.	.sys	Windows System File
20.	.pptx	PowerPoint Open XML Presentation
21.	.xml	XML File
22.	.mp3	MP3 Audio File
23.	.avi	Audio Video Interleave File
24.	.flv	Flash Video File
25.	.bmp	Bitmap Image File
26.	.gif	Graphical Interchange Format File
27.	.jpg	JPEG Image File
28.	.png	Portable Network Graphic File
29.	.psd	Adobe Photoshop Document File
30.	.pdf	Portable Document Format File
31.	.xls	Excel Spreadsheet
32.	.db, .dbf	Database File
33.	.mdb	Microsoft Access Database
34.	.sql	Structured Query Language Data File
35.	.pif	Program Information File
36.	.vb	VBScript File
37.	.wsf	Windows Script File
38.	.php	PHP Source Code File
39.	.css	Cascading Style Sheet
40.	.htm, .html	Hypertext Markup Language File

File Organization: The concept of file organization deals with the arrangement of records in the file and the procedure that is used to access the records in a file. It helps in efficient record access for a specific record access pattern. A file system provides various file organizations, so that the user or the program can select a file organization that best suits the requirements. The efficiency of any file processing system depends on the waiting time per record i.e the time since the request for the record is made by the processor to the time when the record becomes available for the processing. The basic file organization and access methods have been described below:

FILE ACCESS METHODS

The users use files for storing information of various types and the files may be accessed by the user to retrieve data from the files for any type of processing they wish to perform on the files. There are various methods through which the data from the files can be accessed and is known as the file access methods. There are variety of methods which can be used to access file and each has its own advantages and limitations. The user and the system may use the method; they feel to be fit for the particular application.

The common file access methods are:

1. Sequential Access.
2. Direct Access.
3. Index Sequential.
4. Access through Hashed File.

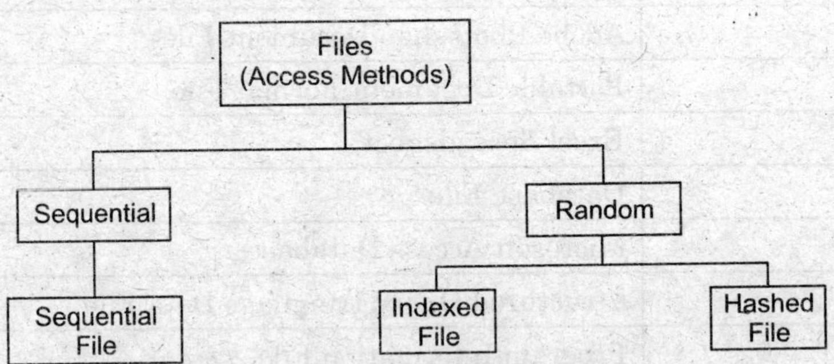

Figure 9.1: *Various File Access Methods*

Sequential Access Method

In this method the information in a file can be accessed sequentially only i.e from the beginning, one record at a time. To change the position in the file, it can be rewinded or forwarded by a number of records or can be reset to the beginning of the file. In the sequential files the records are stored in an ascending or descending sequence by the key field. The sequential file supports two types of operations: read the next or previous record, skip the next or previous record. This method was basically designed for magnetic tapes, which support this method only, but sequential access method also work well on the random access devices like magnetic disks. This is the simplest method for accessing information as records are accessed one after another sequentially only. To perform the read operation the next portion of the file is read and the pointer is incremented automatically. While a write operation appends the data to the end of the file and updates the pointer to the end of newly written material. This method is commonly used by the editors and compliers, which access the data in the sequential order.

Application: This method is useful when the records are to be accessed in a sequential fashion only. Like, the company is willing to prepare the payroll slips of all employees at the end of each month , then the records of all employee are to be fetched starting from the first employee to the last one in a sequential fashion.

A telephone company is to generate the telephone bills of all the customers at the end of the month, then the records of all customers from starting to end and depending upon their usage and tarrif plan chosen, the bills are to be generated one by one. For this to make possible, the sequential access is a good option.

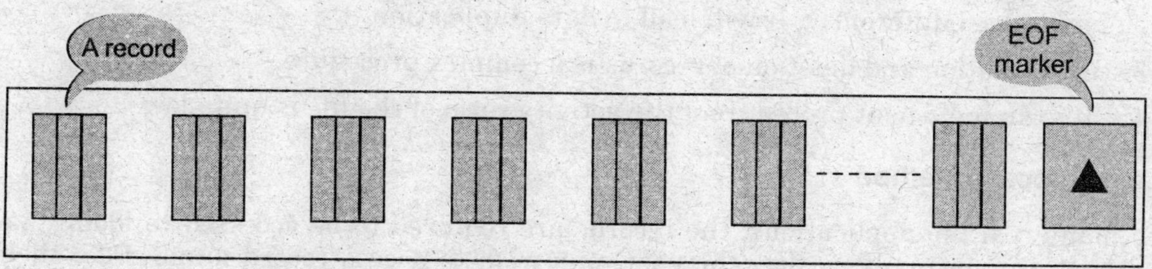

Figure 9.2: *Processing of Records in a Sequential File*

Implementation of Sequential Access

```
While Not EOF
{
Read the Next Record
Process the Record
}
```

Advantage

1. In case the users have to process each record, sequential access is more efficient and easier than random access.
2. The 'NEXT' record can be accessed quickly.
3. Best suited for batch processing systems when all records are to be accessed.
4. Binary Search can be applied in a sorted sequential file.

5. These files can be stored either on serial or direct access devices. Serial access devices are cheaper than direct access devices, so data can be stored economically.
6. It is the most efficient and economical file organization, if large number of records are to be updated at regular intervals like payroll, billing, generation of student mark sheets etc.

Limitations

1. In sequential files, the records can be accessed sequentially only, but in most of the real time applications, the data is to be accessed in random fashion. It is used in batch processing systems rather than in interactive systems.
2. This method suffers from the problem of data duplication. For Example, a user has stored student data in a student file as(rollno, name, marks obtained) and the user needs that the file to be sorted by rollno in ascending order and also require that the file to be sorted by marks in descending order. To satisfy both the needs two sequential files are to be created which will have same set of records but sequenced differently. It will lead to data duplication.
3. The addition and deletion of records is a complex procedure.
4. It is an inefficient procedure if the activity ratio of the file is quite low.

Direct Access Method

In many real life applications, the records are required to be accessed randomly i.e without any particular order, the user may wish to access record number 25, then record number 3 and then record number 78 and so on. This type of access is not possible through sequential access method, so the direct access method was invented which allows the records to be accessed directly, without any particular order. It establishes a relationship between the key used to identify a particular record and location of the record in the file. This method is basically designed for the disks, which allow the direct access to the data. This method is also known as relative access. In this method, file is made up of fixed length logical records that allow the user to read or write records in any order. File is viewed as a numbered sequence of blocks or records and these records are accessed directly without following any particular sequence. In this method, the file access includes the block number as a parameter, so we use read n, where n is the block number from where data is to be read or write n, where n is block where data is to be written. Just compare it with sequential access where we use read next and write next. The access to a record is independent of the record which was accessed prior to it. The direct access file may be used in a sequential fashion, by keeping track of the a variable ptr, which defines our current position, then sequential operations of a) reset, b) read next and c) write next can be performed as:

(a) ptr = 0,

(b) read ptr, ptr = ptr + 1,

(c) write ptr, ptrr = ptr + 1.

A relationship can be used to translate between the key values and physical addresses. The relationship, let it be R is a mapping function defined as:

R (Key Value) -> Address, from key values to the address in the file.

When a record is written in relationship function, the mapping function R is used to translate the key value of the record to an address where the record will be stored. And when the record is to be retrieved, the key value is given to the mapping function that translates it into an address, where the record has been stored.

Applications: This method is suitable to provide immediate access to large amount of data. Now a days, we come across huge sized data bases all around, when we wish to retrieve some particular record through a query, then we search for the block which contains the record information and that particular block is being read. Due to the feature of rapid access to any record directly, relative files are used in interactive processing.

For example: In a student information system, if we have recorded information about 1000 students and we wish to read the details of the student whose record has been stored at the location 854, then by using sequential access we need to access the records from 1to 853 first only then we will be able to access the record at 854. This is quite illogical and cumbersome also. But by using the direct access method we can directly point the pointer to the location number 854 and the data will be accessed at a much faster rate.

Considering the above example of a telephone company again, if we wish to access the record of a particular customer, then direct access will be a better option, lets us consider out of the customers records stored from location 1 to 20000, we wish to access the record of the customer whose data has been stored t the location 12500, then by using direct access the pointer will be pointed to that particular location only and the data stored at that vary location can be accessed.

Advantages of Direct Access Method

1. This method provides fast access to the records as any record can be accessed directly. Like as discussed earlier, if the user wishes to access a record number 100, he/she can access it directly, where as in the sequential access, the user has to visit the records from 0 to 99, to reach up to record number 100.
2. The records can be accessed sequentially by starting at first relative address & incrementing it by one to get to next record.
3. By using this method, the records can be updated more quickly than sequential files because records can be rewritten quickly to original addresses after modifications.
4. There is no need to preserve order of the records, so adding or deleting them takes very little time.

Limitations of Direct Access Methods

1. As the records are accessed in any random fashion, so random address calculation consumes CPU time.
2. If the applications require the sequential access of records, then direct access method is less efficient than sequential access method.
3. The address calculation method used to find the address of next record to be accessed is device dependent, moving the data from one device to another will result in the changes in address calculation formula.

Index Sequential Method

This method combines the best features of sequential & direct access. This method makes use of an index to access a particular record. The index is like a normal index we are familiar with, like an index in the front of the book which has the information about the location of various pages in the book, same way an index of the file will have the pointer to various blocks. To access an entry in the file, the user searches the index and then uses the pointer to access the file directly to find the desired entry. With large files, the index itself may become too large to be kept in the memory, then to solve this problem, an index for the index file is also created. The primary index file will contain pointer to the secondary index files, which in turn will point to the actual data items. Index file is a small file with only two fields:

- The key of the sequential file.
- The address of the corresponding record on the disk.

The Figure 9.3 given below show the snapshot of an index file.

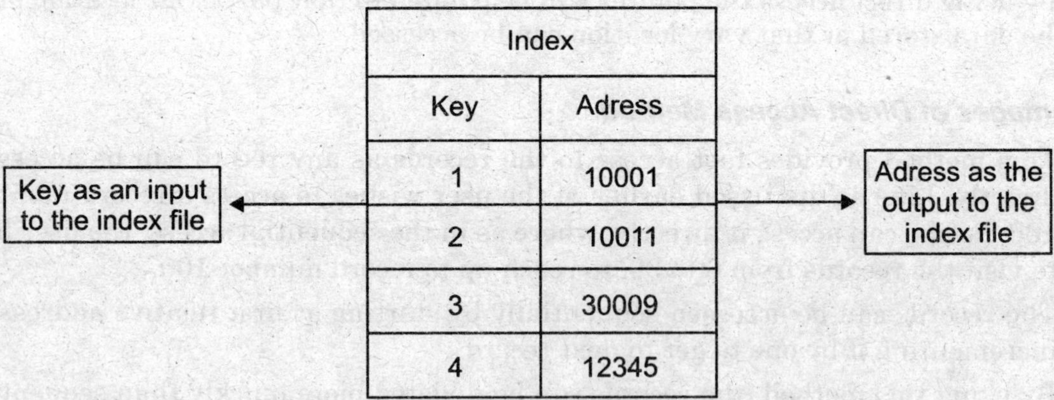

Figure 9.3: *Working of an Indexed Sequential File*

The indexes in this method are created & maintained through Indexed Sequential Access Method (ISAM) software package.

How to access a record in an Indexed File

- Load the entire index file into main memory.
- Search the index file to find the desired key.
- Retrieve the address of the record.
- Retrieve the data record by using the address.

How Indexed Files are implemented: Consider the index table given in Table 9.4

Table 9.4: An Index Table

Index Table	
Key Value	**Address**
12122	105
07091	001
12167	007
	009
	006
	010
34567	123

Let the user wish to access a record with the key value = 34567, then first of all, Index Table will be checked to find the address of key value, in this case it is 123, then the data file will be searched to extract the desired record. The table 9.5 given below is a data file.

Table 9.5: A Logical view of an indexed file

Address field	Key Value	Name	Age	DOB
001	07091			
002				
003				
004				
005				
006	34567			
007	12167			
105	12122			
	.			
123	34567			

Access through Hashed File

In this type of access method a hashed file uses a hash function to map the given key to the address. This eliminates the need for an extra index file and all other overheads associated with it. This technique is known as hashing. The basic purpose is not to search for the correct position of a record but is to compute the position within the array where item is to be stored. In hashing a large key value is translated into a reasonably small range of integers. The function that returns the position is called the hash function and the array is called a hash table. Hashing is used to index, search and hence retrieve items in a database as it is faster to find the item using the shorter hashed key than to find it by using the original value. It is a technique in which address of a data item is computed by executing a function on the search key value.

Let us consider there is a file F of n records with a set K of keys which uniquely determine the records in F.F is stored in the memory by a table T of m memory locations and that L is the set of memory addresses of the locations in T.

The key should be used to determine the address of a record but it must be modified to avoid wastage of memory space. This modification takes the form of a function H from set K of keys into set L of memory addresses. The Translated value of the key is called the Hash Code for the key and it is computed by some Hash Function

H: K → L is called a hash function.

It is a function which, when applied to the key, produces an integer which can be used as an address in a hash table. It is basically "Chopping Up "the Key and selecting certain bits to make up the hash code for that key.

1. **Hash Function**

Definition: It is a function (a mathematical formula) which, when applied to the key, produces an integer or an alphanumeric value which can be used as an address in a hash table.

H: K → L is called a hash function.

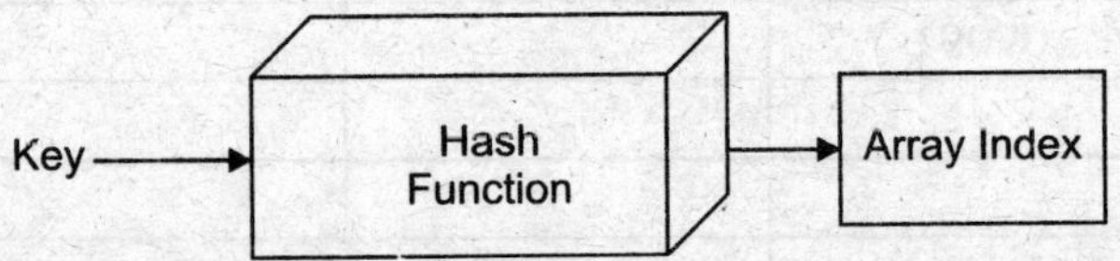

Figure 9.4: *Working of Hash Function*

Let us consider that we wish to access value 400 we can use some hash function that calculates its location

H (400) = 400 DIV 100 = 4

Therefore data is at 4th location and it takes O(1) time to find the key value.

The hash function H may not yield the distinct values, as it may happen that two different keys k1 and k2 will yield same hash address, this situation is known as collision.

Collision is defined as a condition when two or more keys produce the same hash location.

For Example: Suppose with 4 digit key, we want to point to or store data from 0-7 memory indexes. With hash function we will generate a one digit code that point to one of the location from 0-7.

Let the data set be x = 1055, 1492, 1776, 1812, 1918, 1945

The hash function is H(x) = (5*x mod 8)

For Input 1055, the hash address will be computed as:

H (1055) = (5*1055 mod 8) = (5275 mod 8) = 3

Diagrammatically,

0	1	2	3	4	5	6	7
			1055				

Where the values 1492 and 1812 will be addressed to? Both of these values point to same location i.e location number 4, resulting in collision.

0	1	2	3	4	5	6	7
1776			1055	1492 1812	1945	1918	

Method I: Division-Remainder Method

The basic idea of this approach is to divide a key value by an appropriate number, then use the remainder of the division as the computed hash value.

H(k) = k mod m if hash addresses are from 1 to m,

H(k) = k mod m + 1 if hash addresses are from 0 to m – 1

The number m should be a prime number or a number without small divisors, as it will minimize the number of collisions.

For Example: In an organization there are 70 employees, each employee is assigned a unique ID. But in Data Base it is required to store only two digits code. Therefore hash function is:

H (k) = k (mod m)

Let m = 97 i.e greatest prime number from 00 to 99

Let k = 3205, H (3205) = 3205 mod 97 = 4

k = 7148, H (7148) = 7148 mod 97 = 67

That means the data 3205 will be stored at location 4 and 7148 will be stored at location 67.

Method II: Mid Square Method

In this technique the key is squared, and then specified digits are extracted from the middle of the result to take the relative address. Digits are truncated from both sides and some middle digits are taken as address. Generally, 4th and fifth digits from right are chosen. The hash function will be:

$H(K) = l = K^2$

Let K = 3205 $H(K) = K^2$ = 10272025 = 72 i.e 3205 will be stored at 72.

K = 2345 $H(K) = K^2$ = 5499025 = 99 i.e 2345 will be stored at 99.

Method III: Folding Method

In this technique, the key K is chopped into a number of parts and add each part together. Truncate the carry if any.

H(K) = K1 + K2 + K3 + ... + Kn.

Let us consider the key value is K and assume that the target relative address will have 2 digits. The key is partitioned into 2 digits chunks.

H (3205) = 32 + 05 = 37,

H (7148) = 71 + 48 =119 → 19 (truncate higher order digit giving the relative address)

H (36416) = 3 64 16 → folded → 3+64+16= 83

Various Collision Resolution Strategies: The occurrence of a collision is almost inevitable. So we need to adopt some ways and means to resolve the collision, if it has occurred. The various collision resolution strategies are:

1. Linear Probing

If the table position given by the hashed key is already occupied, then move to the next available location. Let us consider a new record R with the key k is to be added to the memory table T, but that memory location with hash address H(k) = h is already filled. The concept of linear probing suggests that assign R to the first available location following T(h) which will be traced out by searching sequentially from the point where collision has occurred. This method is also known as:

Consecutive Spill Method. The linear probe uses the following hash function:

$H(k, i) = [h'(k) + i] \bmod m$ for i = 0, 1, 2...m – 1.

where m is the size of hash table

$h'(k) = k \bmod m$ is the basic hash function

i is the probe number.

For a given key k, the first slot probed is T [h′(k)]. The next slots are T[h′(k) + 1], T[h′(k) + 2], T[h′(k) + 3], and so on up to T[m – 1].

Example 1: Let us suppose with 4 digit key, we want to store data from 0-7 memory indexes. With hash function we will generate a one digit code that point to one of the location from 0-7.

Let x = 1055, 1492, 1776,1812,1918,1945

The hash function is: H(x) = (5*x mod 8)

If 1055 is to be stored, H (1055, 0) = (5*1055 mod 8) = 3

0	1	2	3	4	5	6	7
			1055				

Now if we want to store 1492, H (1492, 0) = (5 *1492 mod 8)

= (7460 mod 8) = 4

If we want to store 1812, H (1812, 0) = (5 *1812 mod 8)

= (9060 mod 8) = 4

0	1	2	3	4	5	6	7
1776			1055	1492 1812			

Clearly, both these values are hashing to the same location i.e 4, Therefore Collision has occurred.

It needs to be resolved by rehashing one value to some new location. The next free location available is 5. Therefore store 1812 at location 5.

It will be computed as h (1812, 1) = (5*1812 mod 8 + 1) = 4 + 1 =5

Advantages

1. This technique is conceptually easy.
2. All elements are available in the contiguous memory locations.
3. The speed of data retrieval is good as only sequential search is to be implemented.

Disadvantages

1. The records tend to cluster around the elements that produce collision. This clustering increases the average search time for a record.
2. As the number of collisions increases, the distance from the array index computed by hash function and the actual location of the element increases, which result in the increase of search time.
3. The array is of fixed size, i.e static memory allocation is present.

2. Closed Address Hashing

It is also called chained hashing. In this case two tables are maintained in the memory. A chained hash table is a table of linked lists. Each entry in the hash table

H[L] is a linked list. i.e each element contains the record and along with that it has an additional field LINK which is used so that all records with the same hash address may be linked in the form of a linked list. Reconsider the Example I, now both the values 1492 and 1812, which has same has address, will be stored with same hash address 4 in the form of a linked list.

0	1	2	3	4	5	6	7
1776			1055	1492	1918	1945	
				1812			

Figure 9.5: *Working of Chained Hashing*

Advantages of Chained Hashing

1. Each cluster is maintained as a separate list.
2. Size of table is not required to be much greater than the number of items.
3. Insertion and deletion of elements is simple.
4. Searching of elements will require lesser time as compared to linear probing. (see example given below).
5. This technique handles collisions very well.

Disadvantages

1. It consumes more space if the number of records to be stored is small.

CRITERIAS FOR THE SELECTION OF AN ACCESS METHOD

1. **Rapid Access:** It deals with the time required to access a particular file. Normally user wishes to access data as early as possible. So the method which will provide rapid access will be selected.
2. **Activity of File:** It deals with frequency with which the file is accessed and percentage of records processed during a given run.
3. **Economy of Storåge:** The cost of storing data and hence the total file system is the another criteria that is kept into mind, while selecting a particular file system, as the cost of maintaining indexed sequential file will be more as compared to the simple direct access method.
4. **Ease of update:** The user may wish to access data in the files for the updation operation also, and this operation should be done with the minimum overhead. Updation is easier and less costly in the direct access and index sequential access methods but is costly and time consuming in sequential access.
5. **Response time:** Another criteria for the choice of file access method is the response time, lesser the response time better will be the method. Sequential

Access will take more time to retrieve the data as compared to the other methods discussed above.

6. **Reliability:** The access method should not interfere with the data stored in the files and only the required data should be searched and accessed.
7. **Security and Integrity:** While accessing a particular file using a particular access method, the data stored in the other files should not be hampered and should remain safe and secure.

FILE PROTECTION

File system contains data of the user or of the organization. In today's information driven world, the data is considered as the most important asset of the organization, so its protection is of paramount importance. It is normally said the persons or the organizations having right access to the right data and at the right time will rule the world. The files containing the user data needs to be protected from the physical harm and the improper access.

Types of threats to files

1. Physical Threats: The files can be damaged by hardware problems, like errors in reading and writing the data, power failures, head crashes, temperature variations.
2. Human Threats: The threats from the authorized access by the intruders into the file system.
3. Operating System Threats: The malfunctioning in the operating system may bring the file system to a halt.
4. Network Threats: The files may be harmed during the transmission in the network or some virus entered into the system through network may harm the file system of the user.

In order to protect the file system, some protection mechanism is required to provide a controlled access to the files. Access request made by the user may be permitted or may be denied, depending upon the authorization rights provided to the user. All of the operations discussed in the table can be controlled.

The file protection is implemented by maintaining the authentication and authorization. The authentication deals with identifying the right person whereas the authorization deals with providing right access to right data.

The authentication of the user means that the user accessing the system an d hence the file system is authorized to do so. It basically deals with the physical access to the system and file system, the various methods for the authentication of the user are:

(a) Password and User id:

(b) Physical Security through Identity Cards:

(c) Use of Magnetic Strips
(d) Use of Biometric Devices
(e) Use of Voice Recognition Systems.

Methods of Access Control

The authorization to the user to access a particular file deals with finding out that whether the user has the sufficient privileges to access the file or not. Each file management system has own file access control method. The various methods in this category are:

(a) Access Control Matrix
(b) Access Control Lists
(c) Capability Lists
(d) Lockword control.

This is made possible by the use of access control list or also known as access matrix.

(a) Access Matrix: An access matrix is associated with each file and directory. It contains the name of the users and type of access allowed for each user. Whenever a user tries to access a file, then the operating system checks this matrix to find out whether the user has the right to access the file in the mode requested. If the number of users are more, then the various users of the system can be combined into the following groups:

- System: It includes the system personnel with unlimited access to all files.
- Owner: The user who created the file is called the owner of the file.
- Group: A set of users who are sharing the file and need similar access is a group.
- World: All other users not included in the first two categories, constitute the world.

Let us consider that a person A has created a file named as operating, then that person will be called as the owner of the file.

If this user has given the permission to execute –only permission to some particular set of users, then all the users constitute a group and all will have same set of rights.

All the other possible users will fall into the category of the World and will have only the read access to the file.

This access control list is maintained by the administrator or the file owner.

In matrix each column identifies a user & each row identifies a file.

Intersection of row & column has access rights for that user to that file.

Upon inspecting the Figure 9.6, we come to know that the User I has read, write, execute and delete access for the file 1, whereas user 2 has just the access of read and execute on the file 2.

	User 1	User 2	User 3	User 4	User 5
File 1	RWED	R-E-	----	RWE-	--E-
File 2	----	R-E-	R-E-	--E-	----
File 3	----	RWED	----	--E-	----
File 4	R-E-	----	----	----	RWED
File 5	----	----	----	----	RWED

R = Read Access

W = Write Access

E = Execute Access

D = Delete Access

- = Access Not Allowed

Figure 9.6: *An Access Matrix*

If the number of user and the number of users are large in number then following methods can be used to shorten list:

1. The users can be grouped together in any of the categories: System, Owner, Group or the World. Rather than mentioning each and every user individually, the users with the similar type of access are grouped together and the entry for the whole group is made once only.
2. Only those who may use file are named; those denied any access are grouped under global heading such as WORLD. Which has been shown below in Figure 9.7.

File	Access
File 1	USER1 (RWED), USER2 (R-E-), USER4 (RWE-), USER5 (--E-), WORLD (----)
File 2	USER2(R-E-), USER3 (R-E-), USER4 (--E-), WORLD (----)
File 3	USER2(RWED), USER4 (--E-), WORLD (----)
File 4	USER1(R-E-), USER5(RWED), WORLD(----)
File 5	USER5(RWED), WORLD (----)

Another way to maintain the matrix is called access control list,

Figure 9.7: *An Access Control List*

3. **Capability Lists:** This is another alternative way to store the access control information, in this case the list shows every user and files which the user can access and in what modes. It requires less storage space than an access control

matrix. It is easier to maintain than an access control list when users are added or deleted from system. A capability list has been shown in the Figure 9.8 given below.

User	Access
User1	File1 (RWED), File4 (R-E-)
User2	File1 (R-E-), File2 (R-E-), File3 (RWED)
User3	File2 (R-E-)
User4	File1 (RWE-), File2 (--E-), File3 (--E-)
User5	File1 (--E-), File4 (RWED), File5 (RWED) \s

Figure 9.8: *A Capability List*

4. **Lockword Control:** Another way of protection is the use of Lockword that is similar to a password. A password is a secret piece of information used to establish the identity of the users. When the file is created, owner protects it via Lockword. It is stored in the directory but is not revealed with directory listing. If a user wishes to access a protected file, then the user needs to provide the correct lockword. It requires smallest amount of storage space for the file protection. If the passwords are chosen randomly and are changed frequently, then it can be an effective method to limit the file access only to the authorized users. But this scheme has many limitations also, as if the user will assign a password to each file then the number of passwords will be very large, making it difficult to remember or manage them, another disadvantage is that anyone who knows it can read, write, delete or execute the file. It can be guessed by hackers and can be used for unauthorized access. Some systems allow the password to be given on directory rather than on a file, another alternative is to provide same password to all files, which make the protection on all – or - nothing basis.

DIRECTORY STRUCTURE

As the amount of data to be stored in the system is increasing day by day, hence the number of files are also becoming un- manageable. So there is a need of some mechanism to manage these all files and keeping track of all files, so that these can be accessed easily whenever it is required. Apart from this in multiuser environment prevailing all around, the user wishes to name the files without being constrained by the file names used by the other users i.e they need freedom to name the files as per their wish and secondly, they wish to share the files of each other but in the constrained fashion only. To perform this task for the users, the operating system provide directories, which are again treated as the files. The complete information about the files is kept in the directories also known as device directory. The directory records complete information of the files such as name, location, size, type and access control information for all the files stored in the memory. The use of directory is important to manage the files. The files of a particular user or file pertaining to a particular function can be grouped together and can be stored together in a group. The directory will contain the information about the files and also a pointer to location where file is stored.

The information stored in a directory

- Name
- Type
- Address.
- Current Length.
- Maximum Length.
- Date of Creation.
- Date of last access.
- Date of last updation.
- Owner Information: Id, Name, Group.
- Protection Information

Directory Operations

The various operations possible on a directory are mentioned below in the table 9.6. These are executed by a number of system calls available in the operating system:

Table 9.6 Description of Various Directory Operations

S.No	Operation	Description
1.	Create	This operation is used to create a directory. It is a two step process: Space for the directory is to be searched It is empty in the beginning except for . and .. which are automatically put in the directory by the system and subsequently the user will keep on adding files to the directory created.
2.	Open	This operation is used to open a directory. As before using a directory for reading purpose, it must be opened. It will show all the files stored in this particular directory. This operation is also known as 'listing a directory'.
3.	Close	This operation is used to close the directory when it is not required any more.
4.	Write	This operation is used to write data into a directory. Given the name of the directory in which file is to be stored, the system searches for the named directory and the data i.e the information about the file is stored in it.

S.No	Operation	Description
5.	Read	This operation is used to read data from a directory. Given the name of the directory from which data is to be read i.e file is to be searched, the system searches for that directory and hence the particular file is searched subsequently.
6.	Delete	This operation is used to delete a directory only an empty directory can be deleted. Here the directory containing the . and .. are considered as empty, But it contains other subdirectories or files then they must be deleted first to delete the directory.
7.	Rename	This operation is used to rename the directories, as we use the similar operation to rename the files.
8.	Link	This system call specifies an existing file and path name, and creates a link from the existing file to the name specified by the path. By doing so the same file may exist in more than one directories.
9.	Unlink	This operation is used to unlink a file from the present directory. If the file being unlinked is present in only one directory, then it is removed from the file system, but if the file is present in multiple directories, then path specified by the current link is removed and other links of the file remain as such.
10.	Traverse	This operation is used to enable the user to visit and access every directory and every file in the directory structure.

Methods for defining the Logical Structure of Directories

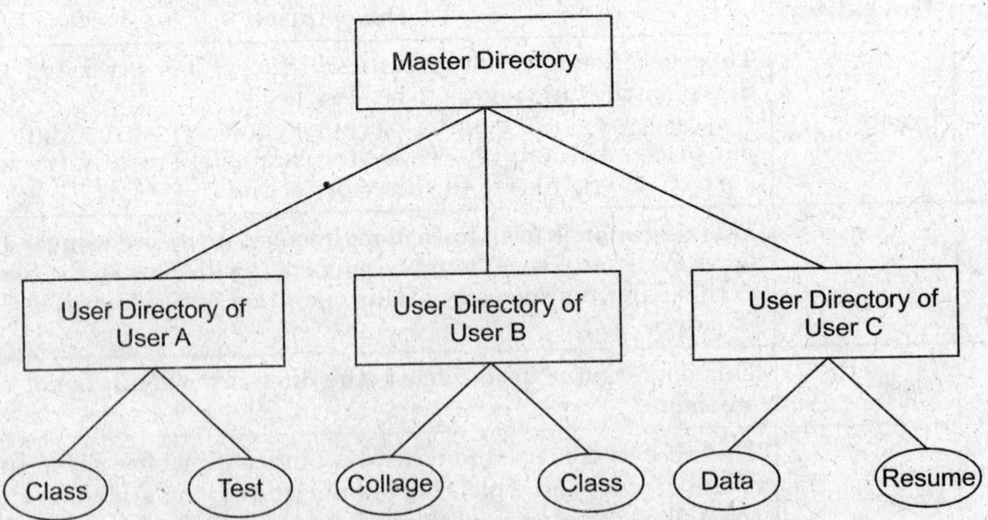

Figure 9.9: *General Structure for Directory Implementation*

The logical structure i.e the way in which the directories and subdirectories and hence the files in them are managed. It varies from system to system. The basic directory structure implementation has been shown in the Figure 9.9 below, here directory is represented by a rectangle and the files are represented by the circles. Figure shows that there are two types of directories: User Directory which contains information about all files owned by a user, and master directory contains information about all user directories of all authorized users of the system. Each entry in master directory contains a pair (userid, UD pointer). Users A and B both have created a file name class. The general directory structure has been shown in the Figure 9.9 given below.

But the most common directory structures are:

Single Level Directory

This is the simplest directory structure. In this case, all files are contained in the same directory. This method is easy to understand and maintain. The figure 9.10 given below show the single level directory structure.

Advantages

1. Easy to understand and maintain.

Limitations

1. If a user has number of files, then the user needs to provide unique name to all of them, it is really a difficult task to name all files with unique names and then to remember them is even more difficult.
2. If multiple users are working on the system, then all the users have to provide unique names to all the files. Two different users cannot give the same name to their files. For example: All the users creating their first program in C as first. c, because normally file names are given to reflect the file contents only. Then unique file name rule is violated.

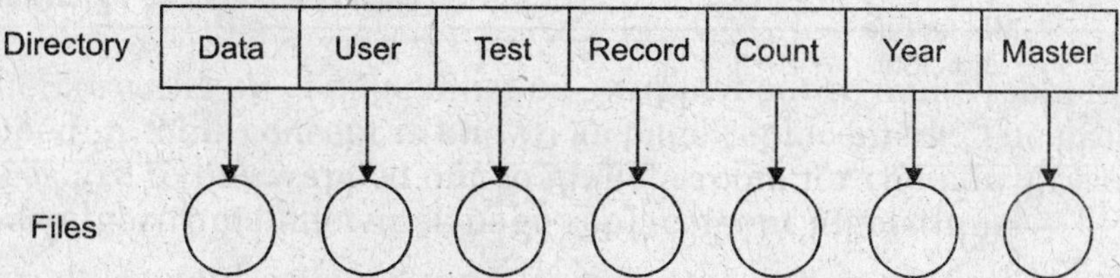

Figure 9.10: *Single Level Directory Structure*

Two Level Directory Structure

In this scheme separate directory for each user is maintained. All the UFD's are stored under the control of Master File Directory(MFD). Each MFD is indexed by the user name or account number and each entry points to the UFD of that user. Whenever the user logs in, the MFD is searched to find the entry of UFD. The various characteristics of two level directory structure are:

1. Each user has his own User File directory(UFD).
2. All UFD's are similar in structure, but contain file of a single user only.
3. To search for the entry of a file then MFD is searched first to find the corresponding entry of UFD and in the UFD of that user the desired file is searched.
4. Different users may have files with the same name in their own UFD.

To create a file for a particular user, the operating system searches the UFD of that user to ensure that the file with this name does not exist earlier in the UFD of that user.

To delete a file, the operating system looks in to the UFD of that user only. It ensures that the file of another user residing in his own UFD with the same name is not deleted even by mistake. Figure 9.11 shows a two level directory structure.

For Example: The user A and user B has their own UFD's as UFDA and UFDB and both of them can create the file with name india,

If user A issues a command to delete his file named as india, then operating system ensures that the file india in UFDA is deleted and the file india in UFDB remain secure as such.

The Figure 9.11 given below the structure of Two level directory structure. The structure shows that there will be a Master File Directory(MFD), containing the information about all the users and corresponding to each entry in MFD, there will be User File directory UFD of that user, which has the information about the files of that user only. Here the two users may have files with similar names. This two level directory structure can be visualized as a tree of height 2. The root of the tree is the master file directory and its children are the various user file directories and their children are the files in that particular UFD.

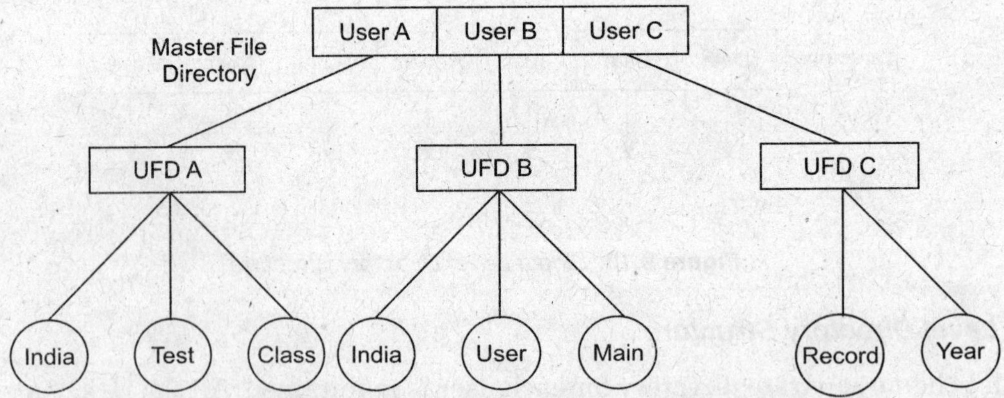

Figure 9.11: *Two Level Directory Structure*

Advantages

1. Each user has the separate space i.e their own directory to store their own directories and files.
2. Two different users can have files with the same name, hence solves the name collision problem present in the single level directory structure.
3. This system ensures isolation when users are working on independent tasks.

Limitations

1. This system does not allow the users to share each others data, which is a disadvantage if two user wish to work on the same file.
2. If this type of access is to be allowed then the users must give both the user name and the file name. This combination of user name and file name is termed as the path name. Like in the example given above the if user A wish to access the file india, he can access it directly, but if wish to access the file of user B, then he has to mention the complete path as /UFDB/india.

Tree Structured Directory

As we have visualized a two level directory structure as a two level tree, then it can be extended to a tree of arbitrary height. It will allow the users to create their own subdirectories and hence files in those subdirectories and more over these subdirectories and hence the files in them can be managed by the respective users directly. It is most common method for directory organization and is used by almost all operating systems. The various characteristics of this type of structure are:

1. Every file has its unique path from the root to that particular file. The root directory will have sub-directories which is quite similar to a file, but its structure is different from the file (as discussed early in the structure of the files and directories). Whereas all directories have same internal format and one special bit in each directory is reserved to depict whether it is a directory or a file,

If this bit = 0, then it is a file and

bit = 1, then it is a directory.

2. Each user has a current directory also known as the working directory. It contains all the files which are being used by the user at present. If a request to search a file is made, then first of all the current directory is searched for the file and if file is not present there then the user will specify the path name to the desired location or can change the directory to the directory containing that file. This operation is performed by the change directory (cd) system call.
3. The path names in the tree structure can be of two types:
   (a) Absolute path names:
   (b) Relative path names.

(c) The absolute path names begin at the root and moves to the desired file, passing through various subdirectories in the path.

(d) The relative path names define the path from the current directory to the desired file.

4. The new files can be created in the current directory only. As the users can create their own subdirectories, so they can impose a structure of their own choice. They may create separate structure for different directories and files.

5. If the user wish to delete a directory in tree structured directory, then

   (a) If the directory is empty, then it can be deleted directly and its entry in the parent directory is deleted.

   (b) If the directory is not empty and it contains some files or subdirectories, then the directory will be deleted only if the files in that directory are deleted first and if the directory contains subdirectories then this procedure is applied to them recursively(that first files in the subdirectories are deleted first and then the subdirectories are deleted in turn).

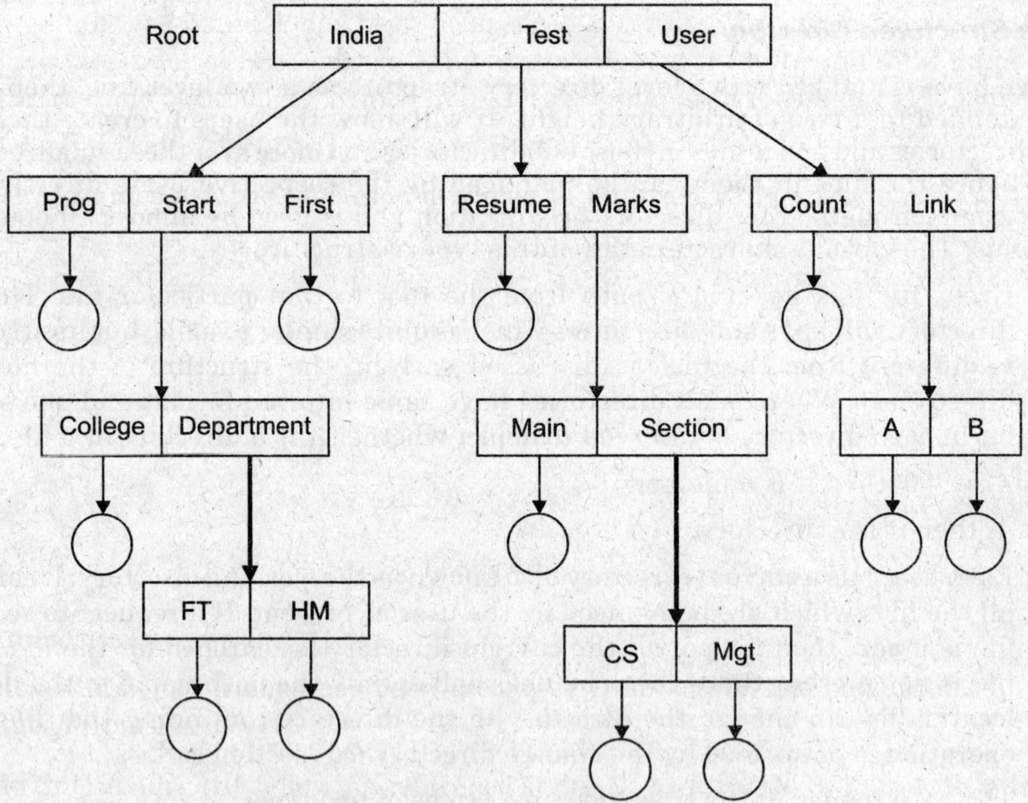

Figure 9.12: *hTree Structured Directory*

(c) Some operating systems also provide an option in which, whenever a command to delete a directory is made then all the subdirectories and files in this directory are deleted i.e the whole directory structure is deleted in one go. This option is quite easy but is very dangerous as may lead to loss of large amount of data.

6. In tree structured directory, the users can access their own files as well as the files of the other users. For doing so both the schemes of absolute path and relative paths can be used. The tree structure

Acyclic Graph Directory

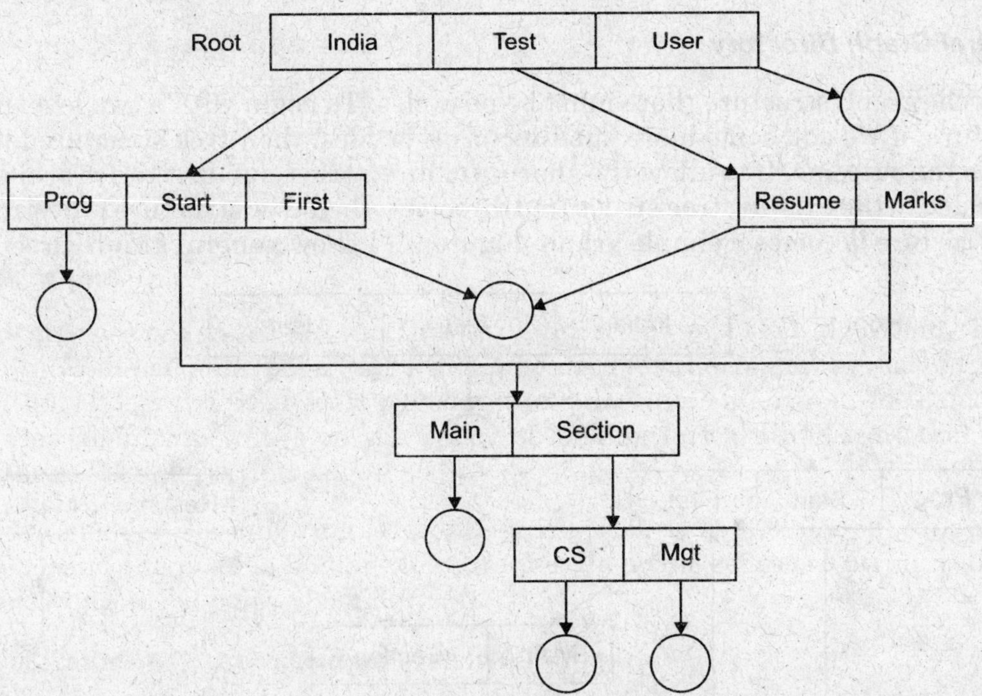

Figure 9.13: *Acyclic Graph Directory*

The tree structure directories do not allow the sharing of files and directories. But there are scenarios in which the two different users who are working on the joint project then they will wish to share the files with each other. The files associated with the joint project can be stored in the subdirectory, separating from the other projects, but both users wish to work on that and want that file should be in their own subdirectories, that means the common subdirectory should be shared. This does not mean that there will be two copies of the same file, rather the common copy will be shared by both the users and changes made by one will be visible to all users sharing that file. If a user has created a new file in the shared subdirectory then it will be visible to all the users immediately. So the acyclic graph directory, allow directories to have shared subdirectories and files. The files to be shared by the users may be put together in one directory and user file directory of all the users will have this directory of shared files as a subdirectory.

The Figure 9.13 given below show the structure of Acyclic Graph Directory.

This directory structure provides flexibility but is complex for the implementation. The biggest problem in this case is that a file may have multiple absolute path names. So a single shared file may be traversed more than once. Another problem is with the deletion of the shared files or subdirectories, when the space allocated to shared file will be considered as deallocated and hence can be used. If the space is freed if any one deletes the file, then it will leave dangling pointers to the non existent file. Another approach is to retain the file till all the references to the file are not deleted.

General Graph Directory

In acyclic graph structure there must be no cycles. To begin with a two level directory structure, if we add some more subdirectories or files, then tree structured directory will be the outcome. If to allow the sharing of directories, subdirectories or files , links are added to the existing tree structured directory, then tree structure is destroyed and the structure becomes a simple graph. Figure 9.14 show general graph directory.

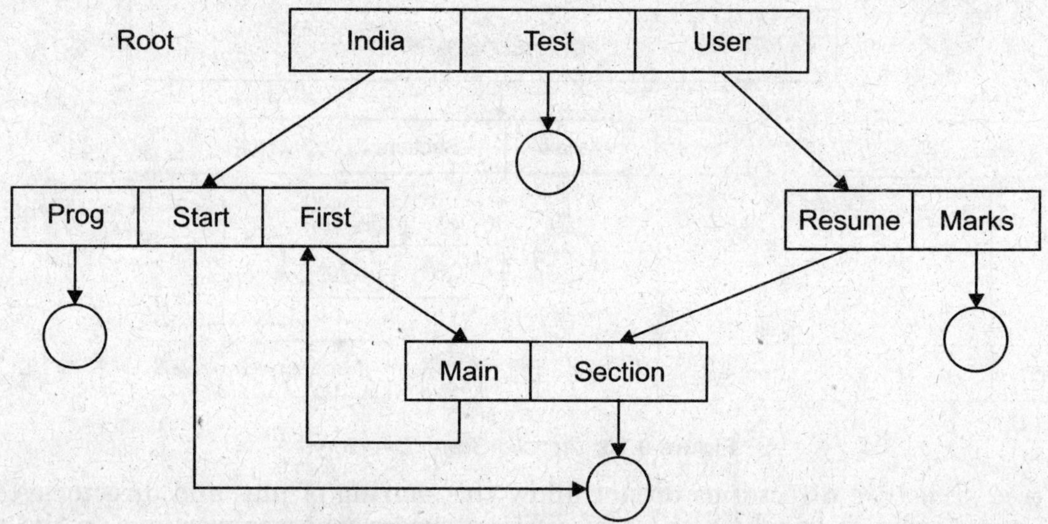

Figure 9.14: *General Graph Directory*

FILE ALLOCATION METHODS

The file system management module is responsible for the creation and management of files, directories and subdirectories as discussed in the previous section. Another major job is to allocate space for these files and directories in the computer system's memory so that the disk space is utilized effectively and files can be accessed quickly.

The view of file and directory management discussed till now deals with the user's view of the file system(which included the naming of files and directories, what operations are possible on them, how the file and directory structure will look alike), the another view is the implementer's view which considers that how the disk space is managed. The various methods used for allocating disk space are:

Contiguous Allocation

This is the simplest method for allocating the disk space for storing the files. In this method files are stored in the contiguous blocks on the disk. The disk addresses allocated follow a linear order. The blocks are accessed one after another, in a sequential fashion. This allocation scheme is defined by the disk address and the length of the first block. If a file is n blocks long, and starts at location b, then it occupies blocks b, b+1, b+2... ....b + n – 1. The directory entry will just store the address of the starting block and the length of the area allocated for this file. As shown in the Figure 9.15(a) given below, the file allocation table show the allocation of files A, B, C, D and E, for file A the size of the block is 3 and the starting address is given as 2, so the blocks 2 to 4 have been allocated to file A and file B need 5 blocks and the starting address is 9, so the blocks 9 to 13 have been allocated to file B. in this example the blocks have been allocated randomly and it may lead to the problem of external fragmentation, as the memory space has been divided in to small memory chunks. But if the requirement of space is known in advance then the allocation can be done as shown in the Figure 9.15(b).

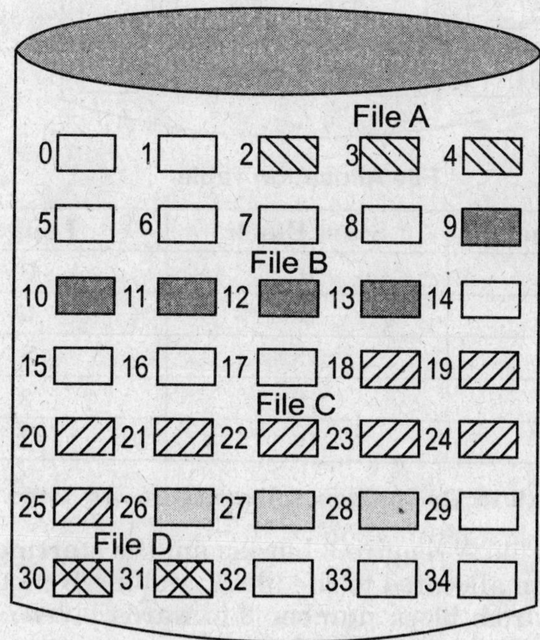

File Allocation Table

File Name	Start Block	Length
File A	2	3
File B	9	5
File C	18	8
File D	30	2
File E	26	3

(a) Contiguous Allocation of Disk Space.

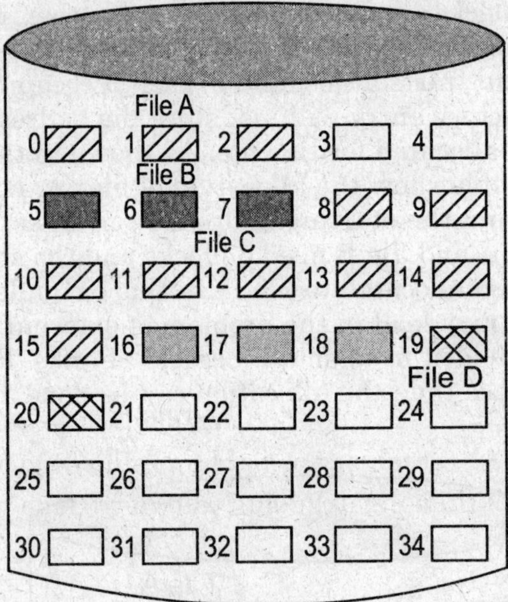

File Allocation Table

File Name	Start Block	Length
File A	0	3
File B	3	5
File C	18	8
File D	19	2
File E	16	3

Figure 9.15: *(b) Contiguous Allocation of Disk Space.*

In Figure 9.15(b) the file A require 3 blocks and the starting address is 0, so the blocks 0, 1 and 2 have been allocated to the file A, and file B require 5 blocks and the next free blocks starting from block number 3 onwards i.e the blocks 3,4,5,6 and 7 have been allocated to file B. by doing so the problem of external fragmentation can be avoided.

Advantages

1. This method is simple to implement because the blocks of a file can be accessed by remembering the disk address of the first block occupied by the file only, as all other block can be accessed just by incrementing the address by 1.
2. The performance of the system will be good as the entire file can be read from the disk in a single operation leading to minimal head movement.

Disadvantages

1. The first major problem in the contiguous allocation method is to find the space for the first free block in the memory. If the file to be stored is of the length n, then the operating system searches for n contiguous free blocks in the memory and allocates them for the file storage. The various strategies for this are:
   (a) First – Fit – This method allocates the first available block of size n.
   (b) Best –Fit – This method allocates the block of size equal to n. It requires searching the entire disk till the block with size n is not found.
   (c) Worst- Fit-This method allocates any block of size greater than n.

   Both first fit and best fit are more efficient than worst-fit in terms of time and storage utilization, first-fit and best-fit are not good, and in terms of the speed the first-fit is better.
2. Another problem is that it is not feasible to know the size of the file at the time of its creation and hence it will be difficult to predict the space required by the file. For example: a file is created to keep a record of the various users logging in to the system, in that case we are not able to predict the exact number of users who will log into the system and the number of records in the file and hence the size of the file will keep on growing and the user will not be able to predict the size in the beginning. But in some cases, like we are copying data from one place to other, then the is known while we are copying the file, so the amount of the space required for storing it to the new location will be known in advance.

   If the user will overestimate the space requirement, then the problem of internal fragmentation will exist.(as discussed below).
3. The third problem with contiguous allocation method is of external fragmentation. In the file system, the files are created every now and then and hence the space is allocated and de-allocated as and when required. Due to which the space is broken down into the little pieces. It becomes a problem when the largest piece of memory space is not sufficient to store the data, but the total space for the storage of data is available. That means enough disk space exists to satisfy a request, but it is not contiguous.

   For example: In the memory snapshot given below in Figure 9.16, the program A and B have been allocated a space of 10 kb and 20 kb respectively, and program C of size 15 kb needs to be stored, but this request will not be fulfilled as a contiguous memory space of 15 kb is not available, although a memory space of 15 kb is lying free in a scattered manner, it is the problem of external fragmentation.

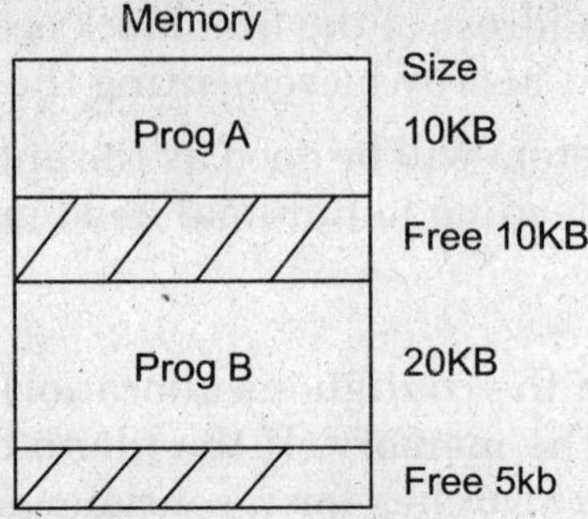

Figure 9.16: *External Fragmentation*

4. Another problem is the problem of internal fragmentation, it exists only if the allocation has been done with first –fit or worst-fit, in these cases the first block of the size >= the required space, or any block of the size >= the required space, is allocated. Then some of the allocated space will always be free, leading to the problem of the internal fragmentation. The space in an allocated block may be lying free whereas the other requests for the space cannot be entertained due to non-availability of free space. Let us consider an example given in the Figure 9.17 given below, The total disk space available to us for storing the data is 60KB and the user wish to store two files A of size 10KB and B of size 20KB and the system has allocated a space of 15K for storing the file A and 30KB for storing the file B(as the operating system has followed the first-fit or worst fit strategies). Now the user wish to store a file C with size 20KB, this request will not be entertained, as the system has only 15 KB of free space, where as a space of 5KB and 10KB is available in the allocation of file A and B respectively. This fragmentation of the memory space is called as the internal fragmentation, where memory space is fragmented into pieces internally.

To overcome these problems, some operating systems use a modified allocation strategy, in which a particular amount of space is allocated in the beginning, when it is found that this space is not sufficient, then another block of contiguous space, also known as chunk is allocated and is added to initial allocation. The location of the file is then recorded as the address of the initial allocation and address of the block allocated later on. The user can predict the size of the extent. But this solution is still have the problem of internal fragmentation, if the extents allocated are too large and the external fragmentation will be present as the extents of varying sizes are allocated and deallocated.

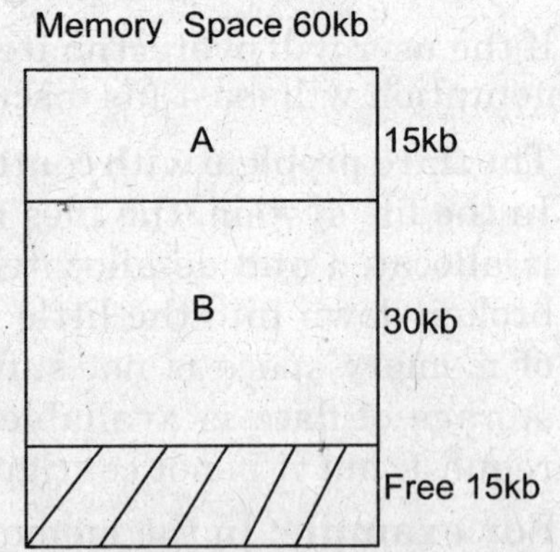

Figure 9.17: *Internal Fragmentation*

Linked Allocation

This method overcomes the problems of contiguous allocation. In this method the file is stored as the link list of disk blocks. These blocks may be scattered anywhere on the disk. The directory contains the pointer to the first and the last block of the file. Each block contains a pointer to the next block. Each block divides its total available space into two parts: one part is used to store the data and the other part stores a pointer to the next block. For example, as shown in the Figure 9.18(a) given below, that there is a file with 5 blocks and the starting address is 1, so the file blocks allocated to file A start with block 1 and the next block allocated is block number 8 and then the pointer points to block number 3 and then to block number 14 and the last block allocated is 28 and this block contains the Null Pointer which shows that this is the last block.

The read operation is quite simple as the user starts with the first block and then traverses block to block till the end of file is not encountered.

For write operation, a free block is found by free space management technique and the new data is written into this block and this new block is then linked to the end of the file.

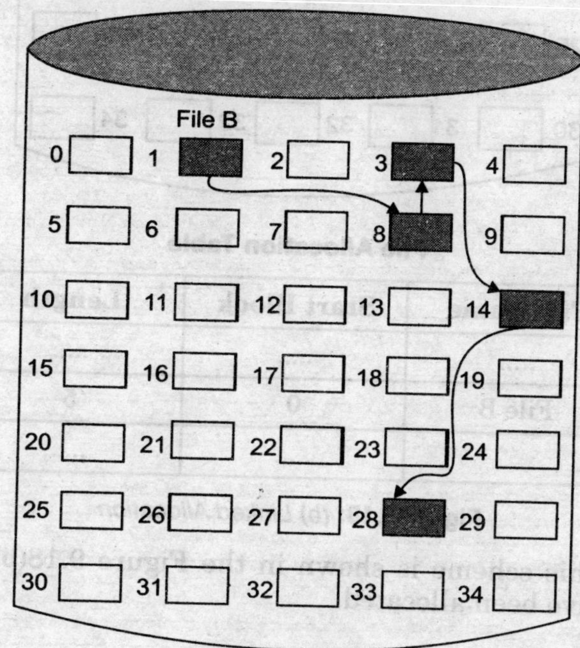

File Allocation Table

File Name	Start Block	Length
.....	.....	.....
File B	1	5
.....	.....	.....

(a) Linked Allocation

File Allocation Table

File Name	Start Block	Length
.....	.....	.....
File B	0	5
.....	.....	.....

Figure 9.18: *(b) Linked Allocation*

Another variant to this scheme is shown in the Figure 9.18(b) in which the blocks consecutive blocks have been allocated.

Advantages

1. There is no need to find contiguous blocks of the required size.
2. The size of the file need not to be known in advance, the size can grow dynamically at the run time.
3. There will be no external fragmentation, as any free block available on the disk can be used to store the data.
4. There will no internal fragmentation, as blocks of equal size are allocated one by one only.

Disadvantages

1. This method is not suitable for direct access, as if we wish to access ith block of a file directly, it is not possible as the user have to start with the first block and then to traverse till the ith block.
2. Another disadvantage is the space allocation for storing the pointers. As each block stores the information and pointer to the next block, then space for storing pointers is just a wastage of storage space.
3. A bug in operating system or a disk failure may result in pointers being lost or damaged. Due to which the system may pick a wrong pointer, which may lead to linking to some another file or even to a free block.

Indexed Allocation Method

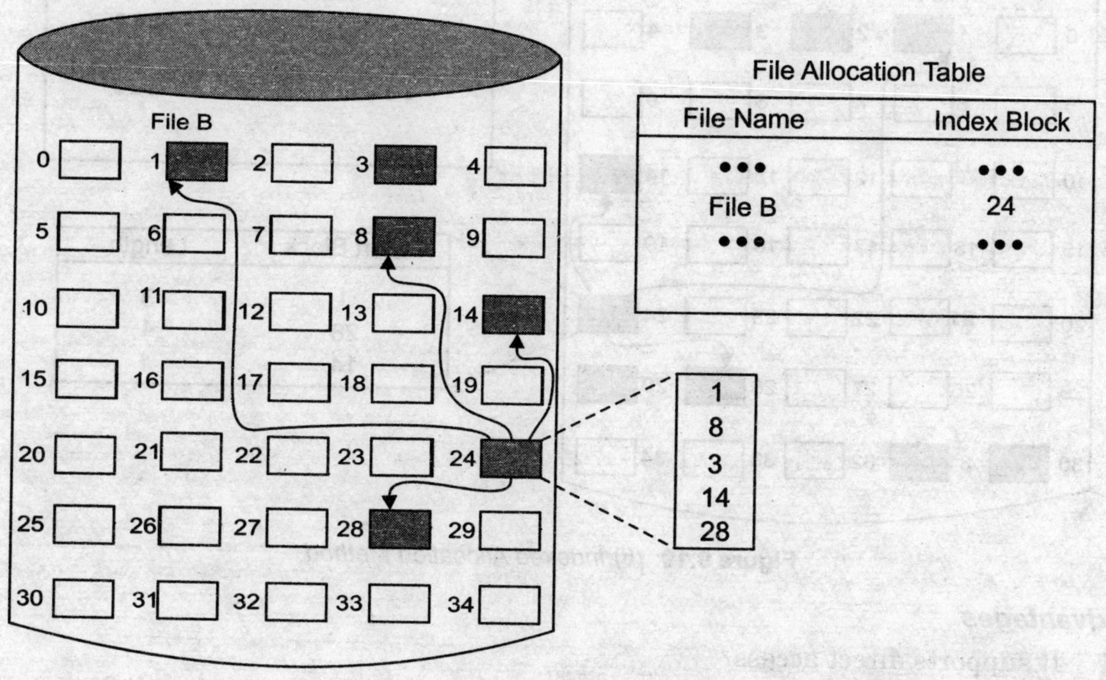

(a) Indexed Allocation Method

The two methods discussed above have some limitations, which are solved with the indexed allocation method. The linked allocation method does not support direct access as blocks and the pointers to the blocks are scattered all over the disk and needs to be accessed in a particular order only. Indexed allocation solves this problem by bringing all pointers together into one block, called the index block. In this method, each file will have its own index block, which is an array of disk block addresses. The directory stores the address of the index block. The ith entry in the index block points to the ith block of the file. To read the ith block, the user uses the pointer in the ith index block entry to find and read the desired block. Figure 9.19(a) given below show an indexed allocation method. The file B has an index block at the location 24 and this block has the details about the allocation of blocks, moving to the index block i.e block number 24, it has the list of allocated blocks as 1, 8, 3, 14 and 28.

Another variant to this scheme is that if a group of blocks are allocated then the index table will have the details about the number of blocks to be allocated to a single file and the starting address of the block. This scheme has been shown in Figure 9.19(b) where the file Allocation table show that the index block is at the location 24, and this index block placed at the location 24 has the details about the various block allocated to the file.

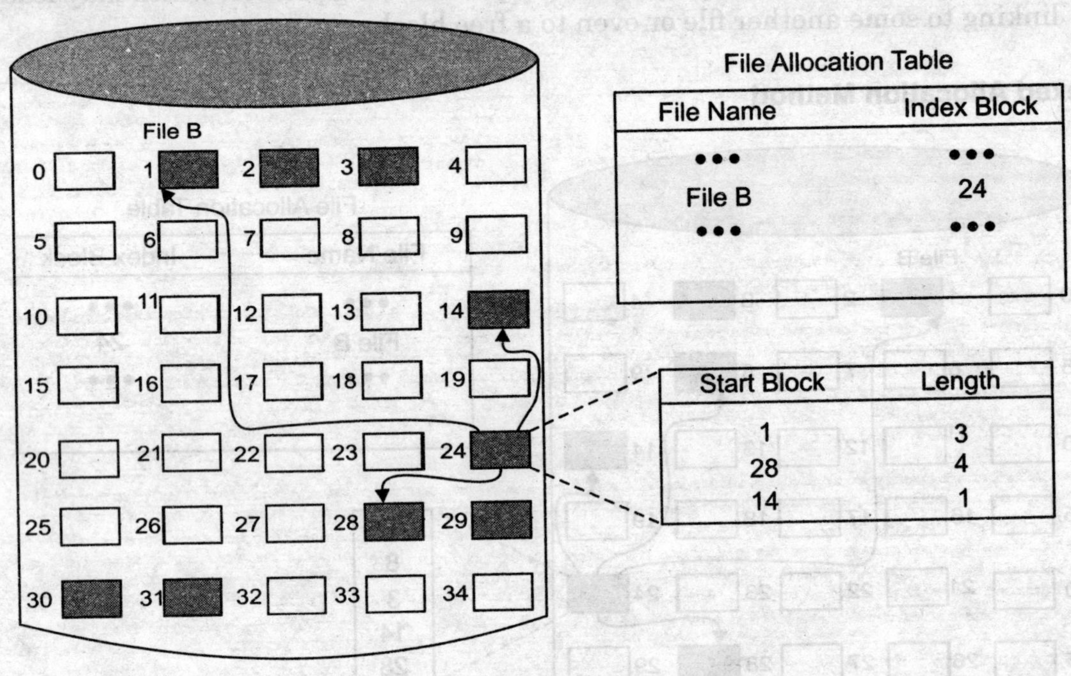

Figure 9.19: *(b) Indexed Allocation Method*

Advantages

1. It supports direct access.
2. No external fragmentation exists, as any free block on the disk may be allocated.
3. No internal fragmentation will exist, as the block of equal size are allocated one at a time.
4. This method also supports sequential access.

Disadvantages

1. The pointer overhead will be there, rather it is more than the linked allocation method. This overhead will be determined by the size of the index block, the system should try to make the index block as small as possible.

FREE SPACE MANAGEMENT TECHNIQUES

The important function of memory management module is to manage the limited memory space, where as the allocation of the required amount of memory space is important (so that sufficient memory space is to allocated), at the same time the management of the free space available is also equally important. It is necessary to reuse the space from the deleted files for the new files. To keep track of the free disk space, the system maintains a free space list, which records all the disk blocks which are free (i.e are not allocated to some another file). To create a file or to allocate a new block to the existing file, the system searches for a free block of the desired size in the free space list. If free space of required size is available in this list then it is allocated to the required file and this block is removed from the free space list. When a file is deleted, its disk space is returned back to the free space list.

Bit Vector

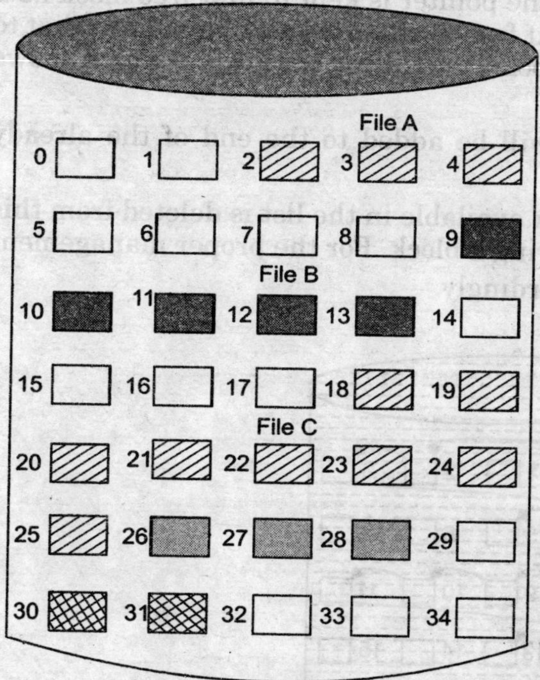

Fil Allocation Table

File Name	Start Block	Length
File A	2	3
File B	9	5
File C	18	8
File D	30	2
File E	26	3

Figure 9.20: *Free Space Management through a Bit Vector*

In this method, each block is represented by a bit. if the block is free, the bit is set to 0, if the block is allocated, then the bit is set to 1. The collection of the bit values for various blocks on a disk is known as bit vector or bit map.

For example: Corresponding to the allocation done in Figure 9.20, the bit map is given below, which show bit has value 1 if the block is allocated and has a value 0 if it is free.

The Corresponding Bit Vector is: 00111000011111000011111111111011000

Advantage

1. This method is simple and it is easy to find the first free block.
2. This method is useful, if n consecutive free blocks are required.

Disadvantages

1. This method requires the entire vector to be kept in the memory, which is not feasible some times, particularly if the disk size is quite large.
2. To find first block with value 1 in a word, requires special hardware support.

Linked List

Another strategy to manage the set of free blocks is to link all the free blocks together. The pointer to the first free block is kept and all the free blocks are linked together.

The Figure 9.21 given below show that the pointer is kept to first free block i.e 2 and then block 2 will have a pointer to the next free block i.e 3,4 and 5 and after that to the block number 8 and so on and the last block 27 will have null value, which shows the end of the list.

To insert a free block, the free block will be added to the end of the already available list.

To delete a free block, the first free block available in the list is deleted from this free list and is allocated to the process requiring a block. For the proper management of the free list, the pointers are updated accordingly.

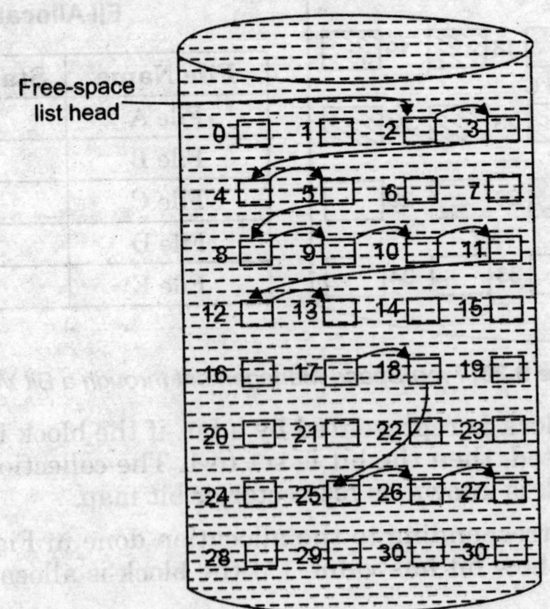

Figure 9.21: *Free Space Management through Linked List.*

Advantages

1. This method is easy to implement, as the user need to keep track of the pointer to the first free node only.
2. N consecutive blocks can be accessed easily.
3. It does not require the caching of the entire bit vector, only the address of the first free node is to be cached.

Disadvantages

1. The pointer overhead associated with each free node.
2. For traversing the list, each block must be read, which is a time consuming activity.

Grouping

In this free space management scheme, the addresses of n free blocks is stored in the first free block, that means first block stores only the addresses of free blocks and the last block contains the addresses of another n free blocks and so on. That means first n-2 blocks of these blocks are actually free.

Advantages

1. By accessing the first free block, the addresses of a large number of free blocks can be found quickly.

Disadvantages

1. A few blocks are storing only the addresses, that is the wastage of disk space.

Counting

Generally, a large number of blocks are allocated and de-allocated at the same time. So to keep the track of these free blocks, this method keeps the track of the first free block, this block stores the number n of contiguous blocks that follow the first block. So each entry consists of a disk address and a count.

Chapter 10

Device Management

Device management is the part of the operating system that manages hardware devices. The device management tries to provide a uniform interface to ease the access to devices with different physical characteristics and optimize the performance of individual devices.

INPUT OUTPUT AND SECONDARY STORAGE STRUCTURE

Device management controls peripheral devices by sending them commands in the language which they can understand. The software routine that knows how to deal with each device is called a driver and the operating system requires drivers for each peripheral attached to the system. Whenever a new peripheral is added, the device driver of that device is installed into the operating system. The operating system has an Input-Output Control System (IOCS) which is responsible for processing the I/O requests from executing processes. It passes the resource requests to the correct device drivers. It performs the check that whether the requested device is available or not. It initiates the status reports of drivers and passes resource requests to the correct device drivers. Device Drivers also known as I/O handler are the programs within the operating system which communicate with the devices. The Input/output control system also offers memory management for devices.

The major device management functions that are performed by an operating system are:

- To track the status of each device like disk drives, printers, plotters and terminals.
- To decide which process will get the device and for how long.
- To allocate the devices.
- To deallocate the device, when it is not required anymore. De-allocation can be done in two ways: at command level, when I/O command has been executed and the device has been released temporarily, at process level, when process has been terminated and the device has been permanently released.

The operating system must issue commands to the devices, handle interrupts and errors and must provide an interface between the devices and rest of the system. There is a great mismatch between the speed at which computers operate and the speed at which users can provide the input. It provides a method for transferring information between internal storage and external I/O devices.

The I/O subsystem is responsible to synchronize and supervise the flow of the data from I/O devices to the central system and is responsible to cover up the following differences between these two. The major differences between I/O Subsystem and the central system are:

1. Peripherals are electromechanical and electromagnetic devices, but CPU is electronic device, so conversion is required.
2. Data transfer rate of peripheral is less than that of the processor, so some Synchronization mechanism is required.
3. Data codes and formats in peripherals differ from word format in CPU and memory.
4. Operating modes of each peripheral is different from each other. So, each must be controlled so as not to disturb the operation of other peripheral.
5. The various peripherals attached to the system have different operating modes, these are designed by a variety of independent companies and each has its individual characteristics and formats and each has its own limitations.

So the input/output subsystem is responsible to bridge up these differences and should be able to synchronize the actions between the various devices and the central system.

DEVICE MANAGEMENT POLICIES

The device management module is responsible to provide uniform interface to ease the access to devices having different characteristics and to optimize the performance of individual device. The basic idea is to organize the software as a series of layers, with lower ones concerned with hiding the internal level details from the upper level layers and the upper layers are concerned with providing an easy to use interface to the users. The various issues in device management are:

1. **Device Independence:** The major issue in the design of I/O software is device independence. The programs written should be device independent i.e the programs written by the user should be executed irrespective of the fact that whether the input files are on hard disks or floppy disks. The program should not to be modified for each device on which it is supposed to run and program should run on different machines without recompiling it.
2. **Uniform Naming:** Another issue is the goal of uniform naming. The name of a file or a device should simply be a string or an integer and should not be dependent on the device. All files and devices must be addressed in the same way i.e by providing a path name.
3. **Error Handling:** The third major design issue is error handling. The errors should be handled by hardware as far as possible. If the controller identifies an error, it should try to correct the error itself and if controller is not able to correct the error by itself, then the device driver should handle the error. Many of the

errors can be handled by just trying to read the block again, as many of the errors can be handled by just repeating the read operation.

4. **Transmission Mode:** Another issue is to decide that whether a synchronous or an asynchronous transfer is required. Most of the physical I/O is asynchronous where the CPU starts the transfer and continues the other job till the interrupt arrives. User programs are easy to write if the I/O operations are synchronous i.e blocking.
5. **Allocation of Devices:** The devices can be allocated by the operating system in any of the following ways:
   (a) *Dedicated Allocation:* In dedicated allocation, a device is assigned to a process dedicatedly and will remain assigned till the process terminates. The device once allocated to one process cannot be allocated to any other process till the process terminates it. This allocation is possible for certain devices that are difficult to be shared like tape drivers, plotters etc. This allocation suffers from the problem of under utilization of the resources as the allocated resource may not be utilized by the process fully, the waiting time of the processes requiring some device may lead to the problem of starvation.
   (b) *Shared Allocation:* In this allocation the operating system assign a device in such a way that it can be shared by many processes at the same time. The various processes can share a device by interleaved execution of their requests. Like printers and hard disks can be shared among various devices. The device manager is responsible for controlling the interleaved process requests and if more than one process arrives at the same time and demand the same resource then the conflict must be resolved with the help of predetermined policy of scheduling and conflict resolution. It may be done by the I/O scheduler/ traffic controller or by the hardware. The biggest advantage of this method is that the device utilization reaches almost 100 percent. But the problems of security and deadlocks may be a major issue to be taken care of.
   (c) *Virtual Allocation:* The devices which are normally dedicated like printers and card readers can be converted into shared devices through the techniques such as SPOOLING i.e Simultaneous Peripheral Operation On Line, a spooling program can read and copy all card input onto a disk at a high speed. When a process tries to read a card, the Spooling program intercepts the requests and converts it to a read from the disk. Then several users may easily share a disk and can convert a dedicated device to a shared device, by changing one card reader into many virtual card readers. Like a printer can be converted to a shared device through Spooling, where the program reroutes all printing requests to the disk and the disk sends the output to the printer only when all of the request that have been lined up before this request have been finished.

The availability of a wide range of I/O devices makes it difficult for the programmers to learn specific commands and interact with the desired devices, or the operating system can implement device encapsulation i.e the abstraction of a device with no particular commands attached to it. It allows application programmers to communicate with any device in a similar manner irrespective of the nature of the device and its make. The logical device presents a virtual representation of any device attached to the system and the user is not aware of the internal implementation and low-level communication details.

COMPONENTS OF I/O SUB SYSTEM

The I/O devices vary in their functions, speed, modes of operations and depending upon this the I/O subsystem of the kernel is formed, where it separates the rest of the kernel from the complexity of managing I/O devices. Figure 10.1 show the components of I/O subsystem. The two basic components of this subsystem are:

1. **I/O Channels:** These are used to provide a path or a channel for the flow of data from I/O devices and the main memory. These channels use programs that specify the action to be performed by the devices and control the transmission of data between the main memory and control units. These are required to resolve the differences between I/O devices and the processor. These units are used to operate the I/O devices and these units are simple, but specialized and are less expensive than the processor. If I/O transfer is performed by the channel then the processor is free to do other jobs like high speed computation, which will increase the CPU utilization and hence the overall system through put will be improved. And moreover several channels may be operated at the same time, so a number of card readers, printers etc can function at the same time. The I/O channels can be divided into two categories: Selector Channel, it can service only one of the devices at a time, these are used for high speed I/O devices like magnetic disks. By using these channels each I/O request can be completed quickly and the other device can be selected for I/O and another type of channels are multiplexer channels, these channels are capable of servicing many devices at the same time. It is feasible for slow I/O devices like card readers and printers etc. and the third type of channels are block multiplexer channels which combines the features of selector channels and multiplexer channels. It allows the multiple channel programs for high speed devices to be active on the same I/O channel. It performs one channel instruction for one device and then automatically switches to perform the instructions for another device and so on. It resembles the selector channels as only one device is serviced at a time and it resembles the multiplexor as it does not wait until the entire channel program is completed.
2. **I/O Control Units:** As there are multiple channels operating at the same time, so all these channels are required to be controlled and supervised and this job is taken care of by the I/O control units. As discussed earlier, that the channels are fewer as compared to the devices, due to the high cost of the channels, so

the channels must be switched from one device to another. The I/O control units perform this job. These control units interprets the signals sent by the channel and then handles the switching from one device to another. A common controller will be responsible for handling a number of similar devices. As shown in the Figure 10.1 a common control unit is managing the various card readers, a common control unit is managing the various tape drives.

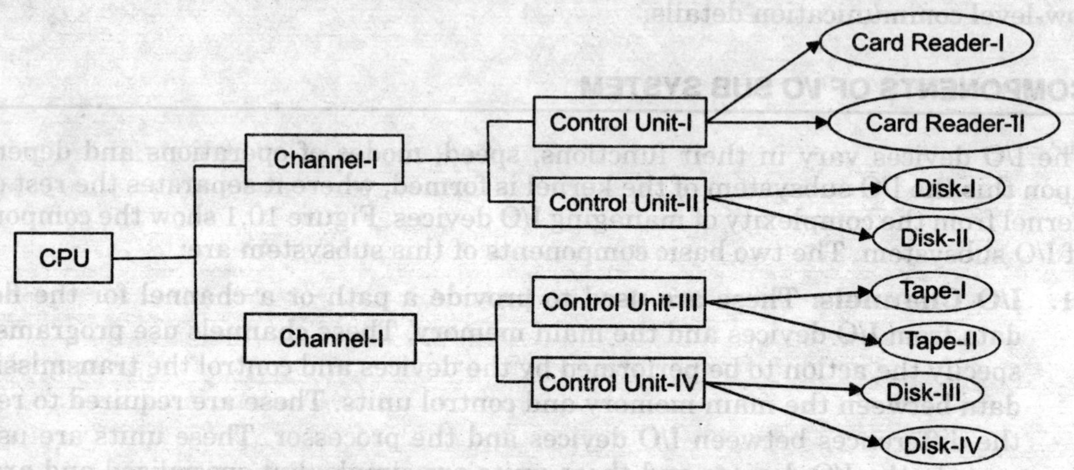

Figure 10.1: *Components of I/O Subsystem*

DEVICE MANAGEMENT TECHNIQUES

The device management module is responsible for managing the various devices in such a way that the overall system productivity can be enhanced, keeping the user convenience in mind. It is responsible for keeping the track of various I/O Channels, control units and devices. As number of devices will be competing for limited resources, then there will be a need to manage the conflicting requests, the various techniques that can be used to reduce these problems are:

- **Independent Device Operation:** There may be sufficient capability in the device to complete an I/O operation without any further assistance from the channel and control unit. When an I/O operation is initiated, the entire path must be available. In order to indicate when parts of the path become available there may be separate I/O completion interrupts, channel end, control unit end and device end. The status bits in the channel Status Word designate completion interrupt. If more than one part of the path becomes available at the same time, there will be only one interrupt but the status bits will indicate all available parts. If a channel end occurs, the channel is no longer busy, although the device may still be busy. An I/O operation can then be initiated on some other device using that channel.
- **Buffering:** The facility of buffering will allow the devices to work independently of the channels. By providing a data buffer in the device or control unit, devices

that would ordinarily require the channel for a long period can be made to perform independently of the channel. For example, a card reader may physically require about 80 ms to read a card and transfer the data to memory through the channel. But if buffering has been used, then card reader always read one card before it is needed and saves 60 bytes in a buffer in the card reader or control unit. When the channel request that a card is to be read, the contents of 60 byte buffer are transferred to memory at high speed and the channel is released. The device then proceeds to read the next card and buffer it independently.

- **Multiple Paths:** The efficiency of overall I/O system can be enhanced by using the channels and control unit in flexible way, which allows multiple paths to each device. Figure 10.2 given below shows an I/O configuration with multiple paths, in this example four different paths to the device F: B-D-F, A-D-F, A-C-F, B-C-F are available, if the channel B and control unit D are busy due to some I/O operation, then a path from A through control unit C can be used alternatively. A completely flexible configuration will make all control units to be accessible to all the channels. Apart from providing the flexibility and the fast transfer of the data, this configuration also provides the benefit of reliability, as if one of the channel and /or control unit is not working properly or is malfunctioning due to some fault, then the other alternative paths may be used.

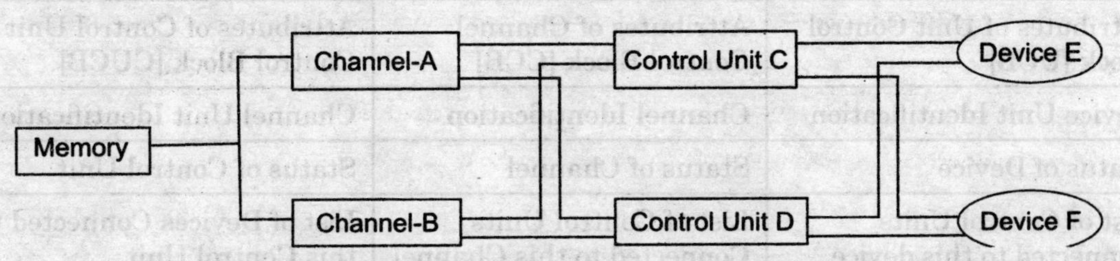

Figure 10.2: *I/O Configurations with Multiple Paths*

FUNCTIONS OF DEVICE MANAGEMENT

The various functions of device management module can be handled by a specific software component, these have been described below:

Role of I/O Traffic Controller

This component is responsible for keeping track of all devices, control units and channels. The traffic controller supervises the flow of data through various devices, channels and control units. When the I/O scheduler takes care of scheduling the devices, i.e which device will get the channel, the I/O traffic controller is concerned with checking whether it is possible to assign the device. The traffic controller maintains all the status information pertaining to the device. The I/O traffic controller has a tough job to perform in the light of limited resources available. The basic jobs of an I/O traffic controller are;

- It checks the availability of the path from the source to the destination.

- If more than one alternative paths are available, then it checks that which one is the most optimal path available.
- If no path is available right now, then it checks when it will be available,
- It maintains the service and waiting queue for all devices and channels attached to it.
- It maintains the database showing the status and connections between devices, channels and control units.

The various data structures maintained by traffic controller are:

1. Unit Control Block
2. Channel Control Block.
3. Control Unit Control Block.

The working starts by searching the desired unit control block and working back through the connected control units and channels trying to find out the possible channels available for the combination right now.

Table 10.1 Attributes of UCB, CCB and CUCB

Attributes of Unit Control Block [UCB]	Attributes of Channel Control Block [CCB]	Attributes of Control Unit Control Block [CUCB]
Device Unit Identification	Channel Identification	Channel Unit Identification
Status of Device	Status of Channel	Status of Control Unit
List of Control Units Connected to this device	List of Control Units Connected to this Channel	List of Devices Connected to this Control Unit
List of Processes Waiting for this particular device	List of Processes Waiting for this Channel	List of Channels Connected to this Control Unit
-	-	List of Processes Waiting for this Control Unit

Role of I/O Scheduler

The job of I/O scheduler will be to schedule the allocation of channels, control units and devices corresponding to the I/O requests received. It follows the various scheduling algorithms discussed in chapter 4. As it may follow, first come first served policy, shortest job first scheduling, or priority scheduling or even entertain the request in the round robin fashion. The scheduler must synchronize its work with the traffic controller so that requests can be handled efficiently and effectively.

I/O Device Handler

I/O device handler is responsible for handling the device completely, As each device has a separate mechanism of construction and modes of operations, type of services it can provide and type of errors which may be encountered, scheduling algorithms possible for the device and the handling of interrupts, so the I/O device handler must be equipped to handle all these issues. Normally there will be different device handler algorithm for each type of I/O device.

DISK STRUCTURE

One of the important functions of the computer is the storage of huge amount of data. For this purpose a variety of devices are used. The choice of the storage device depends on the characteristic features of the device itself, the important features taken into consideration are: permanency of data storage, cost per bit and the access time. The user wants different types of features depending upon the requirements. Based on these criteria, the storage units can be divided in to two broad categories:

1. **Primary Storage Devices:** This provides temporary storage of data at a fast rate but the cost of these devices is comparatively high. The RAM (random Access memory) falls in this category. It is volatile in nature and retains data as long as the power supply is provided. Due to these features, this memory is used to store the data currently being used by the user and size of this memory is less.
2. **Secondary Storage Devices:** Many a times the user wants to store a huge amount of data on the permanent basis. The secondary storage devices solve this problem. These devices provide permanent storage of data, and are comparatively very cheap. The devices come in this category are: magnetic tapes and magnetic disk. The magnetic tapes can provide sequential access of data only, where as the magnetic disk provide the facility of random access. The present context is concerned about the disk structure and the various operations that can be performed on the disks.

The main features of secondary storage devices are:

1. These are used to overcome the limitations of primary storage i. e the volatile nature of primary storage and high cost.
2. It has virtually unlimited capacity because the cost per bit of storage is very low.
3. It is used to store large volumes of data on a permanent basis.
4. Magnetic tapes Support direct access of data. Whereas magnetic tapes are good for sequential access only.
5. Random access property enables them to be used simultaneously by multiple users as a shared device. A tape is not suitable for such type of usage due to its sequential-access property.
6. Due to their low cost and high data recording densities, the cost per bit of storage is low for magnetic disks.
7. Very large amount of data can be stored in a small storage space.

Structure of Magnetic Disk: Magnetic Disk is a commonly used direct-access secondary storage device. A magnetic disk is a thin, circular plate made of metal or plastic that is usually coated on both sides with a magnetizable recording of the material such as iron-oxide. Data is recorded on the disk in the form of tiny invisible magnetized and non-magnetized spots on the coated surfaces of the disk. The disk is stored in a specially designed protective envelope or cartridge, or several of them are stacked together in a sealed, contamination-free container.

The disk surface is divided into a number of invisible concentric circles called tracks. The tracks are numbered consecutively from outermost to innermost starting from zero.

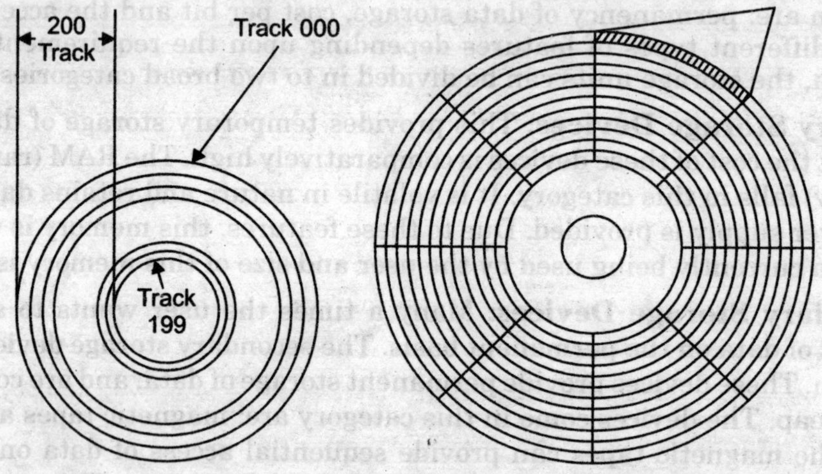

Figure 10.3: *Tracks of a Disk* **Figure 10.4:** *A Sector on a Track*

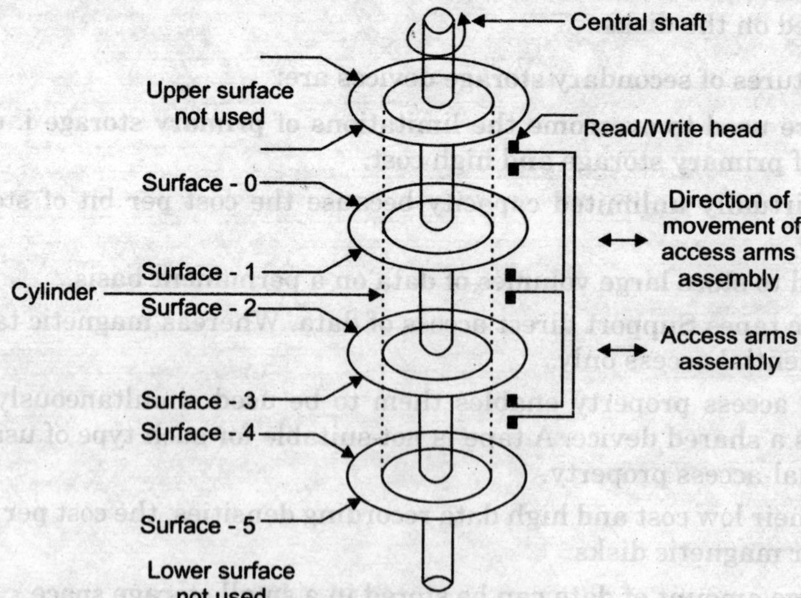

Figure 10.5: *Disk Structure*

Each track of a disk is subdivided into sectors. There are 8 or more sectors per track. A sector typically contains 512 bytes. Disk drives are designed to read/write only whole sectors at a time. So a disk can be defined as an electromechanical device that holds data, there are one or more disk platters and data is written on both sides by heads that read and/or write data using electromagnets, lasers or other technologies.

Storage capacity of a disk system = Number of recording surfaces × Number of tracks per surface × Number of sectors per track × Number of bytes per sector

Parameters to measure the performance of disk

The performance of disk structure depends upon how fast the data can be retrieved from the disk. Faster the access time better is the performance of the disk. When the disk is operating, it is rotating at a constant speed. To read or write the head must be positioned at the desired track and then to the beginning of the desired sector on that track. Track selection deals with moving the head in a moveable head system or selecting one head on a fixed head system. Disk access time is the interval between the instant a computer makes a request for transfer of data from a disk system to the primary storage and the instant this operation is completed.

Disk access time depends on the following three parameters:

1. **Seek Time:** It is the time required to position the read/write head over the desired track, as soon as a read/write command is received by the disk unit.
2. **Latency Time:** It is the time required to spin the desired sector under the read/write head, once the read/write head is positioned on the desired track.
3. **Transfer Rate:** It is the rate at which data are read/written to the disk, once the read/write head is positioned over the desired sector

As the transfer rate is negligible as compared to seek time and latency,

Average access time = Average seek time + Average latency time.

Disk drive is connected to and controlled by a disk controller, which interprets the commands for operating the disk drive.

DISK SCHEDULING

As discussed earlier the efficient utilization of hardware is the primary objective of the operating system. The storage unit is one of such resource which needs to be used optimally. For the disk drives, the objective is that the maximum amount of data should be saved at the minimum cost and should be accessible at a very fast rate. It deals with having fast access time and high disk bandwidth.

The access time comprises of seek time and latency time, which have already been discussed.

The disk bandwidth is the total number of bytes transferred, divided by the total time between the first request for the service and ending of the last transfer.

In order to achieve these objectives, the activities on the disk i.e the I/O requests should be scheduled in such a way that both the above mentioned objectives can be met. Whenever a process issues a request for I/O transfer to or from the disk, the operating system issues a system call, which specifies:

- Whether the operation is for writing data on the disk?
- Whether the operation is for reading data from the disk?
- What is the address of the location where data is to be written?
- What is the address of the location from where data is to be read?
- What is the amount of data to be written or read?

The operating system may follow various types of scheduling schemes in order to achieve the objectives of fast access rate and high bandwidth. If a number of requests have been received, then these will be queued up and then these queued jobs or processes can be executed according to the various scheduling algorithms discussed in the Chapter 4.

But for a particular request, the access to various locations on the disk can be scheduled according to the some scheduling criteria. And for this purpose the various scheduling algorithms which can be used are described below, here we have considered a disk with 300 cylinders numbered from 0-299. And the disk head is at 77 in the starting.

First Come First Served Scheduling

As the name specifies the disk requests are entertained in the order as they are received. The request received first will be served first. It is logically simple and easy to execute scheduling criteria, but it may not provide the fastest service.

For Example: Consider a disk queue with requests for I/O to the blocks on the cylinder as: 95, 37, 23, 283, 7, 130, 250. And the initial position of the disk head is 77.

Then starting from 77, first of all the head moves to the position 95 making a head movement of 95 – 77 = 18 and then the head moves from 95 to 37 making a head movement of 58. Moving in this way from one location to another, the total number of steps in the movement from one location to another can be calculated as:

Table 10.2: Calculation of Head Movement for FCFS Scheduling Algorithm.

Movement from		Head Movement
From	To	
77	95	18
95	37	58
37	23	14
23	283	260
283	07	276
07	130	123
130	250	120
Total Head Movement		869

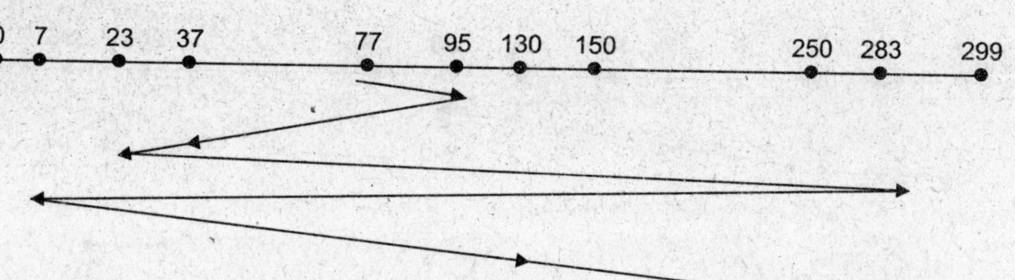

Figure 10.6: *Diagrammatic representation for FCFS Scheduling Algorithm.*

The problem with this scheduling algorithm is that there is very large head movement when the head moves from 23 to 183 and then 183 to 7, the total head movement may be decreased to a large extent if we would have visited the location 23 and 7 in one go. By doing so the efficiency would have been improved to large extent.

Shortest Seek Time First Scheduling

In this algorithm the disk controller selects the request that is close to the current head position. The algorithm which follows this strategy is termed as shortest seek time first algorithm. It selects the request with minimum seek time from the current head position. All the requests close to each other will be processed in one go, but due to this it may be possible that some requests have to wait for long time causing the problem of starvation. This problem occurs when new jobs with shorter seek time keep on arriving causing some of the jobs to wait indefinitely.

In this case, the head movement will start from the starting position of the head i.e 77, And then it will move to the position closest to it, the next position nearer to 77 is 95, so the head will move to the location 95, causing a head movement of 18, and then from 95 the next position closer to it is 130, head will move this position, causing the movement of 35, moving in this way, the head will move the disk position in the following order and the total head movement will be as follows:

Table 10.3: Calculation of Head Movement for SSTF Scheduling Algorithm

Movement from		Head Movement
From	To	
77	95	18
95	130	35
130	37	93
37	23	14
23	07	16
07	250	243
250	283	33
Total Head Movement		452

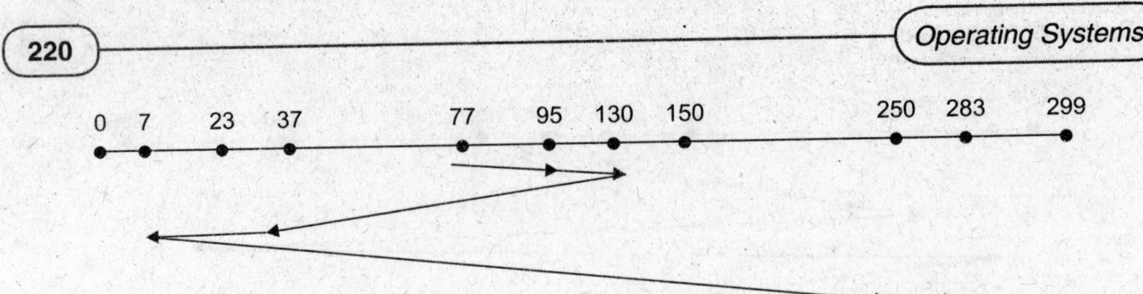

Figure 10.7: *Diagrammatic representation for Shortest Seek Time Scheduling Algorithm*

The total head movement has been reduced to half.

Scan & C-scan

1. **SCAN:** In this algorithm the disk head start from the current head position and move to the either direction to reach the outer cylinder and servicing all requests coming in between and then direction of head movement is reversed and the requests on the other side of the current head position are serviced then. Before starting the traversing, the direction in which the head will move must be known along with the current head position. Due to this behavior of SCAN algorithm, this algorithm is also called as elevator algorithm, as the disk arm behave like an elevator in the building, which service all the requests going up and then reverses its direction to service the requests on the other way.

Case I: Consider that the disk arm is moving towards 0, then head will start from its current position i.e 77 and will move towards 0, satisfying the request coming in between, until it touches the 0 mark, so the requests will be traversed from 77 to 37 and then 23 and then 07 and then it will touch the 0 and from that point onwards the direction of the head will be reversed and the positions 95,130,250 and 283 will be visited, the total head movement in this case can be calculated as:

Table 10.4: Calculation of Head Movement for SCAN Algorithm when the arm is moving towards Left

Movement from		Head Movement
From	To	
77	37	40
37	23	14
23	07	16
07	00	07
00	95	95
95	130	35
130	250	120
250	283	33
Total Head Movement		360

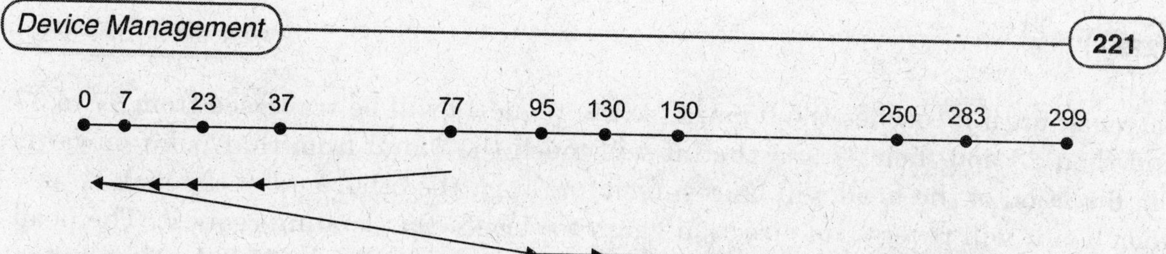

Figure 10.8: *Diagrammatic representation for SCAN Algorithm when the arm is moving towards left*

Case II: Consider the case the disk arm moves to the right side of the current head position: The requests will be entertained in the following order: 77, 95, 130, 250, 283, 299, 37, 23, 07 and the total head movement can be calculated as:

Table 10.5: Calculation of Head Movement for SCAN Algorithm when the arm is moving towards right

Movement from		Head Movement
From	To	
77	95	18
95	130	35
130	250	120
250	283	33
283	299	16
299	37	262
37	23	14
23	07	16
Total Head Movement		514

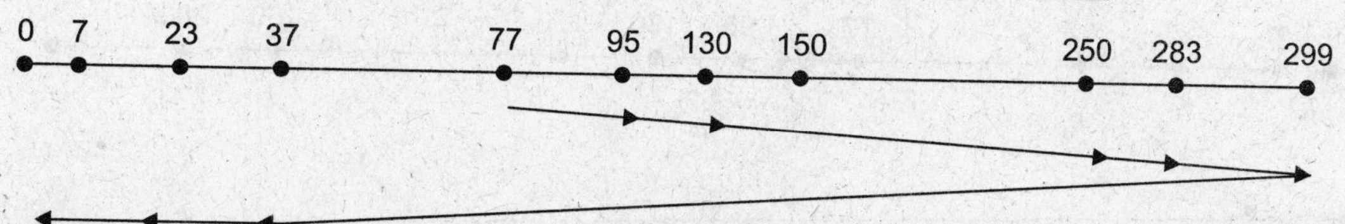

Figure 10.9: *Diagrammatic representation for SCAN Algorithm when the arm is moving towards right*

2. **C-SCAN:** This algorithm works quite similar to the SCAN algorithm, in this algorithm the head moves to any particular direction servicing the requests in between until it reaches the end of the disk, and then it reverses its direction and reaches the other end without servicing any request on the return trip.

Case I: Consider that the disk arm is moving towards 0, then head will start from its current position i.e 77 and will move towards 0, satisfying the request coming in between, until it touches the 0 mark, so the requests will be traversed from 77 to 37 and then 23 and then 07 and then it will touch the 0 and from that point onwards the direction of the head will be reversed and it go the other end of the disk i.e 299 and then it will reverse its direction again to service the pending request. The head movement will be as follows: Starting from 77 the head will visit, 37, 23 , 07 and then it will touch the 0 mark and then the direction of head will be reversed and will touch the other end i.e at 299 and then it goes back to service the requests at 283, 250, 130 and 95 the total head movement in this case can be calculated as:

Table 10.6: Calculation of Head Movement for C-SCAN Algorithm when the arm is moving towards Left

Movement from		Head Movement
From	To	
77	37	40
37	23	14
23	07	16
07	00	07
00	299	300
299	283	36
283	250	33
250	130	120
130	95	35
Total Head Movement		601

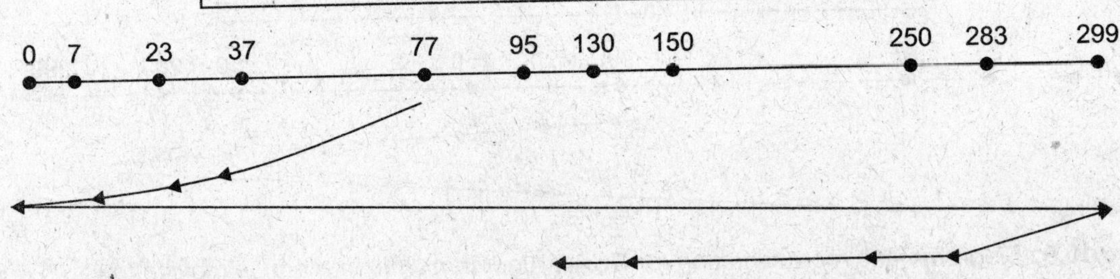

Figure 10.10: *Diagrammatic representation for C-SCAN Algorithm when the arm is moving towards left*

Case II: Consider the case the disk arm moves to the right side of the current head position: The requests will be entertained in the following order: 77, 95, 130, 250, 283, 299, 37, 23, 07 and the total head movement can be calculated as:

Table 10.7: Calculation of Head Movement for SCAN Algorithm when the arm is moving towards right

Movement from		Head Movement
From	To	
77	95	18
95	130	35
130	250	120
250	283	33
283	299	16
299	00	300
00	37	37
37	23	14
23	07	16
Total Head Movement		589

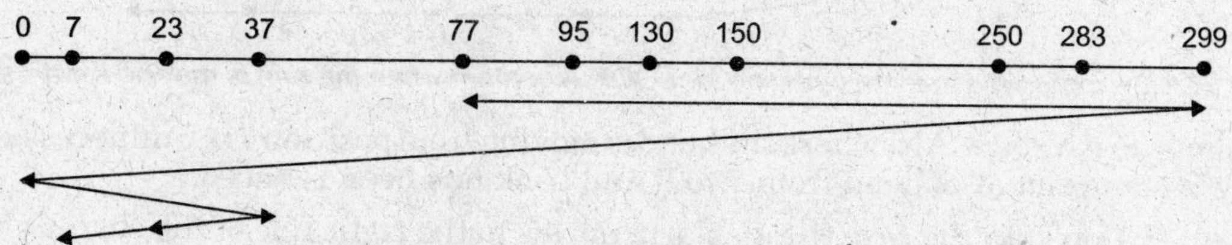

Figure 10.11: *Diagrammatic representation for SCAN Algorithm when the arm is moving towards right*

Look & C-Look

These algorithms are modified form of the SCAN and C-SCAN algorithms.

1. **Look:** Like SCAN algorithm the head starts moving in a particular direction, but it changes its direction, when it knows that there is no requests beyond this point. That means arm goes only as far as the final request in each direction.

Case I: Consider that the disk arm is moving towards 0, then head will start from its current position i.e 77 and will move towards 0, satisfying the request coming in between, until it touches the last request in this direction, so the requests will be traversed from 77 to 37 and then 23 and then 07 and from this point onwards the direction of the head will be reversed and the positions 95,130,250 and 283 will be visited, the total head movement in this case can be calculated as:

Table 10.8: Calculation of Head Movement for LOOK Algorithm when the arm is moving towards left

Movement from		Head Movement
From	To	
77	37	40
37	23	14
23	07	16
07	95	88
95	130	35
130	250	120
250	283	33
Total Head Movement		346

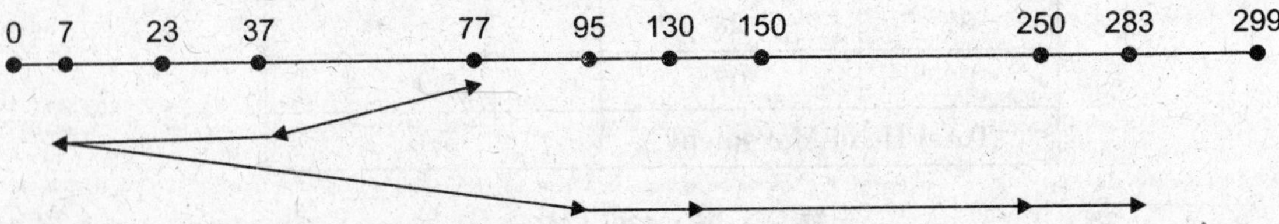

Figure 10.12: *Diagrammatic representation for LOOK Algorithm when the arm is moving towards left*

Compare it with SCAN, where the head is moving from position 7 to 0 unnecessarily. Clearly the movement of head from 7 to 0 and back has been reduced.

Case II: Consider the case the disk arm moves to the right side of the current head position i.e 77, in this case, the requests will be entertained in the following order:

77, 95, 130, 250, 283, 37, 23, 07 and the total head movement can be calculated as:

Table 10.9: Calculation of Head Movement for LOOK Algorithm when the arm is moving towards right

Movement from		Head Movement
From	To	
77	95	18
95	130	35
130	250	120
250	283	33
283	37	246
37	23	14
23	07	16
Total Head Movement		482

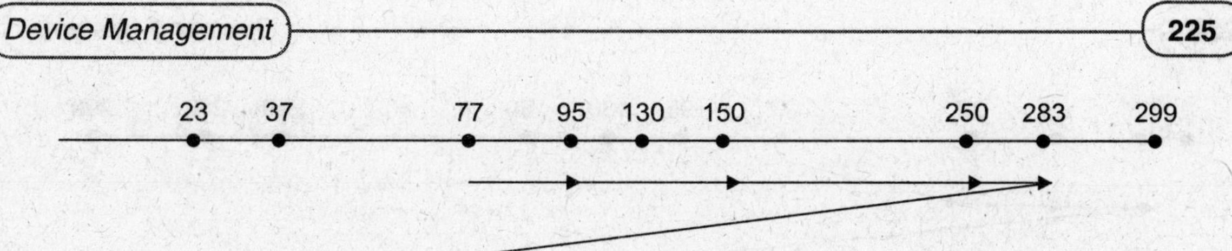

Figure 10.13: *Diagrammatic representation for LOOK Algorithm when the arm is moving towards right*

Here when the head reaches at the position 283, it will reverse back and will start visiting the positions in the back journey.

2. **C-Look:** This algorithm works quite similar to the C-SCAN algorithm, in this algorithm the head moves to any particular direction servicing the requests in between until it reaches the point of last request, and then it reverses its direction and reaches the point of last request in that direction other end without servicing any request on the return trip and then reverses the direction to visit the pending positions.

Case I: Consider that the disk arm is moving towards 0, then head will start from its current position i.e 77 and will move towards 0, satisfying the request coming in between, until it touches the point of last request i.e 7, so the requests will be traversed from 77 to 37 and then 23 and then 07 and from that point onwards the direction of the head will be reversed and it will go to the last request on the other side i.e 283 and then it will reverse its direction again to service the pending requests. The head movement will be as follows: Starting from 77 the head will visit, 37, 23, 07 and then the direction of head will be reversed and will touch the other end at 283 and then it goes back to service the requests at 283, 250, 130 and 95, the total head movement in this case can be calculated as:

Table 10.10: Calculation of Head Movement for C-LOOK Algorithm when the arm is moving towards Left

Movement from		Head Movement
From	To	
77	37	40
37	23	14
23	07	16
07	283	276
283	250	33
250	130	120
130	95	35
Total Head Movement		534

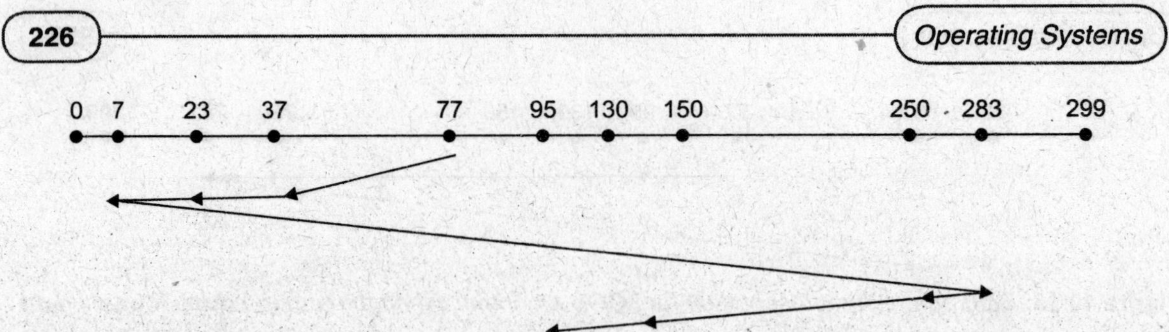

Figure 10.14: *Diagrammatic representation for C-LOOK Algorithm when the arm is moving towards left*

Case II: Consider the case the disk arm moves to the right side of the current head position i.e 77, in this case, the requests will be entertained in the following order:

77, 95, 130, 250, 283, 37, 23, 07 and the total head movement can be calculated as:

Table 10.11: Calculation of Head Movement for C-LOOK Algorithm when the arm is moving towards right

Movement from		Head Movement
From	To	
77	95	18
95	130	35
130	250	120
250	283	33
283	07	276
07	37	30
37	23	14
23	07	16
Total Head Movement		542

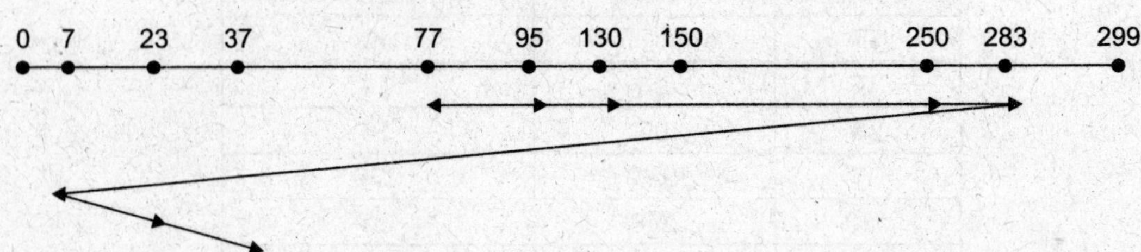

Figure 10.15: *Diagrammatic representation for C-LOOK Algorithm when the arm is moving towards right*

Here when the head reaches at the position 283, it will reverse back and will reach the point 7 and will start visiting the positions in the back journey.

Comparison of all Disk Scheduling Algorithms has been shown below

Algorithm	Total Head Movement
FCFS	869
SSTF	452
SCAN	360 (Left) and 514 (Right)
C-SCAN	601 (Left) and 589 (Right)
LOOK	346 (Left) and 482 (Right)
C-LOOK	534 (Left) and 542 (Right)

CRITERIA FOR CHOOSING THE BEST SCHEDULING ALGORITHM

The various algorithms discussed here have their own advantages and limitations. Generally, visiting the positions according to SSTF algorithm i.e visiting the nodes available at the shortest distance from the current position is always preferred and gives optimal results. But the problem of starvation is also a major area of concern, so the choice of best disk scheduling algorithm depends on many other factors mentioned below:

1. The performance of an algorithm depends on the number and types of requests. The requests may be scattered all over the disk or they may be confined to a particular region. The waiting time and the turnaround times are the major points to be considered.
2. Another factor influencing the performance is the file allocation method, if the contiguous memory allocation scheme has been used, then the requests will be nearer to each other and the disk head movement will be less. But if linked or indexed file allocation methods have been used, then the head movement will be more, as the requests will involve the blocks scattered all over the disk.
3. The third major factor is the position of directories and index blocks. As we know for opening a file, the directory structure will be searched to find out the entry of the required file and then file will be opened then. So the position of the directory and the file itself are the major factor affecting the head movement.
4. The total size of the disk is important if we are following C-SCAN, as the whole disk is traversed from one end to another.

Chapter 11

Protection and Security

Interference in access of resources by the users is a serious threat in an operating system. The two important resources of the system are the system's resources (may be considered as the system itself, or its hardware devices) or the data. The data is considered as the most important asset for an individual and for the organization also. So its protection is of utmost importance. The right user should be provided right access to the right data so that unauthorized access to the data can be avoided. Apart from the data the protection of the system resources is also a major area of concern.

MEANING OF PROTECTION & SECURITY

The protection is required internally and externally. Internally the various processes running in the system whether these are the user processes or the system processes, these must be protected from each other's activities and on the other side the files and data stored in the system must be protected from the outside attacks. The mechanism for controlling the access of programs and data stored in the computer system at the internal level is the problem of protection, whereas the security deals with preventing the unauthorized access of data from the external sources. So we can say that protection is an internal problem, whereas the security is an external problem. So security deals with the threats to the information that are external to the computer system, while protection deals with the threats that are internal.

Security is used in a broad sense to refer to all concerns about controlled access to facilities whereas protection describes special technological mechanisms that support security.

Security refers to the policy of authorizing accesses to various users, whereas the protection refers to the actual mechanism implemented to enforce the designed protection strategy. Internal protection will be of no use if the external source can hamper the data stored in the system. The problem of security is very important in the present scenario, where the distributed environment is prevailing all around and the users are sharing the data with each other and accessing the information from other remote systems. The protection policy for usage of resources may vary from application to application and may vary from time to time. So the design and implementation of protection policy is not a concern of the operating system, but this authority should also be provided to the application programmers, so that they can do this job for the specific application according to the requirements of that application and user's objectives.

There is a thin line of difference between the terms protection and security, and these have been used interchangeably. Security refers to the policy of authorizing accesses, whereas the protection deals with actual mechanisms implemented to enforce the specified policy. The focus area of protection is internal to the system, where as the security deals with the external environment. Commonly, the security is a general term used for security measures implemented internally or externally. Breaches within the system are termed as protection, while breaches from external sources are dealt in security. Security violations may be termed as intentional or un-intentional. It is easy to protect accidental misuse rather than the intentional access. The intentional access may be for reading, modification and destruction of the data or it may be for the resource usage. The security concern is limited to ensuring that only the authorized (i.e registered) users can use the operating system and hence the system itself, so when the user logs in the user is asked to provide some information which will ensure that whether the user is genuine or not, if the user is valid then a userid is assigned to the user, at this point the concept of security stops and all the threats now onwards are the concern area of protection, now protection mechanism takes over the charge to check what the user is authorized to do or what data he can access. Figure 11.1 given below differentiate between the security and protection concerns.

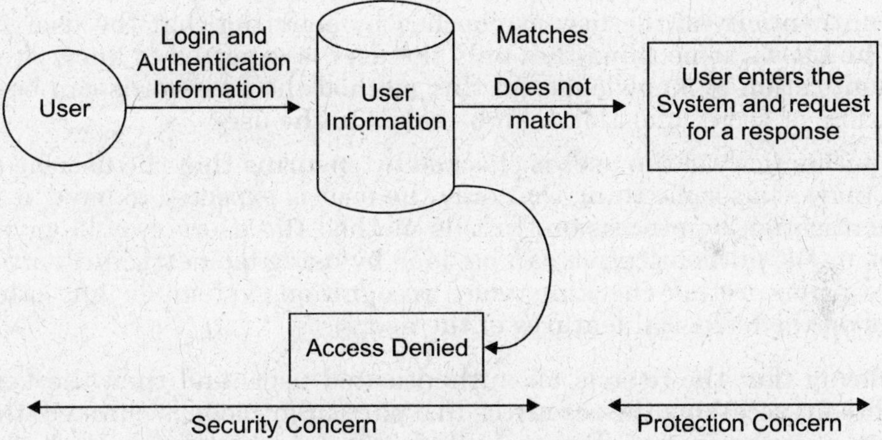

Figure 11.1: *Boundaries between Security and Protection*

Levels of Security

1. **Physical:** The site containing the computer system must be physically secured so that the intruders cannot enter the site.
2. **Human:** It occurs when an unauthorized person is intruding into the system personally. Like an outsider entering into the company office. It must be screened properly. This is usually done by checking the outsiders entering the site. It can be achieved by providing security guards at the sites, the doors may be equipped with the magnetic gadgets or the provision of thumb impressions can be used to ensure that only the authorized users should be allowed to enter the site.

3. **Network:** Most of the data now a days, move from one system to another over private leased lines, shared public lines or any of the other transmission mode. The interception of this data is as harmful as the physical attack on the user's systems. The interruption of these communications could be remote denial-of-service attack.
4. **Operating System:** The system must protect itself from accidental or intentional security breaches.

How the System Implements the Security and Protection

The operating system is responsible to implement the security and the protection mechanism for the user. The process begins with ensuring that the right person is going to access the data, this process is called authentication of the user. Authentication can be defined as the process of verification of identity of a user or the eligibility of a user to access an object. It basically deals with verifying the identity of the user. Earlier physical verification of the identity (i.e human Security) was implemented by checking the user identity at the office gates by checking the user personally or by the identity cards, but now a days it is not possible, so the computer based authentication methods have been used now a days. It can be implemented as:

- The authenticity of the user is checked by ensuring that the user he claims to be if he knows some thing that only the user is expected to know, it is known as authentication by knowledge. In this method the passwords can be assigned to the users or secret questions can be asked to the user.
- The authenticity of the user is checked by ensuring that the user he claims to be if he knows has some thing that only the user is expected to have, it is known as authentication by procession. In this method the users may be given magnetic strips or the authentication can be done by using biometric authentications(like figure prints, retina checking, voice recognition systems or any other measure based on the biological features of the users).

After ensuring that the user is an authenticated user, and then the verification of user's rights for accessing the resources in a particular mode is checked, this is known the problem of authorization. Figure 11.2 given below show the general steps followed in the implementation of security and protection in an operating system, the step by step procedure can be enumerated as follows:

1. The user wishing to access any information in any system, have to prove his identity, it can be done when the user provides the userid and the other authentication information (like password, magnetic strips, or any other biometric measure of identification). This information is provided to the authentication centre, which transform the information in some standard form.
2. The authentication centre checks whether the information provided by the user matches the information already stored in the authentication database or not, where the authentication database stores the loginid, and the other validating information for all the registered users. If the information provided by the user

matches the information already stored, then user is allowed to enter the system otherwise the access is denied.

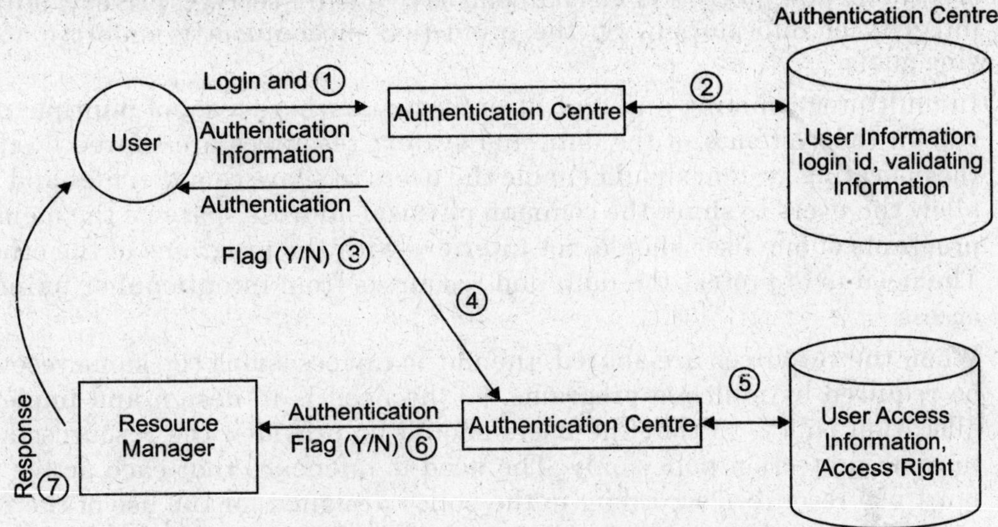

Figure 11.2: *Implementation of Security and Protection*

3. If the permission has been granted, then the authentication centre provides an authentication id.
4. The authentication id generated by authentication centre is passed to authorization centre.
5. The authorization centre passes this information to the authorization database, where it is checked that whether the user has required privileges on the objects requested or not. The authorization database used here stores the authentication id and access rights available on various objects for various subjects. If the user has required privileges as requested then permission is granted otherwise the access is denied.
6. If the permission has been granted then the authorization centre issues an authorization id and passes it to the resource manager.
7. The resource manager reports back to the user about the permission being granted or not.

Here the steps 1 to 4 deal with security mechanism, whereas the remaining steps deal with the protection mechanism.

GOALS OF PROTECTION AND SECURITY

The latest developments in the technology and modes of operations, the sharing of data and resources is common everywhere. In a multiuser environment where a number of users interact with each other, share data and resources, the protection of data and providing authorized access to system's data and resources is gaining importance. The goal of security and protection mechanisms is to ensure secrecy, privacy, authenticity and integrity of information. So the protection mechanism is enforced to achieve following goals:

1. In multiprogramming and multiuser systems, where a set of multiple programs run on the system and the data and system resources are shared by the users, the operating system should enable the users to share common files and it should allow the users to share the common physical address space i.e the memory. The programs of one user should not interfere with the programs of the other users. The need is to protect the data and resources from intentional or unintentional access.
2. When the resources are shared, then at many occasions the same resource may be required by multiple programs, so the need is to design and implement an allocation policy, so that the users should be provided the resources according to some protection policy only. The need is to ensure that each active program must use resources according to the policy designed for the use of the resources only. These policies can be fixed in the design of the system, or can be formulated by the management of the system or can be defined by the individual users to protect their own files and programs.
3. Secrecy is a security concern as it breached when an unauthorized person or process attacks on your system. It ensures that only the authorized users should be allowed to access information. It is enforced to ensure the confidentiality of the data.
4. Privacy is a protection concern, which ensures that the information should be used only for the purpose it is intended to be used. The operating system enforces the privacy through authorization service and resource manager. This system determines the access rights of a user and the resource manager allows or disallows the request for the user. This mechanism is basically designed by the user, who informs the operating system that which information the user wishes to share with the other users.
5. Authenticity ensures that the source and / or destination of information should be verified and the form in which the information is to be sent or preserved should be taken into consideration.
6. The another goal of security and protection mechanism is to maintain the integrity of the data, it should not be possible to destroy or corrupt the information.

The aim of the security mechanism is to ensure:

1. **Confidentiality** i.e the information stored in a computer system should be accessible to the authorized users for the specified access only. The data should be secure from the unauthenticated users and right user should get the right access to the right data only.

2. **Integrity:** The integrity of data will be maintained only if it cannot be changed by everybody. Only the authorized users should be able to modify the data.
3. **Availability:** The data and system resources should be made available to the users who have the privileges to access them. The resource should be made available to the authorized users only in the mode they have the right to access them.

PROTECTION AND ITS IMPLEMENTATION:

The computer system can be visualized as the collection of processes and objects, where objects can be:

- Hardware objects like Processor, memory Units, Printers
- Software objects like files, programs and user data.

Each object is identified by a unique name and each object should be allowed to be accessed only through proper permissions and access rights. The process should be allowed to access the objects which the process is authorized to use. To make this concept feasible, the process is supposed to operate in its protection domain only, which specifies the resources that the process is authorized to access. Each domain specifies a set of objects and the type of operations that can be performed on that object. The permission to perform any operation on an object is known as the access right.

So a domain is defined as a collection of access rights, which is an ordered pair like <object_name, rights>. Like if a domain has the access right <file A,{read}>, then a process executing in this domain can only read the file A. The association of a process and its domain may be either static or dynamic. It will be static if the set of resources available to a process is fixed throughout the life time of the process. In case of dynamic mechanism the process can change the set of resources required in run time also. The process should be allowed to access only those resources it has been authorized to access. Then a process should follow 'need-to-know' principle so that it should be able to access the resources, it needs currently. But in case of dynamic scenario, the domain can be changed at the different instances of a process execution. For example, a process P1 needs read access in one phase and write access in the another phase. Then in the first phase the domain should include only read access on File A like <file A, read> and in the second phase the domain should be modified to <file A,write> . in case of dynamic association the contents of present domain are not changed to satisfy the new request, rather the process is switched from one domain to another.

Methods for Implementing Protection

The authorization to the user to access a particular file deals with finding out that whether the user has the sufficient privileges to access the file or not. The method of storing and using the access control information is known as the protection structure. Each file management system has own file access control method. The various methods in this category are:

1. Access Control Matrix

2. Access Control Lists
3. Capability Lists
4. Lock Word Control

Access Control Matrix

An access matrix is associated with each file. The three basic terms used to specify the access matrix are:

- *Subjects:* The users using the system are known as the subjects, the subjects can be mentioned individually or they may be grouped together into one group.
- *Objects:* Objects can be any resource needs to be protected; objects can be hardware objects like Processor, Memory Units, Printers or may be software objects like files, programs and user data.
- *Access Rights:* It specifies the set of rights permitted to the subject on one particular object. It is also termed as access privileges. These rights are described by an access descriptor denoted by some notation like r for read, w for write and x for execution privileges. It can be represented as a set e.g the descriptor {r,x} indicates the rights to read and execute the file.

The access matrix contains the name of the users (subjects) and type of access allowed for each user on the various objects. This information is known as access control information and is stored in an access control matrix. Whenever a user tries to access a file, then the operating system checks this matrix to find out whether the user has the right to access the file in the mode requested. If the number of users are more, then the various users of the system can be combined into the following groups:

- *System:* It includes the system personnel with unlimited access to all files.
- *Owner:* The user who created the file is called the owner of the file.
- *Group:* A set of users who are sharing the file and need similar access is a group.
- *World:* All other users not included in the first two categories, constitute the world.

1. Let us consider that a person A has created a file named as operating, then that person will be called as the owner of the file.
2. If this user has given the execute –only permission to some particular set of users, then all the users constitute a group and all will have same set of rights.
3. All the other possible users will fall into the category of the World and will have only the read access to the file.
4. This access control list is maintained by the administrator or the file owner.
5. In matrix each column identifies an object & each row identifies a subject.
6. Intersection of row & column defines the access rights for one subject on the particular object.

Subject (Users)/Objects	F1	F2	F3	F4
User I : A	{R,W}			
User II : B	{W}			{R, W, E}
User III : C		{E}		

Figure 11.3: *An Access Matrix*

Upon inspecting the Figure 11.3, we come to know that the User I i.e A has read and write access for the file I, whereas User II has just the access of write privilege for file F1, whereas has user II the rights of Read, write and execute on the file 4.

If the number of users are large in number then following methods can be used to shorten list:

1. The users can be grouped together in any of the categories: System, Owner, Group or the World. Rather than mentioning each and every user individually, the users with the similar type of access are grouped together and the entry for the whole group is made once only.
2. Only those who may use file are named; those denied any access are grouped under global heading such as WORLD.

Protection Domains: The use of access matrix defines the access rights of a user on a number of objects, but here every process created by the user will have same access rights. To facilitate the user to have different access rights for the different processes, the concept of protection domain is used. Instead of defining the access rights on the individual objects, the rows of access matrix may be allowed to represent domains, the entry in the access matrix defines the set of operations that a process executing in domain Di can invoke on the object Oj.

So here the matrix will have Domains in the Rows and the objects in the columns and the entry at the intersection of row and column defines the access rights.

In the access matrix shown below in Figure 11.4, there are three domains D1, D2 and D3 and three objects i.e files F1, F2 and F3. The matrix show that the processes executing in the domain D1 can read the files F1 and F3, whereas the processes executing in the domain D2 can write into File F1 and the processes in domain D3 can read and write the file F1, but can only read the File F2.

Domains/Objects	F1	F2	F3	F4
D1	{R}			{R}
D2	{W}			
D3	{R, W}	{R}		

Figure 11.4: *Access Matrix with Protection Domain*

Change of Protection Domains: The access matrix is an easy and convenient tool to apply the protection on the various objects. It can be used both in the static and dynamic associations between the processes and domains. However, when we switch from one domain to another, then we can execute a switch operation on an object. It can be implemented by including domains among the objects of the access matrix. The Figure 11.5 shown below shows the concept of domain switching, where a process executing in domain D1 can switch to domain D2 and D3 and a process executing in domain D3 can switch to domain D1.

Domains/Objects	F1	F2	F3	F4	D1	D2	D3
D1	{R}			{R}		Switch	Switch
D2	{W}						
D3	{R, W}	{R}			Switch		

Figure 11.5: *An Access Matrix Implementing the Concept of Domain Switching*

The main features of access matrix are:

- It is created by placing on each object the list of users and their access rights. Each object has a list of pairs of the form <subject, access right>.
- As the number of users is quite large, and listing them all will be cumbersome task, so the users can be grouped into classes.
- By default, all users can access a file.

Copying the Rights: The ability to copy the rights from one domain to another can be done by using the copy right. It is denoted by placing an * to the access right. The copy right allows the copying of the access right for that object only, for which it has been defined. In Figure 11.6(a) and 11.6(b), this concept has been demonstrated. In Figure 11.6 (a), a process executing in domain D1 can have a right of write on the file F1 and an * has been placed with this entry, that means this right can be copied to other domains of this file. So a process executing in domain D1 can copy the write permission into any entry associated with the file F1, it has been shown in Figure 11.6(b) that the write permission has been copied to domain D3.

Domains/Objects	F1	F2	F3	F4
D1	Write*		Execute	
D2		Read		
D3			Read	

(a) Copying of Access Rights

Domains/Objects	F1	F2	F3	F4
D1	Write*		Execute	
D2		Read		
D3	Write*		Read	

(b) Copying of Access Rights

Different Versions of Copying the Right Permission: Copy, Transfer & Limited Copy.

(a) *In case of copying the rights,* A right is copied from entry (i, j) to (k, j), that means the rights can be copied to the various domains for the same object only as shown in the Figure 11.6(b), where the write permission has been copied to domain D3 from domain D1.

(b) *In case of transfer the rights,* A right is copied from entry (i, j) to (k, j), it is then removed from (i, j), For example, if the transfer provision is to be carried out, then any process executing in domain D1 will transfer its write permission to any entry associated with file F1 and then the D1 will be deprived of this right. It can be shown in the Figure 11.6 (C) below that D1 has transferred the Write permission to the domain D3 and now D1 has no write permission.

Domains/Objects	F1	F2	F3	F4
D1			Execute	
D2		Read		
D3	Write*		Read	

(c) Transfer of Rights

(c) *In case of limited copy,* When a right is copied from the entry (i, j) to (k,j), only the right R is copied not R*. That means a process executing in domain Dk on receiving the right can enjoy the benefits of that right, but has no authority to transfer this rights to the other domains. As shown in the figure 11.6(d) the domain D1 has transferred the right of write to the file F1 to domain D3, but D3 cannot transfer these rights to the others, it shows a case of limited copy.

Domains/Objects	F1	F2	F3	F4
D1	Write*		Execute	
D2		Read		
D3	Write		Read	

Figure 11.6: *(d) Transfer of Rights(Limited Copy)*

Addition and Deletion of Rights: To manage the access matrix, some mechanism is required to add and remove the rights on various objects for the processes running in various domains. To make this possible the owner right is used to control these operations. If (i, j) includes owner right then any process executing in the domain Di can add or remove any right in any entry in column j. For Example in the Figure 11.7 (a) given below, domain D1 is the owner of F1 so D1 is authorized to change any entry in the column F1 i.e it can add some new right, may delete the existing right or change any right. So the access matrix in Figure 11.7(a) can be modified to the access matrix in Figure 11.7(b), where D1 has taken the read authority from the file F1.

Domains/Objects	F1	F2	F3	F4
D1	Owner		Execute	
D2		Read* Owner		
D3	Read		Read* Write Execute Owner	

(a) Addition and Deletion of Access Rights

Domains/Objects	F1	F2	F3	F4
D1	Owner		Execute	
D2		Read* Owner		
D3			Read* Write Execute Owner	

Figure 11.7: *(b) Addition and Deletion of Access Rights*

The Control Right: The control right allow the processes to change the entries in the rows of the access matrix (compare it with the copy and owner rights which allow the process to change the entries in a column only). If (i, j) includes the control right, then a process executing in domain Di can remove any access right from row i. For Example in the Figure 11.8(a), shows the access matrix in which the user includes control right in (D1, D3), then a process executing in domain D1 can modify the domain D3 as shown in the figure 11.8(a) and 11.8(b) given below:

Domains/Objects	F1	F2	F3	D1	D2	D3
D1	{R}		{R}		Switch	Switch Control
D2	{W}					
D3	{R,W}	{R}		Switch		Switch

(a) Implementation of Control Right

Domains/Objects	F1	F2	F3	D1	D2	D3
D1	{R}		{R}		Switch	Switch Control
D2	{W}					
D3	{R, W}	{R}	{W, E}	Switch		Switch

Figure 11.8: *(b) Implementation of Control Right*

Access matrix can be useful tool to control the user access, when a user creates an object, the user can specify which domains can access the object as well as what operations are allowed on it. But on the other side, the biggest disadvantage of access matrix is that for every access the matrix needs to be checked and when the systems are large then this search can be time consuming. Another disadvantage is that for the large systems the matrix will be a sparse matrix (a matrix is called sparse if most of the entries in the matrix are empty) which will consume large memory space for a fewer entries. If a system has n1 number of users and n2 number of files, the size of access matrix will be n1 * n2, where both n1 and n2 are quite large and large memory space will be required to store this matrix, and normally a user accesses a few files most of the times, so most of the entries in the matrix will be empty, leading to misuse of the memory space. To avoid this wastage, the users having same set of access rights can be grouped together in to groups, so that the rights can be described for the whole group rather than the individual user. An other method to reduce the size of the matrix is to store the access control information in the form of a list rather than in a matrix. The two list structures design approaches possible have been described in the following to section.

Access Control List

The list will contain only the non-null entries from a column of the access control matrix. This list contains access control information for a file in the system. When a user attempts to use a file, the access control list of that file is searched to locate a pair involving that user. It indicates that which user can access the file in what manner. Whenever a user creates a file, he registers the file's access control information with the system. The list for a file stores this information in the form of a set of pairs {userid, access privileges} the figure given below shows the access control lists for files. Let us consider a scenario where the system has three users ravi, ajay and Sonia and the system has four files namely, resume, class, timetable and income. The access control list for these files have been shown below in Figure 11.9, Access Control List for file resume is {(ravi,{read, write)} , {(ajay,{read,write,execute)}, which shows that ravi can read or write the file resume, whereas ajay can either read, write or execute the file, clearly the user Sonia is not allowed to access the file resume in any mode, as the list for the file resume does not has the entry for the user Sonia.

File Name	Protection Information
Resume	{(ravi, {read, write}), (ajay, {read,write,execute})}
Class	{(ajay, {read, write})}
Timetable	{(ajay, {read, write}), (Sonia, {read})}
Income	{(ajay, {read, write}), (ravi, {read, write,execute})}

Figure 11.9: *An Access Control List*

In case the number of users in the system are large in number, then the size of access control list tend to grow and sometimes may become unmanageable, both the memory requirement and the CPU time will be overhead.

Capability Lists

The concept of capability was introduced by Dennis,Van Horn in 1966. This is another alternative way to store the access control information, in this case the list shows every subject with a list of rights the subject has for every object. This list is prepared subject wise. This list stores the entry as a set of pairs as {(fielded/objectid, accessrights)). Where an object can be any hardware or software entity. When some process Pi creates an object Oi, the operating system forms a capability list for object Oi, that contains the entire set of access rights. The process Pi can make copies of this capability list or may create a subset of this capability list and can pass these capabilities to other processes also. It will lead to sharing of object Oi. The capability is defined as a token representing access privileges for an object. The Figure 11.10 given below shows the capability list for the users ravi, ajay and sonia for the example given above.

File Name	Protection Information
Ravi	{(resume,{read, write}),(income,{read,write,execute})}
Ajay	{(class,{read,write}),(resume,{read,write,execute}),(timetable,{read,write})}
Sonia	{(timetable,{read})}
Income	{(ajay,{read,write

Figure 11.10: *A Capability List*

It requires less storage space than an access control matrix. It is easier to maintain than an access control list when users are added or deleted from system. The main features of capability list are:

- It is created by placing on each subject, the list of objects that can be accessed in different modes. Each subject has a list of pairs of the form <object, access rights>.
- The capabilities are the names of the objects, and the objects not required will not be even named in the capability list.

- By default, no one should be able to access a file unless they have been given a capability.
- If a user wishes to access a file the operating system implements the access only if the capability list of that user contains the necessary access privileges for that file.

Lockword Control

Another way of protection is the use of lock word that is similar to a password. A password is a secret piece of information used to establish the identity of the users. Each object has a list of unique bit patterns called locks. Each domain has a list of unique bit patterns called keys. A process executing in domain can access an object only if that domain has a key that matches one of the locks of the object. When the file is created, owner protects it via lock word. It is stored in the directory but is not revealed with directory listing. If a user wishes to access a protected file, then the user needs to provide the correct lock word. It requires smallest amount of storage space for the file protection. If the passwords are chosen randomly and are changed frequently, then it can be an effective method to limit the file access only to the authorized users. But this scheme has many limitations also, as if the user will assign a password to each file then the number of passwords will be very large, making it difficult to remember or manage them, another disadvantage is that anyone who knows it can read, write, delete or execute the file. It can be guessed by hackers and can be used for unauthorized access. Some systems allow the password to be given on directory rather than on a file, another alternative is to provide same password to all files, which make the protection on all or nothing basis.

SECURITY AND ITS IMPLEMENTATION

As discussed earlier, the attacks from the sources outside the system are termed as security attacks. It is an external issue. The attack may be done by persons or entity to breach the security of the system. The number and intensity of attacks increases many fold when the environment is a distributed environment. While ensuring security the user needs to implement:

1. **Attack Prevention:** Attack prevention can be defined as a series of security mechanisms implemented to prevent or defend against various kinds of attacks before they can actually reach and effect the target system. The most common method in this category is access control. Access Control can be defined as the process of limiting access to the resources of an information system only to authorized users, programs, processes or other systems. Firewall is an important access control system that is implemented at the network layer. It prevents the attack from the outside world against the machines in the inside network by preventing connection attempts from unauthorized entities located outside.
2. **Attack Avoidance:** Attack avoidance is the technique in which the information is modified in a way that makes it unusable for the attacker. This is performed

under the assumption that the attacker may access the information. The sender pre-processes the information before it is sent over an unsecure communication channel and it is post-processed at the receiver end. During the communication process, if an intruder tries to capture the data, it will be of no use as it is in encrypted form, the meaning of which can be understood either by the sender or by the receiver.

3. **Attack Detection:** In attack detection, the attacker is able to bypass the installed security measures to access the desired target information. When such incident occur, attack detection program takes on the role of reporting that something wrong has happened and the system tries to identify the type of attack that has occurred.

The most common forms of the security attacks are:

1. **Masquerading:** In this type of attacks an intruder is able to impersonate a registered user of the system. The intruder could access the resources of a registered user of the system and hence can corrupt or destroy the data belonging to that user. The intruder has obtained some information required at the time of logging into the system, like the intruder has stolen the user's password or has guessed the password of the user or has some idea about the security question being asked at the time of logging into the system.
2. **Denial of Service:** In this attack some operations of the operating system are disrupted as a result of which the operating system is not behaving and providing the services as it is expected to do. These attacks can be initiated only by the users of the system, whereas some of the attacks may be initiated by the intruders. Some of these attacks are started in such a sophisticated manner that it is not easy to detect them. In these attacks the programs offering services are destroyed, while in some cases the system resources are overloaded with fake requests to such an extent that the genuine users are denied its use.

Types of Security Attacks

The data on the system is to be secured from the attacks from outside. The attacks may be on the system as a whole or on some program in particular. So these threats can be divided into two categories as:

Program Threats

When a program written by one user may be used by another user, then there are chances that the users may misuse the program. The most common attacks on the programs are:

1. **Trojan Horse:** It is a program that performs a legitimate function that is known to the operating system and its users, but along with that it has a hidden component that attacks on the other data elements stored in the system. Trojan

horse is a program that is written with the intention of disturbances in the computer system. A code segment that misuses its environment is called Trojan Horse. These programs carry out unauthorized actions on computers, such as deleting data on disk drives, can force a system to crash or slow down, stealing the confidential information. These programs are not virus, it cannot break into the system by its own, and rather it is entered in the system as a part of regular software. But the damage caused by them is much more than the damage caused by the viruses. For Example: inside a text editor program, there may be a code to search the file to be edited for certain keywords, if they are found; the entire file may be copied to a special area accessible to the creator of the text editor.

2. **Trap Door:** The designer of the program may leave a hole in the software that can be fixed by that programmer only. The code might check for a specific user Id and it may circumvent normal security procedures. A trap door may be included in the compiler. The compiler can generate standard object code as well as a trap door regardless of the source code being complied. This is a serious problem, as to detect them the user has to analyze the complete source code for all the components of the system. As the system software's consist of millions of lines of code, this type of analysis may be time consuming and tiring.

3. **Stack and Buffer Overflow:** The stack or buffer overflow attack is the most common way to get an unauthorized access to the user system. An unauthorized user may also use this to gain privileges beyond those allowed for the user. The attacker tries to find out a bug in the program. The bug can be as simple as programmer neglected to code bound checking on an input field. It occurs when the attackers sends more data than the program is expected to receive. The attacker tries to exploit the following possibilities:

   (a) Overwrite the current return address on the stack with the address of the exploit code loaded in step 2.

   (b) Write a simple set of code for the next space in the stack that includes the commands that the attacker wishes to execute like a spawn a shell.

   (c) Overflow an input field, command line argument or input buffer.

The result of this will be that the attacker will be able to have an access to the privileged commands, like if a web page needs a user name to be entered in the field, the attacker may enter the user name and some extra characters to overflow the buffer and to have an access to the stack. Along with that a new return address and the malicious code are loaded onto the stack. When the buffer reading subroutine returns from the execution, the return address is the malicious code and it is being run. The buffer overflow attack is quite harmful as it can be run within the system or may travel over allowed communication channels. These attacks may occur in the protocols that move from one system to another over the network and hence are difficult to detect. In order to deal with this problem, CPU may have a feature that disallows execution of the code in a stack section of the memory

System Threats

Most of the operating systems provide a mechanism to generate a number of child processes. In such a scenario it may happen that the operating system files and resources may be misused. The most common methods of creating such an environment are:

1. **Virus:** Viruses are the major problem for computer users. It is a piece of code that is embedded in a legitimate program and spreads itself into other programs and can cause disasters in the system, which may be modifying or destroying the files, causing system crash and program malfunctioning. It alters the way a computer operates and executes without the permission of the user. It replicates itself and may replace other executable files with a copy of virus infected file. While attaching itself to a program, the virus puts its own address as the execution start address of the program. So when the program is activated, the virus runs first and damages the other programs and data and after that it passes the control to the original genuine program for execution. The time for causing the infection is very small and the user has no way of identifying that the program executed carries a virus. In multiuser systems, the chances of virus attacks are less as compared to the single users systems, because in multiuser systems, the executable programs are protected from writing by operating system, and if virus affects the system, the power is limited, whereas in single user systems no such protection mechanism exists, so the viruses run freely and can cause the damage to larger extent. The viruses spread by downloading viral programs from public areas or exchanging the storage media containing an infection. The latest example is an e-mail virus that enters into the computer through an e-mail and sends fake mails to the users whose e-mail ids have been found in the address book. It may cause disturbance as the mail containing unethical material may be sent. The most common types of viruses are:
   (a) *Parasitic:* It is the traditional and most common form of virus. This attaches itself to executable files and replicates when the infected program executes. Due to this the replication occurs in other executable files.
   (b) *Memory Resident Virus:* It lives in main memory as a part of a resident system program. All programs that execute while the virus is in main memory are infected.
   (c) *Boot Sector Virus:* It infects a master boot record or boot record and spreads when the system is booted from the disk containing the virus.
   (d) *Stealth Virus:* It is specifically designed to hide itself from detection by an antivirus software.
   (e) *Polymorphic Virus:* It mutates with every infection and makes the detection of the virus by its signature impossible.
2. **Worms:** A worm is a program that spreads to other computer systems by exploiting security holes like weakness in facilities for creation of remote processes. It uses

spawns mechanism to degrade the system performance. Worms replicate at a very high speed thus will consume a great amount of CPU time. The worms while copying itself uses the system resources and may lock out the other processes from using the system. On computer network, the worms while reproducing themselves may shut down the entire network. Due to its self replicating nature, the worm are even more difficult to trace than a virus. These programs replicate themselves from system to system without the use of a host file.

Methods for Implementing Security Mechanisms:

1. The security attacks created by Trojan Horses, Viruses or Worms can be handled in any of the following ways:
   (a) Be cautious while loading a new software into a computer. Purchasing opened softwares from vendors or getting the pirated copies from the public places may prove to be harmful in long run. The solution is to load programs from original disks on which they are supplied by a vendor or these programs may be supplied on compact disks, as the data on the disk cannot be modified, so it can be prevented from the virus attack.
   (b) The use of antivirus program is the easiest and cheap method for identifying the virus attacks. This program scans all programs on the disk to check whether it has any of the known viruses or not.
   (c) The operating system vendors put the information about the security breaches of their respective operating systems on their websites at the regular intervals of time and also provide the solutions of the same. The user should keep on getting such information so as to safeguard the system from such attacks.
   (d) Another important method is threat monitoring, where the system monitors the activities in order to identify any pattern of activities leading to security breaches.

For example, the system can cause an alarm if the number of attempts to provide correct set of user name and password has exceeded a particular limit, showing that the user is not a legitimate user. The audit log of all the processes can be made, which will record the time of login, user details and types of accesses on an object. If any security attack has been noticed then the audit log can be checked to find out who has created the damage and at what time and in what mode.

The information available through audit logs will be helpful to identify the malicious user and in carrying out the recovery procedures and hence to design the future strategies to avoid such attacks.

(a) The system can be scanned at regular intervals to identify any malicious program installed in the system.

(b) Another method which can be used to ensure security is to implement the concept of firewalls. The firewall can be used to separate trusted and untrusted domains.

1. Another method to handle security is to authenticate the users while they are going to access the system. For this purpose the authentication mechanisms are used, which has already been discussed.

2. Encryption (Cryptography): The third method to maintain security is the method of encryption. It is a technique for protecting the confidentiality of data. Protection and Security mechanisms use it to guard information concerning users and their resources. Encryption is the technique which is used to guard information belonging to the users. The branch of science dealing with the encryption techniques is called cryptography. It is a method which enforces secrecy of the authentication data. The sensitive data needs to be protected, so that if any user receives this data during transition should not be able to comprehend the meaning of the data. To keep such sensitive information secure some mechanism is required to allow a user to protect the data transmitted over the network. The encryption technique is used to protect information transmitted over unreliable links. The steps followed in the encryption process can be enumerated as:
   (a) The original data i.e the data to be transmitted ,also known as the plain text is fed to the encryption algorithm, which convert this plain text to an internal form, known as cipher text or encrypted text with the help of encryption key. This cipher text is readable but is not in user understandable form.
   (b) The encrypted text is transmitted over the transmission channel.
   (c) The receiver will receive the encrypted text as it is not in the understandable form, so the receiver will decode (decrypt) it back to the plain text with the help of decryption algorithm supported by a decryption key.

The process can be shown in the diagram below:

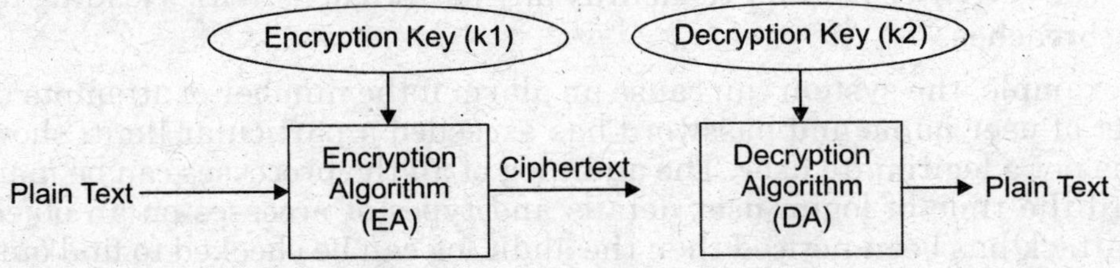

Figure 11.11: *Encryption and Decryption of Data*

The terms used in the Figure 11.11 are:

- Encryption Key: K1.
- Decryption Key: K2.
- Encryption Algorithm: EA
- Decryption Algorithm: DA

The encryption can be of following two types:

(a) *Symmetric Encryption:* In this case the encryption and decryption keys are same, i.e the same key is used to convert plain text to cipher text and then from cipher text to plain text.

(b) *Asymmetric Encryption:* In this case the encryption and decryption keys are different, i.e the key used to convert plain text to cipher text is different from the key used to convert cipher text to plain text.

The technique of encryption ensure that even if encrypted information is accessed by an unauthorized person or program, the user will not be able to read the data as it is in coded form. The biggest problem in this method is to develop an encryption algorithm that can be cracked easily.

Distributed File System

Chapter 12

The advancements in computers and computer technology have showcased a scenario where computer systems distribute computation among several physical processors. There can be two methods to achieve this, in a multiprocessor tightly coupled system, the processors share memory and a clock and communication takes place through the shared memory. On the other hand, in a loosely coupled distributed system, the processors do not share memory or a clock, instead each processor has its own local memory. In this case the processors communicate with one another through various communication networks.

INTRODUCTION TO DISTRIBUTED SYSTEMS

A distributed system consists of several nodes, where each node is a computer system with its own clock and memory, that can communicate among themselves through a network. The distributed systems allow the user to structure his application in a distributed computation, which consists of several processes located at different nodes of the distributed system. In order to service all nodes efficiently, it balances the computational load in various computers by transferring the processes between the nodes. So the processes of the same application can use CPU in different nodes. As a result of which computation speed will increase resulting in better performance of the system. Moreover reliability is provided as there is redundancy of resources and network links.

Definition, Goals and Characteristics of Distributed Systems

Definition: A distributed system consists of two or more computer systems connected through network, each with its own memory, some networking hardware and the capability of performing some of the control functions.

A distributed operating system exploits the use of multiplicity of resources and the presence of network to provide the advantages of resource sharing among computers, reliability of operation, speed up of application execution and communication among the users. For a processor in distributed system, the rest of the processors and their resources are remote, whereas its own resources are local. The processors in a distributed system may vary in size and function. They may include small microprocessors, workstations, minicomputers and large general purpose computer systems. These may be referred as small microprocessors, sites, nodes, computers or hosts. These systems allow the user to access the various hardware resources like printers and tape drives and software resources such as programs and files in a controlled environment provided by the operating system. There are two methods for providing such services, in the first case, the user is aware of the presence of multiple machines and the user can access these resources either by logging into the required remote machine or by transferring the data from the remote machine to their own machines, such a scheme is known as network operating systems, on the other hand, if the user is not aware of the presence of multiple machines, and they are not able to differentiate between the local and global availability of the resources. This is covered in the study of distributed operating systems. The distributed systems have hardware and software components, where hardware components are individual computer systems and other networking hardware such as cables, links and routers and the software components are the programs that handle creation and scheduling of distributed computations and use of distant resources, operating system and programming language features that support writing of distributed computations and networking software which ensures the smooth and reliable communication between the participating units.

The following are the key features of a distributed system:

1. They are loosely coupled and the remote access is many times slower than local access.
2. The nodes in a distributed environment are autonomous.
3. Network connections are maintained using system software and the remote access requires explicit message passing between nodes i.e messages are passed from CPU to CPU.
4. These systems use protocols for reliability, flow control, failure detection, etc., implemented in software.

Goals of Distributed Systems

- *Resource Sharing:* In the distributed systems, a number of sites are connected to each other, then they will be able to share the resources with each other. It provides the facility of sharing data at the remote sites, processing information in a distributed database, using remote specialized hardware etc.
- *Reliability:* In distributed system environment, if one site stops working, then the remaining sites will keep on carrying the jobs. These systems offer enhanced availability of resources through redundancy of resources and communication paths. Hence there will be no threat of failure and ultimately the overall reliability of the system will increase. These systems provide availability i.e continuity of services, despite faults. It is achieved by redundancy in network its resources and services.
- *Increase in Computation Speed:* In distributed environment, a single job can be divided in to number of parts and then can be distributed among the various sites and these sites will be executing their own part at the same time, it will increase the computation speed of the processes and hence the throughput will increase and turnaround time (time between submission of the job and getting

its final results) will decrease. So a number of jobs can be executed in parallel in a stipulated time. Moreover, if a particular site is overloaded with jobs, then some of its jobs may be moved to other lightly loaded sites and this process is termed as load sharing. The distributed systems also provide the facility of automatic load sharing, through which the system automatically moves the job from overloaded site to the less loaded site, in order to maintain the balance and to speed up the execution of the jobs.

- *Better Communication among Systems:* In many cases, the programs need to exchange data with one another. Distributed systems facilitate the sharing and communication of data among the various sites. The processes of the same application may be distributed among various nodes and they will be in need of exchanging the data among them, these systems allow the processes to communicate with one another.
- *Incremental Growth:* In distributed environment it is easy to add the new nodes at a cheaper rate as compared to set up the central systems. The open system standards allow the user to add new subsystems without the need of replacing or upgrading the existing systems.

Characteristics of Distributed Systems

The major characteristics of a distributed system are:

1. **Concurrency:** In a distributed environment multiple processes run at the same time. For example, while the web browser is downloading contents from a web server, it may also be preparing itself for how to present the contents on the screen. The major complexity in the concurrency is that shared resources must be handled properly. Like if more than one user working from their respective nodes may be in need of the same resources at the same time, then conflicts may occur and it may lead to the situation of deadlock. The distributed systems ensure that multiple numbers of users may work at the same time and chances of conflict are reduced to the negligible.
2. **Synchronization:** The processes in a distributed environment must synchronize with each other, the synchronization is required in time, processes must synchronize and coordinate their activities. The synchronization works on the concept that at what time the activities occur.

Techniques used in Distributed Operating Systems

- *Distributed Control:* As the name specifies the control functions of a distributed system are performed by several computers instead of being performed by a single computer. It ensures that if any one node fails in the distributed environment, it does not affect operations of the entire system.
- *Transparency:* It is applicable to both the resources and services, where a user should be able to access them without having to know which node in the distributed system has initiated it. i.e the location of the nodes is hidden for all the processes.

- *Remote Procedure Calls:* These calls are used by an application to execute a procedure in another computer over the distributed system.

Types of Computer Networks

To realize the distributed environment, both the network hardware and software is required. The various issues pertaining to it are the study of types of networks, network topologies and other issues like finding an IP address of the node where the destination process is located, how to enroute the data from source to the destination and ensuring that the message is delivered efficiently and reliably.

A computer network is defined as an interconnected collection of a group of two or more autonomous computers that are linked together to share information and resources. These systems are free to act independent of each other and there is no master and slave relationship between them. The connection between the various computers may be through wires or it can be wireless.

The type of network is determined by the geographical distribution of users and resources in the system. The three basic types of computer networks are:

1. Local Area Network(LAN)
2. Metropolitan Area Network(MAN)
3. Wide Area Network(WAN)

1. **Local Area Network (LAN):** The name specifies the area covered in the network is local only. It covers small distance, typically within a single building or a few adjacent buildings up to a few kilometers. It can be small as a network of 2-3 computers or the link may be between hundreds of computers in the specified geographical area. The LAN came into existence due to the fact that enterprises felt that it is more economical to have a number of small computers with its own self contained applications, rather than a single large system. The small stand alone systems also require the full complement of peripheral devices and they need to share the resources also, so it is a good choice to connect them into a network. To share the network resources and to route the communications on a LAN requires the use of special softwares known as network operating systems. All the sites in a LAN are close to each other so the communication link between them is of high speed and lower error rate as compared to the other types of networks discussed below. To attain the benefits of high speed and reliability, high quality cables will be required. The transmission media used are twisted pair and fiber optical cables. A LAN may consist of number of different computers, from mainframe to laptops and various shared peripheral devices and one or more gateways that provide access to the other networks. LAN will use only one type of transmission media. The topologies used in LAN are bus, ring and star and data rate is between 4-16 Mbps.

Characteristics of LAN

- Small Size: The size of LAN is restricted to a few kilometers. Mostly it is used in a single building.
- Single Owner: The LAN equipment is generally owned by a single organization.
- Physically Secured: LAN is located in the premises of a company, so it is physically protected from the unauthorized physical access.
- Data and Resource Sharing: The users of the same LAN can share the data and resources among themselves.
- Low Cost Data transmission: The LAN uses cable media for transferring the data from one place to another, which is a low cost alternative, hence is cheap.
- Limited Scope: All LAN's support a single group, so the functionality of these systems is limited.

2. **Metropolitan Area Network (MAN):** A MAN often covers a wider geographical area than LAN (upto 50 Km in diameter) and operate at the speeds very close to the speed of LAN. The main objective of MAN is to interconnect the LANs located in an entire city or metropolitan area. The communication links used for MANs are coaxial cable and microwave links. Like a bank with multiple branches may utilize a MAN, it may be a single network such as a cable television network or may be a means of connecting a number of LANs into a larger network so that resources may be shared LAN-to-LAN as well as device-to-device.

Characteristics

- The size of these networks is intermediate of LAN and WAN. These cover an area larger than LAN but smaller than WAN.
- It is a high speed network to allow sharing of regional resources.
- It connects networks in a city into a single larger network.
- Fiber Optics is a popular technology used in MAN.

3. **Wide Area Networks (WAN):** These types of networks came into existence to provide efficient communication between sites allowing hardware and software to be shared conveniently and economically by a wide community of users. The first WAN designed and developed was Arpanet. As WANs are physically distributed over a large geographical area, the communication links are relatively slow, somewhat unreliable and error prone. The range of area covered by WANs may comprise a country, a continent or even the entire globe.

Characteristics

- A WAN generally covers a larger distance than LAN and can cover the distance from a few miles to the entire globe.

- These communication networks are publically available; it has many subscribers that share the common communication media.
- These provide the facilities of e-mail, WWW, file transfer and e-commerce.

Difference between LAN and WAN

Table 12.1 Difference between LAN and WAN

S.No	LAN	WAN
1.	It is restricted to a limited geographical area of a few kilometers, it provide communication within a building or a campus.	It is extended over thousand kilometers and the area covered is nationwide or worldwide.
2.	Data Transmission rate are higher than WAN. It range from 10 Megabits per second(Mbps) to 1 gigabits per second (Gbps)	Data transmission rate is lower than LAN. It ranges from 1200 bits per second to 2 Mbps.
3.	These networks has lower data transmission errors, it range from 10-8 to 10-12.	WAN suffers from higher data transmission errors, it range from 10-5 to 10-7.
4.	The common communication links used are twisted pair, coaxial cable and fiber optics.	The common communication links used are telephone lines, microwave links and satellite channels.
5.	A LAN is owned by a single organization.	A WAN is formed by interconnecting multiple LANs each of which may belong to a different organization.
6.	The cost of data transmission is very less, as the transmission media is owned by a single organization and the distance travelled while moving from one node to another is quite less.	The cost of transmission is comparatively high, as the transmission media used is leased lines or public communication systems, and the distance travelled for sending the data from one location to another is large.
7.	The cost of establishing a LAN is less as compared to WAN.	The comparative cost is high.

Network Topologies

The network topology refers to the way in which the nodes i.e the computers or the other devices which need to communicate are linked together in the network. It determines the data paths, which are used by a node to transfer the data to the other nodes. It is also termed as the physical topology, as it refers to the configuration of cables, computers and other peripherals. On the other side, the method used to pass information between the workstations is termed as logical topology. There are a number of possible configurations to arrange the various nodes in the network, the user or the organization can choose the one most suitable for the organization and its operations. The choice of a particular topology depends on following factors:

1. The desired performance of the system.
2. The required level of reliability.
3. Size of the area to be covered.
4. The need to expand the system.
5. The installation cost and service cost.
6. Availability of communication lines.
7. The required level of delay that can be tolerated.

The various common topologies are

1. **Star:** In the star arrangement of computer network, the multiple computers are connected to a host computer. The computers in a network are not connected to each other, but they can communicate only through a host computer. The host computer provides the communication path between the nodes interested in communication. The host computer is also termed as a server. It may be a hub, switch or concentrator. This host device manages or controls all functions of the network. The Figure 12.1 given below show a Star Configuration of a computer network.

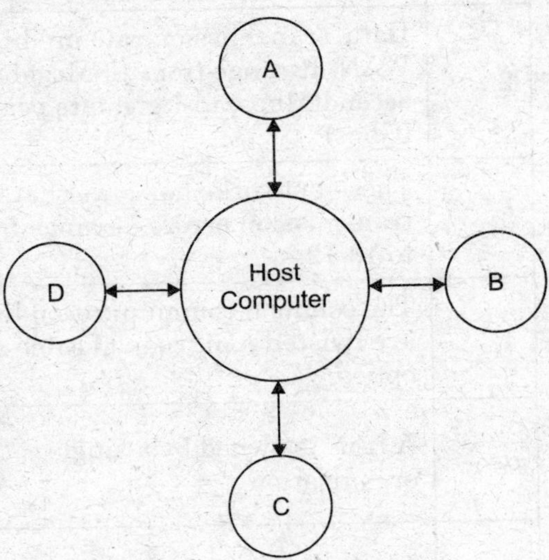

Figure 12.1: *Star Topology*

Advantages

1. Star topology has minimal line cost as only n-1 lines are required to connect n nodes.
2. The communication cost is low, as a message from process A to B requires at most two transfers i.e from A to the central site and then from central site to B.
3. Transmission delay between two nodes does not increase by adding new nodes to the network, as any two nodes may be connected by two links only. (This is an advantage till the central host is capable to handle the nodes attached to it).
4. If any participating computer fails, then it does not affect the whole network. For Example, if the node A in the figure fails, then all other nodes can communicate with each other through the host without any disturbance.

5. It is easy to detect the faults and to remove the faulty computer.
6. The network will remain undistrupted, when the devices are connected or removed.

Disadvantages

1. The system depends on the central host computer badly. As if it fails the whole network fails.
2. Requires more cable length than other topologies.
3. If a large number of systems are attached to the central hub, then it may not be able to cater to the needs of all the systems attached to it. As the number of computers attached to the central system increases, the performance reduces and the time required to satisfy a particular system increases.

2. **Ring Topology:** In the star topology each site is physically connected to exactly two other sites, one to the left of it and another to the right of it. Each computer has communicating subordinates, but there is no master computer for controlling other computers. The node receives the data from one of its two adjacent nodes and decides whether the data is for its own use or not. If it is addressed to it, it utilizes it otherwise it passes it onto the next node. The ring can be either unidirectional orh bidirectional. In unidirectional architecture, a site can transmit information to only one of the neighbors. All sites must send the information in the same direction. Whereas, in bidirectional structure, a site can transmit information to both of its neighbors. A message from source to destination travels around the entire ring until it reaches the destination. In unidirectional ring, this process could require n-1 transfers, whereas in bidirectional ring at most n/2 transfers are needed. The Figure 12.2 given below show a ring configuration of computer network.

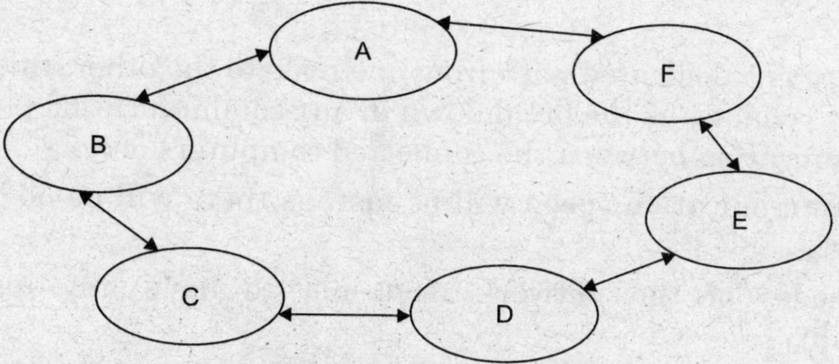

Figure 12.2: *Ring Topology.*

Advantages

1. There is no dependency on the central computer. So it is more reliable than the single host computers.
2. These networks are comparatively easy to install.

Disadvantages

1. A single break in the cable can disrupt the entire network.
2. As the number of nodes in the network increases, the communication delay also increases.
3. Addition and deletion of a node from the network will cause the whole network to halt.
4. It requires complicated control software than the other topologies.

3. **Completely Connected or Mesh Topology:** In a completely connected network each device is directly linked with all other sites in the system. That means there is a physical link from each node to every other node. So each node has a dedicated link called point-to-point link with all other computers in the network. This type of structure provide the benefits of fast and reliable communication. The Figure 12.3 given below show a completely connected computer network.

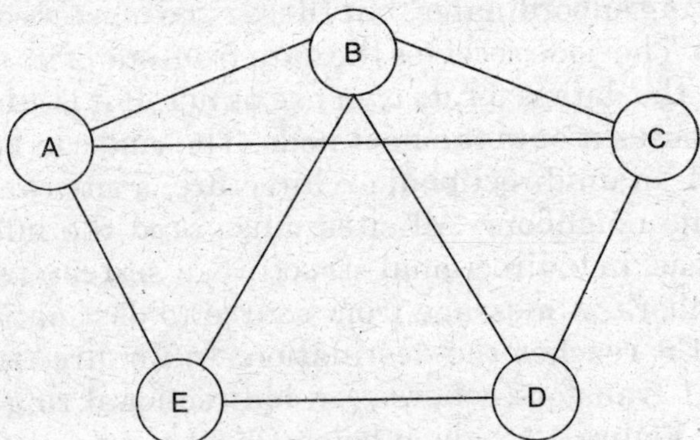

Figure 12.3: *Mesh Topology.*

Advantages

1. As there is a dedicated path from one node to the other, this type of network is very reliable, as the breakdown in any communication path will affect the communication between the connected computers only.
2. The communication speed will be fast, as there will be no congestion in the network.
3. The nodes of the network need not to have any individual routing capability.
4. The messages need to use only one link to travel from the source to the destination.
5. This topology provides security in data transmission, as the messages are sent along the dedicated links only and the intended recipients will receive the message.
6. A point to point link makes the fault identification and isolation easy.

Disadvantages

1. It is most expensive network from the point of view of link cost. If there are n nodes in the network, then n(n-1)/2 links are required. This cost increases as the new nodes are added.
2. A large amount of cabling is required.
3. As the number of nodes increases, the complexity and difficulty in managing the network increases.

4. **Bus Topology:** In this type of network there is a single link and all the devices are directly connected to the link, which may be organized as a straight line or as a ring. The sites can communicate with each other through the link only. The common bus cable has a terminator at the both ends. The Figure 12.4 given below show a network showing bus topology.

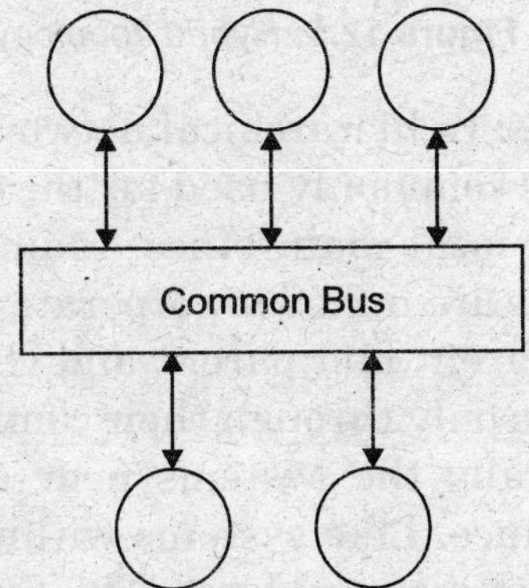

Figure 12.4: *Linear Bus Topology.*

Advantages

1. It helps in reducing the number of physical lines.
2. The failure of one computer does not affect the communication between the other components in the network.
3. Addition and deletion of the nodes is easy.

Disadvantages

1. All computers in the network must have good communication and decision making capability.
2. If the common communication line fails, the entire system will fail.
3. Terminators are required at both ends of the common bus.
4. It is difficult to identify the problem, if entire network fails.

5. **Hybrid Topology:** In this type of structure the various types of networks are connected together, where a combination of two or more different network topologies is used to reap the benefits of all types of topologies. The exact configuration

of the network depends on the needs of the organizations. Communications in such an environment is complex as the multiple protocols must be translated to one another and routing of data is more tricky. In the Figure12.5 given below a ring, star and completely connected network topologies have been connected together.

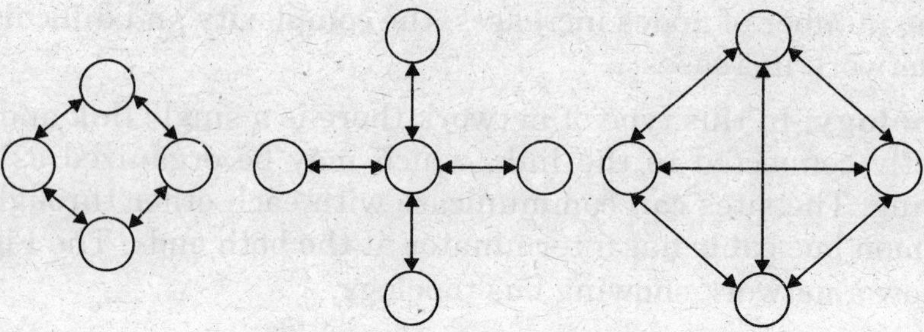

Figure 12.5: *Hybrid Topology.*

6. **Hierarchical Networks:** In hierarchical networks, the sites are organized as a tree. This organization is commonly used for the corporate networks. Individual offices are linked to the local main office. Main offices are linked to regional offices and regional offices are linked to corporate headquarters. Each site(except the root) has a unique parent and parent and child communicate directly. The siblings can communicate only through their common parent. This configuration works well where generally the systems near each other communicate more than those are at a distance. Like systems within a building are more likely to transfer data than those at distant places. The Figure 12.6 given below show the hierarchical network as a tree topology.

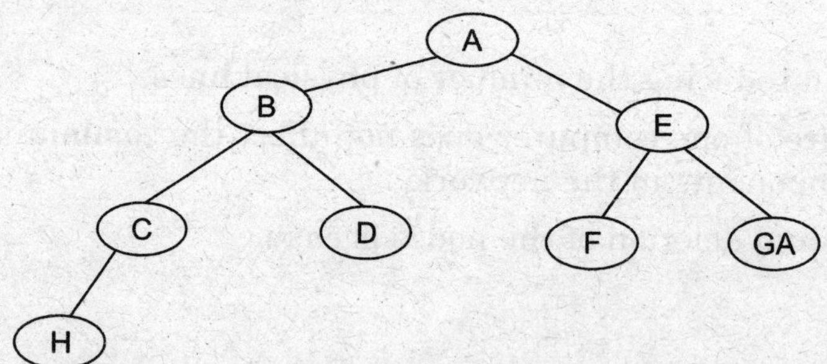

Figure 12.6: *Tree Topology*

Modes of Data Transmission

The communication between the various machines can occur in following different ways. The transmission is characterized by the direction of the exchange, the bandwidth i.e the number of bits transferred at a time and the synchronization between the sender and receiver. Accordingly, there are following transmission modes:

1. **Simplex Mode:** In a simplex transmission mode, the data may flow only in one direction i.e from sender to receiver. It is useful when it is not required to flow the data in both the directions like from the computer to the printer. The Figure 12.7 given below shows the simplex mode of transmission.

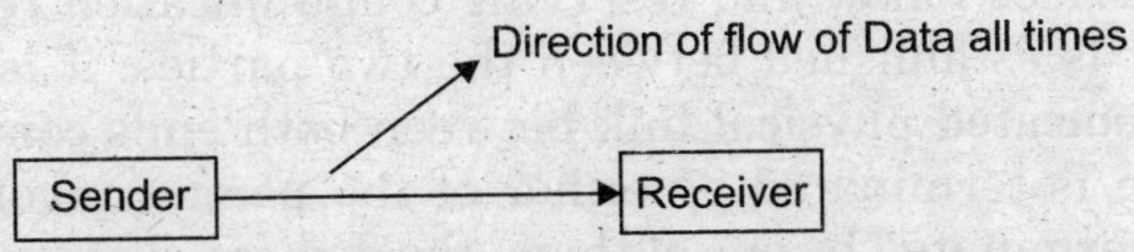

Figure 12.7: *Simplex Mode of Transmission*

2. **Half Duplex Mode:** In half duplex transmission mode, the data may flow in both the directions but not at the same time, i.e it will flow in one direction at a time. It makes it possible to have bidirectional communications using full capacity of the line. The Figure 12.8 given below shows half duplex mode of transmission.

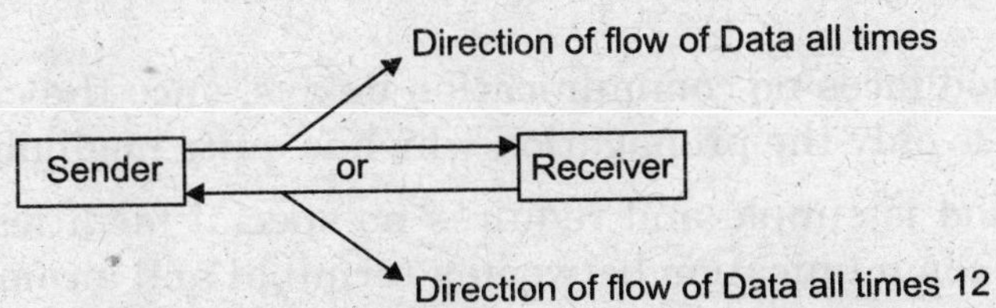

Figure 12.8: *Half Duplex Mode of Transmission*

3. **Full Duplex Mode:** In this mode the data flows in both the directions at the same time. So the bandwidth is divided in two for each direction of data transmission, if the same transmission medium is used for both directions of transmission. The Figure 12.9 given below shows full duplex mode of transmission.

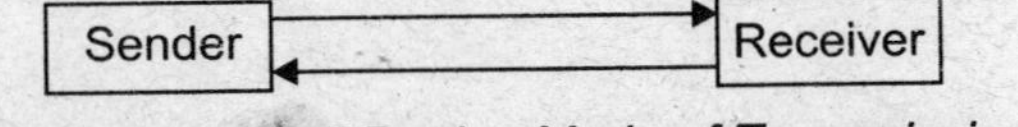

Figure 12.9: *Full Duplex Mode of Transmission*

Network Connection Strategies

A connection is a path between the communicating processes. A connection strategy, also known as a switching technique determines when a connection should be set up between a pair of processes and for how long it will remain active. The choice of switching technology influences efficiency of communication between a pair of processes and throughput of communication links. The three most common switching technologies have been explained here:

1. **Circuit Switching:** A circuit is a connection that is used exclusively by a pair of communicating processes and carries all messages between them. In this type of communication there is a dedicated path which is established between the sender and the receiver through the nodes in the network. This method is used to connect two subscribers for telephone conversation. The computers connected

through a telephone network also use this method of establishing communication path among them. A circuit is established when processes decide to communicate i.e before the first message is sent and is destroyed sometime after the last message has been transmitted. Circuit set up involves deciding the actual network path that messages follow and reserving communication resources accordingly. Once a circuit is established between the two parties, it is exclusively used by them and a dedicated physical link between both ends continues to exist, until the connection is terminated by either of the parties involved. As soon as the connection is terminated by one of them, the dedicated resources are de-allocated and can be used by other nodes. The circuit switching has three phases:

- Circuit Establishment.
- Data Transfer.
- Circuit Disconnection.

Advantages

1. This method faces no communication delays, once the circuit is established. The delay is only the propagation which is quite negligible.
2. This method is simple and requires no special facilities and is suitable for low-speed communication between a terminal and a computer.
3. As a dedicated path is established, the, method is suitable for long continuous transmission.
4. As the full capacity of the circuit is available for use by the connected pair of nodes, the transmission time required to send a message can be known and can be guaranteed once the connection has been established. So this method is suitable for transmission of voice and real time data.

Disadvantages

1. The connection is to be established before the transmission of data starts, this time period may be large in some systems.
2. As a dedicated physical connection is established between the two parties, the channel capacity is dedicated to one source for the entire duration of the connection. So the network resources are not utilized properly.
3. Many a times the communication occur in short bursts with long silent periods in between, during the silent burst the communication line is not used, so this method proves to be very uneconomical.

This method is useful when the overall message density in the system is low but medium to heavy traffic is expected between the pair of processes.

2. **Message Switching:** A message is a logical unit of information and can be of any length. In this method, if a station wishes to send a message to another station, it first appends the destination address to the message. After this the

message is transmitted from the source to the destination either by store-and-forward or broadcast methods. In this case the connection is established for each message sent between a pair of processes. Thus message between the same pair of processes may travel over different paths in the system.

In Store-and-forward method the message is transmitted from the source to an intermediate node. The intermediate node stores the complete message on temporary basis and transmits it to the next node based on the availability of free channel and its routing information. The actual path from the source to destination is dynamic, as the path is created as the, message travels. When the message reaches the destination node, the channel on which it came is released for use by other message.

In the broadcast method, the message is broadcast over a common medium, which is known as broadcast channel. All the stations check the destination address of each message as they pass by and accept only those addressed to them. The routing delays in store-forward method are eliminated in this method.

Advantages

1. No physical connection is required between the source and destination.
2. As the channels are used only when the messages are transmitted, this method uses the channel very effectively.

Disadvantages

1. The message length of various messages varies, so all the switching nodes must have sufficient storage to buffer messages.
2. The message is delayed at every node for the time required to receive the message and at each node the message has to wait in the queue to wait for an opportunity to retransmit the message to the next node.
3. This method is not suitable for interactive real time applications, so it is used when message delays are not critical.

3. **Packet Switching:** A message is split into packets of fixed size. The packet has a block of data to be sent and has a header which contains the destination and source addresses, control information, message number, number of current and last packet, acknowledgement and error checking bits. A connection is established for each packet individually, so packets of the same message may travel along different routes. The packets received at the destination are to be reassembled to make a sense of it. Like message switching the packets may be routed from the sender to the destination nodes either by store-and-forward or broadcast method.

Advantages

1. As the packets are of fixed size, the storage requirement of buffering the packets at the intermediate nodes is minimal.

2. The packets being of small size, the cost of retransmission of a packet due to error is very less.
3. As routing is done on the packet basis, the intermediate nodes need not to wait for the entire message, so the transmission is very fast.
4. This method is very useful for interactive real time applications.
5. It is best suited for bursty communication between computers and is widely used in WAN.
6. Links are not monopolized by specific pairs of processes, so all pairs of communicating processes receive fair and unbiased service.

Disadvantages

1. As the packets are to be reassembled at the destination node, it incurs an overhead.
2. There is no guarantee that how long it takes a message to go from the source to its destination, as time taken for each packet depend on the route chosen for that packet, along with the volume of data being transferred along that route.

Network Routing Strategies

When a process at site A wants to communicate with a process at site B, the routing function is invoked, whenever a connection is to be set up. It decides which network path would be used by the connection. If there is only one physical path from A to B the message must be sent through that path only and if there are multiple physical paths from A to B, then several routing options exist and then the most optimal route must be selected to transfer the data from the source to the destination. Each site has a routing table, which indicates the alternative paths that can be used to send a message to the other site. The table may include information about the speed and cost of the various communication paths and it may be updated as and when required, the three most basic routing strategies are:

1. **Fixed Routing:** In case of fixed routing, a path from source to destination is specified in advance permanently between the nodes wishing to communicate. When processes located at these nodes wish to communicate, a connection is set up using this path. And this path does not change unless a hardware failure disables this path. Fixed routing is simple and efficient to implement. In this case, each node merely contains a table showing paths to all other nodes in the system. But this method lacks flexibility to deal with the changes in traffic densities and faults in nodes or links. If a path has been established between two nodes, then the message must be sent along this path only, even if this path has gone down or some other path is used

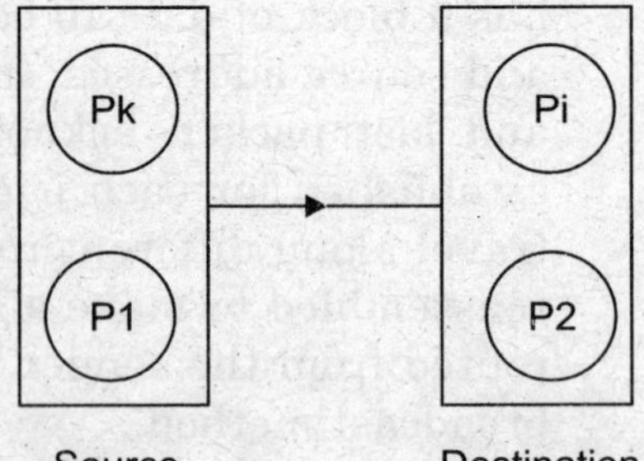

Figure 12.10: *Fixed Routing*

lightly. Hence its use can result in delays or reduction in the throughputs. The Figure 12.10 given below show the Fixed Routing Strategy.

2. **Virtual Routing:** The path between the source and destination is selected for the duration of a session only. A path is selected at the start of the session between a pair of processes and is used for all messages sent during the session. Information related to traffic densities and communication delays along different links in the system are used to decide the best path for a session. So this strategy can adapt to the changing traffic patterns and link faults, due to this feature this method ensure good throughput and response time. The Figure 12.11 given below show the virtual circuit.

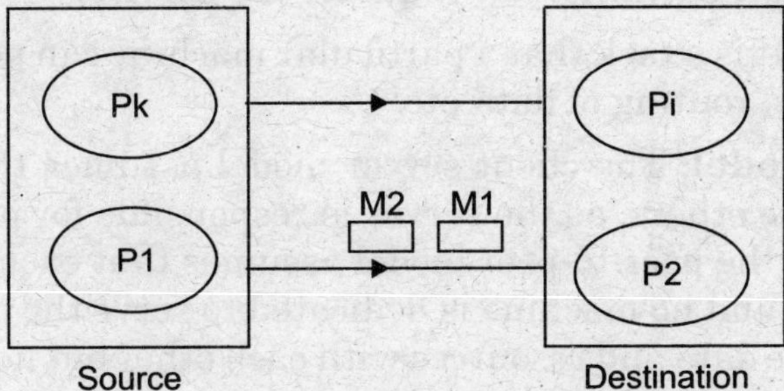

Figure 12.11: *Virtual Circuit.*

3. **Dynamic Routing:** In the case of dynamic routing the path is selected dynamically at the run time only. A path is selected whenever a message or packet is to be sent, so different messages between a pair of processes and different packets of the same message may use different paths. Due to this feature the routing strategy changes with the changes in the traffic patterns and faults in the nodes or links. This strategy ensures better throughput and response time as compared to the other strategies. The Figure 12.12 given below show a dynamic routing scenario.

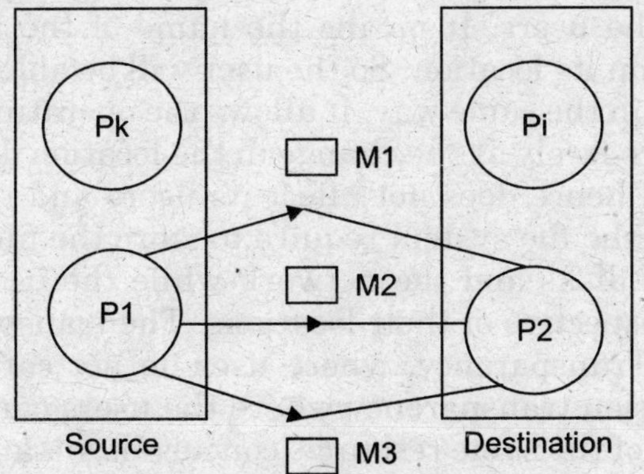

Figure 12.12: *Dynamic Routing*

Architecture of Distributed Systems

1. **Centralized Model:** In a centralized model, there is no networking. All aspects of the application are hosted on one machine and users directly connect to that machine. The main problem with this method is that it is not scalable. There is a limit to the number of processors in a system and problem increases when a number of processes wish to acquire the same resource.
2. **Client-Server Model:** It is very common network model having three major components:
   (a) *A Server:* It is a machine that performs the task and hosts the service.
   (b) *A Client:* It is a machine that requests the service.
   (c) *The Service:* It is a task that a particular machine can perform like execution of commands, routing of data etc.
3. **Peer To Peer Model:** The client server model assumes that certain machines are better than the others, as the server is responsible for providing the services to the clients, but the peer-to-peer model assumes that each machine has almost equal capabilities and no machine is dedicated to serve the others. The machines in this model share data and resources with each other but no machine is regarded as special.

Design Issues in Distributed Systems

The user of a distributed system expects that the system should provide the look and feel of a conventional operating system and must provide the benefits of distributed systems like resource sharing, reliability, computation speed up and faster communications. To meet these expectations data, resources, users and their computations should be distributed effectively among the nodes of the system. The various design issues in distributed systems are:

1. **Transparency of Resources and Services:** Transparency means hiding distribution from the users. It means the name of the resources and services does not depend upon its location. So the user will be able to access the local and non-local resources in the same way. It allows the operating system to change the location of a resource freely as the change in the location does not affect the name of the resource and hence does not affect its users and their applications. This feature is useful as the file system require to store the files at different nodes to optimize the use of disks and the network while the user would like to access files identically irrespective of their locations. The transparency can be of many types as Location Transparency, where user do not care where the resources are located, replication transparency where the users cannot tell whether there are multiple copies of the same resource, concurrency transparency, where users share resources transparently with each other without interference and parallel transparency, where operations can take place in parallel without the users knowing it. It gives the users an illusion that they are using single processor

time sharing system instead of a distributed system. The goal implies that the distributed nature of the system should be transparent. The transparency can be achieved at two different levels:

The concept of transparency can be applied to several aspects of a distributed system. These are explained in the Table 12.2 given below:

Table 12.2 Types of Transparency in Distributed Environment

Kind	Meaning
Location Transparency	The users cannot tell where the resources have been located.
Migration Transparency	The user can move the resources without changing their names.
Replication Transparency	The users are not aware of number of copies that exist.
Concurrency Transparency	Multiple users can share the resources automatically.
Parallelism Transparency	Activities can happen in parallel, but the user is not aware of this parallelism.

2. **Distribution of Control Function:** A control function is a function performed by the kernel to control resources and processes in the system like resource allocation, deadlock handling and scheduling. A distributed operating system performs a control function through a distributed control algorithm, whose actions are performed in different nodes of the system in a coordinated manner.
3. **System Performance:** The optimal performance is a pre-requisite for the system efficiency. In addition to the normal techniques used for maintaining the system performance, the distributed systems provide good system performance through data migration and computation migration. Data migration is used to reduce network latencies and improve response times of processes, whereas computation migration is employed to ensure that equal amount of work load is divided to all processors in the system, through the techniques of load balancing. A distributed system will keep on increasing in size as the new nodes and users are added from time to time, and as the size of the system grows, the response time may degrade and hence the overall performance of the system goes down, in order to maintain the system performance the distributed system should be made scalable.
4. **Availability:** The resources should be available at the nearest site so that the data retrieval function can be performed with a little effort.
5. **Reliability:** The reliability of communication is an obvious requirement. The availability of resources at the multiple sites provide a safeguard against the link or node faults. If a fault occurs in a network path to a resource, the application can use another network path to the resource. The only caution that should be made is that the multiple copies of the data should be consistent, to ensure it the distributed systems use two-phase commit protocol.

6. **Security:** The security in a distributed environment is of paramount importance as the messages may pass through a communication processor that operates under a different operating system. An intruder may gain control of such a computer. So the distributed systems use the techniques of message security, encryption, authentication and authorization to ensure the safe delivery of the data through multiple channels.
7. **Scalability:** The systems tend to grow in size as the new nodes and users are added to the system every now and then. But as the number of users increases the performance of the system goes down and the users tend to be less satisfied. So while designing the distributed systems it should be kept in mind that upto what level the systems are scalable so that the system performance does not come down.
8. **Managing the Heterogeneity:** In the distributed environments, a variety of networks, computer hardware, operating systems and systems developed by different developers work together to achieve their requirements of data and resources. This heterogeneity occurs in:
   - **Networks:** The distributed environment consists of systems under different networks, and all these networks may be using different protocols to communicate and may be using different types of transmission media to transfer data from one location to the other.
   - **Computer Hardware:** The different nodes of the distributed systems may be having different hardware and their data formats and other characteristics will also vary, so synchronization is required between them.
   - **Operating Systems:** The distributed nodes may be using different operating systems.
   - **Programming Language:** Different programming languages use different data representation for characters and data structures, the difference must be taken into account if programs written in different languages are to communicate with each other.

Challenges For Distributed Systems

The major challenges faced by the designers of distributed systems are:

1. **Heterogeneity:** In a distributed environment a number of different sites work together and share resources with each other, but there is a variety of computer networks involved in transferring of data, these networks differ in their working, the participating units also differ in their computer hardware, operating systems, programming languages and implementations of different developers.
2. **Security:** Security is a major issue in distributed environment, protection against open access to the unauthorized individuals, protection against alteration or corruption and protection against interference with the means

to access the resource. Replication of data at the multiple servers and then maintaining the consistency and integrity of data is the major security challenge for the designers of distributed systems.

3. **Scalability:** Most of the time it has been noticed that as number of users in distributed environment increases, the system performance goes down, the turnaround time of the jobs and the waiting time of the users increases manifold, which is not acceptable at any cost. So the designers of distributed systems should keep this requirement in mind that the system performance should not come down as the number of users' increases.
4. **Failure Handling:** Depending upon the architecture used in the design of distributed systems, the havoc and the problems created by the failure of a single or multiple nodes may vary. As the whole system may collapse or some of the nodes in the distributed environment may fail. So the designers must design the strategies for failure detection, failure masking, failure tolerance and then recovery from the failures.
5. **Handling the Concurrency:** In distributed systems scenario, multiple users access the various resources at the same time, the requests from the multiple users must be executed at the same time. Operations on any object must be synchronized such that the object's data remains consistent.
6. **Requirement of Sophisticated Communication Network:** In order to make the efficient use of the distributed system, a strong communication network is required. Network may lose some messages and can become overloaded. When the network saturates, it must be either replaced or new system must be added.
7. **Lack of Software Support:** There is scarcity of sufficient, sophisticated softwares available for the implementation of distributed systems. The experts have different views on kind of operating systems to be used, programming languages to be implemented, distribution of data, control and applications.

DISTRIBUTED FILE SYSTEM

A distributed file system stores users files at several nodes of a distributed system, such that a process and a file required exists at different nodes of the distributed system. It is quite similar to the conventional time sharing model of a file system, where multiple users share file and storage resources. The user here must know the topology of the distributed system to open and get access of the files located at various nodes of the system. The distributed file system administrator allow the users to access and manage the files that are physically distributed across a network and can make the files distributed across multiple servers which appear to the users as if they reside at one location. A distributed file system is a file system whose clients, servers and storage devices are dispersed among the machines of a distributed system. Instead of a single centralized data repository, there are multiple and independent storage devices. A distributed file system can be implemented as a part of distributed operating system or by a software layer whose task is to manage the communication between conventional operating systems and the file systems. The multiplicity and dispersion of the users and storage devices should be transparent and the client should not distinguish between local and remote files. The distributed file system should locate and transport the files from the source to the destination. The performance of distributed file system can be measured as the amount of time required to service various requests. In the conventional systems, this time consists of disk access time and small amount of CPU processing time, in distributed file system, a remote access has additional overhead attributed to the distributed structure, where this overhead includes the time required to deliver the request to a server as well as the time for receiving the response. Along with the time required to transfer the information, processor overhead of running communication protocol software is also taken into consideration. The basic method of file processing in a distributed file systems is shown in the Figure 12.13 below, where a client process in node P1 opens a file named as india, through path name resolution the distributed file systems locates that this file exists at node P2, so a connection is set up to P2 which is termed as a file server. The nodes which are encountered to establish a connection between the client processes to the server process are termed as intermediate nodes. This model is often termed as remote file processing model this processing is done through file accesses through stub processes called file server agent and client agent. When the client opens the file, the request is transferred to the client agent, who communicates the request to the file server agent located at the node P2, it passes the request to the file server, the file server in turn opens the file named india.

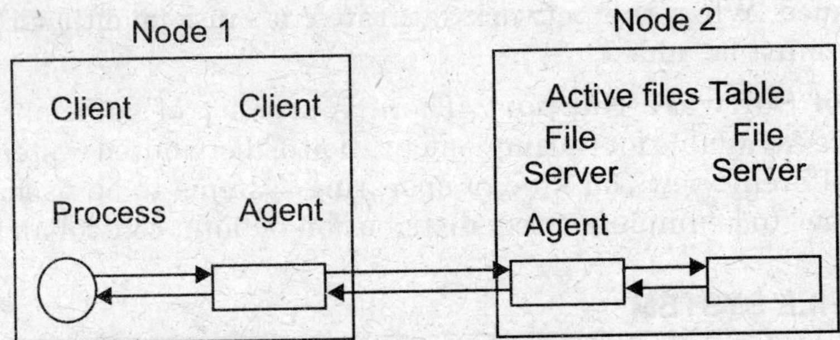

Figure 12.13: *Basic File Processing in Distributed File System*

Features and Design Issues in Distributed File System

The various features of distributed file system are:

1. **Easy Access to Files:** A distributed file system makes it easy to access files located at geographical separated site. The files may be at multiple servers, to access a file the user need to go to one location in the network and through there only he can access the data.
2. **Availability:** The files being distributed at multiple locations can be made available easily.

3. **Server Load Balancing:** The load can be distributed among multiple locations, the distributed file system support multiple targets that are physically distributed across the network. If we have files that are to be accessed heavily by the users, then rather than all users physically accessing these files on a single server and then overloading the server and hence deteriorating the performance, distributed file system ensures that users access to the file is distributed to multiple servers and hence the load of the server can be distributed to multiple locations.

Design Issues in Distributed File System

A distributed file system stores files at several nodes so that a process and a file can be stored at different nodes of the distributed system. The main design issues in distributed file system are:

1. **Transparency:** The transparency here means that the user is not aware of the location of files in the system. A file system finds the location of a file during path name resolution. The main issue here is to know that how much information about the location of a file should be reflected in its path name and can the file system change the location of a file to optimize performance of file access. The main two issues in transparency are:
   - *Location Transparency,* which implies that the name of a file should not reveal its location in the file system. It provides the user the freedom that he need not to be aware of the location of file while assessing it.
   - *Location Independence,* it implies that it should be possible to change the location of a file without changing its name, by doing so the file system can optimize its performance. Like if accesses to some files stored at node cause network congestion then the files may be migrated to some other location in order to improve the system performance.
2. **Fault Tolerance:** A fault may hinder the normal processing of the file processing activity, due to which the consistency of data in files and metadata i.e the control data of the file system may be corrupted. Distributed file system implement journaling techniques to protect the consistency of metadata and implement the mechanisms that ensure the easy recovery whenever some fault occurs.
3. **Performance:** The distributed file systems should be efficient and scalable. The network latency is an important factor affecting the performance of the file system, it is basically the time required to locate the file and then to transfer the file to the specified destination. Normally it is more than the time required to process a file. To improve the performance of distributed file systems the system implements the concept of file caching, which keeps the copy of a remote file in the node of a process from where the file can be assessed easily, the other issue in the performance of distributed file systems is the scalability, which ensures that as the new nodes are added to the system, the performance of the system should not detoriate,

Naming Schemes in Distributed File Systems

The various naming schemes that can be implemented in distributed file systems are:

- In the first approach, the files are named as the combination of their host name and local name, which is a unique system wide name, a file is identified uniquely by host name: local name. This scheme is neither location transparent nor location independent and the same file operations can be used for both the local and remote files.
- In the second approach, the file system provides the facility to attach remote directories to the local ones, which gives an appearance of coherent directory tree, earlier the previously mounted remote directories could be accessed transparently, but the implementation of auto-mount feature allows that the mount can occur on demand based on a table of mount points and file structure names. The components can be integrated to support transparent sharing, but this integration is limited and is not uniform.
- The third approach tries to provide the total integration, where a single global name structure spans all the files in the system.

The implementation of transparent naming requires a provision for mapping the file names to the associated location. To enhance the availability of important mapping information, the concept of replication and local caching can be implemented. But the location independence means that the mapping changes over time, so the replication made at different sites should be consistent. To achieve it low level location independent file identifiers are used, where the textual files are mapped to low level file identifiers that indicate that to which component unit the file belongs to. These identifiers are still location independent and can be replicated and cached freely without being invalidated by migration of component units.

Remote File Access

In remote service mechanism, the requests for the accesses are delivered to the server, the server machine performs the accesses and their results are forwarded back to the user. It is used when a user wishes to access a remote file, the server locates that and then the actual transfer of the data takes place. As we have discussed that in conventional file system the performance of the file system may be improved by caching , where the most recently accessed data is stored on the disk to reduce disk i/o and to improve the system performance, whereas in distributed file systems the goal is to reduce both network traffic congestion and disk i/o.

The basic caching scheme is based on the principle of locality of reference, where the most recently accessed data is cached so that the time to access the data and hence the performance of the system can be improved. It speeds up operations of distributed file systems by reducing the network traffic. It holds some data from a remote file in a buffer in a client node called file cache. The whole or the part of the data is cached from the file server to the file cache, depending upon the requirement of the request and the size of cache. The concept is simple as used in cache memory, where, the availability of data is checked in the cache and if the data needed to satisfy the access request is not already in the cache, then a copy is brought from the server to client system and then the present and the future accesses to the data is made on the cached copy of data. It will reduce the network traffic and the information requests can be handled locally.

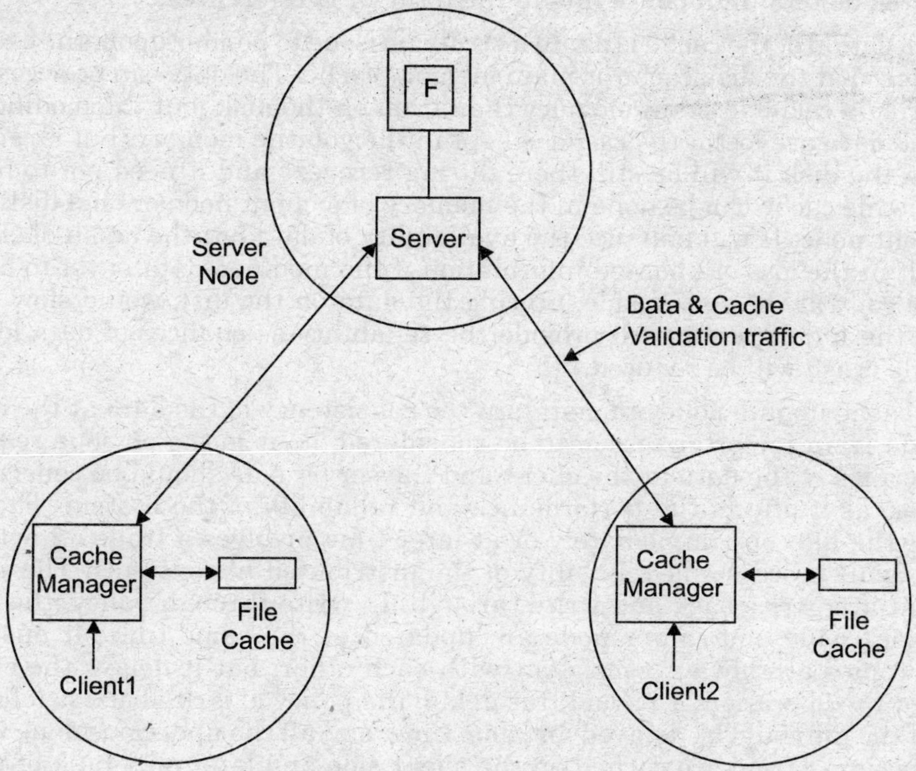

Figure 12.14: *The Concept of File Caching*

Although we have cached a copy of the data at the local site, but the files are still identified by the master copy residing at the server. So the scenario can be visualized as a file being stored at the server and the copies (parts) of it are stored at different caches. But the biggest challenge in the implementation of this scheme is that when cache is modified, the changes must be reflected on the master copy at the server to ensure the consistency of information. The diagram given below, show the concept of file caching. The cache manager exists on the path between a client and server. It loads the chucks of file data into the file cache, supplies data from the cache to the client processes, maintains the file cache using least recently used algorithm to perform the replacement of chunks and write the modified chunks to the server side.

Design Issues: The access to the data through cache memory will enable the data to be accessed easily, whenever a certain data request arises at the client machine, then the local cache is searched for the availability of the data, if the data is available there, it is called as hit and the data is accessed from the fast cache memory rather than getting the data from the server, but if the data is not available at the local cache, it is called as miss, then the request is forwarded to the server and if data is available at the server side, it is provided to the client for processing and a copy of this data is kept at the client cache, so that the data requests in future can be met from the fast cache only. The performance of cache memory is measured by hit ratio, which is calculated as total number of hits to the total CPU references.

The location of the cache is again a strategic issue to ponder upon, the cached data may be stored at the disk cache or main memory cache. The data can be accessed more quickly from a cache in main memory than from on the disk, but the modifications to the cached data are lost if the cache is kept in the volatile memory, but if cached data is kept on the disk it will be still there during recovery and it need not to be fetched again. The file cache can be done in the memory of a client node or on a disk attached to the client node. It will enhance the availability of data but the crash of client node will result in the loss of updated information if the modified data is yet to be written to the file copy at the server side. Storing the data on the disk would slow down the access to the file data, but will provide the reliability as chances of data loss due to client node crash will be reduced.

The cache update policy to maintain the consistency of the data at the client and server side is an important issue to be considered, as it is the obvious requirement that the copies of the data at the client and the server side should be consistent with each other, as it affects the performance and reliability of the system. The decision to update the file copy immediately or at later time involves a trade off between the delay in client process and reliability of the distributed file systems. The policies to implement are: write back and write through. In write through policy, the file cache in the client node and server node are updated at the same time. It ensures that both the copies are always consistent with each other, but it delays the client that performed the operation. To avoid this delay, the policy of write back is followed, the update of the file could be delayed for some time, and all the updations done upto some particular time period are cached on the client side and later on a bulk of updations are copied to the server node later on.

The size of the file cache can be decided on the basis of the user's need of data and the size of the cache available at the client side. The size of the file cache should be large so that locality of data can be increased which will ensure a high hit ratio. But if the size will be too large it will increase the probability of data invalidation due to modifications performed by other clients.

In a distributed file systems environment, the client machine is faced with the problem of deciding whether or not a locally cached copy of the data is consistent with the master copy or not. If the client observes that its cached copy is out of date, so an updated copy needs to be cached. When a file is processed by many clients in parallel, copies of its data would exist in several file caches at the same time. If one client performs a write operation, copies of the other clients become invalid. The cache validation function identifies invalid data and deals with it accordingly. A simple method to identify the invalid data is through time stamps, where a time-stamp is associated with a file and each of its cached chunks. The time stamp of a file indicates the time when the file was modified last. When a chuck of file is copied into a cache, the file's time stamp is also copied, at any time the cached chuck becomes invalid if its time stamp is smaller than the file's time stamp. The other approaches that can be used for cache validation are:

- **Client Initiated Validation:** It is performed by the cache manager at the client side, when a file is accessed by a client, it checks whether the required data is already in the cache, if is available, then it checks that whether it is valid or not, in this validity check the client checks whether the data is consistent with the master copy at the server side or not. This approach leads to cache validation traffic over the network at every file access. The check can be performed at every access to a check on only first access. Every access done through the validity check is delayed as compared to the access done through cache directly. To reduce the traffic, the check can be performed at the regular intervals of time.
- **Server Initiated Validation:** The file server keep track of which client nodes contain what file data in their caches and whenever a client updates some part of a file, the file server sends client nodes that have that file in their file cache and informs the cache manager that their copies of this file have become invalid, each cache manager then has the option of deleting the copy of the file from their cache or to refresh it.

DISTRIBUTED COORDINATION

How the centralized synchronization mechanisms can be extended to a distributed environment.

In a centralized system, it is important to determine the order in which two events have occurred, since there is a single memory and clock. In resource allocation scheme it is important to know that a resource can be used only after the resource has been granted.

Event Ordering

In distributed systems, as there is no common memory and clock then it is not possible to determine which of the two events occurred first, the happened– before relation is only a partial ordering of the events in distributed systems. The happened before relation is defined to provide a consistent total ordering of all the events in the system.

The Happened Before Relation

All events executed in a single process are totally ordered, a message can be received only after it has been sent. We can define the happened – before relation denoted by -> on a set of events as follows:

1. If A and B are events in the same process, and A was executed before B, then A -> B.
2. If A is the event of sending a message by one process and B is the event of receiving that message by another process, then A -> B.
3. If A -> B and B -> C then A -> C.

As an event cannot happen before itself, the -> relation is an irreflexive partial ordering.

If two events A and B are not related by the -> relation, then we say that these two events were executed concurrently. In this case, neither event can usually affect the other, if however A -> B, then it is possible for event A to affect event B casually.

To determine that an event A happened before an event B, the user needs either a common clock or a group of perfectly synchronized clocks. But in a distributed environment neither of these two options will be available, so the happened before relation must be defined without the use of physical clocks. The method used is of time stamps, a time stamp is associated with each system event, for every pair of events A and B, if A -> B, then the time stamp of A is less than the time stamp of B. Within each process Pi a logical clock Ci is defined. This logical clock can be implemented as a simple counter incremented between any two successive events executed within a process. As this logical clock has a monotonically increasing value, it assigns a unique number to every event and if an event A occurs before the event B in process Pi, then Ci(A) < Ci(B), the time stamp for an event is the value of the logical clock for that event.

Mutual Exclusion

If we want to distribute the decision making across the entire system, then an algorithm based on the event ordering scheme can be used. When a process Pi wants to enter its critical section, it generates a new time stamp TS and sends the message request (Pi,TS) to all other processes in the system(including itself). On receiving a request message a process may reply immediately by sending a message back to Pi or it may defer sending a reply back. A process that has received a reply message from all other processes in the system can enter its critical section, queuing incoming requests and deferring them. After exiting its critical section, the process sends reply messages to all its deferred requests. The decision whether process Pi replies immediately to a request (Pj, TS) message or defers its reply is based on three factors:

- If process Pi is in its critical section, then it defers its reply to Pj.
- If process Pi does not want to enter its critical section, then it sends a reply immediately to Pj.
- If process Pi wants to enter its critical section but has not yet entered it, then it compares its own request timestamp with the timestamp TS of the incoming request made by process Pj. If its own request timestamp is greater than TS, then it sends a reply immediately to Pj, else the reply is deferred.

The algorithm described here, ensures that mutual exclusion is obtained, and it is ensured that deadlock will not occur. As the entry to the critical section is scheduled in the time stamp ordering and processes are served in first-come, first served order, so starvation will not occur.

But in a centralized approach for providing the mutual exclusion, one of the processes in the system is chosen to coordinate the entry to the critical section. Every process that wants to begin mutual exclusion sends a request message to the coordinator. When the process receives a reply message from the coordinator it can proceed to enter its critical section. After exiting its critical section, the process sends a release message to the coordinator and proceeds with the execution. On receiving the request message, the coordinator checks to see whether some other process is in its critical section. If no process is in its critical section, the coordinator sends back a reply message, else the request is queued for the processing. When the coordinator gets the release message, it removes one of the request messages from the queue and sends a reply message to the requesting process.

Atomicity

An atomic transaction is a program unit that must be executed atomically, that is either all the operations associated with it are executed to completion or none are performed. In the distributed environment, it is even more important to ensure that atomicity property of the transaction is achieved, because in such a scenario several sites may be participating in the execution of a single transaction. The failure of one site or the communication link between them may hinder the normal completion of the transaction. To ensure this behavior of the distributed system, the transaction coordinator works for it. Where each site has its own local transaction coordinator that is responsible for coordinating the execution of all the transactions. The responsibilities of the transaction coordinator are:

- To initiate the execution of the transaction.
- The main transaction is divided into smaller sub transactions and these sub transactions are divided among various sites for the execution.
- To coordinate the termination of the transactions.

The atomicity of the transaction will be ensured only if T must either commit at all the sites or it may abort at all the sites. To make this possible the transaction coordinator of T must execute a commit protocol. The most common commit protocol is Two-Phase Commit Protocol. The protocol is described as:

Let T be a transaction initiated at site Ai and the transaction coordinator at this site is TCi. When T completes its execution on receiving the completion signal from all the sites at which T has been executed then the transaction coordinator TCi starts the two-phase protocol:

Phase I:

1. TCi prepares a message <prepare T> to the log and stores the message on the storage area.
2. TCi sends this message to all the sites on which T is to be executed.
3. When all the sites receive this message, then the transaction manager of that site decides whether it is willing to commit its portion of transaction T or not.
   (a) If it is willing to commit then, it adds a record <ready T> to the log and forces all the log records corresponding to T on the storage and the transaction manager replies with a ready T message to the transaction manager TCi.

(b) If it is not willing to commit, then it adds a record <no T> to the log and then it responds by sending an abort T message to the transaction coordinator TCi.

Phase II:

When the transaction coordinator TCi receives response to prepare T message from all the sites, or when the specified interval after the prepare T message was sent has passed, then TCi decides whether the transaction T can be committed or aborted.

1. The transaction T can be committed if TCi received a ready T message from all the participating sites, else T must be aborted. And accordingly, either <commit T> or a <abort T> message is added to the log and is stored on the storage media. After this the coordinator TCi sends either a commit T or an abort T message to all participating sites. When a site receives this message it records the message in the log.

A site at which T was executed can unconditionally abort T at any time prior to its sending the message ready T to the coordinator. The ready T message is in effect, a surety by the site to follow the order of the coordinator to either commit T or to abort T. The only situation in which a site can make such a commitment is if the needed information is stored in the stable storage, else the site crashes after sending ready T.

Concurrency Control

The transaction manager of a distributed database system is to manage the execution of those transactions that access data stored in a local site. Each of these transactions may be a part of local transaction that can be executed at that site only or may be a part of the global transaction that will be executed at several sites. Each transaction manager is responsible for managing the log for recovery purposes and to execute the concurrency control scheme to coordinate the concurrent execution of the transactions. The concurrency schemes described earlier in chapter 5 are to be modified to accommodate in the distributed environment.

1. **Locking Protocols:** The two phase locking protocol described earlier can be used in distributed environment, but the only difference is in the way the lock manager is implemented. There are two variants of this schemes, namely:
    - When no replication is allowed.
    - When replication is allowed.

Case I: When no replication is allowed: if no data is replicated then each site maintains a local lock manager, whose role is to manage the lock and unlock requests for those data items that are stored in that site. When a transaction tries to lock a data item A at the site S1, it sends a message to the lock manager at the site S1 requesting a lock, in the mode required i.e either in shared or exclusive mode. If the data item A is locked in an incompatible mode, then the request is delayed until that request can be granted. Once it has been found that the lock request can be granted, the lock manager sends an acknowledgement message to the initiator that the request has been granted. This approach is easy and simple to implement, in this case only two message transfers are required for handling lock requests, and one message transfer for handling the unlock requests. But it deadlock occurs in the case, then it is difficult to handle. In the case of single Coordinator Approach, the system maintains a single lock manager that resides in a single chosen site say Ai. All lock and unlock requests are made to the site Ai. When a transaction needs to lock a data item, it sends a lock request to site Ai. The lock manager determines whether the lock can be granted or not. If it is so, it sends a message to the site from where the lock request was started. The transaction can read the data item from any one of the sites at which a duplicated copy of the data item is present. In case of write all the sites where a duplicated copy of data is present, must be involved in updating the records. This scheme is simple to implement, as it requires two messages for handling lock requests and one message for handling unlock requests. As the requests for locking and unlocking are made at one site, so the deadlocks can be handled easily. But the site where the requests have been made may be overloaded as all sites are making requests to this site only. Another major limitation of this scheme is that if this central site fails, then the processing of all other sites will come to halt. To overcome the limitations of single coordinator scheme, the function of lock manager can be distributed to multiple sites. Where a number of lock managers cater to the needs of a subset of data items. Each lock manager resides at a different site and handles requests independently.

Deadlock Handling

The concept of deadlock, deadlock prevention, avoidance and detection can be used in a distributed environment. The concept and the related algorithms are same and these can be implemented as such, but with little modifications.

Deadlock Prevention: The following two schemes may be used in a distributed environment to handle deadlock prevention.

1. The user can use the resource ordering deadlock prevention by defining a global ordering among the system resources. In this scheme, all resources in the entire system are assigned unique numbers and a process may request a resource with a unique number a only if it is not holding a resource with a unique number greater than a.
2. The banker's algorithm discussed earlier in distributed environment by designating one of the processes in the system as the process that maintains the information necessary to carry out the banker's algorithm. Every resource request must be channeled through the banker's algorithm.

The first scheme is simple to implement and costs a little. The second method is also easy to implement but may require too much overheads. This scheme is not that much suitable for the distributed environment as the messages to and from the process executing banker's algorithm may be large.

To overcome these problems the time-stamp ordering approach can be used, it is defined as follows:

A unique priority number is assigned to each process, Let a process P1 is waiting for process P2 that means P1 has a priority higher than P2, otherwise P1 is rolled back. This scheme prevents deadlock as for every edge P1-> P2 in the wait for graph. P1 has a higher priority than P2. So P1 can wait for P2 but P2 cannot wait for P1, so a cycle cannot exist. This scheme suffers from the problem of starvation, as some processes with extremely low priority may be waiting for a long time and ultimately has to be rolled back. This problem can be avoided by using the concept of time stamping, where a unique time stamp is assigned when it is created. Two schemes using the concept of time-stamping have been described below:

The Wait and Die Scheme: This approach is based on a non-preemptive technique. When process P1 requests a resource currently held by P2, P1 is allowed to wait only if it has smaller timestamp than that of P2. Otherwise P1 is rolled back. An older process must wait for a younger one to release its resources. Thus the older the process gets, the more it tends to wait.

The Wound and Wait Scheme: This approach is based on a preemptive technique. When a process P1 request a resource currently held by P2, P1 is allowed to wait only if it has a larger timestamp than P2, else P2 is rolled back.

Deadlock Detection: Inspite of taking the deadlock prevention measures, if deadlock has occurred then it must be detected and the remedial actions must be taken to remove it so that the smooth working of the various processes of the system can be resumed. As discussed earlier, the deadlock prevention algorithms may preempt the resources even if no deadlock has occurred. To prevent the unnecessary preemption the deadlock detection algorithm can be used. For this purpose, a wait-for-graph is constructed to demonstrate the resource allocation state for the various processes. A cycle in the wait-for-graph will show the presence of deadlock. In the centralized systems, discussed earlier, the maintenance of wait-for-graph is quite easy, but it little bit cumbersome for a distributed environment. In distributed environment, each site should keep a local wait-for-graph. The nodes of the graph correspond to all the processes that are currently holding or requesting any of the resource. The Figure 12.15 given below show that a system consisting of two sites where each site is maintaining its own local wait-for-graph, the processes P2 and P3 are present in both the graphs, which shows that these processes have been requested at both the sites. If these local wait-for-graphs has a cycle, which means deadlock has occurred.

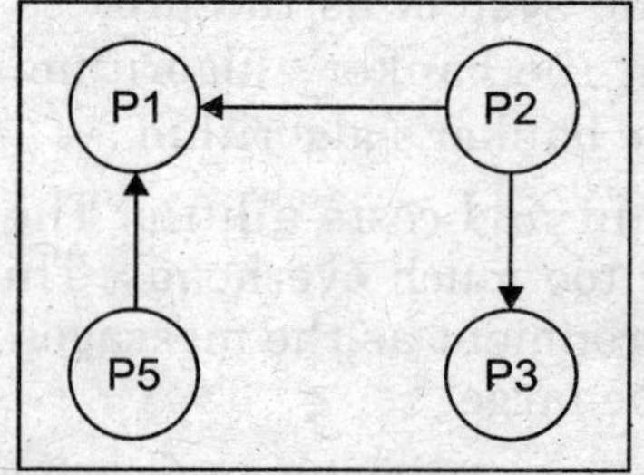

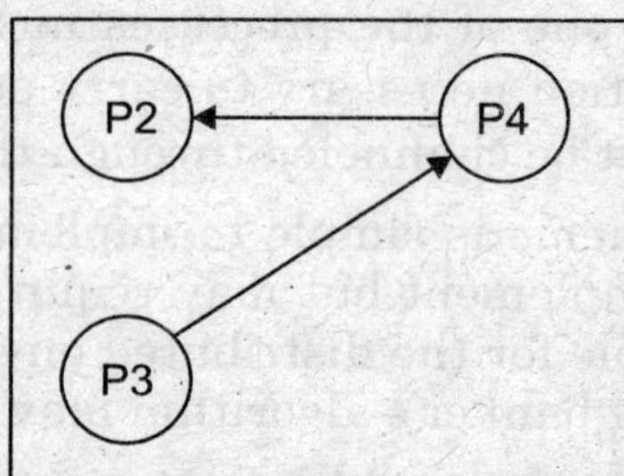

Figure 12.15: *Two Sites managing their own Local Sites and their Wait-for-graph*

But it not the sure shot criteria for deadlock detection, as in the Figure given above, each wait-for-graph is acyclic, but a deadlock is present. So we must ensure that the union of the two wait-for-graphs is cycle free i.e acyclic. The Figure 12.16 given below show the union of the two wait-for-graphs of Figure 12.15, which shows that the system is in a deadlock.

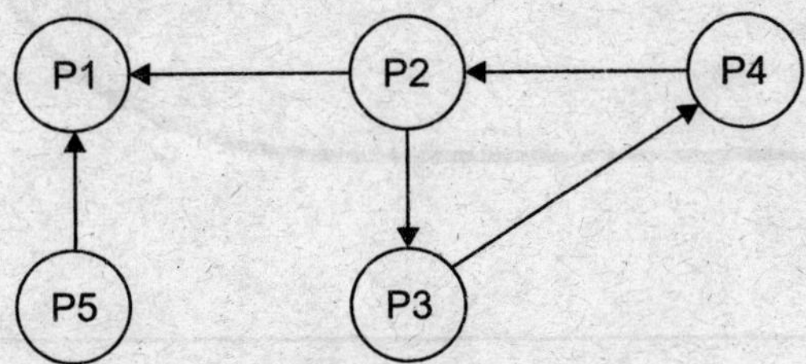

Figure 12.16: *Global Wait for Graph*

Case Study on Disk Operating System (DOS)

Chapter 13

HISTORY OF DOS

DOS or Disk Operating System is an Operating System designed to operate the IBM personal computer or compatibles being an operating system, it works as an interpreter between user and computer. The user provide commands in English like language and it converts it into machine language and after the computer has processed the information, it returns the results back in the user understandable language i.e English. And further it helps to manage the system resources like processor, memory and the input and output devices. MS-DOS is a single-user operating system.

In the beginning, three companies have produced DOS, namely, Microsoft, IBM and Novell. The later two have dropped out of the market. Bill Gates the owner of Microsoft Coorporation purchased 16-bit DOS from Seattle Computer Products for the use in IBM machines and after making a few modifications, Microsoft launched DOS as its own product named as DOS version 1.0. in 1982, Microsoft launched the new version of MS-DOS 1.1 with advanced features. This version supported to work with directories, but this version was not supporting the hard disk. To overcome this limitation Microsoft launched a new version DOS2.0 in 1982, this version allowed the user to work with hard disk. The summary of development and advancement in features of DOS is shown in the table given below. It is designed to operate on machines using the Intel line of 8086 microprocessors. MS-DOS cannot support a large network of users. Because PCs and MS-DOS became so popular, many network operating systems were designed in the mid-1980s to network MS-DOS machines together; working around the operating system limitations through software. MS-DOS is the preferred operating system for most of the Intel processor (currently Pentium) based PCs of the world. MS-DOS does not break out into neat compartments as easily as some operating systems do. This is partially due to its simplicity -- no multi-user or multitasking ability. It is also partly due to the way MS-DOS has evolved over the years. So in many respects DOS was a primitive OS. The majority of computer users today use graphical systems, but users of Windows, for instance, have the ability to interact with the computer through DOS to do things which are difficult or impossible to accomplish through the graphical interface. For this reason, familiarity with DOS is still considered essential for anyone supporting Intel-based machines running Windows.

Version	Year	Features
1.0	1981	First Operating System for IBM-PC
1.1	1982	Support for Directories.
2.0	1983	Support for Subdirectories and Hard Disk.
2.01	1983	Support for International Symbols
2.25	1983	Support for Bug Fixing.
3.0	1984	Support for Floppy and Large Hard Disk
3.1	1984	Support for PC Networks.
3.2	1986	Support for 3.5 inch disks.
3.3	1987	Support for PS/2 Computers.
4.0	1988	Support for Large Partitions
5.0	1990	New Editor, Disk and Memory Management.
6.0	1993	Support Disk Compression, Better Memory Management and Antivirus Software included in the operating system.
6.2	1993	Microsoft claimed it the operating system with advanced commands.

FEATURES OF DISK OPERATING SYSTEM: THE MAIN FEATURES OF DOS ARE

1. It provides an interface between the user and machine, and tries to overcome the differences between the two.
2. DOS has a rich collection of commands to perform various types of functions, moreover, the DOS commands are easy to understand and use.
3. It allows the user to manage files using directories and subdirectories.
4. It allows the user to recover the deleted data through the 'Undelete' Command.
5. It can remember the commands submitted by the user, it is made possible with the 'DOSKEY' command.
6. It has a full screen user friendly text editor, which allow the user to open, edit and save the text files.
7. It has an efficient set of commands like Fdisk, Format and Defrag to manage the disk space efficiently.
8. It has the capability for backup and restoring the data.
9. By using MEM command, the user can view the memory status/
10. It has the ability to check errors on the disk, diagnosing it and fixing the bad clusters. It is made possible with the SCANDISK command.

COMPONENTS OF MS-DOS

MS-DOS consists of following three files, the disk that contains all these three files are called as bootable disk or system disk.

1. **COMMAND.COM File:** It is the DOS shell and is known as the command processor. It is that part of DOS that executes the commands. These commands are either internal or external. The code of an internal command is available in computer's RAM at all the times as a part of operating system boot up, where as the external commands exist as a separate executable program. When the user wishes to execute an external command, DOS reads the appropriate program file into memory and control is passed to that command for its execution.
2. **CONFIG.SYS File:** This file configures DOS at startup and allows the user to customize the settings of DOS as well as load device drivers to support additional hardware. After the DOS system files are loaded, the computer reads the device driver settings from this file and automatically executes the statements in the file.
3. **AUTOEXEC.BAT File:** After DOS is loaded, the computer looks for a batch file called AUTOEXEC.BAT. This file contains a series of DOS commands and these are automatically executed after DOS is loaded. It is also used to run programs on start up that may be required to perform some tasks on start-up. The user can write a group of commands to be executed on start up, for example, setting the path, loading keyboard and mouse drivers or running a virus checker etc.
4. **IO.SYS File:** It defines the basic input/output routines for the processor. This file is a hidden file located in the root and runs the MSDOS.SYS, CONFIG.SYS and COMMNAD.COM files.

BOOTING PROCESS OF DOS

The booting process of a computer involves loading the operating system into computer's RAM. Process that starts up a computer is called booting. When the user first power up a PC, the machine goes through several internal processes before it's ready for the use. This is called the boot process, or booting the PC. Boot is short for bootstrap, a reference to the old idea, "Pull yourself up by the bootstraps," which means to start something from the very beginning. It checks for proper functioning of all the peripheral devices attached with the system. It searches for the operating system and, when located, loads it into the main memory. When the user turns on the PC, it runs a series of routines that are located in the BIOS ROM and these routines perform the following functions:

1. Test Hardware.
2. Identify the computer's configuration and record the details.
3. Setup programmable I/O devices.
4. Load the operating system from a boot disk.

The boot process is controlled by the PC's basic input-output system BIOS. The BIOS is a software stored on a flash memory chip. In a PC, the BIOS is embedded on the motherboard. Occasionally, a PC manufacturer will release an update for the BIOS, and you can carefully follow instructions to "flash the BIOS" with the updated software. Besides controlling the boot process, the BIOS provide a basic configuration interface for the PC's hardware components. In that interface, you can configure such things as the order to read drives during boot and how fast the processor should be allowed to run.

Steps in Booting Process

The following is a summary of the boot process in a PC:

1. The power button activates the power supply in the PC, sending power to the motherboard and other components.
2. The PC performs a Power-On-Self-Test (POST). The POST is a small computer program within the BIOS that checks for hardware failures. A single beep after the POST signal signify that everything is fine. Other beep sequences signal a hardware failure, and PC repair specialists compare these sequences with a chart to determine which component has failed.
3. The PC displays information on the attached monitor showing details about the boot process. These include the BIOS manufacturer and revision, processor specs, the amount of RAM installed, and the drives detected. Many PCs have replaced displaying this information with a splash screen showing the manufacturer's logo. The user can turn off the splash screen in the BIOS settings if the users see the text.
4. The BIOS attempts to access the first sector of the drive designated as the boot disk. The first sector is the first kilobytes of the disk in sequence, if the drive is read sequentially starting with the first available storage address. The boot disk is typically the same hard disk or solid-state drive that contains the operating system. The user can change the boot disk by configuring the BIOS or interrupting the boot process with a key sequence (often indicated on the boot screens).
5. The BIOS confirms there's a bootstrap loader, or boot loader, in that first sector of the boot disk, and it loads that boot loader into memory (RAM). The boot loader is a small program designed to find and launch the PC's operating system.
6. Once the boot loader is in memory, the BIOS hands over its work to the boot loader, which in turn begins loading the operating system into memory.
7. When the boot loader finishes its task, it turns control of the PC over to the operating system. Then, the OS is ready for user interaction.

Types of Booting

1. **Cold Booting:** It is a process of turning on or restarting the computer without performing any shut down procedure first. Like rebooting the computer

automatically after a sudden failure in power supply or intentionally switching off and then switching on. The cold booting is also known as hard booting.

2. **Warm Booting:** It is a process of restarting the computer under software control without switching off the power supply. Like restarting the computer by pressing Ctrl+Alt+Del keys simultaneously. It is also known as soft booting.

Naming the DOS Files: The file name in DOS consists of two parts:

1. Primary Name
2. Secondary Name or Extension.

Primary name is separated from the Secondary name extension with the help of a dot (.) look at the following example.

Example: ENVOICE. TXT

Primary name can be from 1 to 8 characters long and

Secondary name contains 3 or less than 3 characters and is optional. The extension tells DOS about what kind of file it is.

A valid Character for naming a file are: from A to Z and the digit 0 to 9

BASIC DOS COMMANDS

The DOS commands can be divided into two parts:

1. Internal Commands or Memory-Resident Commands
2. External Command or Disk-Residence Commands

Internal Command

These are also called memory-resident commands. These commands are automatically loaded into the computer's memory during the booting process. These are present in the system and is a part of COMMNAD.COM program actually included in the Command.com file.

These commands are available at all the times. A list of few internal commands is given below:

VER	TIME	MD	CD	PATH
VOL	DATE	CLS	DIR	COPY CON
DEL	REN	PROMPT		

A command can be given in Capital letters or Small letters also. The internal commands can execute immediately but External Commands require special files for their execution without which it is not possible to execute them.

External Commands

These are also called Disk-Resident Commands. These commands are meant for special purpose. These are found in separate files on Hard Disk or Floppy Disk, these must be loaded into RAM as and when required. So that these don't typically consume valuable memory space. They are loaded into memory only when called.

Some External Commands are:

XCOPY	MOVE	FC	DOSKEY	MEM
FILTER	ATTRIB	DELTREE	EDIT	TREE
UNFORMAT	MODE	BACKUP	XCOPY	MORE
SYS	RESTORE			

Description of Internal Commands

1. **VER:** The version number indicates which edition of operating system the user is working on.

   Syntax: VER <Enter>

   Example: C:\> Ver <Enter>

   Result will be: Microsoft Windows XP [Version 5.1.2600]

2. **VOL:** It is used to display volume label and serial number of the current drive

   Syntax: Vol [drive:]

   Example: C:\> VOL

3. **DATE:** Used to display the current system date and prompt for entering new date.

   Syntax: Date <Enter>

   Example: C:\> date <Enter>

4. **TIME:** Displays the current system Time and prompt for entering new time.

   Syntax: Time <Enter>

   Example: C:\> Time <Enter>

5. **CLS:** Clears the cluster screen.

   Syntax: CLS <Enter>

   Example: C:\> CLS <Enter>

6. **DIR:** This command displays the list of directories and files with details like date of creation whether it is directory or file etc.

   Syntax: DIR <Enter>

   Switches:

/p : To view one screen of files at a time.

/w : Displays only five columns of filenames and directories.

/b : Display only file and directory.

/l : Display all the information in lower case letters.

/a — stands for attributes that are given below.

/-h - Hidden (or not hidden) files

s/-s - System (or not systems) files

d/-d - Directory (or not Directory) names

r/-r - Read only(or not read only) files

7. **MD OR MKDIR:** Used to create a new Directory or nested Directories.

   Syntax: MKDIR OR MD [DRIVE:] PATH DIRECTORY NAME

   Example: C:\> MD SAMS <Enter>

8. **CD OR CHDIR:** This command allows the user to change present directory to another directory.

   Syntax: CD [DRIVE:] PATH

   Example: C:\> CD SAMS and press <Enter>

9. **PATH:** This command defines a list of directories.

   Syntax: PATH (Display the current Search Path)

   PATH; : - (Clear the search path so DOS will search for external commands only in the current directory)

10. **RD:** To delete the empty directory.

    Syntax: RD [DRIVE:] PATH

    Note: The directory must be empty when we use RD.

    Example: C:\> RD SAMS and press <Enter>

11. **COPY CON:** This command is used to create a new file.

    Syntax: COPY CON <FILENAME>

    Example: C:\> Copy Con sams.txt <Enter>

12. **TYPE:** This command allows the user to see the contents of an existing file on the screen.

    Syntax: TYPE <file name>

    Example: C:\> TYPE SAMS

13. **COPY:** Using this command the user can make duplicate files of an existing file from one location to another or one directory to another with different name or exiting name.

    Syntax: COPY < SOURCE FILE NAME> <TARGET FILENAME>

14. **DEL/ERASE:** This command removes one or more files from the disk or current working directories.

    Syntax: DEL filespec [/p] or ERASE filespec [/p]

15. **REN:** Used to change the name of the file or directory.

    Syntax: REN <file name>

16. **PROMPT:** This command allows the user to customize the DOS prompt.

    Syntax: PROMPT

    Example: PROMPT PG <Enter>

17. **TREE:** It is used to display directory structure of a specified directory graphically.

    Syntax: TREE [drive:] [path] [/f]

Description of External Commands

1. **XCOPY:** This command is faster than Copy Command and allows the user to copy entire directories/disk including all the sub directories and files to destination.

   Syntax: XCOPY Source [Target][/Y][-Y] [/P][/E]

   Switches:

   /-Y : Prompts before copying over existing files.

   /y : Overwrites existing files without prompting.

   /p : Ask before copying each file.

   /e : Copying empty directory also.

   /s : Copying subfolders.

   Example: XCOPY C:\SAMS D:\SAMS /S/E

2. **MOVE:** This command moves a file or group of files from one directory to another and also one disk to another disk. It can also be used to rename directories.

   Syntax: Move [Path File Name] [Destination file name path]

   Swiches:

   /-Y : Prompt before it overwrites while it copies file that already exists.

   /Y : Overwrites existing files without prompting.

3. **FC:** Stands for File Compare. If you wish to compare two files or two sets of files then the user may use this command. This command has the capability to differentiate between the files and display the difference

   Syntax: FC <files spec 1> <files spec2> [/a][/b][/c][l][/n]

   Switches:

   /a : This switch displays only the first and last line of each group.

   /b : Compare the files in library mode (byte-by-byte)

/c : Ignore the case of letters.

/l : Compare the files in text mode.

/n : Displays the line number for lines that are different.

4. **DOSKEY:** DOS can remember only the last command entered. But in order to make DOS remember all the commands entered by the user, the DOSKEY utility has to be loaded.

   Syntax: DOSKEY and Press <Enter>

   Display message on the screen.

   DOSKEY Installed.

5. **MEM:** This command displays amount of total available memory (Low, Expanded and Extended) and all currently programs.

   Syntax: MEM [/f][/p][/m]

   Switches:

   /f : Using this switch MEM display all the areas of memory that are free.

   /p : Use this option to display the information one screen at a time.

   /m : Display information about how a specified program is using memory.

6. **FILTER:** A Powerful feature of DOS is its use of filters to process data directly. A DOS FILTER can process in unique way any data that passes through it and can change what the user sees on the screen.

There are three FILTERS included in DOS:

(a) *MORE:* More command is used to pause Vertical Scrolling on the display screen, after each screenful, The display pauses and the message - - More - - appears.

Pressing any key display the next screen.

Example: C:\> MORE < TYPE FILE.TXT and then press <Enter>

(b) *SORT:* Reads, Sorts in Order and sends the data to the screen, file or to another device. Sort to arrange data in an order.

Syntax: SORT [drive:][Path][filename][/r][+n]

Switches:

[drive:][Path][filename]: Specifies the name and location of the file to be searches.

[/r] : Sort lines in reverse ASCII Order (Z-A)

[+n] : Sorts line starting with the contents in column n. The default is 1.

Example: C:\> SORT < NAME .TXT and then press <Enter>

(c) *FIND:* The find Filter is used to search a file one or more designated character (called a text string) Depending upon the form of the FIND Command. Each line having (or not having) the text string is sent to an output devices. Such as the Screen, a file or the printer. The text string is always typed within quotes ("Text String").

Syntax: FIND [/v][/c][/n] "String " [d:] [path][filename]

Switches:

[/v] : Displays all the lines that do not contain string.

[/c] : Display the total number of lines found to contain the string.

[/n] : Display the line number as well as the line that contains the string.

[/i] : Ignores uppercase or lowercase during the search.

7. **ATTRIB:** Every file on the disk has its own description like size, space occupied, the type, the date it was created, etc. Likewise, every file has few attributes. The attributes of a file indicates whether it is a

   i. Read-Only File: r

   ii. Archive File: a

   iii. Hidden File: h

   iv. System File: s

   With the ATTRIB command you can check the attributes of a file.

   Syntax: ATTRIB [+r][+a][+h][/+s] [filename]

   Switches:

   +r, -r : +r Read-Only attribute or, -r turn of Read-Only attribute

   +a,-a : +a archive attribute, or -a turn of archive attribute

   +h,-h : +h hidden attribute, or –h turn of hidden attribute

   +s, -s : +s system attribute and it should not be used generally.

   Note:

   Example: C:\> ATTRIB my.txt +R and then press <Enter>

8. **DELTREE:** This command is used for deleting the entire directory whether the directory contains files or subdirectories and also it will delete hidden files.

   Syntax: DELTREE [drive:][path] directories [/y]

   Example: C:\> DELTREE my.txt and then press <Enter>

9. **EDIT:** This is the DOS Editor, which the user can use to edit the text file.

   Syntax: Edit [drive:][path][filename]

   Example: C:\> EDIT c:\sams\FO.TXT and then press <Enter>

   Example: C:\> Edit NEW FILE and then press <Enter>

Case Study on Windows Operating System

Chapter 14

HISTORY OF WINDOWS OPERATING SYSTEM

Inspired by the user interface of the Apple Lisa, the forerunner to the Apple Macintosh, Microsoft decided to give MS-DOS a graphical user interface (shell) that it called Windows. Windows 1.0, released in 1985, was something of a dud. Windows 2.0, designed for the PC-AT and released in 1987, was not much better. Finally, Windows 3.0 for the 386 (released in 1990), and especially its successors 3.1 and 3.11, caught on and were huge commercial successes. None of these early versions of Windows were true operating systems, but more like graphical user interfaces on top of MS-DOS, which was still in control of the machine and the file system. All programs ran in the same address space and a bug in any one of them could bring the whole system to a halt.

The release of Windows 95 in August 1995 still did not completely eliminate MS-DOS, although it transferred nearly all the features from the MS-DOS part to the Windows part. Together, Windows 95 and the new MS-DOS 7.0 contained most of the features of a full-blown operating system, including virtual memory, process management, and multiprogramming. However, Windows 95 was not a full 32-bit program. It contained large chunks of old 16-bit assembly code (as well as some 32-bit code) and still used the MS-DOS file system, with nearly all its limitations. The only major change to the file system was the addition of long file names in place of the 8 + 3 character file names allowed in MS-DOS.

Even with the release of Windows 98 in June 1998, MS-DOS was still there (now called version 7.1) and running 16-bit code. Although yet more functionality migrated from the MS-DOS part to the Windows part, and a disk layout suitable for larger disks was now standard. The main difference was the user interface, which integrated the desktop and the Internet more closely. It was precisely this integration that attracted the attention of the U.S. Dept. of Justice, which then sued Microsoft claiming that it was an illegal monopoly, an accusation Microsoft vigorously denied. In April 2000, a U.S. Federal court agreed with the government.

In addition to containing a large lump of old 16-bit assembly code in the kernel, Windows 98 had two other serious problems. First, although it was a multiprogramming system, the kernel itself was not reentrant. If a process was busy manipulating some kernel data structure and then suddenly its quantum ran out and another process started running, the new process might find the data structure in an inconsistent state. To prevent this type of problem, after entering the kernel, most processes first acquired a giant mutex covering the whole system before doing anything. While this approach eliminated potential inconsistencies, it also eliminated much of the value of multiprogramming since processes were frequently forced to wait for unrelated processes to leave the kernel before they could enter it.

Second, each Windows 98 process had a 4-GB virtual address space. Of this, 2 GB was completely private to the process. However, the next 1 GB was shared among all other processes in the system. The bottom 1 MB was also shared among all processes to allow all of them to access the MS-DOS interrupt vectors. This sharing facility was heavily used by most Windows 98 applications. As a consequence, a bug in one program could wipe out key data structures used by unrelated processes, leading them to crash. Worse yet, the last 1 GB was shared (writably) with the kernel and contained some critical kernel data structures. Any rogue program that overwrote these data structures with garbage could bring down the system. The obvious solution of not putting kernel data structures in user space was not possible because this feature was essential to make old MS-DOS programs work under Windows 98.

In the millennium year, 2000, Microsoft brought out a minor revision to Windows 98 called Windows Me (Windows Millennium Edition). Although it fixed a few bugs and added a few features, under the covers it is essentially Windows 98. The new features included better ways to catalog and share images, music, and movies, more support for home networking and multiuser games, and more Internet-related features, such as support for instant messaging and broadband connections (cable modems and ADSL). One interesting new feature was the ability to restore the computer to its previous settings after a misconfiguration. If a user reconfigures the system (e.g., changing the screen from 640 × 480 to 1024 × 768) and it no longer works, this feature makes it possible to revert to the last known working configuration.

Windows NT

By the late 1980s, Microsoft realized that building a modern 32-bit operating system on top of the leaky 16-bit MS-DOS probably was not the best way to go. It recruited David Cutler, one of the key designers of DEC's VMS operating system, to work for Microsoft and gave him the job of leading a team to produce a brand-new 32-bit Windows compatible operating system from the ground up. This new system, later called Windows NT (Windows New Technology), was intended for mission-critical business applications as well as for home users. At the time, mainframes still ruled the business world, so designing an operating system on the assumption that companies would use personal computers for anything important was a visionary goal, but one that history has shown to be a very good one. Features such as security and high reliability, clearly lacking on the MS-DOS-based versions of Windows, were high on the agenda for Windows NT. Cutler's background with VMS clearly shows in various places, with there being more than a passing similarity between the design of NT and that of VMS.

The project succeeded and the first version, called Windows NT 3.1, was released in 1993. This initial release number was chosen to match the number of Microsoft's then popular 16-bit Windows 3.1 system. Microsoft expected that NT would rapidly replace Windows 3.1 because it was technically a far superior system.

Much to its surprise, nearly all users preferred to stick with the old 16-bit system they knew, rather than upgrading to an unknown 32-bit system they did not know, however better it might be. The failure of NT 3.1 to catch on in the marketplace was the reason Microsoft decided to build a 32-bit version of Windows 3.1, namely Windows 95. The continued user resistance to NT then caused Microsoft to produce Windows 98 and finally Windows Me; each one claimed to be the very last release of the MS-DOS-based systems.

The first major upgrade to NT came with NT 4.0 in 1996. This system had the power, security, and reliability of the new operating system, but also sported the same user interface as the by-then very popular Windows 95. This compatibility made it much easier for users to migrate from Windows 95 to NT, and many of them did so.

From the beginning, NT was designed to be portable, so it was written almost entirely in C, with only a tiny bit of assembly code for low-level functions such as interrupt handling. The initial release consisted of 3.1 million lines of C for the operating system, libraries, and the environment subsystems (discussed below). When NT 4.0 came out, the code base had grown to 16 million lines of code, still mostly C, but with a small amount of C++ in the user interface part. By this time the system was highly portable, with versions running on the Pentium, Alpha, MIPS, and PowerPC, among other CPUs. Some of these have been dropped since then.

ARCHITECTURE OF WINDOWS NT

NT's Kernel operates more closely with hardware than the Executive does, and it contains CPU-specific code. NT's thread scheduler, called the dispatcher by NT's developers, resides in the Kernel. The dispatcher implements 32 priority levels, 0-31. The dispatcher reserves priority level 0 for a system thread that zeros memory pages as a background task. Priority levels 1 through 15 are variable (with some fixed priority levels) and are where programs execute; priority levels 16 through 31 are fixed priority levels that only administrators can access. The NT dispatcher is a preemptive scheduler. The CPU's time is divided into slices called quantum. When a thread runs to the end of its quantum and doesn't yield the CPU, the dispatcher will step in and preempt it or schedule another thread of equal priority that is waiting to run.

NT implements most synchronization primitives in the Kernel. NT has a rich set of synchronization types, including mutexes, semaphores, events, and spin locks. The Kernel implements and manages its own object types, and Kernel objects represent NT's synchronization primitives. In most cases, NT wraps Kernel objects with Executive objects so that applications can access them from user mode through the native API.

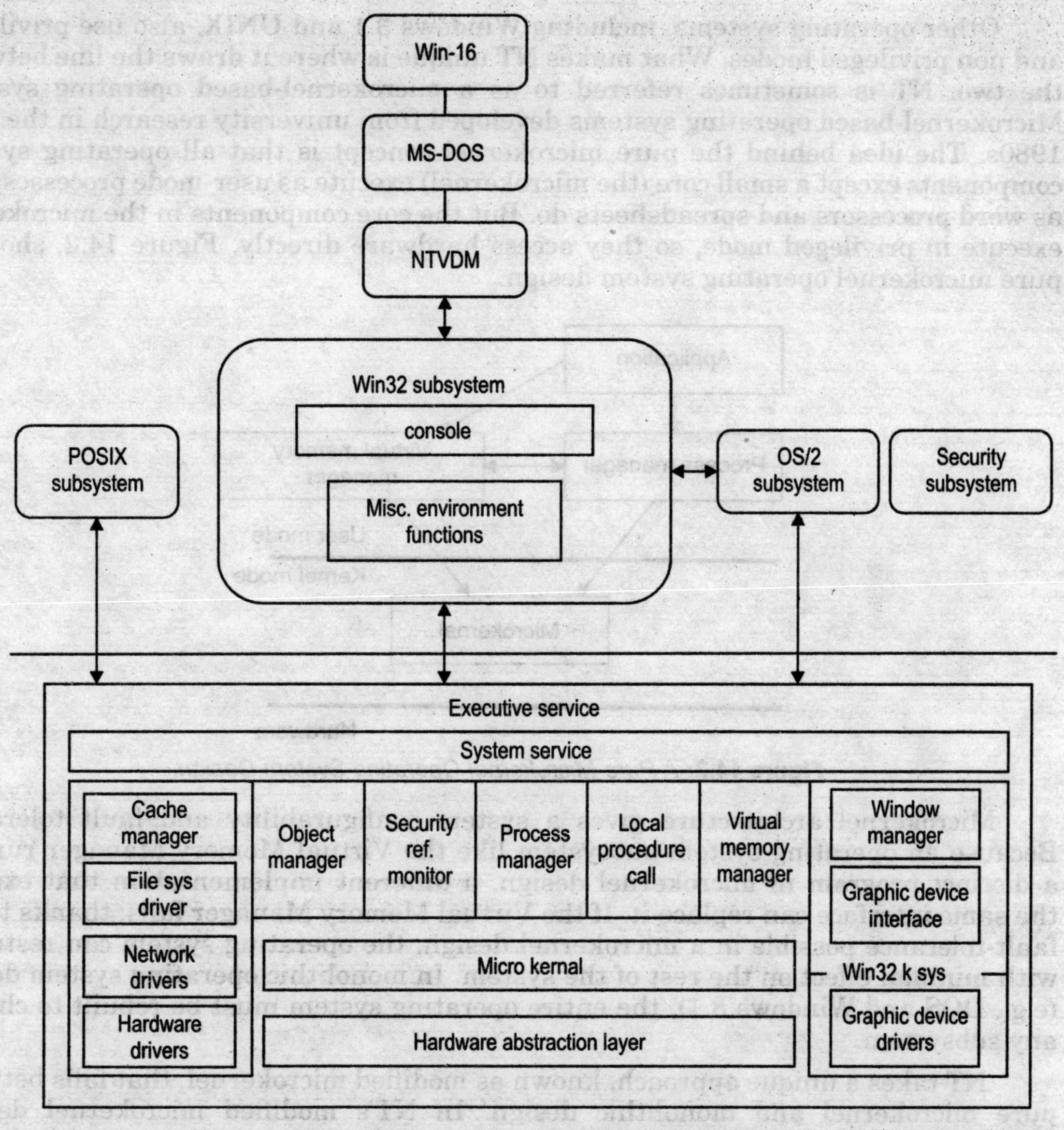

Figure 14.1: *Architecture of Windows NT*

User mode is the least-privileged mode NT supports; it has no direct access to hardware and only restricted access to memory. For example, when programs such as Word and Lotus Notes execute in user mode, they are confined to sandboxes with well-defined restrictions. They don't have direct access to hardware devices, and they can't touch parts of memory that are not specifically assigned to them. Kernel mode is a privileged mode. Those parts of NT that execute in kernel mode, such as device drivers and subsystems such as the Virtual Memory Manager, have direct access to all hardware and memory.

Other operating systems, including Windows 3.1 and UNIX, also use privileged and non privileged modes. What makes NT unique is where it draws the line between the two. NT is sometimes referred to as a microkernel-based operating system. Microkernel-based operating systems developed from university research in the mid-1980s. The idea behind the pure microkernel concept is that all operating system components except a small core (the microkernel) execute as user-mode processes, just as word processors and spreadsheets do. But the core components in the microkernel execute in privileged mode, so they access hardware directly. Figure 14.2, shows a pure microkernel operating system design.

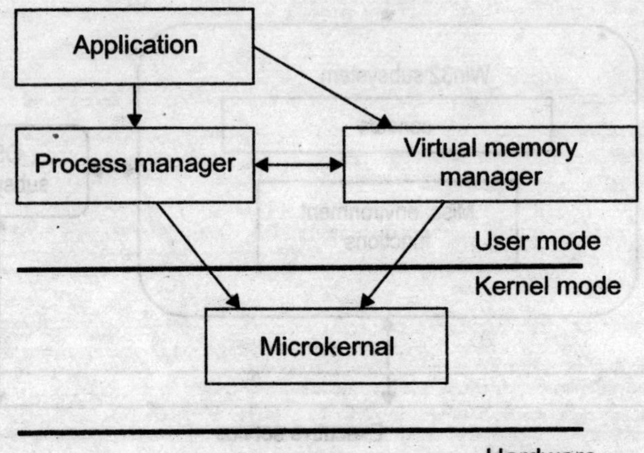

Figure 14.2: *A Pure Microkernel Operating System Design.*

Microkernel architecture gives a system configurability and fault tolerance. Because an operating system subsystem like the Virtual Memory Manager runs as a distinct program in microkernel design, a different implementation that exports the same interface can replace it. If the Virtual Memory Manager fails, thanks to the fault-tolerance possible in a microkernel design, the operating system can restart it with minimal effect on the rest of the system. In monolithic operating system design (e.g., DOS and Windows 3.1), the entire operating system must be rebuilt to change any subsystem.

NT takes a unique approach, known as modified microkernel, that falls between pure microkernel and monolithic design. In NT's modified microkernel design, operating system environments execute in user mode as discrete processes, including DOS, Win16, Win32, OS/2, and POSIX. The basic operating system subsystems, including the Process Manager and the Virtual Memory Manager, execute in kernel mode, and they are compiled into one file image. These kernel-mode subsystems are not separate processes, and they can communicate with one another by using function calls for maximum performance.

NT's user-mode operating system environments implement separate operating system APIs. The degree of NT support for each environment varies, however. Support for DOS is limited to the DOS programs that do not attempt to access the computer's hardware directly. OS/2 and POSIX support user-interface functions and the advanced features of the APIs. Win32 is really the official language of NT, and it's the only API Microsoft has expanded since NT was first released.

NT's operating system environments rely on services that the kernel mode exports to carry out tasks that they can't carry out in user mode. The services invoked in kernel mode are known as NT's native API. This API is made up of about 250 functions that NT's operating systems access through software-exception system calls. A software-exception system call is a hardware-assisted way to change execution modes from user mode to kernel mode; it gives NT control over the data that passes between the two modes.

NT's Executive components use basic hardware functionality implemented in the microkernel. The microkernel, which is known in NT as the Kernel, contains the scheduler. The Kernel also manages the Executive's use of NT's hardware and software interrupt handlers and exports synchronization primitives. Device drivers and the Kernel use the HAL to interact with the computer's hardware. The HAL exports its own API, which translates abstract data into processor-specific commands. NT is portable across processor types because processor-specific code is restricted to the Kernel and the HAL. This situation means that when NT is ported to a new processor, only the Kernel and the HAL must be converted. The rest of NT's code is written in C and C++ and can simply be recompiled for the new processor.

SYSTEM SERVICES

System services export the native API from kernel mode so that user-mode portions of NT can use it. The native API is intended for use by operating system environments, but nothing prevents an application from bypassing the operating system environment API and accessing the native API directly. However, the native API is usually undocumented, is very similar to the Win32 API, and would not give an application privileges or powers its operating system environment would not give it.

System services have names that begin with NT. For example, Win32 has an API function called Create Process, which the Win32 server handles. CreateProcess calls the native API function, Nt Create Process. The parameter lists for both functions are similar; however, Create Process performs significant amounts of work on behalf of the environment. For instance, it sets up the process's environment variables and command line and fills in the process address map with the program to be executed. System services validate parameters that are passed from user mode and then usually call functions within Executive subsystems. For example, NtCreateProcess calls the Process Manager Executive subsystem, invoking its PsCreateProcess function. Most system services are short because they serve primarily as thin interfaces between user mode and Executive subsystems. There can be a one-for-one correspondence between Win32 calls and native calls, but many Win32 functions make more than one native call to carry out a task.

Applications and operating system environments that use the native API access it through a DLL named ntdll.dll. This DLL is linked to every process in an NT system and consists of entry points for every system service. These entry points don't do much other than preparing variables and causing a system service software exception. The

System Service Exception Handler in kernel mode is executed in response to system service exceptions, and it uses a number associated with the requested service to index the System Service Table and find the function that implements the service. Thus, adding a new system service requires updates of that table and ntdll.dll. Microsoft continues to add to the number of system services in NT, and almost two dozen new calls will appear in NT 5.0.

Process Management

The logical boundary that separates user-mode and kernel-mode processes is designed to make the system robust by preventing direct access to hardware and protecting the core operating system from bugs and unauthorized access by user-mode processes. A failing application will not interfere with the operating system or its support of other applications.

To cross this boundary, user-mode processes must use well-documented application program interfaces (APIs) to switch their threads from user mode to kernel mode. Such a conversion is called a kernel-mode transition. Kernel-mode threads can use Executive services but must be switched back to user mode to return control to the application.

Accessing an environment subsystem involves several kernel/user mode transitions and consumes substantial memory and processor time. This is an example of a graphics call in previous versions of Windows NT. It demonstrates that interprocess communication can be quite complex, even when optimized:

- The application uses an API to make a graphics call to a user-mode dynamic link library. The component that implements the call makes a kernel-mode trap call to the Executive to switch its thread and copy its call parameters from its user mode stack to its kernel mode stack. Then, the processor's stack register is switched to point to kernel mode. Now the thread can run in the Executive mode.
- Applications communicate with protected subsystems by using local procedure calls (LPC), an application-independent method of communication between components on the same computer. After the thread is switched to kernel mode, the Microkernel schedules the LPC for delivery.
- The graphics call parameters are passed to the receiving subsystem thread. The receiving thread switches back to user mode to fulfill the graphics request.
- The subsystem completes its task and then returns control to the waiting calling thread in the application by the same method.
- The calling thread (from the DLL) is switched back to user mode before returning control to the application.

Microsoft operating-system engineers also used the concept of a shared memory window to speed up communication. Data is placed in a temporary shared memory window administered by the Process Manager in the Executive. This lets the application see into the subsystem's memory and share data without using LPCs. However, because the application thread must still run in the Executive, kernel/user mode transitions and thread switches are still required.

Memory Management

As the size of applications and the operating systems that run them grow larger and larger, so do their demand for memory. Consequently, all modern operating systems provide a form of virtual memory to applications. Being the newest of the operating systems to hit the main stream, Windows NT™ will likely have applications ported to it that will evolve into larger monstrosities that require even more memory than they did on the last operating system on which they ran. Even applications being written exclusively for Windows NT will be written with the future in mind and will no doubt take advantage of all the memory that is available to them.

Fortunately, Windows NT does, in fact, offer virtual memory to its applications (or processes) and subsystems. Windows NT provides a page-based virtual memory management scheme that allows applications to realize a 32-bit linear address space for 4 gigabytes (GB) of memory. As a result, each application has its own private address space from which it can use the lower 2 GB—the system reserves the upper 2 GB of every process's address space for its own use.

The Win32™ subsystem provides user services that are loaded as dynamic-link libraries (DLLs) into the lower portion of the address space of a process. These DLLs exist in addition to the system DLLs that occupy the upper portion of the address space. Depending on which DLLs an application links or loads, the DLLs that are mapped into the lower portion of a process's address space will vary from one application to the next within a subsystem.

Windows Version 3.x has realizable limitations to the maximum amount of memory available to it and all of its applications; these are often barriers to large applications for this environment. Windows NT's limits are far more theoretical. Windows NT employs the PC's hard disk as the memory-backing store and, as such, has a practical limit imposed only by available disk space. So, it is reasonable to assume that a Windows NT system could have an extremely large hard disk or array of disks amounting to 2 GB or more of physical memory and provide that much virtual memory to each of its applications (minus the portions used by the system, occupied by the file system, and allocated by files stored within the file system). In short, Windows NT provides a seemingly endless supply of memory to all of the applications running on it.

VIRTUAL MEMORY IN WINDOWS NT

The Virtual-Memory Manager (VMM) in Windows NT is nothing like the memory managers used in previous versions of the Windows operating system. Relying on a 32-bit address model, Windows NT is able to drop the segmented architecture of previous versions of Windows. Instead, the VMM employs 32-bit virtual addresses for directly manipulating the entire 4-GB process. At first this appears to be a restriction because, without segment selectors for relative addressing, there is no way to move a chunk of memory without having to change the address that references it. In reality, the VMM is able to do exactly that by implementing virtual addresses. Each application is able to reference a physical chunk of memory, at a specific virtual address, throughout the life of the application. The VMM takes care of whether the memory should be moved to a new location or swapped to disk completely independently of the application, much like updating a selector entry in the local descriptor table (LDT).

Windows versions 3.1 and earlier employed a scheme for moving segments of memory to other locations in memory both to maximize the amount of available contiguous memory and to place executable segments in the location where they could be executed. An equivalent operation is unnecessary in Windows NT's virtual memory management system for three reasons. One, code segments are no longer required to reside in the 0-640K range of memory in order for Windows NT to execute them. Windows NT does require that the hardware have at least a 32-bit address bus, so it is able to address all of physical memory, regardless of location. Two, the VMM virtualizes the address space such that two processes can use the same virtual address to refer to distinct locations in physical memory. Virtual address locations are not a commodity, especially considering that a process has 2 GB available for the application. So, each process may use any or all of its virtual addresses without regard to other processes in the system. Three, contiguous virtual memory in Windows NT can be allocated discontiguously in physical memory. So, there is no need to move chunks to make room for a large allocation.

The foundation for the system provides the answer to how VMM is able to perform these seemingly miraculous functions. VMM is constructed upon a page-based memory management scheme that divides all of memory into equal chunks called pages. Each page is 4096 bytes (4K) in size with no discrimination applied as to how a page is used. Everything in Windows NT—code, data, resources, files, dynamic memory, and so forth—is implemented using pages of physical memory.

Because everything in the system is realized via pages of physical memory, it is easy to see that pages of memory become scarce rather quickly. VMM employs the use of the hard disk to store unneeded pages of memory in one or more files called page files. Page files represent pages of data that are not currently being used, but may be needed spontaneously at any time. By swapping pages to and from page files, the VMM is able to make pages of memory available to applications on demand and provide much more virtual memory than the available physical memory. Also, page files in Windows NT are dynamic in size, allowing them to grow as the demand for pages of memory grow. In this way, Windows NT is able to provide virtually unlimited memory to the system.

WINDOWS NT FILE SYSTEM

The Windows file system is called NTFS, and was introduced with Windows NT 4.0 and is the standard file system on Windows 2000 and later systems, such as Windows XP. Its goal was to solve the size, performance, reliability, and flexibility limitations in DOS.

It has a general similarity to the FAT file system in that all files are described in a single table, called the Master File Table (MFT). However, it has more modern characteristics in that all components are files, including:

- Master File Table
- Data Files
- Directories
- Free List (bit map)
- Boot Images
- Recovery Logs

Disks are divide in fixed size regions:

- Each region is called a volume.
- Each volume can contain a different kind of file system, such as NTFS, FAT, or even Unix.
- Since each volume is a separate file system, it has its own root directory.
- Multiple volumes allow for fixed limits on the growth of a particular file tree, such as limiting the size of temporary file space.
- Multiple volumes also allow a single disk to contain multiple, separating bootable operating system.

Master File Table (MFT)

Clusters are the key element to allocation:

- Logically, the disk consists of allocation units called clusters.
- A cluster is a power-of-two multiple of the physical disk block size. The cluster size is set when the disk is formatted. A small cluster provides a finer granularity of allocation, but may require more space to describe the file and more separate operations to transfer data to or from memory.
- The free list is a bitmap, each of whose bits describe one cluster.
- Clusters on the disk are numbered starting from zero to the maximum number of clusters (minus one). These numbers are called logical cluster numbers (LCN) and are used to name blocks (clusters) on disk.

The MFT is the major, and in some ways, the only data structure on disk:

- All files, and therefore all objects stored on disk are described by the MFT.
- All files are logically stored in the MFT and, small files are physically within the bounds of the MFT. In this sense, the MFT is the file system.
- The MFT logically can be described as a table with one row per file.
- The first row in the table described important configuration files, including the MFT itself.

As stated previously, each row or entry in the MFT (called a record) describes a file and logically contains the file. In the case of small files, the entry actually contains the contents of the file. Each entry consists of (attribute, value) pairs. While the conceptual design of NTFS is such that this set of pairs is extensible to include user-defined attributes, current version of NTFS have a fixed set. The main attributes are:

- **Standard Information:** This attribute includes the information that was standard in the MS-DOS world:
  - read/write permissions,
  - creation time,
  - last modification time,
  - count of how many directories point to this this file (hard link count.
- **File Name:** This attribute describes the file's name in the Unicode character set. Multiple file names are possible, such as when:
  - The file has multiple links, or
  - The file has an MS-DOS short name.
- **Security Descriptor:** This attribute lists which user owns the file and which users can access it (and how they can access it).
- **Data:** This attribute either contains the actual file data in the case of a small file or points to the data (or points to the objects that point to the data) in the case of larger files.

  For small files, this design is extremely efficient. By looking no further than the MFT entry, you have the complete contents of the file.

However, the Data field gets interesting when the data contained in the file is larger than an MFT entry. When dealing with large data, the Data attribute contains pointers to the data, rather than the data itself. The pointers to data are actually pointers to sequences of logical clusters on the disk. Each sequence is identified by three parts:

  - Starting cluster in the file, called the virtual cluster number (VCN),
  - Starting logical cluster (LCN) of the sequence on disk,
  - Length, counted as the number of clusters.
- The run of clusters is called an extent.
- NTFS allocates new extents as necessary. When there is no more space left in the MFT entry, then another MFT entry is allocated. This design is effectively a list of extents, rather than the Unix or DEMOS tree of extents.

Directories

As with other modern file systems, a directory in NTFS is a file whose data contains a collection of name/file mappings.

- A directory entry contains the name of the file and file reference. The file references indentifies the file on this volume. In other words, it is an internal name for the file.

A reference is a (file number, sequence number) pair. The file number is the offset of the file's entry in the MFT table.

- The list of file names in the directories is not stored in a simple list, but rather as a lexigraphically-sorted tree, called a B+ tree. The data structure is called an *index* in NFTS.
- The NTFS design specifies that an index can be constructed for any attribute, but currently only file name indices are supported.
- The name for a file appears both in its directory entry and in the MFT entry for the file itself.
- As with regular files, if the directory is small enough, it can fit entirely within the MFT entry.

INTER-PROCESS COMMUNICATION

Inter process communication (IPC) refers to the coordination of activities among cooperating processes. A common example of this need is managing access to a given system resource. To carry out IPC, some form of active or passive communication is required. The increasing important role that distributed systems play in modern computing environments increases the need for IPC. Systems for managing communication and synchronization between cooperating processes are essential to many modern software systems. IPC has always played a prominent role in UNIX-variant operating systems, but it has been largely overlooked for systems running the Windows NT operating system.

Pipes

Pipes are a simple synchronized way of passing information between two processes. A pipe can be viewed as a special file that can store only a limited amount of data and uses a FIFO access scheme to retrieve data. In a logical view of a pipe, data is written to one end and read from the other. The processes on the end of a pipe have no easy way to identify what process is on the other end of the pipe.

The system provides synchronization between the reading and writing process. It also solves the producer/consumer problem: writing to a full pipe automatically blocks, as does reading from an empty pipe. The system also assures that there are processes on both ends of the pipe at all times. The programmer is still responsible, however, for preventing deadlock between processes. Pipes come in two varieties:

- **Unnamed:** Unnamed pipes can only be used by related processes (i.e. a process and one of its child processes, or two of its children). Unnamed pipes cease to exist after the processes are done using them.
- **Named:** Named pipes exist as directory entries, complete with permissions. This means that they are persistent and that unrelated processes can use them.

* **Windows NT** supports both named and unnamed pipes, although it refers to the latter as anonymous pipes. The CreatePipe() function creates an anonymous pipe and returns two handles. One handle is a read handle to the pipe and the other is a write handle to the pipe; neither pipe can perform the opposite operation. When the pipe is created the server requests that it should be implemented using a programmer-defined buffer size. To communicate using the pipe, the server must pass one of the handles to another process. Usually, this is done through inheritance; that is, the process allows the handle to be inherited by a child process. The process can also send the handle to an unrelated process using another form of inter process communication, such as shared memory. A server can send either the read handle or the write handle to the pipe client, depending on whether the client should use the anonymous pipe to send information or receive information. To read from the pipe, the pipe's read handle is used as a parameter to the call ReadFile(). The ReadFile() call returns when another process has written to the pipe. ReadFile() call can also return if all write handles to the pipe have been closed or if an error occurs before the read operation has been completed.

Sockets

A socket is a software abstraction that is used to create a channel-like interface between processes. The channel allows bi-directional communication between processes, but does little to structure the data being transmitted. In general, the serving machine in a system that uses socket communication follows several steps to initiate communication:

* Create a socket
* Map the socket to a local address
* Listen for client requests

When the client process wishes to begin a transaction with the server, it follows similar steps:

* Create a socket
* Determine the location (system name and port number) of the server
* Begin sending and/or receiving data

Types of Sockets

Communication between processes via sockets can be viewed as streams or data grams. Stream based communication views transmitted data as a sequence of bytes, whereas datagram-based communication deals with small discrete packets of information. These packets typically contain header and trailer information in addition to the data being transmitted. Choosing a socket type is important, because each has different performance and reliability characteristics, and two communicating sockets must be of the same type.

- **Stream:** Stream sockets are reliable; that is, data is guaranteed to be delivered in the same order it was sent. An underlying mechanism that the programmer need not be concerned with handles duplicate data, performs error checking, and controls flow. When using stream sockets, a connection is established. This means that two processes must logically agree to communicate before information can be transferred between the two of them. This connection is maintained by both processes throughout the communication session.
- **Datagram:** Datagram sockets provide unreliable communication between the two processes, meaning that data could be received out of order. Datagram sockets provide no notion of a connection, so each datagram is sent and processed independently. This has a host of implications, one of the most significant of which is that individual data grams can take different paths to their ultimate destination. Another important implication is that there is no flow control. Datagram packets are typically quite small and usually are fixed in size. No error correction is mandated, and when optional error connection is used, it is weak.

Case Study on Unix

Chapter 15

HISTORY OF UNIX

The birth of Unix is the most finest things that has happened in the computing industry in the recent times. If has a large number of outstanding and diverse features, which are simple yet powerful. Unix was developed at Bell Laboratories as a private research project by a small group of people in 1969. Unix was originally developed in 1969 by a group of AT&T employees at Bell Labs, including Ken Thompson, Dennis Ritchie, Douglas McIlroy, and Joe Ossanna.

There are various Unix variants available in the market. Solaris Unix, AIX, UP Unix and BSD are few examples. Linux is also a flavor of Unix which is freely available. By 1980 Unix could be moved to virtually any computer system and was available as System III. In 1983, it was introduced to minicomputers as XENIX, due to the efforts of Microsoft Corporation. A large number of systems and millions of users are using UNIX and various versions of UNIX like 3.2, 4.0 and 5.0 are available in the market. The OPEN systems standards imply and offer:

1. Portability of data from one hardware platform to another.
2. Interoperability of systems of fundamentally different designs.
3. Application to be moved among systems of different levels of computing power.
4. Availability of extensive software solutions.

The OPEN system is necessary, to protect capital assets and investment on computer resources, to move quickly to the systems of higher power and capability and to integrate the products from multiple vendors and thus eliminating the dependency on a single vendor.

Several people can use a UNIX computer at the same time; hence UNIX is called a multiuser system. This group has experience with a number of different operating system research efforts in 1970s. The goal of the group was to design an operating system that satisfy the objectives of a simple and elegant set of programs written in a high level language rather than assembly language and which must allow reusability of code.

The Unix system can be divided into two parts, one interacting with the users and the other one with the hardware of the machine. These jobs are done by the kernel and the shell. The kernel is the heart of the system, it is a collection of programs written in C, which communicate with the hardware directly. There is only kernel for any system. It is loaded into the memory when system is booted. It manages the system resources, allocates time between the users and processes, decides process priorities and performs other house keeping jobs on behalf of the user. It is independent of the user programs and is independent of the hardware used. Actually, the kernel is known as the operating system. The shell is called the 'sleeping beauty'. It is the interpreter of commands given by the user. It receives the commands from the users and converts them into the form kernel can understand. It is an interface between the user and the kernel. It insulates the user from the knowledge of kernel functions.

FEATURES OF UNIX OPERATING SYSTEM

The popularity of UNIX is due to the simplicity of its design and functioning. The salient features of the system are:

1. **Multiuser Capability:** UNIX is a multiuser operating system. User can view different programs, send messages among themselves or to the users outside the system. They can access the saved database and get the queries answered, reports generated, update and modify data and moreover all these jobs can be done simultaneously. Users can share resources such as printers, tapes and discs. Unix verifies and checks at the login, whether the user is an authorized user or not. Unix allows the access to programs and files only if the user has the sufficient access rights.
2. **Time Sharing:** Unix operates on the principle of time sharing. The programs of each user are loaded into the memory from the disc and the scheduler provides a time slice for each user, executes his programs for the assigned time slice and then moves to the programs of the other users turn by turn in a cycle. As the clock speed is very fast, each user feels that he/she is the only user of the system and the system is responding to their requests only. Although many programs reside in the memory at the same time, the operating system ensures that the jobs and the processes do not get mixed up with each other.
3. **Command Interpreter:** Unix provides a built-in shell, which interprets the commands typed by the user and enables the operating system to execute the commands. When the user enters the command, the shell locates the corresponding files and gets it executed by the operating system. An expert programmer can even change the name of these commands and can use it as per the ease.
4. **Portability:** Portability means that Unix can be implemented on different computers easily. Unix design has a very small portion that depends on the actual hardware which is to be written in assembly code and proves to be much easier and less time consuming than writing the full operating system in assembly language. The ability to port Unix from one type, brand or manufacture of one computer to another has been a major reason for the success and acceptance of Unix as a multiuser operating system.

5. **Multitasking and Background Processing:** As Unix can fulfil the requirements of the different users, and these users can assign multiple tasks, this feature is known as multitasking. Even an individual user can perform different tasks simultaneously. Like if the user is printing a document, at the same he can edit the source program or can give a command for compiling another program. Some of the processes can be executed in the background as these do not require any interaction with the user.
6. **Simple Command Structure:** Unix system commands are user friendly and consist of a simple command structure for most of the user commands. Commands are entered in lower case. These commands are easy to remember and an ordinary user has to know only 15 to 20 basic commands.
7. **Hierarchical File System:** Unix Provides an excellent multiple directory file system. The directory in Unix can have subdirectories and files. Unix does not distinguish between the text, program and data files and represent all of them by their file names.
8. **File Security and Protection:** Unix provides protection to the user's files and directories from accidental or intentional damage by the other users. Access permissions can be provided for read, write or execute. Users working as a group in a software project can share files and directories. These permissions can be changed by the owner of the files. Login and password protection provided by Unix prevents the unauthorized users from gaining access to the system, for directories and files of another user.
9. **System Administration and Job Accounting:** Unix provides the excellent feature for monitoring and controlling the use of a multiuser system. System administration relates to various activities needed to control, coordinate and maintain the system. Once it has been started up, it does not require a constant attention, as there are commands and utilities available through which the user will be able to identify if any abnormal condition like system crashes, hardware failure etc occurs.
10. **Job Accounting:** It provides the feature for maintenance of job accounting of various users of the system, by monitoring the CPU utilization, memory space utilization, terminal logged on time etc.
11. **DOS/Unix Interface:** Unix supports the DOS merge utility, where a user can switch from Unix to DOS in his terminal and execute programs available under DOS and user can store DOS data files and programs in the Unix system hardware, thus providing an integration between DOS and Unix.
12. **Tools and Utilities:** Unix tools can be defined as any command that is executable in Unix. All commands are macros. There are hundreds of tools available in Unix and the number is increasing as new tools are being added. Even users can create their own tools also. Unix allow large software projects to be broken into smaller

manageable program modules, allowing separate compilation of modules, storing of different versions of modules as well using Source Code Control System. Some of the tools of Unix are termed as utilities. Commands for printing a text, finding difference between the files, scanning files, sorting files are considered as utilities.

13. **Shell and Shell Programming:** The command interpreter of Unix is known as shell. The various types of shell in Unix are C shell, Bourne shell. The shell not only interpret the commands for the Kernel, but also includes a complete programming language that can be used to create new commands. It is possible to store a set of shell commands to a file in proper order and get them executed one by one, like a batch file in DOS.

14. **Online Documentation:** Unix provides an online help to understand the proper syntax or expression of system commands, tools and utilities with their description. These are covered in man and learn commands which provide help to the user.

15. **Library of Application Packages:** Various application packages are available which provide the facility of word processing, data base management and spreadsheet. Powerful graphic workstations used for engineering and 3D graphics prefer Unix as the operating system.

THE UNIX SYSTEM LIFE CYCLE

Unlike a small computer operating system, the UNIX system is designed to run continuously. Constant operation allows it to schedule tasks a long way in advance, and ensures that the services it provide are available on demand, whenever they are needed.

Unix boot process has these main phases:

- Basic hardware detection (memory, disk, keyboard, mouse, and the like).
- Executing the firmware system initialization program (happens automatically).
- Locating and running the initial boot program (by the firmware boot program), usually from a predetermined location on disk. This program may perform additional hardware checks prior to loading the kernel.
- Locating and Starting the Unix kernel (by the first-stage boot program). The kernel image file to execute may be determined automatically or via input to the boot program.
- The kernel initializes itself and then performs final, high-level hardware checks, loading device drivers and/or kernel modules as required.
- The kernel starts the init process, which in turn starts system processes (daemons) and initializes all active subsystems. When everything is ready, the system begins accepting user logins.

Whenever the user starts up a UNIX system, it goes through the following complex life cycle:

Startup

When the user switches the computer on, it is not yet ready to run the UNIX system. The machine contains a library of programs stored in read-only memory (or ROM) which are known collectively as the BIOS (or basic input-output system). These programs serve two purposes; they are used by DOS (but not by the UNIX system) to access peripheral devices, and they carry out a Power-On Self-Test (or POST) of the computer's hardware. If all is well, the light on the computer's first floppy disk drive flashes. If a disk containing a small program called a boot program is present in the drive, it will then read the program in and proceed to the next stage; if there is a hardware fault and the POST fails, the computer will either beep a series of tones at you or display a message on its monitor, and refuse to go any further.

Boot

If the power-on self-test was successful, the boot process commences. The term ``boot'' is a traditional reference to the way in which the system must pull itself up by its own bootstraps, loading a short program that runs and loads a more elaborate program, and so on. The first step in the boot process is for the computer to read in a short program stored in the first sector of either a floppy disk or the first hard drive on the computer. This is carried out by part of the BIOS. The boot sector program then loads another short program, which is just intelligent enough to search the disk for a program called /boot, and read that program into the computer's main memory. At this stage, the computer is minimally functional. The /boot program cannot make use of virtual memory, mount file systems, or do any of the other tasks associated with the system; neither can it run under the system when it is operational. What it can do is prompt the user for the name of a file to execute, then search the root directory of the root file system for that file and load it. To do this it places a prompt on the system console and then it waits for the user to type the name of the kernel, or any additional instructions that it recognizes. If the user do not type anything, it will time out after a specified period and load the default file listed in /etc/default/boot.

Loading the Kernel

The kernel is visible on user system as a file in the root directory, usually called / unix. The boot program copies the kernel into the computer's memory, then starts it running. When the kernel begins to run, it starts by setting up a number of internal lists, or tables. These tables are used to keep track of running processes, memory allocation, open files, and a number of other things; they are not directly accessible to the user. However, two of them which are of interest are the process table and the buffer cache. After initializing its tables, the kernel creates three dummy processes; sched, vhand and bdflush (with process IDs 0, 2 and 3 respectively). These processes are sections of kernel code which must be called periodically; vhand provides virtual memory paging services, sched provides swapping services, and bdflush flushes the buffer cache periodically. None of these processes can be killed; they are part of the kernel, and are essential to the correct running of the UNIX system. Finally the kernel creates a third process; init, or process 1. init starts up as a dummy process, then achieves independence: it runs as the first true process on the system. init runs continuously; it is the parent of all other processes on the system. Other activities performed by init include the following:

- Checking the integrity of the file systems, traditionally using the fsck utility.
- Mounting local disks.
- Designating and initializing paging areas.
- Performing file system cleanup activities: checking disk quotas, preserving editor recovery files, and deleting temporary files in /tmp and elsewhere.
- Starting system server processes (daemons) for subsystems like printing, electronic mail, accounting, error logging, and cron.
- Starting networking daemons and mounting remote disks.
- Enabling user logins, usually by starting getty processes and/or the graphical login interface on the system console (e.g., xdm), and removing the file /etc/nologin, if present.

Run levels

Run Levels define the behavior of init, and by extension those processes which run on the system when it is at any given level. The system starts at run level 0 (shutdown) and then enters run level 1, single user mode. At level 1, only the root file system is mounted and only processes connected to the console can run; this means that it is safe to check the un-mounted file systems for integrity without risking any other processes altering them. At other run levels, init starts up the daemon processes that provide various services, and enters multiuser mode.

init executes other programs via the fork system call. Each time init calls fork, it passes control to the kernel, which creates a new entry in the process table, allocates a temporary storage area called a U-area, and copies the calling processes' local data (including the stack) into the U-area. The kernel then returns control to the child process, which may make an exec call, overwriting itself with a new program. init periodically reads a file called /etc/inittab, which tells it which programs to execute at any given run level.

The init (M) program should not be confused with the init process; the former is an executable program which can be used by the administrator to change the run level of the system or cause the init process to reread the /etc/inittab file.

Multiuser Mode

When the system reaches a suitable run level (2 or higher), init starts a series of processes called gettys. (In /etc/inittab each line specifying a getty process includes the option respawn. This means that whenever a getty process dies, init spawns a replacement with the same parameters immediately. The getty options include a tty serial line, which it serves. The job of the getty process is to display a login prompt, then wait for input. If the user try to log in on the terminal, getty works out the serial line speed as the user type the name, then execs a login process. The login process reads the password; if it is incorrect the process dies, and init spawns another getty on the terminal. If the user enters a valid password, login then runs a shell, which inherits user's terminal, his identity and his access permissions. When the login shell finishes, there are no processes left attached to your terminal, so init re-spawns another getty to wait for a login. Thus, while the system is in multiuser mode, each terminal continually executes a four stage cycle: init-getty-login-shell. It is not uncommon for a system to remain in multiuser mode for days or weeks at a time. However, it is necessary for the system administrator to shut it down for maintenance at regular intervals. (Performance is likely to suffer if a system is kept running for several weeks without a shutdown.)

Shutdown

When the administrator shuts down a system, it follows a set procedure. Because the system may be supporting a number of users, warning messages are broadcasted to all terminals before a shutdown. After a short time, init switches to run level 1, killing all the processes linked to terminals and flushing and un-mounting all the mounted file systems. The buffer cache is then flushed (by the sync program), and the system drops to run level 0, or shutdown.

It is important to understand that unless the user is running on a multiprocessor system only one process is actually being executed at any given instant. Although the system is multitasking, a single processor can only carry out one instruction at a time.

The kernel effectively mediates the demands of each process, by scheduling the processes to run one after another. The signal for the kernel to take over is sent by the system clock; every hundredth of a second the kernel wakes up and checks to see if the current process has completed its time allocation. If so, the kernel suspends the process and switches execution to the process on the queue with the highest priority. The kernel also mediates all requests for memory and requests to load and run other processes. The requesting process (be it init or any other process) issues a ``system call", a request to the kernel to deliver a service; it then suspends execution (sleeps) until the kernel can deliver the requested facility.

ARCHITECTURE OF UNIX

Various parts of Unix are arranged around the hardware. The core of Unix is the kernel which schedules jobs and manages the data storage and it is very closely interfaced with the hardware. The hardware functions according to the machine instructions released by the kernel. Surrounding the kernel there is a shell which is a program that collects and interprets the user commands, invokes the concerned program files from memory and directs the kernel to execute them. The main concept that unites all versions of UNIX is the following four basics:

1. **Kernel:** The kernel is the heart of the operating system. It interacts with hardware and most of the tasks like memory management process scheduling and file management.

The kernel runs the show, i.e. it manages all the operations in a Unix flavored environment. The computer programs that allocate the system resources and coordinate all the details of the computer's internals is called the operating system or kernel. Users communicate with the kernel through a program known as the shell. The shell is a command line interpreter; it translates commands entered by the user and converts them into a language that is understood by the kernel. The kernel architecture must support the primary Unix requirements. These requirements fall in two categories namely, functions for process management and functions for file management (files include device files). Process management entails allocation of resources including CPU, memory, and offers services that processes may need. The file management in itself involves handling all the files required by processes, communication with device drives and regulating transmission of data to and from peripherals. The kernel operation gives the user processes a feel of synchronous operation, hiding all underlying details in peripheral and hardware operations (like the time slicing by clock). In summary, we can say that the kernel handles the following operations:

1. It is responsible for scheduling running of user and other processes.
2. It is responsible for allocating memory.
3. It is responsible for managing the swapping between memory and disk.
4. It is responsible for moving data to and from the peripherals.
5. It receives service requests from the processes and honors them.

All these services are provided by the kernel through a call to a system utility. As a result, kernel by itself is rather a small program that just maintains enough data structures to pass arguments, receive the results from a call and then pass them on to the calling process. Most of the data structure is tables. The chore of management involves keeping the tables updated.

2. **Shell:** The shell is the utility that processes your requests. As the name suggests, it envelops the kernel. Most of the users are not aware of various complexities of the operating system or the hardware. The user sees the shell command and the shell command interpreter and finally talks with the kernel. Every user once accepted by the kernel as an authorized user is issued a shell prompt. And the commands issued by the user are counted and numbered serially. When the user type in a command at the terminal, the shell interprets the command and calls the program that the user wants. The shell uses standard syntax for all commands. C Shell, Bourne Shell and Korn Shell are the most famous shells which are available with most of the Unix variants. The shell environment consists of following to ensure proper interaction between the user and the system:
   - The name of the users and a working directory (i.e the directory allotted to the user by the operating system).
   - A List of system directories to be searched to locate the commands given by the user.
   - The file access permission modes.
   - A record of users identification and group identification numbers.

3. **Commands and Utilities:** There are various command and utilities which the user would use in your day to day activities. cp, mv, cat and grep etc. are few examples of commands and utilities. There are over 250 standard commands plus numerous others provided through 3rd party software. All the commands come along with various options.
4. **Files and Directories:** All data in UNIX is organized into files. All files are organized into directories. These directories are organized into a tree-like structure called the file system.

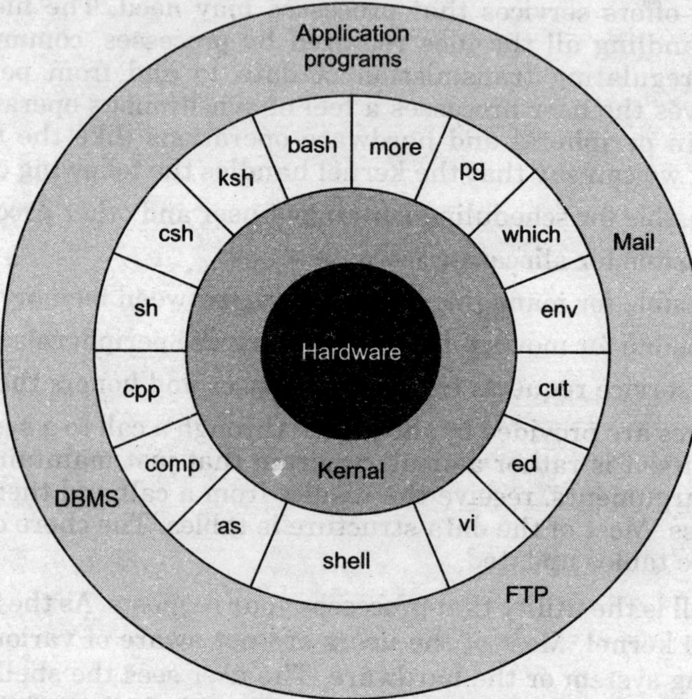

Figure 15.1: *Unix Architecture*

UNIX FILE SYSTEM

Directories are central to the use of Unix system and directory structure is of a great and unique strength to Unix. The directory system of Unix is in the form of an inverted tree shown in the Figure 15.2 given below. The directory at the top most position is called the root. It is the source from which all directories emerge. Under root, there are several system directories as branches. The system directories are known as bin, dev, lib, etc, unix and usr.

The usr directory has further system subdirectories. These are called as subdirectories of usr directory. Under this directory, there are various users with their login names located, with one directory allocated for each user. Whenever the user creates a directory for storing his files, they are stored in his login directory called home directory. The users should be aware of his own private files and directories and need not to know the data of the other users in the system. The details of system directories and their contents are shown in the Table 15.1 given below. Generally there is no limit to the number of subdirectories one can create under his/her directory. They are restricted to the disc space allocation provided by the system administrator.

Table 15.1 : The System Subdirectories, their Files and Function.

/	Root
/bin	Most commonly used Unix Commands and tools compilers, assemblers, editors, program development tools.
/dev	Devices including terminals. Contains special files that represent peripheral devices such as console, printer etc.
/etc	System Administrative Files
/lib	Library Functions for C program and languages, system calls and I/O routines.
/tmp	Temporary files and word space for any user, using editors, compilers and assemblers.
/unix	Unix kernel.
/usr	All user accounts
/usr/man	Online user manual and information.
/usr/mail	All the mails.
/usr/bin	Less used utility programs
/usr/lib	Library files
/user1, /user2	User's Home Directories

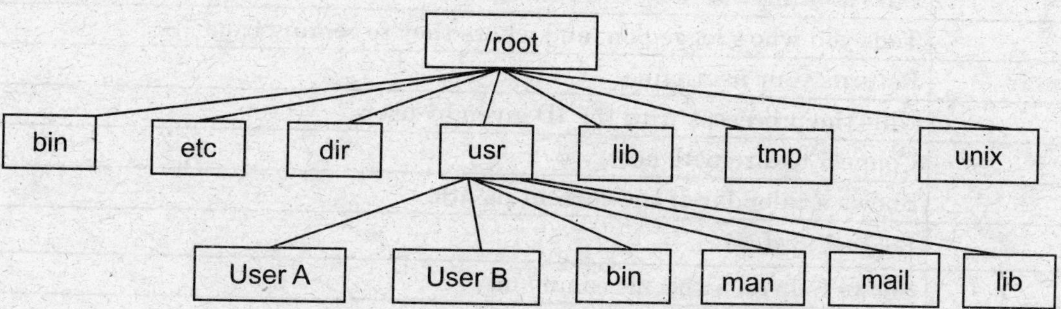

Figure 15.2: *Unix System Directories*

BASIC UNIX COMMANDS

Unix is rich in commands, some of the basic commands are given below in the Table 15.2.

Table 15.2: Basic Unix Commands.

Command	Purpose
mkdir	Make a directory
mv	Move or rename a file
rm	Remove a file
pwd	Displays Present Working Directory
bc	Programmable Calculator
cat	Concatenate files and Write them to Standard Output
cmp	Compare two files
chmod	Change Protection Mode for Files
comm	Returns lines common to two Sorted Files
date	Returns Date and Time
ed	Text Editor
find	Find all files meeting a given condition
cp	Make a copy of the file
diff	Return all differences between two Files.
grep	Search a file for lines containing a given pattern.
ls	List files in a Directory.
phr	Format a file for printing.
sh	Invoke the Shell.
sleep	Suspend the execution for a given number of Seconds.
wc	Count Characters, Words and Lines in a file.
ff	Find files anywhere on the system.
who	Tells you who's logged on, and where they're coming from
Who am i	Returns your username
kill	Kills the processes with the ID given by user.
telnet	Connect to a remote host.
cal	Shows a calendar of the current month.
logout	Logs off system
man	Shows help on a specific command
ftp	Connects to a FTP site
tar	Combines multiple files into one or vice-versa
ps	Prints the status of various processes.
nice	Sets command execution priority.
cc	Invoke a C Compiler.
tty	Show reference and name of the terminal.
news	Send message to all the users.

Chapter 16

Case Study on Linux Operating System

HISTORY OF LINUX

In 1991 Linus Torvalds began developing an operating system kernel, which he named "Linux" . This kernel could be combined with the FSF material and other components (in particular some of the BSD components and MIT's X-windows software) to produce a freely-modifiable and very useful operating system. This book will term the kernel itself the "Linux kernel" and an entire combination as "Linux".Many use the term "GNU/Linux" instead for this combination.

In the Linux community, different organizations have combined the available componentsdifferently. Eachcombinationiscalleda "distribution", andtheorganizations that develop distributions are called "distributors". Common distributions include Red Hat, Mandrake, SuSE, Caldera, Corel, and Debian. There are differences between the various distributions, but all distributions are based on the same foundation: the Linux kernel and the GNU glibc libraries. Since both are covered by ``copyleft" style licenses, changes to these foundations generally must be made available to all, a unifying force between the Linux distributions at their foundation that does not exist between the BSD and AT&T-derived Unix system. Increased interest in software that is freely shared has made it increasing ly necessary to define and explain it. A widely used term is "open source software". Another widely-used term is "free software", where the "free" is short for "freedom": the usual explanation is "free speech, not free beer." Neither phrase is perfect. The term "free software" is often confused with programs whose executables are given away at no charge, but whose source code cannot be viewed, modified, or redistributed. Conversely, the term "open source" is sometime (ab) used to mean software whose source code is visible, but for which there are limitations on use, modification, or redistribution. This book uses the term ``open source" for its usual meaning, that is, software which has its source code freely available for use, viewing, modification, and redistribution; a more detailed definition is contained in the Open Source Definition. In some cases, a difference in motive is suggested; those preferring the term "free software" wish to strongly emphasize the need for freedom, while those using the term may have other motives (e.g., higher reliability) or simply wish to appear less strident.

CHARACTERISTICS OF LINUX OPERATING SYSTEM:

- **Multiuser:** allows number of users to work with the system at the same time.

- **Multitasking:** supports true preemptive multitasking. All processes independently of each other.
- **Multiprocessing:** from kernel Version2.0 onwards, linux supports multiprocessor architectures. Applications are distributed across several processors.
- **Architecture Independent:** runs almost on all platform that are able to process bits and bytes. examples like IBM s390, Sparc, ARM, etc .
- **Demand Load Executables:** only those parts of a program actually required for execution are loaded into memory. Support POSIX1003.1 standard - Linux since version. onwards supports POSIX1003.1,which defines a minimum interface to a Unix like operating system.
- **Memory Protected Mode:** uses the processor's memory protection mechanisms to prevent the process from accessing memory allocated to the system kernel or other processes. This is for the security of the system.
- **Shared Libraries:** it is a collection of routines needed by a program to work. There are number of standard libraries used by more than one process at the same time. so these libraries are made to load into memory for once and all the programs can make use of it.
- **Support to various file systems:** supports various file systems like Proc, Ext2, Ext3 and Ext4. The most commonly used file system is Ext3 and Ext4 also developed, both are journaling file systems.

COMPONENTS OF LINUX OPERATING SYSTEM

Linux is designed to be compliant with the relevant POSIX documents; at least two Linux distributions have achieved official POSIX certification.

The Linux programming interface adheres to the SVR4 UNIX semantics, rather than to BSD behavior.

Like most UNIX implementations, Linux is composed of three main bodies of code; the most important distinction between the kernel and all other components.

The kernel is responsible for maintaining the important abstractions of the operating system.

1. Kernel code executes in kernel mode with full access to all the physical resources of the computer.
2. All kernel code and data structures are kept in the same single address space.

The system libraries define a standard set of functions through which applications interact with the kernel, and which implement much of the operating-system functionality that does not need the full privileges of kernel code as shown in figure 16.1 The system utilities perform individual specialized management tasks.

Components of a Linux System

System management programs	User processes	User utility programs	compilers
System shared libraries			
Linux kernal			
Loadable kernel modules			

Figure 16.1: *Components of Linux System*

ARCHITECTURE OF LINUX KERNEL

The Linux or the unix kernel is just developed under the microkernel architecture. The Microkernel provides only the necessary minimum of functionality (inter process communication and the memory management) and can be accordingly be implemented in a small and compact form.

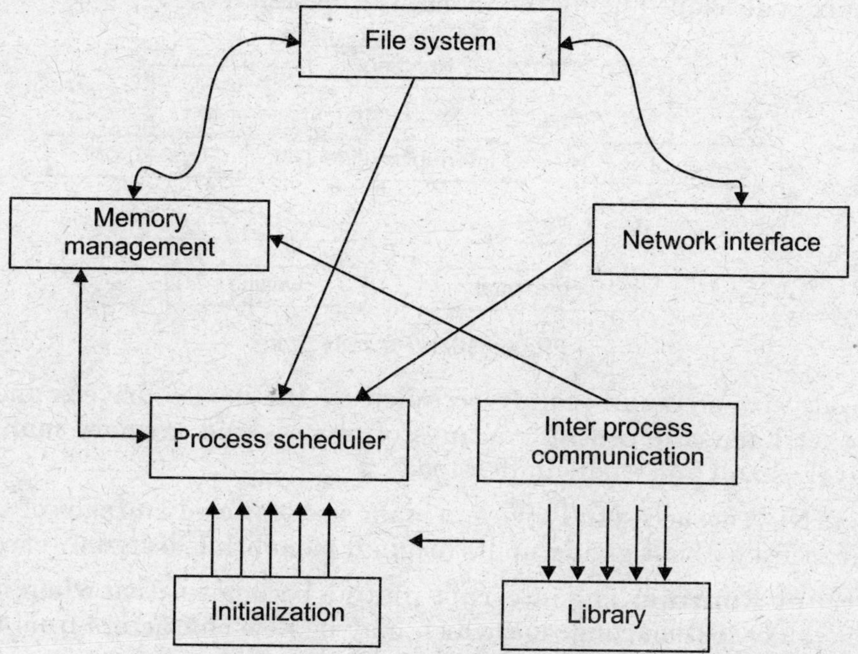

Figure 16.2: *Conceptual Architecture of Linux Kernal*

Building on this microkernel, the remaining functions of the operating system are relocated to the autonomous processes communicating with the microkernel via a well defied interface. Generally, microkernel systems have been created whose performance can be improved by the monolithic systems. Since Linux provides slow i386 architecture, so Linux is developed using the monolithic design. The code size of linux mainly occupied by the device drivers and similar. On the other hand, the central routines of process and memory management are relatively small and easily understood, with 13000 lines of C code in each. Thus LINUX is successfully tries to make use of the advantages of a microkernel architecture without giving up its original monolithic design. In Figure 16.2, process scheduler initialize the process with the help of memory management, file system and network interface and execute the process with inter process communication and library of functions.

The Linux or the Unix kernel is just developed under the microkernel architecture.

- The Microkernel provides only the necessary minimum of functionality (inter process communication and the memory management) and can be accordingly be implemented in a small and compact form. Building on this microkernel, the remaining functions of the operating system are relocated to the autonomous processes communicating with the microkernel via a well defied interface.
- Generally, microkernel systems have been created whose performance can be improved by the monolithic systems. Since linux provides slow i386 architecture, so Linux is developed using the monolithic design.

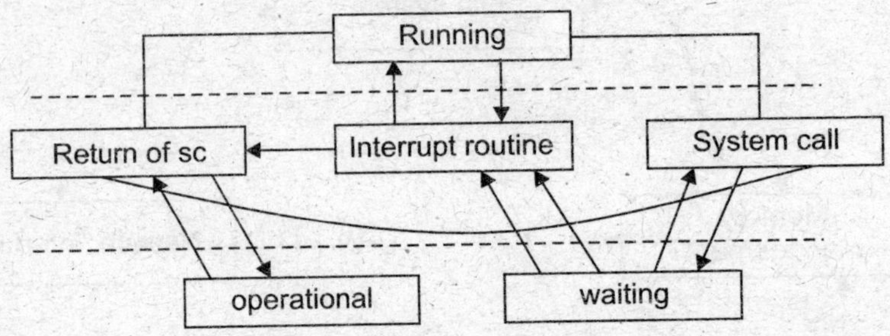

Figure 16.3: *Process State*

- The code size of Linux mainly occupied by the device drivers and similar. on the other hand, the central routines of process and memory management are relatively small and easily understood.
- Thus LINUX is successfully tries to make use of the advantages of a microkernel architecture without giving up its original monolithic design.interrupt
- **Interrupt Routine:** The interrupt routine becomes active when the hardware signals an exception condition which may be new characters from the keyboard or any other hardware interrupt.
- **System calls:** System calls are initiated by software interrupts

- **Waiting:** The process is waiting for an external event. E.g. waiting for a button press.
- **Ready:** The process is ready to run under the CPU, but some other process is currently running under the CPU.
- **Return from System Call:** This state is adopted after the end of the system call or end of the interrupts.

Kernel Directory Structure in Linux

In Linux the Kernel source is available under /usr/src/linux.

- Architecture dependent code is available in the following directory structure
  - arch/alpha – for the DEC Alpha Architecture
  - arch/x86 – for the Intel 32 bit Architecture
  - arch/arm – for the ARM Architecture
  - arch/ia64 – for the intel 64 bit architecture
  - arch/m68k – for the 68000 architecture and compatible processors.
- init/ directory contains all the functions needed to start the kernel.
- kernel/ – central sections of the kernel. Most important system calls are implemented here.
- arch/x86/mm or mm/ – takes care of memory management by requesting and releasing kernel memories.
- fs/ is the virtual file system interface. Some important file systems are proc, ext2,ext3,. The proc file systems is used for system management.
- drivers/ – every operating system requires drivers for its hardware component.

These are held in this directory and classified into group according to their subdirectories like the following:

- drivers/char – character oriented devices
- drivers/block – block oriented devices
- drivers/i2c – a generic i2c driver
- drivers/scsi – the SCSI interface
- drivers/usb – drivers for the USB subsystem
- ipc/ – indicates the Inter process communication
- lib/ – indicates the standard C library functions scheduler

All the components of linux directory are explained below as in figure 16.4.

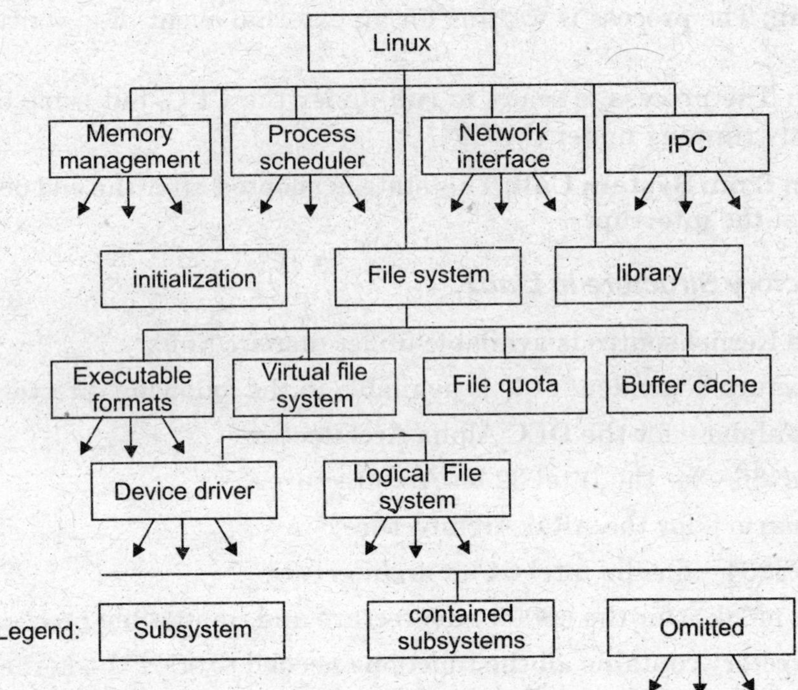

Figure 16.4: *Partial Subsystem Hierracrchy*

Kernel Data Structures

Task Structure

The fundamental entity of any operating system is the task or a process. The task structure is defined in the linux / sched.h and it is the important data structure and following are some of its parameters.

struct task_struct {

volatile long state; //determines the current state of the process like unrunnable, runnable and stopped.

unsigned long flags; // various flags for accounting purpose like PF_STARTIN, PF_MEMALLOC

unsigned long ptrace; // process is being monitored by other process.

int sigpending; //define when the signals must be handed over to this process mm_segment_t addr_limit;

struct exec_domain *exec_domain; //domain other than x86

long need_resched; //flag in4dicates that scheduling must be executed

int lock_depth; //structure is protected before simulataneous access can take place long counter; //dynamic priority of a process

long nice; //static priority of a process
unsigned long policy; //scheduling policy like SCHED_RR, SCHED_FIFO, SCHED_OTHER
unsigned long rt_priority;
};

Scheduling

Schedulers control the access to CPU by implementing some policy such that the CPU is shared in a way that is fair and also the system stability is maintained. In Linux scheduling is required for the user processes and the kernel tasks. Kernel tasks may be internal tasks on behalf of the drivers or initiated by user processes requiring specific OS services as shown in figure 16.5. Examples are: a page fault (induced by a user process) or because some device driver raises an interrupt. In Linux, normally, the kernel mode of operation can not be pre-empted. Kernel code runs to completion - unless it results in a page fault, or an interrupt of some kind or kernel code it self calls the scheduler. Linux is a time sharing system. So a timer interrupt happens and rescheduling may be initiated at that time. Linux uses a credit based scheduling algorithm. The process with the highest credits gets scheduled. The credits are revised after every run. If all run-able processes exhaust all the credits a priority based fresh credit allocation takes place. The crediting system usually gives higher credits to interactive or IO bound processes – as these require immediate responses from a user. Linux also implements Unix like nice process characterization.

MEMORY MANAGEMENT (LINUX KERNEL)

The data related to the processes are to be stored in the memory somehow by the operating system. In the olden days, primary memory is a scarce resource and the application demands increases, so store the data of a process, it is necessary to use other forms of memory, either we can use

- Physical address space or
- virtual address space

Mapping the virtual addresses onto the physical addresses is the responsibility of the operating system's memory management system. Memory protection prevents two processes exchanging data by changing the areas of memory used by both. The program code of a process can be executed in different threads at the same time. In principle, these threads share a common virtual address space.

FILE SYSTEM IN LINUX

Over the years conventions have been built on ``what files to place where". Where possible, please follow conventional use when placing information in the hierarchy. For example, place global configuration information in /etc. The File system Hierarchy Standard (FHS) tries to define these conventions in a logical manner, and is widely used by Linux systems. The FHS is an update to the previous Linux File system Structure standard (FSSTND), incorporating lessons learned and approaches from Linux, BSD, and System V systems. See http://www.pathname.com/fhs for more information about the FHS. A summary of these conventions is in hier(5) for Linux and hier(7) for Solaris. Sometimes different conventions disagree; where possible, make these situations configurable at compile or installation time.

INTERPROCESS COMMUNICATION (IPC)

When two processes trying to access a resource is called race condition. Main challenge is to avoid the race condition, the following method is usually adopted to avoid the race condition.

1. Use of shared memory can prevent race condition
2. Use of threads: Threads use the same address space when switching it to other threads (so same page directories and tables), whereas processes uses different address which leads to exchange of page directories and page tables. This is made with the help of POSIX Threads.

There are four forms of IPC. Linux implements all forms of IPC.

1. Resource Sharing (system V Shared memory)
2. Synchronization (Mutex, Semaphores)
3. Connection oriented data exchange (Virtual Sockets, Pipes, named Pipes(FIFO))
4. Connectionless data exchange (Signals)

Synchronization in the Kernel

When multiple processors are used, how each processor is synchronized in the kernel is what described in this section. Processor can acquire a spinlock whenever it wanted to access a resource.

```
typedef struct
{
volatile unsigned int lock; //default value is 1
}
spinlock_t;
```

Whenever a lock is wanted, it is set to 0 and during unlock it is set to 1.

The bus access to the other processors is blocked during the processing of this command (spinlock).

If spinlock cannot be set, the processor waits in a loop until a lock variable is released again.

Single processor does not need spinlock.

Multiple Choice Questions

Set

I

1. Which of the following is the function of an operating system?
   A. To provide an interface between the user and machine.
   B. To make the computer system convenient to use by providing a user friendly interface.
   C. To hide the hardware level details from the user.
   D. To manage the resources (i.e Allocation and Assignment) of computer resources efficiently.
   E. All of the above.
2. What is the main objective of a multi-programming operating system?
   A. Resource Sharing.
   B. Resource Utilization.
   C. Meeting the Time constraints.
   D. None of these.
3. Which of the following is the main objective of Time Sharing Systems?
   A. Resource Sharing.
   B. Resource Utilization.
   C. Better Response Time.
   D. None of these.
4. Which of the following is not an operating system?
   A. DOS
   B. Windows
   C. Unix
   D. Java.
5. Operating System is a/an:
   A. Application Software.
   B. System software.
   C. Depend upon the hardware used.
   D. None of These.
6. The jobs which use CPU most of the time, and amount of input output operations is quiet less are termed as:
   A. CPU bound Jobs
   B. I/O bound Jobs.
   C. No Specific Categorization is possible.
   D. Depends on operating system used.
7. Which of the following is an example of parallel systems?
   A. Increased Throughput
   B. Reduced Cost
   C. Increased Reliability
   D. All of the Above.
8. A program is a passive entity, whereas, a process is an active entity.
   A. True.
   B. False.

9. The running process is preempted and processor is taken from the running process, as processor decides to execute some other process. Which of the following process transition has occurred:
   A. Ready -> Running.
   B. Waiting -> Ready.
   C. Running -> Ready.
   D. Running -> Waiting.

10. Which of the following is stored in a Process Control Block?
   A. Process ID.
   B. PSW.
   C. Process Priority.
   D. Process State.
   E. All of the above.

11. Which of the following scheduler selects the processes from the secondary storage device and loads them into the memory for the execution?
   A. Short term Scheduler.
   B. Medium Term Scheduler.
   C. Long Term Scheduler.
   D. None of these.

12. Which of the following is the technique to allow the processes to communicate with each other and to synchronize their actions?
   A. Process Scheduling.
   B. Inter Process Communication.
   C. Process Counting.
   D. None of these.

13. In which of the following addressing scheme, only the sender names the receiver but the receiver need not to know the sender.
   A. Symmetric Addressing.
   B. Asymmetric Addressing.
   C. Bi-directional Addressing.
   D. Virtual Addressing.

14. A thread consists of:
   A. A program counter.
   B. A register set and
   C. A stack space.
   D. All of Above.

15. Threads of a task share the same address space.
   A. True.
   B. False.

16. The threads of a program are created to assist each other, but they require mutual protection.
   A. True.
   B. False.

17. In which of the following scheduling, CPU can be taken away forcibly from the process to which it has been allocated and can be allocated to some other process.
   A. Preemptive Scheduling.
   B. Non-Preemptive Scheduling.
   C. User defined Scheduling.
   D. None of the Above.

18. The objective of CPU Scheduling is to ________ the CPU utilization and through put and to ________ the turnaround time, waiting time and response time.
   A. Minimize, Maximize.
   B. Maximize, Minimize.

C. Minimize, Minimize.

D. Maximize, Maximize.

19. The turn around time can be caluculated as:

A. Time of Submission of Job – Time of Completion of Job.

B. Time of submission of Job.

C. Time of Completion of Job – Time of Submission of Job.

D. None of these.

20. Priorities assigned depending on memory requirements, burst time are termed as:

A. Internally Defined Priorities.

B. Externally Defined Priorities

C. No Specific difference is terms.

D. None of these.

21. A small time span allocated to each process in a round robin scheduling is termed as:

A. Time Slot.

B. Time Slice.

C. Time Quantum.

D. All of the above.

22. The resources which can be safely used by one process at a time and is not consumed by that use.

A. Reusable.

B. Consumable.

C. Preemptive.

D. None of these.

23. The resources which cannot be taken away from its current owner without causing the computation to fail.

A. Resusable.

B. Preemptable.

C. Non-Preemptble.

D. None of These.

24. Round Robin scheduling is essentially the preemptive version of ________.

A. FIFO

B. Shortest job first

C. Shortest remaining time first

D. Longest time first

25. Which of the following is the main objective of Real time Systems?

A. Resource Sharing.

B. Resource Utilization.

C. Meeting the time constraints.

D. None of these.

26. Which of the following criteria is most important for the selection of systems software?

A. Is the applications software you want to use compatible with it?

B. Is it expensive?

C. Is it compatible with your hardware?

D. Both A and C

27. In the blocked state

A. The processes waiting for I/O are found.

B. The process which is running is found.

C. The processes waiting for the processor are found.

D. None of the above.

28. Which of the following is the main objective of Distributed Systems?

A. Resource Sharing.

B. Resource Utilization.

C. Better Response Time.
D. None of these.

29. Which of the following is a necessary condition for occurance of deadlock.
A. Mutual Exclusion.
B. No-preemption.
C. Circular Wait.
D. Hold and Wait.
E. All of the above.

30. An edge from a process to resource, in a resource allocation graph is called,
A. Assignment edge.
B. Request edge.
C. Commitment edge.
D. Priority edge.

31. In a resource allocation graph, the process is shown by:
A. Square.
B. Rectangle.
C. Circle.
D. Straight Line.

32. Banker's algorithm can be used for:
A. Deadlock Prevention.
B. Deadlock Avoidance.
C. Deadlock Detection.
D. Deadlock Recovery.

33. Multiprogramming systems ______.
A. Are easier to develop than single programming systems
B. Execute each job faster
C. Execute more jobs in the same time
D. Are used only on large main frame computers

34. Which is not the state of the process?
A. Blocked
B. Running
C. Ready
D. Privileged

35. The solution to Critical Section Problem is: Mutual Exclusion, Progress and Bounded Waiting.
A. The statement is false
B. The statement is true.
C. The statement is contradictory.
D. None of the above

36. The state of a process after it encounters an I/O instruction is ________.
A. Ready
B. Blocked/Waiting
C. Idle
D. Running

37. The number of processes completed per unit of time is known as ________.
A. Output
B. Throughput
C. Efficiency
D. Capacity

38. ________ is the situation in which a process is waiting for another process,which is also waiting for another process . which is waiting on the first process. None of the processes involved in this circular wait are making progress.
A. Deadlock
B. Starvation
C. Dormant
D. None of the above

39. Which technique was introduced because a single job could not keep both the CPU and the I/O devices busy?

A. Time-sharing

B. SPOOLing

C. Preemptive scheduling

D. Multiprogramming

40. If the wait-for-graph for a system has a cycle, that means the system is deadlocked.

A. True.

B. False.

41. Let S and Q be two semaphores initialized to 1, where P0 and P1 processes the following statements wait(S); wait(Q); ---; signal(S); signal(Q) and wait(Q); wait(S); ---; signal(Q); signal(S); respectively. The above situation depicts a ________ .

A. Semaphore

B. Deadlock

C. Signal

D. Interrupt

42. A critical region

A. Is a piece of code which only one process executes at a time

B. Is a region prone to deadlock

C. Is a piece of code which only a finite number of processes execute

D. Is found only in Windows NT operation system

43. PCB is

A. Program Control Block

B. Process Control Block

C. Process Communication Block

D. None of the above

44. FIFO scheduling is ________.

A. Preemptive Scheduling

B. Non Preemptive Scheduling

C. Deadline Scheduling

D. Fair share scheduling

45. Switching the CPU to another Process requires to save state of the old process and loading new process state is called as ________.

A. Process Blocking

B. Context Switch

C. Time Sharing

D. None of the above

46. Which directory implementation is used in most Operating System?

A. Single level directory structure

B. Two level directory structure

C. Tree directory structure

D. Acyclic directory structure

47. A thread

A. Is a lightweight process where the context switching is low

B. Is a lightweight process where the context swithching is high

C. Is used to speed up paging

D. None of the above

48. A tree structured file directory system

A. Allows easy storage and retrieval of file names

B. Is a much debated unnecessary feature

C. Is not essential when we have millions of files

D. None of the above

49. The high paging activity is termed as:

A. Multiprogramming.

B. Scheduling.

C. Thrashing.

D. None of these.

50. The problem of thrashing is affected scientifically by ________.

A. Program structure

B. Program size

C. Primary storage size

D. None of the above

51. Virtual memory is __________.

A. An extremely large main memory

B. An extremely large secondary memory

C. An illusion of extremely large main memory

D. A type of memory used in super computers.

52. The mechanism that bring a page into memory only when it is needed is called ___________.

A. Segmentation

B. Fragmentation

C. Demand Paging

D. Page Replacement

53. Which of the following memory allocation scheme suffers from External fragmentation?

A. Segmentation

B. Pure demand paging

C. Swapping

D. Paging

54. Information about a process is maintained in a _________.

A. Stack

B. Translation Lookaside Buffer

C. Process Control Block

D. Program Control Block

55. A page fault occurs

A. When the page is not in the memory

B. When the page is in the memory

C. When the process enters the blocked state

D. When the process is in the ready state

56. Which of the following is not advantage of multiprogramming?

A. Increased throughput

B. Shorter response time

C. Decreased operating system overhead

D. Ability to assign priorities to jobs

57. In which of the following operating systems, the response time is very critical.

A. Multitasking

B. Batch

C. Online

D. Real-time

58. An optimal scheduling algorithm in terms of minimizing the average waiting time of a given set of processes is ________.

A. FCFS scheduling algorithm

B. Round robin scheduling algorithm
C. Shortest job - first scheduling algorithm
D. None of the above

59. Real time systems are ________.
A. Primarily used on mainframe computers
B. Used for monitoring events as they occur
C. Used for program development
D. Used for real time interactive users

60. Which of the following techniques can be used to over come the problem of starvation?
A. Terminating the process.
B. Aging
C. Mutual Exclusion
D. Semaphore .

61. CPU performance is measured through ________.
A. Throughput
B. MHz
C. Flaps
D. None of the above .

62. The belady's anomaly is present if,
A. The page faults increases with the increase in number of frames.
B. The page faults decreases with the increase in number of frames.
C. The page faults increases with the decreases in number of frames.
D. None of these.

63. Which of the following is a valid file operation?
A. Read.
B. Append.
C. Getattributes
D. All of the above.

64. Which of the following file name extension suggests that the file is Backup copy of another file?
A. TXT
B. COM
C. BAS
D. BAK .

65. Which of the following file name extension suggests the file contains the text for help command?
A. TXT.
B. BIN.
C. HLP
D. EXE.

66. The situation in which two or more keys to the same hash functions point to the same location is termed as:
A. Thrashing.
B. Deadlock.
C. Collision.
D. Starvation.

67. Identify the odd thing in the services of operating system.
A. Accounting
B. Protection
C. Error detection and correction
D. Dead lock handling

68. Cryptography technique is used in ________.

A. Polling
B. Job Scheduling
C. Protection
D. File Management

69. A ________ is a software that manages the time of a microprocessor to ensure that all time critical events are processed as efficiently as possible. This software allows the system activities to be divided into multiple independent elements called tasks.

A. Kernel
B. Shell
C. Processor
D. Device Driver

70. The primary job of the operating system of a computer is to ________.

A. Command Resources
B. Manage Resources
C. Provide Utilities
D. Be user friendly

71. With the round robin CPU scheduling in a time-shared system ________.

A. Using very large time slice degenerates in to first come first served algorithm
B. Using extremely small time slices improve performance
C. Using extremely small time slices degenerate in to last in first out algorithm
D. Using medium sized time slices leads to shortest request time first algorithm

72. Which of the following is a criterion to evaluate a scheduling algorithm?

A. CPU Utilization: Keep CPU utilization as high as possible.
B. Throughput: number of processes completed per unit time.
C. Waiting Time: Amount of time spent ready to run but not running.
D. All of the above

73. Which of the following is contained in Process Control Block (PCB)?

A. Process Number
B. List of Open files
C. Memory Limits
D. All of the Above

74. Super computers typically employ ________.

A. Real time Operating system
B. Multiprocessors OS
C. Desktop OS
D. None of the above

75. Which of the following is crucial time while accessing data on the disk?

A. Seek time
B. Rotational time
C. Transmission time
D. Waiting time

ANSWERS

1. E	2. B	3. C	4. D	5. B	6. A	7. D	8. A	9. C	10. E
11. C	12. B	13. B	14. D	15. A	16. B	17. A	18. B	19. C	20. A
21. D	22. A	23. C	24. A	25. C	26. D	27. A	28. A	29. E	30. B
31. C	32. B	33. C	34. D	35. B	36. B	37. B	38. A	39. D	40. A
41. B	42. A	43. B	44. B	45. B	46. C	47. A	48. A	49. C	50. A
51. C	52. C	53. A	54. C	55. A	56. C	57. D	58. C	59. B	60. B
61. A	62. B	63. D	64. D	65. C	66. C	67. C	68. C	69. A	70. B
71. A	72. D	73. D	74. B	75. A					

Multiple Choice Questions

1. Initially __________ was separated into two products: one designated for user computers the other a network server.
   A. Linux
   B. Windows XP
   C. Windows NT
   D. Novell

2. If you need an operating system that provides data redundancy, you should select a __________ operating system.
   A. Network
   B. Embedded
   C. Linux
   D. Windows

3. A database that contains the users, shares and features of a network.
   A. shell
   B. enterprise directory
   C. distributed application
   D. operating environment

4. A program that runs in parts on several computers is said to be __________.
   A. delegated
   B. spread
   C. distributed
   D. recursive

5. When a computer is first turned on or restarted, a special type of absolute loader called ____ is executed
   A. Compile and Go loader
   B. Boot loader
   C. Bootstrap loader
   D. Relating loader

6. Which of the following Operating systems is better for implementing a Client-Server network
   A. MS DOS
   B. Windows 95
   C. Windows 98
   D. Windows 2000

7. The operating system manages
   A. Memory
   B. Processes
   C. Disks and I/O devices
   D. All of the above

8. Usually, in MSDOS, the primary hard disk drives has the drive letter ____
   A. A
   B. B

C. C

D. D

9. What is the function of an operating system?

A. Manages computer's resources very efficiently

B. Takes care of scheduling jobs for execution

C. Manages the flow of data and instructions

D. All of the above

10. Which is not the function of the Operating System?

A. Memory management

B. Disk management

C. Application management

D. Virus Protection

11. Which file keeps commands to execute automatically when OS is started?

A. command.com

B. any batch file

C. autoexec.bat

D. config.sys

12. What should be the extension to execute files?

A. EXE

B. BAT

C. COM

D. All of the above

13. Which one of the following is not the function of Operating System?

A. Resource Management

B. File Management

C. Networking

D. Processor Management

14. The Banker's algorithm is used

A. to rectify deadlock

B. to detect deadlock

C. to prevent deadlock

D. to slove deadlock

15. Which of the following concept is best for preventing page faults?

A. Paging

B. The working set

C. Hit ratios

D. Address location resolution

16. Which of the following memory unit that processor can access more rapidly

A. Main Memory

B. Virtual Memory

C. Cache memory

D. Read Only Memory

17. A page fault occurs when

A. the Deadlock happens

B. the Segmentation starts

C. the page is found in the memory

D. the page is not found in the memory

18. Bringing a page into memory only when it is needed, this mechanism is called

A. Deadlock

B. Page Fault

C. Dormant Paging

D. Demand Paging

19. First-in-First-Out (FIFO) scheduling is

A. Non Preemptive Scheduling

B. Preemptive Scheduling

C. Fair Share Scheduling

D. Deadline Scheduling

20. Copying a process from memory to disk to allow space for other processes is Called

A. Swapping

B. Deadlock

C. Demand Paging

D. Page Fault

21. The necessary conditions needed before deadlock can occur?

A. No Mutual Exclusion, Hold and wait, Preemption, Circular Wait

B. Mutual Exclusion, No Hold and wait, Preemption, Circular Wait

C. Mutual Exclusion, Hold and wait, No Preemption, Circular Wait

D. Mutual Exclusion, Hold and wait, Preemption, No Circular Wait

22. A program in execution is called

A. A Paging

B. A Process

C. A virtual memory

D. A Demand Page

23. An operating system is a program or a group of programs that

A. Helps in checking the spelling of Word

B. Maintain the relationship in Database

C. Manages the resources of the Computer

D. Performs the calculations of cells in Excel

24. What is contained in the page table?

A. Base address of each frame and corresponding page number

B. Memory address and corresponding page number

C. File name and corresponding page number

D. None of Above

25. The chunks of a memory are known as

A. Sector

B. Offset

C. Page

D. Frame

26. Which of the following is an essential file of a MS-DOS boot disk?

A. COMMAND.COM

B. START.COM

C. TREE.COM

D. VER.COM

27. Which of the following operating system reads and reacts in actual time?

A. Quick Response System

B. Real Time System

C. Time Sharing System

D. Batch Processing System

28. Which of the following resources must be protected by the operating system?

A. I/O

B. Memory

C. CPU

D. All of the above

29. Command Interpreter is also known as

A. Prompt

B. Shell

C. Command

D. DOS Prompt

30. Which of the following is major activities of an operating system in regard to secondary-storage management?

A. Free-space management

B. Storage allocation

C. Disk scheduling

D. All of the above

31. Which of the following is System Programming Language?

A. C

B. PL/C60

C. Pascal

D. All of the above

32. The operating system keeps the information of files in a table called

A. File Folder Table (FFT)

B. File Index Table (FIT)

C. File Allocation Table (FAT)

D. Directory Index Table (DIT)

33. Round robin scheduling is essentially the preemptive version of ________.

A. FIFO

B. Shortest job first

C. Shortest remaining

D. Longest time first

34. A page fault occurs

A. when the page is not in the memory

B. when the page is in the memory

C. when the process enters the blocked state

D. when the process is in the ready state

35. Which of the following will determine your choice of systems software for your computer ?

A. Is the applications software you want to use compatible with it ?

B. Is it expensive ?

C. Is it compatible with your hardware?

D. Both A and C

36. Let S and Q be two semaphores initialized to A, where P0 and PA processes the following statements wait(S); wait(Q); ---; signal(S); signal(Q) and wait(Q); wait(S); ---; signal(Q); signal(S); respectively. The above situation depicts a ________.

A. Semaphore

B. Deadlock

C. Signal

D. Interrupt

37. What is a shell?

A. It is a hardware component

B. It is a command interpreter

C. It is a part in compiler

D. It is a tool in CPU scheduling

38. Routine is not loaded until it is called. All routines are kept on disk in a relocatable load format. The main program is loaded into memory & is executed. This type of loading is called ________

A. Static loading
B. Dynamic loading
C. Dynamic linking
D. Overlays

39. In the blocked state

A. the processes waiting for I/O are found
B. the process which is running is found
C. the processes waiting for the processor are found
D. none of the above

40. What is the memory from AK - 6D0K called ?

A. Extended Memory
B. Normal Memory
C. Low Memory
D. Conventional Memory

41. Virtual memory is __________.

A. An extremely large main memory
B. An extremely large secondary memory
C. An illusion of extremely large main memory
D. A type of memory used in super computers.

42. The process related to process control, file management, device management, information about system and communication that is requested by any higher level language can be performed by __________.

A. Editors
B. Compilers
C. System Call
D. Caching

43. If the Disk head is located initially at CB, find the number of disk moves required with FCFS if the disk queue of I/O blocks requests are 98,C7,AD,ABD,65,67.

A. CA0
B. CBD
C. CA5
D. CBA

44. Multiprogramming systems ______.

A. Are easier to develop than single programming systems
B. Execute each job faster
C. Execute more jobs in the same time
D. Are used only on large main frame computers

45. Which is not the state of the process?

A. Blocked
B. Running
C. Ready
D. Privileged

46. The solution to Critical Section Problem is: Mutual Exclusion, Progress and Bounded Waiting.

A. The statement is false
B. The statement is true.
C. The statement is contradictory.
D. None of the above

47. The problem of thrashing is effected scientifically by ________.
    A. Program structure
    B. Program size
    C. Primary storage size
    D. None of the above

48. The state of a process after it encounters an I/O instruction is ________.
    A. Ready
    B. Blocked/Waiting
    C. Idle
    D. Running

49. The number of processes completed per unit time is known as ________.
    A. Output
    B. Throughput
    C. Efficiency
    D. Capacity

50. ________ is the situation in which a process is waiting on another process, which is also waiting on another process which is waiting on the first process. None of the processes involved in this circular wait are making progress.
    A. Deadlock
    B. Starvation
    C. Dormant
    D. None of the above

51. Which of the following file name extension suggests that the file is Backup copy of another file ?
    A. TXT
    B. COM
    C. BAS
    D. BAK

52. Which technique was introduced because a single job could not keep both the CPU and the I/O devices busy?
    A. Time-sharing
    B. SPOOLing
    C. Preemptive scheduling
    D. Multiprogramming

53. A critical region
    A. is a piece of code which only one process executes at a time
    B. is a region prone to deadlock
    C. is a piece of code which only a finite number of processes execute
    D. is found only in Windows NT operation system

54. The mechanism that bring a page into memory only when it is needed is called ________
    A. Segmentation
    B. Fragmentation
    C. Demand Paging
    D. Page Replacement

55. PCB =
    A. Program Control Block
    B. Process Control Block
    C. Process Communication Block
    D. None of the above

56. FIFO scheduling is ________.
    A. Preemptive Scheduling
    B. Non Preemptive Scheduling
    C. Deadline Scheduling
    D. Fair share scheduling

57. Switching the CPU to another Process requires to save state of the old process and loading new process state is called as ________.

A. Process Blocking

B. Context Switch

C. Time Sharing

D. None of the above

58. Which directory implementation is used in most Operating System?

A. Single level directory structure

B. Two level directory structure

C. Tree directory structure

D. Acyclic directory structure

59. The Banker's algorithm is used

A. to prevent deadlock in operating systems

B. to detect deadlock in operating systems

C. to rectify a deadlocked state

D. none of the above

60. A thread

A. is a lightweight process where the context switching is low

B. is a lightweight process where the context swithching is high

C. is used to speed up paging

D. none of the above

61. ______ is a high level abstraction over Semaphore.

A. Shared memory

B. Message passing

C. Monitor

D. Mutual exclusion

62. A tree sturctured file directory system

A. allows easy storage and retrieval of file names

B. is a much debated unecessary feature

C. is not essential when we have millions of files

D. none of the above

63. The part of machine level instruction, which tells the central processor what has to be done, is

A. Operation code

B. Address

C. Locator

D. Flip-Flop

E. None of the above

64. To avoid the race condition, the number of processes that may be simultaneously inside their critical section is

A. 8

B. 1

C. 16

D. 0

E. None of the above

65. Process is

A. program in High level language kept on disk

B. contents of main memory

C. a program in execution

D. a job in secondary memory

E. None of the above

66. The Memory Buffer Register (MBR)

A. Is a hardware memory device which denotes the location of the current instruction being executed.

B. Is a group of electrical circuits (hardware), that performs the intent of instructions fetched from memory.

C. Contains the address of the memory location that is to be read from or stored into.

D. Contains a copy of the designated memory location specified by the MAR after a "read" or the new contents of the memory prior to a "write".

E. None of the above

67. The LRU algorithm

A. pages out pages that have been used recently

B. pages out pages that have not been used recently

C. pages out pages that have been least used recently

D. pages out the first page in a given area

E. None of the above

68. Which of the following systems software does the job of merging the records from two files into one?

A. Security software

B. Utility program

C. Networking software

D. Documentation system

E. None of the above

69. Fork is

A. the dispatching of a task

B. the creation of a new job

C. the creation of a new process

D. increasing the priority of a task

E. None of the above

70. Thrashing

A. is a natural consequence of virtual memory systems

B. can always be avoided by swapping

C. always occurs on large computers

D. can be caused by poor paging algorithms

E. None of the above

71. Supervisor state is

A. never used

B. entered by programs when they enter the processor

C. required to perform any I/O

D. only allowed to the operating system

E. None of the above

72. Interprocess communication

A. is required for all processes

B. is usually done via disk drives

C. is never necessary

D. allows processes to synchronize activity

73. Memory

A. is a device that performs a sequence of operations specified by instructions in memory.

B. is the device where information is stored

C. is a sequence of instructions

D. is typically characterized by interactive processing and time-slicing of the CPU's time to allow quick response to each user.

E. None of the above

74. Which of the following are loaded into main memory when the computer is booted?

A. internal command instructions

B. external command instructions

C. utility programs

D. word processing instructions

E. None of the above

75. The FIFO algorithm

A. executes first the job that last entered the queue

B. executes first the job that first entered the queue

C. execute first the job that has been in the queue the longest

D. executes first the job with the least processor needs

E. None of the above

ANSWERS

1. C	**2.** A	**3.** B	**4.** C	**5.** C	**6.** D	**7.** D	**8.** C	**9,** D	**10.** D
11. C	**12.** D	**13.** C	**14.** C	**15.** B	**16.** C	**17.** D	**18.** C	**19.** A	**20.** A
21. C	**22.** B	**23.** C	**24.** A	**25.** D	**26.** A	**27.** B	**28.** D	**29.** B	**30.** D
31. D	**32.** C	**33.** A	**34.** A	**35.** D	**36.** B	**37.** B	**38.** C	**39.** A	**40.** D
41. C	**42.** C	**43.** D	**44.** C	**45.** D	**46.** B	**47.** A	**48.** B	**49.** B	**50.** A
51. D	**52.** D	**53.** A	**54.** C	**55.** B	**56.** B	**57.** B	**58.** C	**59.** A	**60.** A
61. C	**62.** A	**63.** A	**64.** B	**65.** C	**66.** D	**67.** C	**68.** B	**69.** C	**70.** D
71. D	**72.** D	**73.** B	**74.** A	**75.** B					

Model Question Paper I

Note: *The candidates are required to attempt ONE question each from Sections A,B,C and D carrying 10 marks each and the entire Section E consisting of 5 short answer type questions carrying 2 marks each.*

SECTION A

1. (a) In brief, discuss the layered structure of an OS.

   (b) How does an IPC takes place? What are the various parameters involved in it?

2. (a) Discuss the different process states during CPU scheduling.

   (b) What are the various access methods to access a file ? Discuss by giving suitable examples.

SECTION B

3. (a) What are the goals of a good scheduling algorithm? Discuss Preemptive Scheduling and Non-preemptive Scheduling.

   (b) Differentiate between Disk Scheduling and CPU Scheduling.

4. (a) Provide the solution to the following synchronization problem, known as "cigarette smoker's problem:

There are four processes, namely, three smoker processes and an agent process. Each of the smoker processes will make a cigarette and smoke it. To make a cigarette tobacco, paper and matchbox are required. Each smoker process has one of the three items, i.e one process has tobacco, another has paper and the third one has matchbox. The agent has sufficient supply of all three. The agent places two of the three items on the table and the smoker has third item required to make a cigarette.

   (b) What are the various access methods to access a file ? Discuss by giving suitable examples.

SECTION C

5. Differentiate between:
   (a) Contiguous and Non-Contiguous Memory.
   (b) Physical Address and Logical Address.

6. Discuss segmentation with paging. How can we secure an OS memory implementing in such a way?

SECTION D

7. What is the importance of Remote File Access? How an OS does provide it?
8. How is concurrency control handled in a distributed OS? Also, discuss the deadlock handling issue.

SECTION E

9. Write short notes on:
   (a) Differentiate between Buffering and Spooling.
   (b) What is a Resource Allocation Graph? Depict two different scenarios of research graph in which five different process are i) deadlocked and ii) not deadlocked.
   (c) Assuming a cluster size of 512 bytes calculate the percentage wastage in file space due to incomplete filling of last cluster for a file of size 10000 bytes.
   (d) What is meant by an 'alias filename' and explain its Linux/Unix implementation?
   (e) (i) Name any one OS used in modern day mobiles.
       (ii) Differentiate between FAT 16 and FAT 32.

Model Question Paper

Note: *The candidates are required to attempt ONE question each from Sections A, B, C and D carrying 10 marks each and the entire Section E consisting of 5 short answer type questions carrying 2 marks each.*

SECTION A

1. (a) In brief, discuss the layered structure of an OS.

   (b) What are system calls? What is their purpose? How are they implemented? Discuss, any two system calls.

2. If a multithreaded process forks, a problem might occur if the child gets copies of all the parent threads. Let us suppose that one of the thread was waiting for a mouse input and after the fork command we have two such threads.i.e one in each process. How can we solve a problem? Write an algorithm for the same.

SECTION B

3. Suppose, a disk drive has 5000 cylinders(0 through 4999). The drive is currently serving a request at cylinder 516 and the previous request was at cylinder 714. The queue of pending requests is:

   233, 456, 125, 91, 789, 1600, 2345, 13.

   Starting from the current head position. What is the total distance (in cylinders) that the disk arm moves to satisfy the entire request for FCFS, SCAN and LOOK algorithms?

4. Discuss the i-node structure of Unix file system. Compare it with DOS/Windows file system.

SECTION C

5. What is demand paging? How do we calculate the effective access time. Discuss, the second chance algorithm by taking a suitable example.

6. How is Cryptography useful in security?

SECTION D

7. How is deadlock handled in distributed system? Give one relevant example.
8. How is process management and Memory Management different in Linux as compared to any other OS (e.g., LINUX/UNIX).

SECTION E

9. Write the following in brief:
   (a) Differentiate between Buffering and Spooling.
   (b) What is a kernel (or nucleus) of an operating system? Why is it maintained in the primary storage? What functions does a kernel normally perform.
   (c) (i) Name any one OS used in modern day mobiles.
   (ii) Differentiate between FAT 16 and FAT 32
   (d) Security classification as viewed by the OS.
   (e) Simplex, Half duplex and Full duplex modes of communication.